READING THE BIBLE MISSIONALLY

THE GOSPEL AND OUR CULTURE SERIES

A series to foster the missional encounter of the gospel with North American culture

John R. Franke
Series Editor

• •

Volumes Published to Date

Lois Y. Barrett, editor, *Treasure in Clay Jars: Patterns in Missional Faithfulness*

James V. Brownson et al., *StormFront: The Good News of God*

Michael W. Goheen, editor, *Reading the Bible Missionally*

Michael J. Gorman, *Becoming the Gospel: Paul, Participation, and Mission*

Darrell L. Guder, *Called to Witness: Doing Missional Theology*

Darrell L. Guder, *The Continuing Conversion of the Church*

Darrell L. Guder, editor, *Missional Church: A Vision for the Sending of the Church in North America*

George R. Hunsberger, *Bearing the Witness of the Spirit: Lesslie Newbigin's Theology of Cultural Plurality*

George R. Hunsberger, *The Story That Chooses Us: A Tapestry of Missional Vision*

George R. Hunsberger and Craig Van Gelder, editors, *The Church between Gospel and Culture: The Emerging Mission in North America*

Stefan Paas, *Church Planting in the Secular West: Learning from the European Experience*

Craig Van Gelder, editor, *Confident Witness — Changing World: Rediscovering the Gospel in North America*

Reading the Bible Missionally

Edited by

Michael W. Goheen

William B. Eerdmans Publishing Company
Grand Rapids, Michigan

Wm. B. Eerdmans Publishing Co.
2140 Oak Industrial Drive N.E., Grand Rapids, Michigan 49505
www.eerdmans.com

Published 2016
Printed in the United States of America

22 21 20 19 18 17 16 1 2 3 4 5 6 7

ISBN 978-0-8028-7225-8

Library of Congress Cataloging-in-Publication Data

Names: Goheen, Michael W., 1955- editor.
Title: Reading the Bible missionally / edited by Michael W. Goheen.
Description: Grand Rapids, Michigan : William B. Eerdmans Publishing Company, 2016. | Series: The Gospel and our culture series | Includes bibliographical references and index.
Identifiers: LCCN 2016028013 | ISBN 9780802872258
Subjects: LCSH: Missions—Biblical teaching.
Classification: LCC BV2073 .R43 2016 | DDC 266—dc23
LC record available at https://lccn.loc.gov/2016028013

To Norman Shepherd,

Beloved professor, theologian, and preacher

who has set an example of faithfulness to the gospel for many

Contents

Preface

The term "missional" has become pervasive in North America, to the point where it is now being used to describe church, theology, hermeneutics, theological education—even motherhood.[1] We might be tempted to remark (as one British newspaper editor did, in reference to the word "postmodernism"): "The word has no meaning. Use it as often as possible." It is true that a word can be used so much that it becomes emptied of meaning. But, on the other hand, that a term has come to be adopted by so many people so quickly may also indicate that something important is being recovered from obscurity. I believe this to be the case with the term "missional."

Darrell Guder offers a helpful perspective when he says that the term "missional" is a kind of scaffolding that holds up our ecclesiology, theology, interpretation of Scripture, and theological education. We would not need that scaffolding if those things were all shaped as they should be by the *missio Dei* and by a robust understanding of the church's missional nature. Speaking of theology in particular, Guder says, "If mission were truly the mother of our theology, if our theological disciplines were intentionally conceived and developed as components of the formation of the church for its biblical vocation, we would never need to use the term 'missional.'"[2] The trouble is, of course, that it is not so: we've lost much of the sense of connection between mission and theology. Our use of the word "missional" points

1. Helen Lee, *The Missional Mom: Living with Purpose at Home and in the World* (Chicago: Moody, 2011).

2. Darrell Guder, "*Missio Dei*: Integrating Theological Formation for Apostolic Vocation," *Missiology: An International Review* 37.1 (January 2009): 66.

us to something biblically significant that has been, if not lost completely, certainly long misplaced. Likewise, concerning biblical hermeneutics, Guder says that the "practice of hermeneutics should be missional by its very nature. But it clearly is not, and so we must speak of 'missional hermeneutics,' propping up the enterprise with this conceptual scaffolding."[3]

The problem is that our ecclesiology and theology developed at a time when mission was not a central concern, as Lesslie Newbigin comments: "The period in which our thinking about the Church received its main features was the period in which Christianity had practically ceased to be a missionary religion . . . the dimensions of the ends of the earth had ceased to exist as a practical reality in the minds of Christians."[4] Similarly, David Bosch says of current theological curriculum: "A major problem is that the present division of theological subjects was canonized in a period when the church in Europe was completely introverted."[5]

And so the word "missional" may be helpful as scaffolding, a reminder to us of a kind of biblical interpretation that views the participation of God's people in his redemptive mission as a central theme in Scripture, a reminder of the true nature of the church as it exists for the sake of the world and of the kind of theology needed to equip the church for its vocation. Of course, scaffolding is a temporary structure that supports a building until it can stand on its own. It is to be hoped that someday our understanding of church, theology, scriptural interpretation, and theological education will be so suffused with our sense of missional vocation that we no longer need the reminder of the term "missional." Perhaps one day we may even be able to say, as Chris Wright does, that to speak of "missional church" or "missional hermeneutic" is like saying "female woman"—that's the only kind there is!

This book probes a missional hermeneutic. Its beginnings were in the conference "A Missional Reading of Scripture" hosted by Calvin Theological Seminary in Grand Rapids, Michigan, in November 2013. Four keynote addresses opened up the theme of a missional reading of Scripture and its implications for preaching and theological education: Christopher Wright spoke on a missional reading of the Old Testament, N. T. Wright spoke on the New Testament, Michael Goheen addressed the implications

3. Guder, "*Missio Dei*," 66.

4. Lesslie Newbigin, *Honest Religion for Secular Man* (Philadelphia: Westminster, 1966), 102.

5. David J. Bosch, "Theological Education in Missional Perspective," *Missiology: An International Review* 10.1 (January 1982): 26.

of a missional reading of Scripture for preaching, and Darrell Guder on its importance for theological education. Various workshops examined the significance of a missional hermeneutic for the ministry of the church, for preaching and for worship. Over seven hundred participants made the conference a significant and memorable event.

The keynote addresses and some of the workshops given at that conference have been reworked into chapters for this book. In addition, other scholars whose voices have been significant in this conversation were invited to contribute their own chapters. The book's first section examines the general nature and meaning of a missional hermeneutic from a variety of angles. The next two sections wrestle with a missional reading of the Old and New Testaments respectively; in both sections, an opening chapter addresses the issue more generally and is then followed by two chapters that give a missional reading of specific books of the Bible. The last two sections investigate the significance of a missional reading of Scripture for preaching and for theological education.

I am grateful to all those who willingly contributed to this book. Also my thanks goes to Calvin Theological Seminary—especially Jul Medenblik and Carl Bosma, who envisioned and hosted this conference—and to the many cosponsors who also helped to see it through: Missional Training Center–Phoenix, Institute for Global Church Planting and Renewal, Christian Reformed Church Home Missions, Newbigin House of Studies, and the Gospel and Our Culture Network (GOCN). I am thankful also to Doug Loney for giving his excellent editing skills to the task of making this a better book, and to Erin Glanville for the many hours she put in transcribing and also creating the index.

I dedicate this book to Norman Shepherd, my professor at Westminster Theological Seminary thirty-five years ago. His lectures had a profound impact on me in a variety of ways. In terms of the theme of this book, his understanding of the covenant was deeply formative for the way I would learn to read God's word, and so for what would later develop into a missional reading of Scripture. Norman was a theological educator in the first stage of his professional career and a preacher in the second, and thus his career path reflects the concerns of this book. Norman was almost eighty when he attended the 2013 conference, and he still took time between sessions to interact with younger students, pastors, and scholars. In my experience it is rare to see an older scholar remain flexible and willing to hear the word of God afresh in new contexts. It seems that with age one's convictions and patterns of thinking often become hardened and stiff—very much like our bodies—and new ideas can be met with fear or suspicion. Old, familiar formulations, rather than the word of God, can become the basis on which we judge anything new to us. But it is not so with Norman! He continues to listen and reflect appreciatively on the importance of a missional reading of Scripture in our time. It has been a joy to interact with him on this topic. It is my prayer that this book may encourage others to continue in the path Norman Shepherd has walked so faithfully: listening again and again to the address of God in the Scriptures in new settings, and then letting it speak into the new currents of our contemporary context so that the church may be led more and more into a living and vibrant faith.

Michael W. Goheen

Contributors

Craig G. Bartholomew is the H. Evan Runner Professor of Philosophy and professor of theology and religious studies at Redeemer University College in Ancaster, Ontario, and teaches hermeneutics at the Missional Training Center in Phoenix, Arizona.

Richard Bauckham is emeritus professor of New Testament studies at University of St. Andrews, Scotland, and Senior Scholar at Ridley Hall, Cambridge.

Carl J. Bosma is emeritus associate professor of Old Testament at Calvin Theological Seminary in Grand Rapids, Michigan.

Tim J. Davy is lecturer in biblical studies and mission and director of the Centre for the Study of the Bible and Mission at Redcliffe College in Gloucester, United Kingdom.

Dean Flemming is professor of New Testament and missions at MidAmerica Nazarene University in Olathe, Kansas, and teaches New Testament at the Missional Training Center in Phoenix, Arizona.

John R. Franke is theologian in residence at Second Presbyterian Church in Indianapolis, Indiana, and general coordinator of the Gospel and Our Culture Network.

Mark Glanville is pastor of Grandview Calvary Church in Vancouver, British Columbia, and teaches Old Testament at the Missional Training Center in Phoenix, Arizona.

Michael W. Goheen is theological director at the Missional Training Center and scholar in residence of the Surge Network in Phoenix, Arizona.

Joel B. Green is dean of the School of Theology and professor of New Testament interpretation at Fuller Theological Seminary in Pasadena, California.

Darrell L. Guder is Henry Winters Luce Emeritus Professor of Missional and Ecumenical Theology at Princeton Theological Seminary in Princeton, New Jersey.

George R. Hunsberger is emeritus professor of missiology at Western Theological Seminary in Holland, Michigan.

Timothy M. Sheridan is pastor of Maple Ridge Christian Reformed Church in Maple Ridge, British Columbia, and teaches congregational theology at the Missional Training Center in Phoenix, Arizona.

Christopher J. H. Wright is international ministries director of Langham Partnership International and teaches Old Testament at the Missional Training Center in Phoenix, Arizona.

N. T. Wright is research professor of New Testament and early Christianity at St. Mary's College, University of St Andrews in Scotland.

A Missional Hermeneutic

CHAPTER 1

A History and Introduction to a Missional Reading of the Bible

Michael W. Goheen

This book will probe a missional reading of Scripture and demonstrate the importance and fruitfulness of encountering the text in this way. This kind of missional hermeneutic has been gaining ground in missiological circles for over a half century. But it remains relatively uncommon to see biblical scholarship take seriously the insights of missiology. As one New Testament scholar sympathetic to a missional hermeneutic puts it: "Biblical scholars have yet to be persuaded that mission can and should serve as a fundamental rubric for biblical interpretation."[1] Many biblical scholars go on about their business paying little attention to this insight of their missiological colleagues: that mission is a central category in the Bible that needs to be taken seriously if our interpretation is to be faithful.

Biblical Scholarship and Mission—Not Yet Persuaded

Why are so many biblical scholars not yet persuaded of the importance of mission for interpreting Scripture? The following reasons became evident to me as I participated, often as the token missiologist, in various meetings with biblical scholars.[2] It seems that the first fundamental problem is con-

1. Michael Barram, "The Bible, Mission, and Social Location: Toward a Missional Hermeneutic," *Interpretation* (January 2007): 50.

2. See also the reflections on the relationship of biblical scholarship to missiology of David J. Bosch, "Mission in Biblical Perspective," *International Review of Mission* 74 (1985): 531–38; Bosch, "Toward a Hermeneutic for 'Biblical Studies and Mission,'" *Mission Studies* 3.2 (1986): 65–79; and Barram, "Bible, Mission, and Social Location," 42–58.

fusion about what the word "mission" means. For centuries, the word was used to describe the intentional efforts of the church to spread the Christian faith among unbelievers. This might have meant evangelistic efforts at home but more often it referred to cross-cultural activities to establish a witnessing presence in places where there had been none. There was some movement in the mid-twentieth century toward a broader understanding of mission that moved beyond evangelism and cross-cultural missions and included deeds of justice and mercy.[3] But these too were "missional" in the sense of being intentional activities on the part of the church to spread the gospel beyond its walls.

Massive changes in theological reflection on mission developed in the middle part of the twentieth century and culminated in the description of the *missio Dei* as a framework for mission. But these developments seem to be little known among biblical scholars. And as long as "mission" means intentional efforts at spreading the Christian faith by word or deed, certainly it cannot be a central rubric for interpreting Scripture—especially not the Old Testament. "Mission" so defined may be a very important task for the church to engage in, or merely a leftover relic from past colonial times: either way, it can hardly merit serious consideration as a basis for biblical hermeneutics.

A second problem flows from the first: missiology is often not taken seriously as an academic discipline because it is considered limited to the practical issues of outreach, the "how to" of evangelism and cross-cultural mission. In theological institutions enslaved to the *theoria-praxis* dichotomy of the Enlightenment, mission is considered to be divorced from the complex rigors of the more theoretical theological disciplines. "The 'practical' American," laments Harvie Conn, "has placed missions in 'practical theology.' The basic 'four great theological disciplines' remain OT study, NT research, church history, and doctrine. And missions maintains its toolshed appearance behind the 'stately mansions' of theology."[4]

Missiologists, too, have contributed to the caricature—and this is the third problem. It is not uncommon for missiologists simply to accept their relegation to the back benches: to teach the practical side of outreach and to refuse to engage the theological curriculum at a deep level. But more

3. For definitions of mission, missions, evangelism, relation between word and deed, see Michael W. Goheen, *Introducing Christian Mission Today: Scripture, History, and Issues* (Downers Grove, IL: InterVarsity, 2014), especially chaps. 6 and 11.

4. Harvie Conn, "The Missionary Task of Theology: A Love/Hate Relationship?" *Westminster Theological Journal* 45 (1983): 6.

problematically, when missiologists sometimes use Scripture to construct a biblical and theological foundation for mission, their use of the biblical text is often considered naïve. There are at least two ways this happens.

The first concerns the *historical conditioning* of the biblical text, the seeming gulf between the ancient text and the contemporary situation. Biblical scholars oriented to the spirit of the Enlightenment, which separated the subject and object of knowledge, insist on an uncommitted approach to Scripture. This produces a distancing effect by which the text becomes a strange object to be examined and dissected rather than one to be heard and obeyed. Consequently, many biblical scholars employ a historical-critical method as a bridge to cross over the great gulf fixed between the ancient text and today. Rarely do they make the journey back, and so they are reticent to draw any kind of direct connection between this alien text and the present.

Missiologists rightly react against this distancing, but in seeking the contemporary relevance of biblical texts they frequently fail to respect the cultural distance, and so read their own missional concerns back into the biblical text. They dismiss the rigorous methodological approach of biblical scholars. This can make them vulnerable to simplistic applications of the biblical text to the contemporary missionary setting. This lack of attention to hermeneutical rigor certainly will not impress biblical scholars—especially those who remain uncritically immersed in the Enlightenment worldview.

Further, biblical scholars stress the tremendous literary, theological, and semantic *diversity* of the scriptural record. To get hold of such variety, study of the Bible can become an increasingly specialized set of sciences in which biblical scholarship becomes focused on increasingly narrow fields of competence. Frustrated with this fragmentation and specialization, and lamenting its debilitating impact on the church, missiologists tend to overlook this rich diversity and may reduce their biblical foundation for mission to a single word, idea, or text as the unifying hermeneutical lens through which to see Scripture. A failure on the part of missiologists to respect the diversity of Scripture will not draw biblical scholars to the insights of missiology.

A final problem affects not just biblical scholars but the whole church in Western culture. Our Christendom and Enlightenment heritage has clouded our missional consciousness. Our missional identity has been suppressed, and so nonmissional assumptions inevitably influence biblical scholarship. There is, of course, no such thing as methodological neutrality. We carry our assumptions about the world into our reading and they largely determine what we see. To the degree that biblical scholars have not recognized their missional located situation, as Scripture presents it, they will not have eyes to see the centrality of mission in Scripture. In an article written almost forty years ago, Elisabeth Schüssler Fiorenza diagnoses the problem precisely: "Exegetical inquiry often depends upon the theological and cultural presuppositions with which it approaches its texts. Historical scholarship therefore judges the past from the perspective of its own concepts and values. Since for various reasons religious propaganda, mission, and apologetics are not very fashionable topics in the contemporary religious scene, these issues have also been widely neglected in New Testament scholarship."[5] For these reasons, mission has not been recognized as a crucial rubric for biblical interpretation.

Hopeful Signs for the Development of a Missional Hermeneutic

The historical neglect of mission in biblical scholarship cannot but have a negative effect on theological education and on the local congregation. Is there any hope that things might change? In fact, there are hopeful signs of late, and I will consider four such signs here.

The Changing Situation of the Church in Western Culture and in the World

Perhaps the most important factor that may help to stimulate a missional reading of Scripture is the changing setting of the church in Western culture. The influence of the gospel and the Christian faith on Western culture continues to decline, and the church is losing its former place of influence. The Western church finds itself increasingly in a situation that can only be characterized as missionary: it has become a culturally disenfranchised church in a neo-pagan culture. Or perhaps it is more accurate to say (since, of course, the church is always situated in a missional setting) that our missional context has changed. It is now more obvious and harder to ignore.

The church in the non-Western part of the world, moreover, has experienced spectacular growth and now dwarfs the church in the West both

5. Elisabeth Schüssler Fiorenza, "Miracles, Mission, and Apologetics: An Introduction," in *Aspects of Religious Propaganda in Judaism and Early Christianity*, ed. Elisabeth Schüssler Fiorenza (Notre Dame: University of Notre Dame Press, 1976), 1.

in terms of numbers and vitality. The church in the southern hemisphere does not have a Christendom heritage and so has always been more aware of its missional situation. So it is much more deeply attuned to the centrality of mission to the Christian faith. The sheer size of the non-Western church means that it is inevitable that their voices will be heard sooner or later. This will bring a growing challenge to the Western church.

Together, then, the expanding awareness of our newly discovered missional setting and the decisive shift of the center of gravity in the church to the global south are leading to a "raised consciousness of mission" in the Western church.[6] This new situation has the potential to reopen our missional categories when reading Scripture. I have witnessed on more than one occasion, in the case of biblical scholars, a missional reading of Scripture arise out of extended contact with the third world church or from a missional engagement with their own culture in a local church setting.

Growing Convergence on a New Understanding of Mission

A second hopeful sign is that the twentieth century has witnessed the emergence of a new biblical and theological framework for mission that has garnered widespread recognition. This new view of mission embraces much more than outreach activities, and it has serious implications for the interpretation of Scripture. As this continues to be the subject of reflection in various theological traditions, its presence will be felt in biblical studies.

A colonial framework shaped the church's view of mission well into the twentieth century, generating an introverted life in the local congregation. The following assumptions were widespread: (1) mission is a task for parachurch organizations while the church has only a pastoral role; (2) the world is divided into the Christian West (home base) and the non-Christian non-West (mission field); (3) mission takes place on the non-Western mission field; and (4) there is no need for mission in the West, since it is already Christian: the only necessary outreach effort is the evangelism of individuals, and there is little need for a prophetic challenge to what is considered to be a Christian culture.

Clearly these assumptions had to fall away if there was to be a fresh understanding of mission. And this is what happened in the early and mid-

6. Lucien LeGrand, *Unity and Plurality: Mission in the Bible*, trans. Robert R. Barr (Maryknoll, NY: Orbis, 1990), xiv.

dle part of the twentieth century in missiological discussion. The church in the non-Western part of the world began to grow and mature. In Western culture, the growth of demonic ideologies, two world wars, and unspeakable atrocities during the twentieth century signaled that the secular West was far from Christian. Colonialism collapsed, and uncertainty pervaded the Western missionary enterprise. The church in the West weakened as its numbers dwindled, and its life was deeply compromised by the powerful idols of Western culture.

The meetings of the global missionary body, the International Missionary Council, tell the story of theological reflection on mission. As one traces the results of these meetings it is clear that all the twentieth-century assumptions about mission were gradually dismantled. The question that faced the church in the early 1950s was: What new framework could replace the obsolete colonial one? The 1952 meeting of the International Missionary Council in Willingen, Germany, was a turning point, because there a new framework for mission emerged that would dominate mission thinking to the present. Lesslie Newbigin observes that "subsequent history has shown that Willingen was in fact one of the most significant in the series of world missionary conferences."[7]

The most important legacy of Willingen was the new concept of God's mission. Mission has its source in the love of the Father who sent his Son to reconcile all things to himself. The Son sent the Spirit to gather his church together and empower it to participate in his mission. This church is sent by Jesus to continue his mission, and this sending defines its very nature.

Our mission thus begins with the mission of the triune God. But this Trinitarian mission must be understood in the narrative context of the biblical story. The Scriptures tell the story of God's work to restore the entire creation, and a people from all nations, from the debilitating impact of human rebellion. God chose a people to play a role in this mission. This means that mission is more than simple activity: it is an identity that comes from the role that God's covenant people are called to play in the biblical story. Mission, then, is not merely a set of outreach activities: *it defines the very being of God's people.* To say that their missional identity comes from the role they are called to play in the biblical story already points to the centrality of mission in reading Scripture.

7. Lesslie Newbigin, "Mission to Six Continents," in *The Ecumenical Advance: A History of the Ecumenical Movement*, vol. 2: *1948–1968*, ed. Harold Fey (London: SPCK, 1970), 178.

Changes in the Discipline of Biblical Studies

A further hopeful sign is the changes taking place in the discipline of biblical studies. At least three hold promise for the development of a missional hermeneutic. All three are responses to the atomistic and naturalistic approaches of much higher critical scholarship that has been the dominant paradigm for the last two centuries.

First, there is growing interest in a theological interpretation of Scripture.[8] At its heart, theological interpretation is concerned to recover a reading of the Bible as the Christian Scriptures, a reading that listens to the Bible as God's address to his people. One of the chief characteristics of biblical scholarship in the last two centuries, as a result of the religious conversion of Western culture to the Enlightenment faith, had been the opening of a chasm between a critical reading of Scripture that was considered religiously neutral and a committed Christian reading. That is, attention to the historical, cultural, literary, and even theological details of the text was separated from hearing God speak to his people in the text. While historical-critical scholarship brings much insight to reading Scripture, it often capitulated to the Enlightenment story as its controlling religious narrative. While it claims to be objective and neutral, in fact much biblical scholarship is "a move from one confessional stance to another, a move from one creed to another."[9] In truth, the "Enlightenment did not (as it is sometimes supposed) simply free the scholar from the influence of 'dogma'; it replaced one dogma by another." The compelling power of the Enlightenment story is such that it is difficult to convince many modern biblical scholars "to recognize the creedal character of their approach."[10] The goal of theological interpretation is to wrest the Bible from an Enlightenment creedal reading and return it to its proper place: a Christian reading of Scripture to nurture the church, one that recognizes God's speech and human interpretation as complementary.

A second trend in reaction to the dominance of a methodology shaped by the Enlightenment dogma is the recognition that all readings are *located* readings that cannot escape their own cultural or historical limitations. In post-Enlightenment hermeneutical approaches there was the belief one could

8. Craig G. Bartholomew and Heath Thomas, *A Manifesto for Theological Interpretation* (Grand Rapids: Baker, 2016).

9. Lesslie Newbigin, *Proper Confidence: Faith, Doubt, and Certainty in Christian Discipleship* (Grand Rapids: Eerdmans, 1995), 80.

10. Lesslie Newbigin, "The Role of the Bible in Our Church" (remarks given at the URC Forward Policy Group, 17–18 April 1985), 1.

create critical distance ("spectator exegesis") so as to approach the text in a neutral way ("the principle of the empty head").[11] But, of course, this is simply naïve. We are, each of us, woven into a particular historical place, and that context will always shape our interpretation. Our reading of any text will always be affected by what Hans Georg Gadamer refers to as prejudices or anticipatory fore-structures: established categories the interpreter necessarily employs to make sense of the text. These prejudices may be enabling or disabling. They may open our eyes to see what is in the text, but they may also blind us to what is there. The problem is that our missional prejudices were clouded by a nonmissional self-understanding that closed us off to an important element at the heart of the scriptural story. Our increased awareness of mission in a new context puts us in a new location and may open us up to this central theme. Awareness of the importance of our own horizons in interpretation may enable biblical scholars to take stock of the way our nonmissional effective history has led to a blinkered vision of mission.

A final trend in biblical scholarship favorable to a missional reading of Scripture is the development of hermeneutical approaches that take seriously longitudinal themes in Scripture and the message of the entire canon. Richard Bauckham points specifically to canonical and narrative critical approaches that come to Scripture with an awareness of the storied nature of the entire biblical canon. For a missional reading to develop, this kind of awareness is essential, since both the mission of God and the role of God's people develop precisely in the unfolding of the biblical narrative. Even more promising is the recognition by some biblical scholars that the narrative unity of Scripture is not simply a hermeneutical or biblical-theological approach, but is a worldview-story[12] or a metanarrative[13] in which we are called to live the whole of our lives—including our scholarship.

11. Bernard J. F. Lonergan, *Method in Theology* (London: Darton, Longman & Todd, 1971), 157.

12. This is the language of N. T. Wright, *The New Testament and the People of God* (Minneapolis: Fortress, 1992), 135 (see his whole discussion on pp. 121–44). Cf. also this statement found in various forms in many parts of his writing: "The whole point of Christianity is that it offers a story which is the story of the whole world. It is public truth" (41–42).

13. This is the language of Richard Bauckham. A metanarrative is "a story about the meaning of reality as a whole. . . . [It] is an attempt to grasp the meaning and destiny of human history as a whole by telling a single story about it; to encompass, as it were, all the immense diversity of human stories in a single, overall story which integrates them into a single meaning." The Bible is such a metanarrative, for Bauckham, because it "tells a story that in some sense encompasses all other human stories, draws them into the meaning that God's story with the world gives them"; *Bible and Mission: Christian Witness in a Postmodern World*

The Growing Contribution of Biblical Scholars to the Conversation

A final hopeful sign is the growing contribution of biblical scholars to the missional hermeneutic conversation. During the nineteenth and early twentieth centuries, when mission was generally understood rather narrowly, most of those who treated the topic of mission and Scripture were mission scholars or practitioners. The primary approach was to focus on scriptural texts that would authenticate the enterprise they were already practicing. But toward the middle of the twentieth century a broadening understanding of mission caused mission scholars to return to the Bible afresh. The concept of the *missio Dei* that emerged in the mid-twentieth century as an organizing structure allowed a number of biblical insights from the early part of the century to be gathered together into a new unifying framework for mission.

It was not accidental that this coincided with the biblical theology movement, which shaped the ecumenical movement during the 1940s and 1950s.[14] Johannes Blauw was commissioned by the World Council of Churches to survey and appraise the current work in biblical scholarship and to harness those insights into the service of this new understanding of mission. Blauw's doctoral work, at the intersection of biblical studies and missiology, was done under J. H. Bavinck. In response to the commission, Blauw produced a fine little book that demonstrates the centrality of mission to the main story line of the Bible.[15] It became the nucleus of a growing consensus in mission studies and served as the major work for Bible and mission until the mid–1970s.[16]

Late developments in biblical studies and significant changes in the world church have rendered Blauw's work somewhat inadequate. During the 1970s and 1980s, many scholars with combined expertise in both mis-

---

(Grand Rapids: Baker, 2003), 4–5. See also his chapter "Authority and Scripture," in *God and the Crisis of Freedom: Biblical and Contemporary Perspectives* (Louisville: Westminster John Knox, 2002), 50–77.

14. Michael G. Cartwright, "Hermeneutics," in *Dictionary of the Ecumenical Movement*, ed. Nicholas Lossky et al. (Grand Rapids: Eerdmans, 1991), 454.

15. Johannes Blauw, *The Missionary Nature of the Church* (New York: McGraw-Hill, 1961).

16. Many other fine works appeared at this time; e.g., Robert Martin-Achard, *A Light to the Nations: A Study of the Old Testament Conception of Israel's Mission to the World*, trans. John Penney Smith (London: Oliver & Boyd, 1962); and Richard De Ridder, *Discipling the Nations* (Grand Rapids: Baker, 1971). But Blauw's book was the "received text" at this time.

sion and biblical studies addressed the issue of the Bible and mission, producing a number of valuable studies; of these, perhaps *The Biblical Foundations for Mission* by Roman Catholic scholars Donald Senior and Carroll Stuhlmueller is the most noteworthy.[17] But during this period the name of David Bosch truly stands out.[18]

Bosch was trained as a New Testament scholar, completing his doctoral work under Oscar Cullmann. He was an outstanding scholar in both missiology and biblical studies.[19] The topic of Bible and mission occupied Bosch's attention for over three decades,[20] but the arrival of *Transforming Mission* was a watershed not only in theology of mission, but also in the area of a missional hermeneutic. It gathered up the scattered insights toward a missional hermeneutic already achieved and gave sophisticated expression to a missional reading of Matthew, Luke, and Paul.[21]

Bosch rightly critiques a "foundations of mission" approach that considers isolated texts important for missionary activity; instead, he attends to the missional thrust of Scripture as a canonical whole and of particular books as whole literary units. A number of significant themes in his work advance a consistent missional hermeneutic: mission as a central thrust of Scripture's message, the centrality of the *missio Dei*, the mission theologies of various New Testament books all rooted in the mission of Jesus, the mis-

17. Donald Senior and Carroll Stuhlmueller, *The Biblical Foundations for Mission* (Maryknoll, NY: Orbis, 1983). In fact, because of Vatican II, which defined the church as missionary by its very nature, Roman Catholic scholars were well ahead of Protestant scholars in working toward a missional hermeneutic.

18. See Michael W. Goheen, "A Critical Examination of David Bosch's Missional Reading of Luke," in *Reading Luke: Interpretation, Reflection, Formation*, ed. Craig G. Bartholomew, Joel B. Green, and Anthony Thiselton; Scripture and Hermeneutics 6 (Grand Rapids: Zondervan, 2005), 229–64.

19. J. G. Du Plessis notes that Bosch's "extensive bibliography leaves the professional exegete somewhat astounded at the range of his biblical scholarship" and that he must be "reckoned as a formidable exegete with a comprehensive and penetrating knowledge of trends in biblical scholarship"; "For Reasons of the Heart: A Critical Appraisal of David J. Bosch's Use of Scripture in the Foundation of Christian Mission," *Missionalia* 18.1 (April 1990): 76.

20. See the following by David Bosch: "The Why and How of a True Biblical Foundation for Mission," in *Zending op Weg Naar de Toekomst*, ed. J. Verkuyl (Kampen: Kok, 1978); "Mission in Biblical Perspective," *International Review of Mission* (1985): 531–38; "Toward a Hermeneutic for 'Biblical Studies and Mission,'" *Mission Studies* 3.2 (1986): 65–79; and "Reflections on Biblical Models of Mission," in *Toward the Twenty-First Century in Christian Mission*, ed. James M. Phillips and Robert T. Coote (Grand Rapids: Eerdmans, 1993), 175–92.

21. David Bosch, *Transforming Mission: Paradigm Shifts in Theology of Mission* (Maryknoll, NY: Orbis, 1991).

sionary identity of the church, the broad scope of mission centered in the comprehensive salvation of the kingdom of God, the communal dimension of mission, and a hermeneutic of "consonance" or historical logic that enables the ancient missionary paradigms of the New Testament to speak authentically to the present.

Bosch's work was groundbreaking. Yet from where we stand today we can discern in it some of the weaknesses and inconsistencies that inevitably come with trailblazing. Sometimes his work seems to study the theme of mission or various themes relevant to mission rather than *reading the whole text through the lens* of mission. But perhaps the weakest area is his meager treatment of the Old Testament and its importance for the New Testament. Since Bosch's time, work on a missional hermeneutic continued along the path he pioneered, carried on with greater consistency and wider scope. The nature of a missional hermeneutic became more carefully defined and expanded in scope with work done on the Old Testament and more of the New Testament canon.

In this post-Bosch era, once again, one name stands out: Christopher Wright. Wright, like Bosch and Blauw, has one foot in missiology and one in biblical studies. His PhD work at Cambridge was in Old Testament ethics, and so he is by training a biblical scholar. As well, Wright taught in India and later at All Nations Christian College, a training school in the United Kingdom for cross-cultural missionaries. Wright produced a number of essays on a missional hermeneutic[22] and brought it to bear on various Old Testament books in his commentaries.[23] The publication of his (almost 600-page) *The Mission of God: Unlocking the Bible's Grand Narrative*[24] was another watershed for missional hermeneutics. With this book the conversation was brought to a new level. What is especially important is the way this book demonstrates

22. See the following by Christopher J. H. Wright: "Mission as a Matrix for Hermeneutics and Biblical Theology," in *Out of Egypt: Biblical Theology and Biblical Interpretation*, ed. Craig Bartholomew, Mary Healy, Karl Möller, and Robin Parry; Scripture and Hermeneutics Series 5 (Grand Rapids: Zondervan, 2004), 102–43; "Truth with a Mission: Reading All Scripture Missiologically," *Southern Baptist Journal of Theology* 15.2 (2011): 4–15; and "Mission and Old Testament Interpretation," in *Hearing the Old Testament: Listening for God's Address*, ed. Craig G. Bartholomew and David J. H. Beldman (Grand Rapids: Eerdmans, 2012), 180–203.

23. Christopher J. H. Wright, *Deuteronomy*, New International Biblical Commentary (Peabody, MA: Hendrickson, 1996), 8–17; idem, *The Message of Ezekiel*, Bible Speaks Today (Downers Grove, IL: InterVarsity, 2001), 35–38; idem, *The Message of Jeremiah*, Bible Speaks Today (Downers Grove, IL: InterVarsity, 2014), 35–39.

24. Christopher J. H. Wright, *The Mission of God: Unlocking the Bible's Grand Narrative* (Downers Grove, IL: InterVarsity, 2006).

both the crucial importance of the Old Testament and how central biblical-theological themes relate to a missional hermeneutic.

In the last decade, the conversation around a missional hermeneutic was more visible in the discipline of biblical studies, in many blogs, articles, chapters, and books (see bibliography). A group of biblical scholars and missiologists came together at the annual meetings of the Society of Biblical Literature (SBL) for over a decade to discuss this theme.[25] In the important eight-volume Scripture and Hermeneutics series, at least three chapters are explicitly devoted to the topic.[26] Participating in the discussion are a good number of first-class biblical scholars who do not have the same connection to cross-cultural missions and missiology that Wright, Bosch, Blauw, and many of the earlier authors had. Biblical scholars like N. T. Wright,[27] Richard Bauckham,[28] and Joel Green,[29] among many others, advocate a missional reading of Scripture.[30] A comment made by Tom Wright expresses what is true of many: that he was led to pursue a mis-

25. George Hunsberger maps the various proposals that are part of that ongoing conversation in "Proposals for a Missional Hermeneutic: Mapping a Conversation," *Missiology* 39.3 (July 2011): 309–21. Cf. also Hunsberger, "Exploring Missional Hermeneutics: Tracing a Conversation," chap. 3 in this book.

26. Harry Daniel Beeby, "A Missional Approach to Renewed Interpretation," in *Renewing Biblical Interpretation*, ed. Craig Bartholomew, Colin Greene, and Karl Möller; Scripture and Hermeneutics Series 1 (Grand Rapids: Zondervan, 2000), 268–83; Wright, "Mission as Matrix"; Goheen, "Bosch's Missional Reading of Luke."

27. See Michael W. Goheen, "The Mission of God's People and Biblical Interpretation: Exploring N. T. Wright's Missional Hermeneutic," paper for "A Dialogue with N. T. Wright. Jesus: A Public Figure Making a Public Announcement. Mission, Worldview, and the People of God," Scripture and Hermeneutics Seminar, San Francisco, 18 November 2011; available at 64.64.27.114/~mission/wp-content/uploads/2013/01/Missional-Hermeneutic-A-Dialogue-with-NT-Wright.pdf.

28. Richard Bauckham, "Mission as Hermeneutic for Scriptural Interpretation," *Currents in World Christianity Position Paper* 106 (1999); Bauckham, *Bible and Mission: Christian Witness in a Postmodern World* (Grand Rapids: Baker, 2003).

29. Joel B. Green, "Scripture in the Church: Reconstructing the Authority of Scripture for Christian Formation and Mission," in *The Wesleyan Tradition: A Paradigm for Renewal*, ed. Paul Wesley Chilcote (Nashville: Abingdon, 2002), 38–51; Green, "Recovering Mission-Church: Reframing Ecclesiology in Luke-Acts," *We Confess* 9.5 (2003): 3–5; and Green, "Neglecting Widows and Serving the Word? Acts 6:1–7 as a Test Case for a Missional Hermeneutic," in *Jesus Christ, Lord and Savior: Essays in Honor of I. Howard Marshall*, ed. Jon Laansma, Grant Osborne, and Ray Van Neste (Carlisle: Paternoster/Eugene, OR: Wipf & Stock, 2011), 151–60.

30. Other prominent biblical scholars attending to a missional hermeneutic are Dean Flemming, Michael Gorman, Jim Miller, Brian Russell, Ross Wagner, and Michael Barram.

sional hermeneutic not by missionary experience in a foreign country, but by his study of the data of Scripture itself. He says: "When I was planning my big series I thought at the beginning I was writing a 'New Testament Theology' but gradually have realised that, in fact, it is, if anything, a 'New Testament missiology.'"[31]

Contours of a Missional Hermeneutic

In this last section, by way of introduction to the chapters that follow, I am going to give a brief sketch of a missional hermeneutic.[32] To structure this section I employ the threefold description of a missional hermeneutic that Bauckham suggests. He describes a missional hermeneutic as

> a way of reading the Bible for which mission is the hermeneutical key. . . . [It is not] simply a study of the theme of mission in the biblical writings, but a way of reading the whole of Scripture with mission as its central interest and goal. . . . [It] would be a way of reading Scripture which sought to understand what the church's mission really is in the world as Scripture depicts it and thereby to inspire and to inform the church's missionary praxis.[33]

There are three dimensions of a missional hermeneutic in this definition: reading the whole of Scripture with mission as a central theme, reading Scripture to understand what mission really is, and reading Scripture to equip the church for its missional task.

Mission as Central to the Biblical Story

A missional hermeneutic begins with the triune God and his mission to restore the world and a people from all nations. God's mission is disclosed in a historical narrative in which he chooses and covenants with a people to be part of what he is doing. This point is central: at the heart of a

31. Private email correspondence, 11 April 2012.

32. For a fuller description see Michael W. Goheen and Christopher J. H. Wright, "Theological Interpretation and a Missional Hermeneutic," in *A Manifesto for Theological Interpretation*, ed. Bartholomew and Thomas, 171–96.

33. Bauckham, "Mission as Hermeneutic," 1.

missional hermeneutic is the recognition that God chooses and covenants with a *particular people* to fulfill his universal purpose of restoration. Both words, "particular" and "people," are important. The direction of the biblical story is a movement from one people to all nations. The church is caught up in this movement of God's redemptive work from the particular to the universal.

Two crucial texts—Genesis 12:1–3 and Exodus 19:3–6—give us a hermeneutic lens through which to see the role of God's people in the biblical story.[34] Genesis 12 tells us why God chooses and covenants with Abraham and Israel, as well as how he will carry out his redemptive plan. In Exodus 19, God delineates Israel's vocation and place in his redemptive purpose.

The grammatical structure of Genesis 12:1–3 (cf. 18:18–19) shows that God's plan of redemption will unfold in two stages: first God will restore his creational blessing to Abraham and his descendants, and then through that nation God will bless all the nations on the earth. "What is being offered in these few verses is a theological blueprint for the redemptive history of the world."[35]

Exodus 19:3–6 more carefully delineates the narrative trajectory given in Genesis 12. Here we find "the unique identity of the people of God."[36] This text stands at the center of the book of Exodus, preceded by Israel's liberation from Egyptian idolatry, and followed by the giving of the law and God's establishing his presence in their midst. Redemption, covenant, law, divine presence—these are the foundation stones of God's people. And all of them must be interpreted in terms of a missional trajectory in the story of God's work in the world.

God frees Israel from bondage to pagan idolatry and takes them to Sinai. There he tells them that out of all nations he will make them his treasured possession, "because the whole earth is mine" (19:5). The whole earth belongs to God, and through Israel he is going to reclaim it.

The unique identity of Israel is found in two titles: "priestly kingdom" and "holy nation." As a priestly kingdom, Israel is to mediate and embody God's holy presence and blessing to the surrounding nations by being a

34. Many books see the central significance of these two texts for the rest of the Old Testament narrative; e.g., William Dumbrell, *Covenant and Creation: A Theology of Old Testament Covenants* (Nashville: Nelson, 1984); and Bauckham, *Bible and Mission*.

35. Dumbrell, *Covenant and Creation*, 66.

36. Jo Bailey Wells, *God's Holy People: A Theme in Biblical Theology* (Sheffield: Sheffield Academic Press, 2000), 34–35.

distinctive people.[37] As a holy nation, "they are to be a people set apart, different from all other people by what they are and are becoming—a display people, a showcase to the world of how being in covenant with Yahweh changes a people."[38] These words are critical for the subsequent story: "The history of Israel from this point on is in reality merely a commentary upon the degree of fidelity with which Israel adhered to their Sinai-given vocation."[39] Israel's calling is the means by which the Abrahamic promise will be fulfilled. It sets out a hermeneutical framework by which to understand the rest of the story in the Old Testament.

God gives the law (Exod. 20–23) immediately following his call to Israel, for the law is to shape Israel into a new society so they can fulfill their vocation amidst the nations (cf. Deut. 4:5–8). Exodus ends with the building of the tabernacle and God's coming to dwell among them (Exod. 25–40). God's mission is a matter of "*the presence of the People of God in the midst of mankind and the presence of God in the midst of His people.*"[40]

On the land, Israel is placed at the crossroads of the world to be a display people visible to the nations. The visibility of Israel on the land is integral to their theological identity, to their role as a priestly nation among the nations.

Israel's mission is eschatological: while the promise that Israel will be a blessing to all nations is first set before them as a task, it finds little fulfillment throughout the Old Testament and will ultimately be fulfilled only in the eschatological future. When Israel fails to carry out its vocation faithfully and is exiled from the land, God does not abandon his intention to use Israel to bring blessing to the nations. Rather, through the prophets he promises to gather and renew Israel to fulfill their calling (e.g., Ezek. 36:16–27). Thus, the prophets look forward to "two successive events, first the call to Israel, and subsequently the redemptive incorporation of the Gentiles in the kingdom of God."[41]

This incorporation of the gentiles into a renewed Israel will be carried out when God establishes his universal rule over the whole earth. The associations between the coming of the kingdom and the gathering of Israel became stronger during the centuries leading up to the coming of Christ.

37. Cf. Wells, *God's Holy People*, 98–129.

38. John Durham, *Exodus*, Word Biblical Commentary (Waco: Word, 1987), 263.

39. Dumbrell, *Covenant and Creation*, 80.

40. Martin-Achard, *Light to the Nations*, 79 (emphasis original).

41. Joachim Jeremias, *Jesus' Promise to the Nations*, trans. S. H. Hooke, Studies in Biblical Theology 24 (London: SCM, 1958), 71.

However, the additional element of the Abrahamic promise—that *all* nations would be blessed—was lost in the increasingly ethnocentric separatism of the Jewish people during their domination by one repressive foreign regime after another. Election and covenant increasingly became a matter of exclusive Jewish privilege.

Then Jesus steps onto the stage of redemptive history and announces the good news of the kingdom (Mark 1:14–15). It is commonplace to speak of the "already–not yet" era of the kingdom. What is not so commonplace is reflection on *why* God delays the end. What stands out in the Gospels is the central activity of gathering. God keeps the walls of history open so that an eschatological gathering might take place. Three images permeate the Gospels: the gathering of sheep into the fold, the gathering of guests to the banquet table, and the gathering of wheat into the barn. "That God has chosen and sanctified his people in order to make it a contrast-society in the midst of the other nations was for Jesus the self-evident background of all his actions," says Gerhard Lohfink. Jesus's gathering activity is God's "eschatological action" to "restore or even re-establish his people, in order to carry out definitively and irrevocably his plan of having a holy people in the mist of the nations."[42]

This begins to clarify why Jesus restricts his mission to the Jews (Matt. 10:5–6; 15:24). Jesus's "apparent particularism is an expression of his universalism—it is because his mission concerns the whole world that he comes to Israel."[43] But more than gathering is needed. Israel first must be restored to their missional vocation, liberated from their ethnocentric exclusivism, and empowered to live distinctive lives. Jesus's mission in both his ministry and his death and resurrection is to accomplish these things.

A major part of Jesus's mission is to restore Israel to their missional vocation. We get a glimpse of this in the Sermon on the Mount. The whole sermon is a challenge to Israel to take up their eschatological calling to be a light to the nations and to reject the nationalist and separatist way of the other Jewish leaders of the day: "You are the light of the world. A town built on a hill cannot be hidden. . . . In the same way, let your light shine before others, that they may see your good deeds and glorify your Father in heaven" (Matt. 5:14–16; cf. Isa. 2:2–5).

42. Gerhard Lohfink, *Jesus and Community: The Social Dimension of the Christian Faith*, trans. John P. Galvin (Philadelphia: Fortress, 1982), 123.

43. Johannes Munck, *Paul and the Salvation of Mankind*, trans. Frank Clarke (Atlanta: John Knox, 1959), 272.

Yet this newly gathered eschatological Israel, symbolized by the appointment of the twelve,[44] is as weak and sinful as the covenant people of God in the Old Testament. A new mighty work of God is needed. And this is what is accomplished in the death and resurrection of Jesus. "For what the law was powerless to do because it was weakened by the sinful nature, God did by sending his own Son in the likeness of sinful humanity to be a sin offering. And so he condemned sin in human flesh in order that the righteous requirement of the law might be fully met in us, who do not live according to the sinful nature but according to the Spirit" (Rom. 8:3–4). Newly gathered Israel now participates in the two mightiest acts of God that stand at the center of the story: in his death, Jesus conquers the sin and evil of the old age and invites his people to share in that victory; in his resurrection, he inaugurates the age to come and gives his Spirit that his people might enjoy new life.

The story of Israel culminates not only in the death and resurrection of Jesus (Luke 24:46) but also in mission to all nations (24:47). A redemptive-historical logic runs from the work of Christ to the eschatological mission of God's people. Thus, the Gospels end with a commission that leads to a "great change of direction" in redemptive history (Matt. 28:16–20; Luke 24:45–59; John 20:19–23).[45] According to the Old Testament prophets, the nations would *come* to Israel. But with the words of Jesus, that is now reversed: now eschatological Israel is *sent* to the ends of the earth, beginning in Jerusalem (Acts 1:8).[46]

The book of Acts narrates the way the prophetic promise of the incorporation of the nations into Israel is fulfilled. Eschatological Israel will do for the nations what Jesus has done for Israel: through the witness of their life, word, and deed empowered by the Spirit they will gather sheep into the covenant fold of blessing. The "already–not yet" era of the kingdom will continue for this reason (Acts 1:6–7). As Newbigin writes:

> The meaning of this "overlap of the ages" in which we live, the time between the coming of Christ and His coming again, is that it is a time given for the witness of the apostolic Church to the ends of the earth. . . .

44. Ben Meier, "Jesus, the Twelve, and Restoration," in *Restoration: Old Testament, Jewish, and Christian Perspectives*, ed. James M. Scott (Boston: Brill, 2001), 404; N. T. Wright, *Jesus and the Victory of God* (London: SPCK, 1996), 275.

45. Blauw, *Missionary Nature of the Church*, 85.

46. Charles Scobie, "Israel and the Nations: An Essay in Biblical Theology," *Tyndale Bulletin* 43.2 (1992): 291–92.

> The implication of a true eschatological perspective will be missionary obedience, and the eschatology which does not issue in such obedience is a false eschatology.[47]

Four themes in the book of Acts make clear the main lines of the ongoing story of God's mission. The first is that the gospel is the power of God that brings salvation *first to the Jew, then to the gentile*. "The mission to Jews is a necessary stage through which the history of salvation must pass in order that salvation might proceed from the restored Israel to the Gentiles."[48] What unfolds in the narrative of Acts is a division in Israel (cf. Luke 2:34) between those who embrace the Messiah and those who reject him and thus exclude themselves from membership in the people of God. Pauline language in Romans provides imagery for what takes place in Acts: some Jews reject the gospel and are broken off, and gentiles are grafted on (Rom. 11:17–21).[49]

A second theme in Acts is the interplay of the *centripetal and centrifugal* dimensions of mission. On the one hand, the centripetal aspect of mission observed in the Old Testament continues. People in Jerusalem are drawn to the attractive lives of restored Israel (Acts 2:43–47; 4:32–35). On the other hand, a centrifugal dynamic is new. The church in Antioch, inspired by the Holy Spirit, lifts up its eyes and sees many places throughout the Roman Empire where there are not communities to draw people into covenant blessing. They send Paul and Barnabas (Acts 13:1–3), who "preach the gospel where it is not known" (Rom. 15:20), establishing new missional communities.

A third theme in Acts is *transformation of the people of God* into a new kind of community. The goal of the biblical story from the beginning was that all nations would be drawn into the covenant that God made with Abraham. That goal is realized in the book of Acts, but not without some painful struggle: a controversy develops over whether gentiles have to become Jews to become part of the people of God. The Council of Jerusalem (Acts 15) settles the issue: "Not even the original, divinely sanctioned culture of God's elect nation has the right to universalize its particular expres-

47. Lesslie Newbigin, *The Household of God: Lectures on the Nature of the Church* (New York: Friendship, 1953), 153–54.

48. Jacob Jervell, *Luke and the People of God: A New Look at Luke-Acts* (Minneapolis: Augsburg, 1972), 43.

49. David Seccombe, "The New People of God," in *Witness to the Gospel: The Theology of Acts*, ed. I. Howard Marshall and David Peterson (Grand Rapids: Eerdmans, 1998), 371.

sion of Christianity."[50] The people of God are no longer bound to one land and one cultural way of life.

The story of God's mission through his people—and this is the fourth theme—is an *unfinished story* in which we are invited to take our place. The book of Acts draws to a close with Paul in Rome, yet it is a puzzling conclusion. Why does it end so abruptly? It is because Luke invites us into the mission, "to the ends of the earth." Acts portrays the ongoing progress of the gospel, and the sudden ending in Rome invites us into this story to complete the task not yet finished. "In effect," Brian Rosner says, Luke "finishes with the subliminal message, 'to be continued,'"[51] and, I might add, "with you, the reader, as a participant."

The Meaning of Mission

A missional hermeneutic helps us to understand what the church's mission in the world really is. A brief survey of mission in the biblical story enables us to describe it in a number of overlapping ways. In the past two centuries, definitions of mission often began with the concept of mission as the initiative of the church to reach those outside the covenant community. During the twentieth century, fresh exposure to the Scripture led to a new starting point: mission begins not with the task of a people, but with the redemptive activity of God. The Bible narrates the work of the triune God to restore the whole of creation and the whole life of humankind from the corrupting effects of sin. If we are to understand mission properly we must begin with this work of God. Only then may we ask: How does the church participate in this mission?

The mission of God's people is their calling to participate in this story of God's work. They take their place and play their role in this story according to God's elective purpose. So mission is not first of all the activities of individual members of God's people to bring outsiders to the faith—although it involves that at a later stage of God's mission—but the vocation of a whole people who play a part in God's salvation on behalf of the whole world.

The direction of the biblical story makes this clear. The narrative flow

50. Dean Flemming, *Contextualization in the New Testament: Patterns for Theology and Mission* (Downers Grove, IL: InterVarsity, 2005), 52.

51. Brian Rosner, "The Progress of the Word," in *Witness to the Gospel: The Theology of Acts*, ed. I. Howard Marshall and David Peterson (Grand Rapids: Eerdmans, 1998), 231.

of the biblical story is from the particular to the universal: mission is the church finding itself within, and faithfully participating within, this narrative direction. The narrative direction of the biblical story can be discerned in two biblical phrases: "the ends of the earth" and "all nations." Both of these phrases denote the universal goal implicit in the biblical story. The movement of God's mission is from one place (Israel) to the ends of the earth, and from one nation (Israel) to all nations.

Another way to describe mission is in terms of a people chosen by God for the sake of the world. This describes the people of God in terms of their two most significant (and closely connected) relationships: with God first, and also with the world. Their identity is defined by God's election and covenant. What is clear in the biblical story is that neither election nor covenant is an end in itself: they are fundamentally missional in that their purpose is not for the salvation of God's people alone but for the rest of the world also. From the beginning, both election and covenant envisaged a people chosen for the sake of the world. To forget this missional aim of election and the covenant is to misunderstand and misrepresent their very purpose. God's people are blessed so that they may be a blessing. God begins by working *in* a people to save them, but always with a view to work *through* them to draw others into the blessings of his covenant. In much biblical scholarship, it is the first element—of a people blessed by God—that receives attention and the latter element—of God's working through a people that they may be a blessing—is neglected. But the people of God are defined by their relationship to God's elective and covenantal purpose, which means that they exist for the sake of (and are oriented to) the world. The ultimate goal of their existence is the blessing of all nations on earth.

We've not yet considered *how* the people of God are to be a blessing to the nations. In the first instance, the vocation of God's people is to be a distinctive people on display to the nations. God calls Abraham to direct his household to keep the way of the Lord, doing what is right and just (Gen. 18:19), and then God gives Israel his law to enable them to be a holy nation (Exod. 20–23; 19:3–6). Both this calling and this gift focus our attention on how being a distinctive people with changed lives is the key to God's missional work through his people.

The distinctiveness, first of Abraham's clan and then of Israel as a nation, has three facets. First, it looks back to creation, for these people are called to embody God's *creational* design and intention for all humanity. Then it looks forward to the coming kingdom, for they are also called to be a sign or preview of the *restoration* God will accomplish in the new creation. Finally it looks outward to the nations, for this people are called to engage in missionary encounter the idolatrous cultures in the midst of which they are set.

For the people called to this task, mission will be comprehensive in scope. God's people embody his renewing work across the whole spectrum of their lives, private and public. Since God's salvation is as wide as human life, so is the mission of the church. This means, moreover, that being a distinctive people across the breadth of human life will entail a missionary encounter with the surrounding culture. A missionary encounter is a meeting of different and comprehensive visions of life. Thus, the comprehensive claims of the gospel will call for a lifestyle that challenges and calls into question the fundamental assumptions and totality claims of the ultimate faith commitments of other visions of life. This happened too seldom in the past, since the gospel was too often relegated to the private sphere of life, and the church meekly accepted a place within a wider pluralistic vision of life. A missionary encounter calls the church to recover an alternative, all-encompassing vision of life based on the gospel of Jesus Christ. Such a vision will counter and challenge all other visions of life not based on the gospel. But this is to be a *missionary* encounter: not coercive, but compelling attention by an attractiveness of life.

So, on the one hand, the church is called to be a distinctive and attractive people across the breadth of their lives. On the other, they are a distinctive people on display before the nations. They are not to retreat and live their lives in a corner far from the gaze of outsiders. They are to live as a community visible to the world. This is God's design for them. God attaches his name to his people. They live before others, aware that the glory of God is at stake in their lives.

To this point I have defined mission in a way that embraces the old and new covenant peoples of God. However, sensitivity to the progress of the biblical story and especially to its fulfillment in Jesus Christ leads us to recognize a richer view of mission with which the New Testament church is tasked. With the coming of Jesus Christ, the kingdom of God breaks into history. What leads to a fuller perspective on mission is the eschatological vision: the kingdom of God as the goal of history is now present. This means four things for mission.

First, the coming of the kingdom means that the biblical story reaches the climactic point where "the nations" are to be incorporated within the covenant people of God. This is the point toward which the whole story has been moving. The time between the first and second comings of Jesus is a time defined precisely by what the biblical story anticipates from the beginning: the gathering in of the nations.

A second implication of the coming of the kingdom for mission is that God's people now have a foretaste of the life of the age to come. They are incorporated into the death and resurrection of Jesus Christ, and they are given the Spirit, so that now they share in the life of the kingdom. This renewing power equips and enables the people of God to embody the good news and to fulfill the task they were given from the beginning: to be a distinctive people embodying God's intention for humanity.

Third, the gathering of the nations means that the form of God's people changed. They are now a multiethnic community scattered throughout the world, and this new form brings fresh challenges. Throughout the Old Testament, God's people were given the Torah to govern and shape their social, economic, political, and cultural lives. They existed as a self-contained cultural unit, and the threat of pagan cultures was external to their community. Paganism posed a grave danger to them, as is clear from the Old Testament story, but that threat came from outside. Now that God's people inhabit every culture of the world, the gospel is lived out in a rich diversity of ways. But as the church lives in the very midst of the cultures of the world—cultures that are shaped by very different visions of life—it forfeits the protection of cultural isolation that ancient Israel experienced, and thus the threat of idolatry is nearer to us than it was to them. Clearly, it is God's intention that his people should *not* be culturally isolated forever, but we do well to note that our new situation means that *missionary encounter will be for us the everyday experience of life.*

Finally, the gathering of the nations in this eschatological time means that the church must engage in intentional evangelistic activities. A couple of distinctions by Newbigin help us at this point.[52] The first is between a missional *dimension* for all of life and a missional *intention* for specific elements of life. There is a missional dimension to the whole of our lives, since every part is being renewed, and therefore every part is a sign of the coming kingdom. However, there are also activities that have an explicit missional intention, words and deeds whose intent is to invite those outside the faith to believe in Jesus Christ. The second distinction is between mission and missions.[53] *Mission* is the vocation to embody God's renewing work before the nations across the breadth of human life. *Missions* is the activity

52. Cf. Goheen, *Introducing Christian Mission Today*, 82–86.

53. Cf. Goheen, *Introducing Christian Mission Today*, 401–35.

of establishing a witnessing presence in places and among peoples where there is currently no Christian presence. Missions is what dominated the nineteenth- and early-twentieth-century church's view: taking the gospel to places in Africa and Asia where there was no Christian presence. Today with a church established in most parts of the world and a Western church embarrassed by its colonial past, this important dimension of mission is in danger of being neglected. Yet missions remains part of the church's mission. The "ends of the earth" is the horizon, and there are still peoples and places without a witnessing community to make known the gospel.

Reading Scripture to Equip the Church for Missional Praxis

The final dimension of a missional hermeneutic, Bauckham notes, is that the Scriptures are to inspire and inform the church for its missionary praxis. The contemporary testimony of the Christian Reformed Church, "Our World Belongs to God," helpfully speaks of Scripture as a record and a tool of God's redeeming work. Wright makes a similar distinction, commenting that the books of Scripture "were not simply about the coming of God's Kingdom into all the world; they were, and were designed to be, part of the means whereby that happened."[54]

The authority of Scripture thus is a "sub-branch of the mission of the church. . . . God's self-revelation is always to be understood within the category of God's mission to the world, God's saving sovereignty let loose through Jesus and the Spirit and aimed at the healing and renewal of the creation."[55] To rightly understand the nature and authority of Scripture, then, is to understand its formative role, how it powerfully works to shape a faithful people and through them to bring healing to the world.

Darrell Guder, too, wants us to recognize that the Bible is a tool or instrument that shapes God's people for their missionary calling: "The writings that became the canonic New Testament all functioned basically as instruments for the continuing formation of these communities for the faithful fulfilment of their missional vocation." And so this must be a fundamental perspective for reading Scripture: "This biblical formation of the church requires a missional hermeneutic that constantly asks, 'How did this

54. N. T. Wright, *Scripture and the Authority of God* (New York: HarperCollins, 2011), 51.

55. Wright, *Scripture and the Authority of God*, 27–29.

written testimony form and equip God's people for their missional vocation then, and how does it do so today?'" Moreover, this will have a formative influence on the whole nature of biblical scholarship: "All the resources of historical, critical, and literary research on the biblical testimony can and must contribute to the church's formation by illumining all the dimensions of this fundamental question."[56]

Formation for missional calling—that is why the various books of the scriptural canon were written. Again, do not hear the word "mission" in terms of a traditional understanding. What is here meant by "formation for mission" is not an equipping to carry out various evangelistic and outreach activities; rather, the vocation of God's people is to be a distinctive people for the sake of the world. God works first of all *in* his people and only thereafter *through* his people, for the sake of the nations.

The biblical books are products of God's mission: they arise out of various needs, threats, and crises that faced God's people in the course of living out their calling. For example, the Pentateuch is addressed to a people in danger of being engulfed by the pagan religions of the ancient Near East. Thus, Genesis 1 is a polemic against ancient Near Eastern creation myths, enabling Israel to understand the nature of the one true God, what it really means to be human, and what the world is really like. Similarly, the Exodus account of the redemption of Israel from Egypt is portrayed as God's victory over the Egyptian gods. Historical and prophetic books are addressed to a people in a crisis of faith so as to shape their identity and call them to faithfulness in a new setting: 1–2 Kings and Jeremiah address a people in exile who wonder what they're doing there after God's promises about a people, land, king, and temple seem to have been abandoned; Ezra-Nehemiah, Chronicles, and Haggai are addressed to a postexilic people struggling to understand why the grand fulfillment promised earlier in Scripture has not materialized. The Torah is designed to shape Israel into a people embodying God's creational purposes for human society in a particular cultural and historical context. The prophets are covenant enforcers who call Israel back to their original vocation by warning them of judgment and by nurturing hope with visions of God's marvelous future. The book of Psalms forms a covenant mindset and identity in various ways, giving Israel songs and words for their worship. Wisdom literature forms a people to live in accordance with the wisdom of God's creation order across the whole spectrum

56. Darrell Guder, "From Mission and Theology to Missional Theology," *Princeton Seminary Bulletin* 24.1 (2003): 48.

of human life. The Gospels craft their narratives to proclaim and witness to the Christ event in a way that equips the church for faithful witness. The Epistles address the church as it exists in various cultural contexts, bringing the good news of Jesus Christ to bear on their experience so that they might be a faithful preview of the kingdom where God has planted them. And so on. The scriptural books form Israel and the church to be a faithful covenant people. And if we properly understand that covenant and election are always for the sake of the world, then it will be clear that these books are intended to form a people who exist for the sake of the world.

Conclusion

This overview is intended to introduce readers to the history of and ongoing conversation surrounding a missional reading of Scripture, a reading to be developed in the chapters that follow. It is my conviction that this is urgently needed for the health of the church today. The Bible is the vehicle by which God's kingdom comes into the world. If the Bible is to play that role in the church we must read its texts, and this will involve, in part, a missional reading. A nonmissional reading of the Bible is crippling the church in the West, often fostering self-centeredness and thwarting a missional encounter with our culture. Reading the Bible missionally can aid the church in various ways, inspire preaching that shapes congregations, and foster theological education that forms future leaders. This volume is offered to stimulate a missional reading of Scripture for the sake of the church and, through the church, for the sake of the world.

CHAPTER 2

Mission as Hermeneutic for Scriptural Interpretation

Richard Bauckham

The title of this chapter could be read in at least two ways, which are certainly not mutually exclusive. One could take it to mean that the church's practice of mission is a form of scriptural interpretation. The Bible is the sort of text that calls for interpretation not only by means of more text but also by the practice of what it preaches. Could anyone really understand what it means to love enemies without doing it, or at least seeing it done? That the church's mission in and to the world is the *practice* of the biblical text in which the text is constantly being interpreted is important, and I shall return to it at the end of the chapter.[1] But it depends, I think, on the other possible meaning of my title. In this case the title refers to a missionary hermeneutic of Scripture: in other words, a way of reading the Bible for which mission is the hermeneutical key, much as, for example, liberation is the hermeneutical key for the way of reading the Bible that liberation theology advocates. A missionary hermeneutic of this kind would not be simply a study of the theme of mission in the biblical writings, but a way of reading the whole of Scripture with mission as its central interest and goal.[2] Of course, such a missionary hermeneutic could and should be only one way of reading Scripture among others, since mission itself is not the comprehensive subject of the whole Bible. But a missionary hermeneutic would be a way of reading Scripture that sought to understand what the church's mis-

1. Cf. Lesslie Newbigin's notion of "the congregation as hermeneutic of the Gospel," in *The Gospel in a Pluralist Society* (Grand Rapids: Eerdmans, 1989), chap. 18.

2. A useful example of such a study is Johannes Blauw, *The Missionary Nature of the Church: A Survey of the Biblical Theology of Mission* (Guildford/London: Lutterworth, 1962).

sion really is in the world as Scripture depicts that mission, and thereby to inspire and inform the church's missionary praxis. Such a hermeneutic, one that reads the Bible with a view to mission, should properly be developed in reciprocal relationship with the practice of mission as itself a practice of interpreting Scripture. In the preliminary sketch I am offering now of the character of a missionary hermeneutic, it will be possible to indicate only one major aspect of that relationship with praxis, at the end of the chapter.

A Missionary Hermeneutic and Biblical Studies

To situate such a missionary hermeneutic within the academic discipline (or disciplines) of biblical studies as practiced in the Western world today, it is important to stress that its hermeneutical context would not be the academic guild of biblical scholars itself, whose largely self-generated agenda increasingly excludes the church from its context and implied audience. This agenda often reflects the interests and concerns of nonbelieving scholars in the context of the academy, usually adopting the newest items on the agenda of other academic disciplines, and it addresses Christians only insofar as they can be trained or persuaded to limit their interests in the Bible to those that are also of secular interest. The context in the academy has much to offer the believing scholar and a Christian audience, but a missionary hermeneutic must also transcend it. It must address the church in its mission to the world. More specifically, I suggest, its dialogue partners—not simply its audience—should be those who seek to live Christianity as a countercultural movement in our particular post-Christian society. It must share the recognition, now relatively widespread among Western Christians, that the church in the West is now in a missionary situation, in the sense in which Christians in the West once regarded the situation of churches in many other parts of the world as missionary. While it was a mistake to suppose that the church in any situation ever lacks a missionary vocation in that situation, the recent recognition of our current situation as missionary is recognition of a real change, from a society at least aspiring to the description "Christian," to a culture largely indifferent or even positively hostile to the Christian faith. A missionary hermeneutic in the West today must address such a situation without by any means neglecting the global context in which the various churches find themselves situated both similarly and differently.

Two current trends in biblical hermeneutics are especially favorable to a missionary hermeneutic. These are canonical interpretation (the reading of Scripture as a canonical whole) and narrative interpretation (which recognizes the way narrative creates its own world in front of the text and so interprets our world for us, how narrative opens up new possibilities of living that change us and our world, how we are given our identities by the narratives of our own lives and the wider narratives to which they relate). Scripture read as a canonical whole tells a story, a metanarrative about all reality, within which are told many other stories and within which, of course, nonnarrative literature also finds its place. In the interests of a missionary hermeneutic I suggest we focus on one prominent aspect of the narrative shape of the biblical story: its movement from the particular to the universal. This direction of the biblical story corresponds to the biblical God, who is the God of the one people Israel and the one human being Jesus Christ, and is also the Creator and Lord of all things. The identity of this God is itself a narrative identity, a particular identity God gives himself in the particular story of Israel and Jesus, and an identity that itself drives the narrative toward the universal realization of God's kingdom in all creation. In the narrative world of the Bible the people of God are also given their identity in this movement from the particular to the universal, an identity whose God-given dynamic has traditionally been summed up in the word "mission."

From Particular to Universal: Temporal, Spatial, and Social Aspects

The movement of the biblical narrative from the particular to the universal has three aspects: the temporal, the spatial, and the social. The *temporal* movement of the narrative runs from creation to the eschatological future, from the old to the new, reconstructing the past in memory and constructing the future in expectation. Within this movement, mission is movement into the new future of God. It is the movement of the people of God whose identity is found not only in the narrative of the past but also in their being turned by that narrative toward the coming of God's kingdom. The possibilities the narrative opens up for them, when they find themselves in it, are those God gives as they live toward his future. Temporally, mission is movement into the ever new future.

Temporal movement is not, as such, necessarily from the particular to the universal, but in the case of the biblical narrative it is. From Genesis 12 to Revelation the narrative is always in transition from a particular past toward the universal future. This is so definitively in the movement from the history of Jesus to his parousia and the coming of the kingdom in all creation. It is his life, death, and resurrection that open up God's new future for all creation, and so it is only as the universal future of Jesus, as the future projected by his particular story, that the New Testament knows the future. Mission is the movement that takes place between the sending of Jesus by his Father and the future coming of Jesus in the kingdom of his Father.

The *spatial* or *geographical* movement of the biblical narrative runs from one place to every place, from the center to the periphery, from Jerusalem to the ends of the earth. This too is the divine movement of God's saving purpose from his particular presence in the temple in the midst of his own people toward the coming of his universal kingdom. The church finds its identity also within this geographical movement. Spatially, mission is movement toward ever new horizons.

I shall discuss this geographical aspect of mission in more detail shortly. Biblical scholars who usually take history seriously rarely take geography equally seriously, but literal and theological geography forms a very significant aspect of the biblical narrative. A missionary hermeneutic requires not only a biblical-theological version of Paul Ricoeur's *Time and Narrative*, but also a biblical-theological version of his (nonexistent) *Space and Narrative*.

Movement in time and space is also movement of people, movement from person to person, people to people. The Old Testament typically reckons time in genealogies, and the New Testament measures space in journeys. The *social* or, we could say, numerical movement of the biblical narrative is from the one to the many, from Abraham to the nations, from Jesus to every creature in heaven, on earth, and under the earth. Socially, mission is a movement that is always being joined by others: the movement, therefore, of an ever new people.

Anticipating the Universal Goal: The Mission of the Church

Many biblical narratives portray instances of temporal, spatial, and social movement from the particular toward the universal. Historical or even realistic fictional narratives cannot, of course, portray the attainment of the universal goal of the movement. They can portray only the ever-recurrent setting out from the particular toward the universal in a movement that can move in a universal direction only by way of other particulars, since the goal is not an abstract universal but the gathering of all particulars into the one kingdom of the one God. This goal is portrayed not in realistic narrative but in a rich variety of narrative images. We can sample these now by attending to three, each representing one aspect of the movement, to be found in the Gospels.

In Jesus's parable of the seed that grows by itself (Mark 4:26–29), the temporal aspect is most prominent. While the farmer lives his normal life from day to day, the seed he sows sprouts and grows until the moment for harvest—a common image of the eschatological consummation—arrives. He does not know how it grows. Jewish farmers in first-century Palestine would think less of a process of natural cause and effect, more of an annual miracle, the direct act of God's power and generosity, as in Paul's observation that he planted and Apollos watered, but it was God who gave the growth (1 Cor. 3:6). From the seed planted in Jesus's ministry to the eschatological harvest, the movement is not humanly calculable or achievable: it is the gift of God. The church in its missionary vocation is not so much the agent of the process as its product on the way to its God-given goal.

Second, in the parable of the mustard seed (Mark 4:30–33 and parallels), the spatial aspect is stressed, in the contrast between the smallest of all seeds and the greatest of all shrubs into which it grows. The sizeable shrub that the mustard plant actually is, is so described as to evoke the image of the mythological world tree, which from its trunk at the center of the world overshadows the whole world with its branches. In Daniel (4:10–12) and Ezekiel (17:22–23) it was already an image of God's universal kingdom, the birds in its branches representing the nations that enjoy the blessings of God's rule. Here it is not the process of growth that is the point, but that the insignificant beginnings will lead to the astonishingly great end result. No more than in the case of our first parable should we assimilate this parable to a modern ideology of progress. The church is never far from the insignificance of Jesus and his band of unimpressive followers. It is always setting out from the particular in the direction of God's incalculable gift of everything.

The third parabolic story from the Gospels is an acted parable: the miraculous catch of fish that in both Luke and John is intended to illustrate Jesus's designation of the disciples as fishers of people. In the epilogue to John (21:2–11), the fishing story serves a similar function to the great commission at the end of Matthew's Gospel. It previews the church's mission that lies ahead of the gospel narrative itself. Also, in John the emphasis is on the social or numerical aspect of the metanarrative movement: the fishing disciples are seven (the number of completeness) and so representative of all, while the catch is counted and numbers 153 fish. If this number is rightly considered the number of kinds of fish there are, it suggests the inclusion of people of all nations in the church, and in any case it suggests a large number.[3] Unlike the two parables of growth, in this case the activity of the church itself in the movement from particular to universal is pictured, but the fishing is futile until Jesus intervenes. The results of mission are always the gift of God.

In these three examples we see how the church's mission takes place between its commissioning by God and the coming of the kingdom of God. It lives from the God who gives and sends and toward the God who gives and comes. We can see how the world of possibilities the biblical narratives create for their readers is not simply a different way of seeing the world (though it is that), nor are the possibilities such as the church's mission itself can achieve. The missionary church's "passion for the possible"[4] is a passion for what is possible with God: for what the church, living faithfully and expectantly, receives as divine gift in every anticipation of the coming kingdom. The movement from the particular to the universal in which the church's mission belongs should not be confused with the progressivism of the modern world. It is not a steadily cumulative process in which we move ever further away from the biblical narratives. We are always beginning again from the biblical narratives that still open up unexpected possibilities for our own future within the future of Jesus Christ. We are always figuratively starting again from Jerusalem on our way to the ends of the earth; we are always starting again from Jesus, who is the one human for all others; and we are always starting again from Pentecost, the event that gives birth to the new community on its way to the new future.

The New Testament has a surprising way of speaking of the universal goal of mission as though it were almost or even already achieved. In terms of our three aspects of the movement from particular to universal, we can say that the New Testament indulges in temporal, geographical, and numerical hyperbole. Temporally, as is well known, it anticipates the parousia of Jesus in the near future. Geographically, Paul can tell the Roman Christians that their "faith is proclaimed throughout the whole world" (Rom. 1:8; cf. 1 Pet. 5:9), even though he was particularly conscious when writing Romans that there were not yet churches in parts of the Roman Empire.

3. This was Jerome's explanation, but his statement that the Greek biologists reckoned 153 kinds of fish is open to question; for this and other explanations, see Raymond E. Brown, *The Gospel according to John*, Anchor Bible 29a (London: Chapman, 1971), 1074–76.

4. Ernst Bloch, "Zur Ontologie des Noch-Nicht Seines," in *Auswahl aus Seinem Schriften*, ed. Hans Heinz Holz (Hamburg: Fischer, 1967), 41.

Socially or numerically, Colossians 1:23 can claim that the gospel "has been proclaimed to every creature under heaven."

All three forms of hyperbole are especially evident in the book of Revelation if read as addressing its first readers. In some respects they parallel the Roman Empire's patently exaggerated claim to rule the world—exaggerated not because of our own knowledge of continents unknown to the ancients, but because much of the well-known world of the time lay beyond the empire's borders. Much as the empire's political theology required the claim to universal rule, so the early church's eagerness for the coming universal kingdom of God found expression in hyperbole.

But at the same time the New Testament's story of the church's mission in the New Testament period noticeably stops short of its universal goal. In terms of narrative function, we could say that it stops short at the point where we come in. Just as many interpreters of the Hebrew Bible suppose that the Pentateuch reached its final form in the period of the Babylonian exile and so ends its story of the Israelites of old at a point comparable with the position of the Israelites in Babylon, poised to reenter and to repossess the promised land, so the New Testament narrative leaves the task of mission incomplete, as it has been for every generation of readers. Paul's intention of going on from Rome to Spain is not fulfilled, at least within the pages of Scripture. That in Christ "there is no longer Greek and Jew, . . . barbarian [and] Scythian" (Col. 3:11) opens up a whole vista of as yet unevangelized savages (for as savages, worse than barbarians, Scythians were conventionally regarded) in the little-known northern reaches of the world beyond the Black Sea. The "great multitude that no one could count, from every nation, from all tribes and peoples and languages" (depicted in Rev. 7) is far from the reality of the church at the end of the first century, when the number of Christians probably could have been counted at least as accurately as Josephus numbers the Essenes and the Pharisees. The New Testament gives the church in every age its missionary identity by plunging it *in medias res* where the words of the great commission still ring in its ears.

Two Directions of the Church's Mission: Centripetal and Centrifugal

I do not, of course, mean that the New Testament finds us literally with Paul in Rome or with Titus in Dalmatia (cf. 2 Tim. 4:10). At this point we need to look more closely at the geographical aspect of the movement from the particular to the universal. Studies of the precedents for missionary thinking in the Old Testament and of the beginnings of missionary practice in the New Testament frequently contrast two directions of movement: the centripetal and the centrifugal.[5] The expectation in the Old Testament prophets, that the nations will come to acknowledge and to serve the God of Israel, is usually depicted as the coming of the nations to Jerusalem, to the center where God is present and worshiped. It is this expectation that appears, for example, in Jesus's saying that many will come from the east and from the west and eat with the patriarchs in the kingdom of God (Matt. 8:11). The New Testament understanding of mission is said to be novel, not in its expectation of the conversion of the gentile nations, but in the idea of mission to them: that is, of going out from the center to the periphery. In fact, there are hints of this in the prophets (Isa. 2:3b; 66:19; Jonah), while conversely the centripetal image also appears in the New Testament (see below). The two are not mutually exclusive, especially when, as we shall see, the geography becomes more metaphorical than literal.

The dominant centrifugal image is that of the sending of an individual. Frequently used of God's sending a prophet to God's own people (Moses, Isaiah, Ezekiel, Jesus himself), its sense is of authorization to speak and act in God's name, a meaning retained in the sending of disciples by God or Jesus (John 20:21; Rom. 10:15; 1 Cor. 1:17). Especially when used of sending to other nations, it acquires a more strongly geographical nuance, as already in Isaiah's prophecy of the survivors who will be sent to the nations (Isa. 66:19) and then in the sending of apostles (Acts 13:4; 22:21; 26:17), though authorization to speak remains the more important meaning. Major centripetal images are the city set on a high mountain for all to see (Isa. 2:2–3; Matt. 5:14), and the light whose shining into the darkness draws people to it (Isa. 60:1–3; Tobit 13:11; Matt. 5:14–16; Phil. 2:15; Rev. 21:23–24), both taken up from Isaiah in the Gospels and in other parts of the New Testament. While both types of image are used of Jesus himself (e.g., John 8:12; 12:32, 46; 20:21), normal biblical usage reserves the centrifugal image for individuals and the centripetal image for the community.

The literal geographical use of these images depends on the idea of the centrality of Jerusalem, which the earliest Christian mission certainly assumed and to which the book of Acts continues to refer when Jesus tells the apostles they are to be his witnesses in Jerusalem, in Judea and Samaria,

5. E.g., Blauw, *Missionary Nature*; and Joachim Jeremias, *Jesus' Promise to the Nations*, trans. S. H. Hooke, Studies in Biblical Theology 24 (London: SCM, 1958).

and to the ends of the earth (Acts 1:8). This is the geography of the book of Isaiah, in which the ends of the earth (e.g., Isa. 45:22) are the furthest extent of the earth as viewed from its geographical and theological center on mount Zion. This geography is important even for the way Paul conceived his mission (Rom. 15:19). But with the fall of Jerusalem, if not earlier for some, the Christian movement lost its physical center. We can observe the spatial imagery thereby losing its literal spatial sense but retaining a metaphorical meaning when Ephesians speaks of "those who were near" and "those who were far off" (Eph. 2:13, 17), language borrowed from Isaiah 57:19, to refer to Israel and the gentiles, respectively insiders and outsiders to God's covenant with Israel, able and not able to enter God's presence in the temple (Eph. 2:12). But in the church, both have access to God in Christ. God's presence is now among his people in the metaphorical temple they compose (2:21). This new center is everywhere and nowhere, just as with the advent of modern geography and postmodern globalization the ends of the earth are everywhere and nowhere. To substitute another physical center for Jerusalem, whether Rome or Byzantium in earlier times, or western Europe in the modern age of missions, was always a mistake. God's people move from place to place, but not from a geographical center to a geographical periphery. The permanent value of the two kinds of image—centrifugal and centripetal—is not tied to any particular geography, though it will always, like all human life, have geographical contexts. The church's mission requires both the individuals who, authorized by God to communicate his message, go out from the community to others, near or far, and also the community that manifests God's presence in its midst by its life together and its relationships to others. The image of witness, which lies near the heart of the biblical understanding of mission, transcends the two aspects.

Another Missionary Image: Exiles among the Nations

There is, however, also a third geographical image, which comes into its own with the loss or the lack of a physical center. This is the image of God's people as exiles among the nations. Luke's account of the movement of the gospel from Jerusalem outward depicts a literal diaspora of the Jerusalem church, driven by persecution from Jerusalem, some as far as Antioch, where the gentile mission first began in earnest. With the loss of a sense of a physical center of the Christian movement in Jerusalem, the way is clear for writers like the authors of Hebrews and 1 Peter to represent Christians anywhere as aliens and exiles among the nations, sojourning like the patriarchs in lands that are not their own, awaiting their homecoming to the heavenly Jerusalem that will come down to earth in the future. In recent times the image has suffered from association with a nonbiblical kind of otherworldliness, but its positive significance for mission is its call to the church to be a countercultural movement, living for a different God in a different way and with a different future in view. It may be that this image will come into its own again as the church in the postmodern West reconceptualizes its missionary relationship to a post-Christian society. The church in the West may have to get used to the idea that its own center in God, from which it goes out to others in proclamation and compassion, is actually a position of social and cultural marginality. This may improve its witness to the Christ who was himself usually also found at the margins.

Is the Universality of the Biblical Story and Mission Oppressive?

In considering all three aspects of the biblical narrative's movement from the particular to the universal I have spoken in ways that, in our contemporary cultural context, almost invite the postmodern critique of all metanarratives as oppressive. Isn't this movement a kind of narrative imperialism or ecclesiastical globalization, a form of self-aggrandizement on the church's part, in which the church universalizes its own story, foists it on others, subjects others to it, suppresses their own stories, and deprives them of the opportunity to write their own stories? Is it not even the case, it might be asked, that the Christian church's drive to universalize its own story at others' expense is the root of the whole modern phenomenon of totalizing narratives, from the Enlightenment idea of progress, through European imperialism, Marxism, Nazism, down to global capitalism and the Americanization of the world, with all the implications for violent suppression and ideological repression of human freedom and diversity?

That some of these narratives have indeed applied a veneer of Christianity to justify themselves, and that the church and its mission have sometimes been implicated in both the brighter and the darker sides of these manifestations of modernity, cannot be denied. Our question must be whether the biblical narrative of movement from the particular to the universal has anything that essentially distinguishes it from such dubious totalization. Or must we take refuge in a radical pluralism that can tolerate only local narratives with no pretensions to wider relevance and renounce altogether the desire for meaning that requires some sketch of the meaning of the whole if we are to live meaningful stories of our own? At stake is not only the human quest for narrative meaning but also the claims of a God who is other than radically unknowable. I take the postmodern critique not as a prescription of what is thinkable or not, but as a critique that can assist Christian and biblical theology, so long as it does not overstep the limits of critique.

This charge is answerable only by considering the content of the church's witness. This motif of witness, drawn like so much of the New Testament's missionary conceptuality and vocabulary from Deutero-Isaiah and developed especially in the Gospel of John and the book of Revelation, imagines history as a global contest for the truth in which the God of Israel and Jesus will demonstrate his true and sole deity to the nations. God's people are the witnesses to his truth and his great acts of salvation. The emphasis in this image is not so much on the authorization of a spokesperson, but on the ability to speak from observation and experience of the God whose identity is not universally evident in the mere nature of things but must be known from his particular history with Israel and Jesus. He is indeed the Creator and Lord of all things, never more emphatically than in the calls for all to acknowledge his true deity in Deutero-Isaiah and Revelation, but who this Creator and Lord truly is appears from his particular history with Israel and Jesus. This is why the Scriptures often associate mission with the making known of God's name, as in the command to baptize in Matthew's great commission: God's name names the narrative identity he gives himself in the biblical story.

Witness to this God is always also witness against idolatry, contending with the false witnesses to the idols who are no-gods.[6] The projects of the idols are indeed often projections of the aspirations and frustrations of the human will to power. We might think today, for example, of the greedy, never-satisfied idols that lurk behind the ideology of consumerism in its project to dominate the whole of life and the whole globe. To the domination of the no-gods, the rule of the true God is opposed not as a rival of the same kind but as qualitatively different. It must be characterized by telling the stories of the exodus from pharaoh's tyranny, of the forms of human living together that are nourished by the Sinai covenant, of the suffering

6. Cf. Vinoth Ramachandra, *Gods That Fail: Modern Idolatry and the Christian Mission* (Carlisle: Paternoster; Downers Grove, IL: InterVarsity, 1996).

servant, of Jesus's proclamation and enactment of the kingdom, of his rejection and cross, of the discipleship and martyrdom of his followers. For resisting the subversion of mission by the human will to power, the first four chapters of 1 Corinthians are seminal. What Paul encounters there is not some gnostic spiritualizing of the gospel message, but a desire that the gospel message serve the projects of self-promotion and self-advancement that formed the social dynamic of Corinthian society. Paul confronts such projects with the cross of Christ that shows the gospel to be radically unassimilable to such projects. When he states that in his preaching at Corinth he decided to know nothing but Christ crucified (1 Cor. 2:2), he does not mean that he said nothing about God except the cross. He means that he spoke of that God whose narrative identity inescapably includes the cross. It is significant that Paul's account in fact appeals not only to the cross but also extensively to the Old Testament characterization of God as the God who characteristically chooses the powerless and the insignificant (1:19–21, 27–31; 3:18–20). In the cross, God acts in character, insofar as he is known from the biblical story, but also in a way that is decisive for the plot of the biblical narrative's movement from the particular to the universal. Here is God's self-identification as one human being identified with all human beings, the particular that is also the universally salvific; and that self-identification is not with humanity in its self-aggrandizement, but with humanity in its degradation, humanity victimized by the human will to power.

Paul's account of the cross as the critical test of the content of the church's witness is also—the themes are intertwined in these early chapters of 1 Corinthians—an account of the cross as the critical test of the form of the church's witness. The way that, as an apostle of Christ, Paul lived and preached could serve the gospel only by not conforming to the social values and strategies that the message of the cross contradicts but that the Corinthian Christians still espoused. That the church's mission is inseparable from the church's community life as the living of an alternative way in contradistinction to its sociocultural context is not always noticed to be as important in Paul as it is in the Sermon on the Mount or in James. But whereas God has, so to speak, plotted his own narrative identity irrevocably in the cross of Christ, the church's narrative identity in its mission remains unstable, insofar as its conformity to the cross is in question at every new juncture of its story, and its faithfulness to the crucified God has to be sought and received in the face of ever new temptations to self-aggrandizement.

A further twist of the postmodern critique regards even the message of the cross as a sophisticated form of manipulation of others.[7] In the notion that the cross has a transformative effect on human lives is hidden, it is alleged, the same inescapable will to power, seeking only a more subtle way of dominating others. But here the real issue becomes the nature of human autonomy and its absolutizing in postmodern thought. Such an application of the hermeneutic of suspicion can never be satisfied, for it presupposes that the hidden agenda in all human relationships is the will to power and must therefore never cease to suspect. Against this corrosive cynicism, so prevalent in our culture, the biblical message of the cross asks us to trust that the will to power is not the ultimate reality of things, that the true God is the God who is different.

Further Reflection on the Nature of the Biblical Metanarrative

Although the biblical narrative has a plot—I have mentioned some key elements in the plot—the narrative is by no means as simple and obviously coherent as any attempt to summarize it might suggest. Remarkably, I think that nowhere in Scripture itself is there anything we could call a summary of the whole story from creation to consummation. In the collection of many narratives of different kinds, and of other kinds of literature that compose the canon, it is easy to lose sight of any overall direction in the larger narrative. For example, the movement from the particular to the universal that has been my main concern is by no means apparent in large parts of the Old Testament histories read apart from their larger canonical context. As well as the relative coherence, the relative incoherence of the biblical story needs stressing against the suspicion that the coherence is achieved at the expense of suppressing the incalculable diversity, the aporias and resistance to meaning that belong to all human experience of life. The biblical plot is not a procrustean bed, but more like a compass on a highly adventurous and dangerous journey. Scripture does not always make it easy for us to find the way, and it gives far more space and attention to those we might suppose to have lost the way or never known it than a narrow orthodoxy might expect. There is the book of Job confronting a perplexity at the heart of biblical faith, but virtually without reference to the Old Testament story of

7. E.g., Stephen D. Moore, "God's Own (Pri)son: The Disciplinary Technology of the Cross," in *The Open Text: New Directions for Biblical Studies?* ed. Francis Watson (London: SCM, 1993), 121–39.

God and his people. There is Ecclesiastes, almost postmodern in its inability to make sense of the story. There is the book of Esther, in which something like the Old Testament story goes on, but in a narrative world as apparently godless as that of contemporary secular people. From the perspective of the main plot of the biblical narrative, these and others may seem marginal books, but they should not be too readily pushed to the neglected edge of the canon or too easily assimilated to the rest of Scripture. Actually in their problematic and marginal character they too may be resources for a missionary church.

As well as this complexity and diversity in Scripture, we should notice also the relative openness of the biblical narrative. The conclusion of the story, though describable only figuratively, is in important respects specified, and alone makes it possible for the biblical writers or ourselves to construe the world as a narrative. But, *in medias res* and on the way to this conclusion, the church's immediate future is always open. If Scripture, as some recent writers propose, can be seen as a script that we are to perform, then there is not only scope for improvisation; there are directions from the author that positively *require* improvisation. The narrative identity of the church in its mission, I said before, is unstable. That suggests the possibilities for failure and apostasy, but more positively we can say it is unfinished, on the way to the conclusion that in some sense we know, but open to all kinds of possible ingredients in the making of that conclusion. The biblical narratives constantly set the church's mission moving from the right starting point and in the right direction, but every subplot is unique, and its contributions to the whole and to the conclusion are not calculable.

This is where, to our canonical and narrative hermeneutic, we must add, as essential to the church's mission, an important element of contextualization. Not all practitioners of narrative hermeneutics take the contexts of the readers of Scripture seriously. There is a real danger of absorbing these contexts into the narrative world of Scripture in a way that suppresses their own narrative particularity. A missionary hermeneutic cannot tolerate that. Rather, we must stress that the biblical narrative in its openness to the future is open to the inclusion of other narratives in their own particularity and diversity, narratives of other times and places, other groups and individuals, narratives with which the church's mission brings the biblical metanarrative into relationship. From the New Testament itself we could tell very different stories of the church of Jerusalem or Corinth or Antioch, or of the lives of Lydia or Apollos or Barnabas. The diversity can only increase with the diversity of times and places and cultures encountered as the church follows its calling to universality via every particularity. Of course the gospel's encounter with other narratives is far from uncritical. We have noticed how the message of the cross in Corinth proved so alien as to threaten the Corinthian Christians with a degree of narrative disruption they at first strongly resisted. The biblical particularity of God's own narrative identity is nonnegotiable. But the effect of its encounter with other narratives is not uniform or predictable, since they each have their own particularity. This is where the element of contextualization in a missionary hermeneutic is required. It is also the point at which missionary praxis turns out to be itself a necessary part of a missionary hermeneutic.

Summary Argument

I offer the following as a summary argument of the chapter above.[8]

1. A Hermeneutic for the Kingdom of God

Following the events of September 11, 2001, Jonathan Sacks (then the Chief Rabbi in the United Kingdom) spoke of these events as the clash of two universalizing cultures and their metanarratives: Islam, on the one hand, and global capitalism, on the other. (Since 2003, Sacks's comments have become, if anything, even more relevant to the catastrophic dynamics of our contemporary world.) Sacks made a contrast between such universalizing metanarratives, with their intolerance of diversity, and a postmodern valuing of diversity and particularity. This argument raises a key contemporary question about Christianity and its biblical metanarrative. Does the evident universalism of the biblical metanarrative align it with universalizing ideologies that suppress diversity and override the particular? We might pursue an answer by exploring the relationship of the universal and the particular in the biblical metanarrative, with specific reference to Christian mission. This takes the shape of a missionary hermeneutic or hermeneutic for the kingdom of God, with the three forms of movement from the particular to the universal that were discussed earlier in

8. These themes have been developed at greater length in my *Bible and Mission: Christian Witness in a Postmodern World* (Carlisle: Paternoster; Grand Rapids: Baker, 2003).

the chapter: the temporal movement, the geographical movement, and the movement of people.

2. *From the One to the Many*

Three broad patterns in the movement of God's purpose in history according to the biblical narrative are identified as having the same shape: in each case God's purpose moves from the choice of a particular and singular person or group and moves toward the universal. They are "from Abraham to the ends of the earth," "from Israel to all the nations," and "from the king who rules from Zion to the ends of the earth." In all three cases the movement of God's purpose is already established in the Old Testament with the choice of one person (Abraham), one nation (Israel), one king (David), and one place (Zion), but in each case, already in the Old Testament, the particular starting point has a universal direction. The fourth biblical movement from the particular to the universal has a different shape: it is "to all by way of the least." The priority of the poor and the unimportant in God's mission is also for the sake of all, such that his saving purpose can reach the wealthy and the powerful only by way of the least.

3. *Geography—Sacred and Symbolic*

The relationship of the particular to the universal is elaborated in Scripture, not only in history, but also in geography. Biblical geography must be given its due place in our understanding of the biblical narrative. While the literal geographical horizon of the biblical world is naturally limited to the actual known world of the Bible's times and places, this geography also has a representative character that enables it to stand for the furthest possible geographical horizon. The biblical narrative works with the idea of a center of the world (Zion) and how this relates to images of mission as centripetal (the nations come to Zion) and centrifugal (the word of God goes out from Zion). In the New Testament, this orientation to a literally geographical center is transcended by metaphor. This does not deprive mission of the geographical particularity that is essential to human life, but it clears the way for an understanding of mission as from *this* particular place (wherever it may be) to *that* (wherever it may be).

4. Witness to the Truth in a Postmodern and Globalized World

In engaging the postmodern critique of all metanarratives as oppressive, it is important to distinguish the biblical metanarrative from the modern metanarratives at which the postmodern critique was originally directed. The former has distinctive characteristics that resist assimilation to such modern grand narratives as the Enlightenment idea of progress. In particular, the direction of the biblical metanarrative toward the universal is a quite different sort of globalization from the economic globalization that is the dominant global force in the contemporary world. In the light of its own metanarrative, including the priority of the poor, Christianity should be critical of, and actively resist, key aspects of global capitalism. Finally, in the face of the postmodern critique of all claims to universal truth, the concept of noncoercive witness to the truth needs emphasis. The biblical story is apt to clash with global narratives of power and with local narratives that ape them, but it is not opposed to cultural diversity as such. Its universalism does not erase the integrity of the particular, but gives the particular its essential place on the way to and within the universal kingdom of God.

CHAPTER 3

Mapping the Missional Hermeneutics Conversation

George R. Hunsberger

Proposals for developing what came to be called a missional hermeneutic reflect a range of basic notions about what such a hermeneutic is and how it affects biblical interpretation. In a set of recent conversations among biblical scholars, missiologists, and scholars in other theological fields, four distinct emphases can be observed for defining a missional hermeneutic: the *missio Dei* as the unitive narrative theme of the Bible, the purpose of biblical writings to equip the church for its witness, the contextual and missional locatedness of the Christian community, and the dynamic of the gospel's engagement with human cultures. In their convergence, these streams of emphasis provide foundations for the continuing development of a robust missional hermeneutic.

Prologue: "Why Isn't Bible Study More Transformational?"

Several years ago, I was invited by a friend to lead a couple of workshops among congregational leaders, clergy and otherwise, on the theme of biblical engagement. He had been a fellow traveler with many of these leaders in his capacity as director of a lay and clergy learning program at Grand View University (Iowa). Groups of pastors had for some time worked to cultivate Bible study in their congregations, believing as he did that this would be the key to transformation for the churches. After some time, they reflected on their respective experiences, and for the most part, they found that this hoped-for outcome had not materialized. As if with one voice, they asked, "Why isn't Bible study more transformational?"

I was invited to engage that daunting question with them. By that time, the Gospel and Our Culture Network (GOCN) conversation about a missional hermeneutic, which this chapter reports, had gained considerable momentum. In the prior year, it had been my role in the conversation to trace the proposals of previous years for defining "missional hermeneutics" and to explore whether some emerging framework could be discerned. I argued that in fact the seemingly disparate proposals, if taken together, displayed an intriguing confluence and gave promise for developing a robust vision for being engaged by the Scriptures in light of the missionary nature of the church.

It seemed to me that the fruit of that more academic conversation had relevance to the practical, grounded concerns of these leaders. The question and the occasion, however, demanded something more of me. What was the connection between an appropriately missional hermeneutic for reading Scripture, and the formation—the transformation—of the church? Might it be that a missional hermeneutic breaks assumed approaches to a study of the Bible? Is there inherent in a missional hermeneutic a different way of studying the Bible, a way that isn't any longer studying so much as it is imbibing? I was convinced that the answer was "yes" and that a missional hermeneutic turns on at least these three hinges.

1. *We inherit habits of a subject/object relationship to texts, ancient texts, sacred texts.* Treating the Bible as the object of our rational inquiry has brought many gains, to be sure. We have grown to treat biblical texts as occurring in particular times and places, among particular people. But along the way, the habits have the unfortunate consequence of producing a *psychological distance* between us and the text: *we* consider *it*. It is something out there, beyond us. But what if the Bible *is the acting subject*? What if we are being addressed here by God? What if God intends the reading of it to change us and makes of us a different kind of student—a disciple, in fact?
2. *We make judgments about what the text may have meant originally and what it might mean now, here, for us.* We must, of course, come to such conclusions, or at least to a sense of our difficulty in arriving at them. But along the way, this habit settles us into the judgment seat. We decide what meanings texts may have had when they were written, and what meanings they have for us now. We hold *interpretive control* in the process. But what if the Bible *makes judgments about us*? What if it calls into question our most basic assumptions, our most

cherished commitments? What if it judges that our hopes are misplaced and determines for us a new and living hope? What if we don't read *it* so much as it reads *us*?

3. *We think about interpretation and application in largely individual terms.* It is true enough that each one who hears the biblical texts is brought to a place of decision: "Do I receive this, do I believe this, do I commit myself to this?" But along the way, in a society that has so deeply ingrained in us a sense of our individual identity, we get in the habit of asking "What does this mean to me? How does this apply to my life?" Even in group Bible study, we each share what we see to be the application to "my life" and are hardly capable of considering what this means to, about, and for *us*, or how it applies to our life together. Our approach to the Bible is oriented to the expectation that it speaks with *personal*, not communal, reference. But what if the Bible addresses *communities*, and not only people as individuals? What if its point of reference is to communities of people called into faithful life as the body of Christ and to each member as part of that called community?

On all three accounts, what if Lesslie Newbigin is right that the Bible is "that body of literature which—primarily but not only in narrative form—renders accessible to us the character and actions and purposes of God"?[1] What if God is *doing* something by presenting us with these scriptural words and texts? What if God is "rendering accessible" to us what God is like, what God is doing, and what God purposes for the world?

Tracing the Formative GOCN Conversation

What difference does it make if the Bible is approached from the perspective of the mission of God and the missionary nature of the church? This question has been at the center of a deliberate and serious conversation among scores of scholars who have been meeting annually since 2002 within the context of the annual meetings of the Society of Biblical Literature (SBL) and the American Academy of Religion (AAR).[2] From its beginnings as an

1. Lesslie Newbigin, *Foolishness to the Greeks* (Grand Rapids: Eerdmans, 1986), 59.

2. These two large academic associations (AAR and SBL) draw upward of ten thousand people in combined attendance for their annual meetings, which until 2008 were held

informal, early-morning breakfast meeting hosted by Tyndale Seminary of Toronto, the conversation became from 2005 onward a semiformal Additional Meeting in the AAR/SBL program under the sponsorship of GOCN.[3] In 2009 the conversation was formalized as an "Affiliate Organization" related to SBL and continues annually as the "GOCN Forum on Missional Hermeneutics."

As this conversation unfolded over its first six years, there were signs that two things were true of the various presentations.[4] On the one hand,

---

jointly on the same dates and in a common venue. Since then, they have met on different dates and at different places, but they resumed meeting jointly in November 2015.

3. The conversation began in response to an invitation extended by Tyndale Seminary of Toronto and its then Academic Dean Jeff Greenman to gather for an early-morning breakfast meeting each year. Greenman and others at Tyndale were associated with developments in the North American Gospel and Our Culture Network (GOCN) and particularly proposals for testing a model for "Missional Bible Study" (George Hunsberger, "Missional Bible Study: Discerning and Following God's Call," *The Gospel and Our Culture* 11.3 [1999]; available at gocn.org). They wanted to encourage scholars in biblical and other theological fields to give explicit attention to a missional hermeneutic for biblical engagement.

4. The breakfast conversations included presentations in 2002 by James V. Brownson (entitled "An Adequate Missional Hermeneutic"), in 2003 by Michael D. Barram ("Toward a Missiological Hermeneutic: The Bible and Mission in Current and Future Discussion"), and in 2004 by Grant LeMarquand (based on his "From Creation to New Creation: The Mission of God in the Biblical Story," in *Waging Reconciliation: God's Mission in a Time of Globalization and Crisis*, ed. Ian T. Douglas [New York: Church Publishing, 2002], 9–34). The upgrade to an Additional Meeting in 2005 meant that there would be more time for extending the conversation (a two-and-a half-hour session). In 2005, three papers were accepted for presentation, response, and discussion: by Christopher Wright ("Making Missional Sense of the Old Testament: Does It Work?"; available at galileo.stmarys-ca.edu/mbarram/Chris-Wright-SBL.htm), Colin Yuckman ("An Ulterior Gospel: The Mission of Critical Hermeneutics and the Critical Hermeneutics of Mission"; available at galileo.stmarys-ca.edu/mbarram/ColinYuckman-AARSBL2005.htm), and James Miller ("Missional Hermeneutics: An Experiment in Implementation and Reflection"; available at galileo.stmarys-ca.edu/mbarram/JimMiller-AARSBL2005.htm), with responses by James Brownson, Michael Barram, and Grant LeMarquand, respectively. In the next two meetings, keynote speakers were invited to give presentations: in 2006 by Michael Goheen ("Notes toward a Framework for a Missional Hermeneutic"; available at gocn.org/resources/articles/notes-toward-framework-missional-hermeneutic) and Michael Barram ("'Located Questions' for a Missional Hermeneutic"; available at gocn.org/resources/articles/located-questions-missional-hermeneutic), and in 2007 by Darrell Guder (cf. "Missional Hermeneutics: The Missional Authority of Scripture—Interpreting Scripture as Missional Formation," *Mission Focus: Annual Review* 15 [2007]: 106–21) and Ross Wagner (cf. "*Missio Dei*: Envisioning an Apostolic Reading of Scripture," *Missiology* 37.1 [2009]: 19–32), faculty colleagues presenting their experience of team-teaching a seminary course on Philippians.

there seemed to be some sharp differences emerging between the various proposals being made about what a missional hermeneutic *is*. As both participant and observer, it seemed to me that we had not achieved a uniform definition, and perhaps not even a uniform way to pose the question. Increasingly, some of the proposals were beginning to speak to and about each other, cordially, but with some degree of candor as well. Even where the proposals did not present themselves in that way, distinctions of approach and nuance and accent and aim were becoming more apparent, at least to me. All of this is a sign of maturation in this emerging field of hermeneutical reference.

On the other hand, there was a richness of texture and nuance with which each presentation addressed the matter of a missional hermeneutic. Apart from any other reflections about their respective accents or differences, this seemed significant. There *is* a swelling tide of imagination that converges here, arising from the influence of many disciplines and out of varieties of lived experience; we begin to see in more crisp ways than would have been the case even a few years ago how fully missional life and biblical interpretation overlap and interpenetrate in their concerns and methodologies. The time is ripe for a rigorous and robust missional hermeneutic!

My aim here is to tease out from these conversations what I believe to be four different streams of thought about what a missional hermeneutic is and how it affects biblical interpretation. I do this in order to explore how each of the foci relates to the others and to test whether these differences represent alternative and incommensurate paths, or complementary and synergistic ones. Or maybe both.

Four Streams of Emphasis

Each proposal for a missional hermeneutic, I suggest, tends to exhibit a gravitational pull toward what is believed by the proponent to be the most essential aspect of what makes biblical interpretation missional. While a range of dimensions and facets might also be brought into view, those tend to remain closely allied with what is taken to be the fundamental point of it all. It is that gravitational center, that controlling impulse, in each of the proposals we have heard that I will examine. I sense at least four differing streams of emphasis. The primary exemplars of each do in fact reflect on a missional hermeneutic in broader terms, and there is considerable overlap among them. Yet, I argue, the diversity of primary accent is sufficiently strong that teasing out the differences can allow us to see something of the range of the territory we are engaging. I suggest that these four points of gravity comprise an expanding and rich force field. Their spheres of interest and imagination intersect and produce synergy. And there is an important corollary to this thesis: none of these is sufficient on its own to provide a robust hermeneutic.

I will describe each of the four according to what is stressed as the orienting vision for the approach a missional hermeneutic should take.

The Missional Direction of the Story

The *framework* for biblical interpretation is the story the Bible tells of the mission of God and the formation of a community sent to participate in it.

Christopher Wright is perhaps the prime exemplar of this model and the one who most thoroughly and extensively plays it out. His 2005 presentation, published previously[5] and later incorporated as the introduction to his book *The Mission of God*,[6] offers a detailed rationale for interpreting the Bible in light of the mission of God as the heart and core of the biblical narrative. It is what the Bible is about. He does not deny that the narrative is multivocal and comes in a variety of literary expressions. But taken as a canonical whole, the Bible, he says, tells the story of God's mission in and for the whole world, and with it the story of the people of God whom God has called and sent to be implicated in that mission. Interpreting any specific biblical material requires attending to this pervading story of which it is a part. The parts must be read in light of the whole. That, he says, is what comprises a missional hermeneutic. The mission of God provides the framework, the clue, the hermeneutical key for biblical interpretation.

Wright envisions a shift from speaking of "the biblical basis for mission" to speaking of "the missional basis of the Bible."[7] "Mission is not just one of a list of things that the Bible happens to talk about, only a bit more urgently than some. Mission is, in that much-abused phrase, 'what it's all

5. Christopher Wright, "Mission as a Matrix for Hermeneutics and Biblical Theology," in *Out of Egypt: Biblical Theology and Biblical Interpretation*, ed. Craig Bartholomew et al. (Carlisle: Paternoster; Grand Rapids: Zondervan, 2004), 102–43.

6. Christopher Wright, *The Mission of God: Unlocking the Bible's Grand Narrative* (Downers Grove, IL: InterVarsity, 2006).

7. Wright, "Mission as a Matrix," 103–6.

about.'"[8] "We are thinking," he says, "of the purpose for which the Bible exists, the God the Bible renders to us, the people whose identity and mission the Bible invites us to share, and the story the Bible tells about this God and this people and indeed about the whole world and its future."[9] "For that reason, mission could provide the framework both for our hermeneutical approach to reading the Bible and for organizing our account of biblical theology."[10]

This frames for Wright a sense of the project on which a missional hermeneutic embarks: it "sets out to explore that divine mission and all that lies behind it and flows from it in relation to God himself, God's people, and God's world."[11] It rests on the fundamental judgment about "the writings that now comprise our Bible," that they "are themselves the product of, and witness to, the ultimate mission of God—The Bible is the drama," he says, "of this God of purpose engaged in the mission of achieving that purpose universally."[12] He concludes: "In short, a missional hermeneutic proceeds from the assumption that the whole Bible renders to us the story of God's mission through God's people in their engagement with God's world for the sake of the whole of God's creation."[13]

Two other presenters in this series followed essentially this same path. Grant LeMarquand's 2004 presentation reflected on the general topic "What the Bible Says about Mission."[14] The straightforward simplicity of that stated topic belies the richness of the nuances that follow. He is deliberate about reading the Bible from the situation and experience of missional engagement, in his case in East Africa. He wrestles with holding together what often are two competing notions of mission: great commission, and liberation from oppression. He works to put them together in the context of a comprehensive sense of the biblical narrative. For that purpose, he provides a reading of fundamental, paradigmatic texts, particularly the beginning (Gen. 1–12) and the ending (Rev. 4–5) of the story. In this way, he is not declaring the principle of a missional narrative core as fundamental to a missional hermeneutic, but he is illustrating and underscoring the princi-

8. Wright, "Mission as a Matrix," 104.

9. Wright, "Mission as a Matrix," 108–9.

10. Wright, "Mission as a Matrix," 104.

11. Wright, "Mission as a Matrix," 105.

12. Wright, "Mission as a Matrix," 103–4.

13. Wright, "Mission as a Matrix," 122.

14. LeMarquand's presentation was based on his earlier publication: "From Creation to New Creation."

ple by engaging particular themes internal to that narrative and crucial for understanding it.

Michael Goheen is more direct in his acknowledgment that he follows Wright's lead, defining a missional hermeneutic in a similar way and stressing what he calls elsewhere "the urgency of reading the Bible as one story."[15] He echoes and receives Wright's framework as the starting point for his own reading of Scripture in a missional way, while adding notes that anticipate what will be said shortly about three other streams of emphasis.

Goheen takes note of Wright's very conscious choice to understand the phrase *missio Dei*, the "mission of God," in a way different from what has become the traditional way of understanding it in terms of "sending"—in reference both to the mutual sending among the persons of the Trinity and to God's sending of Israel and the church.[16] Wright fears the close association of the idea of sending with the church's sending of the few ("missionaries") and, in the interest of involving the whole church in a sense of its mission, moves in a different direction. He chooses rather to use the term "mission" "in its more general sense of a long-term purpose or goal that is to be achieved through proximate objectives and planned actions."[17] This he does with reference both to the mission of God and to the mission of the church.

Goheen does not explore Wright's observation further, even though his own sense of the importance of God's sending is more present throughout his own work, and the missional ecclesiology that results from that is evident, as his excellent book on Lesslie Newbigin's "missionary ecclesiology" shows.[18] This subtle difference between Wright and Goheen is worth further exploration.

Two comments may be added with respect to this first stream of emphasis. First, this framework is fundamental to all the other proposals, and they all have in one way or another affirmed this understanding of the Bible as a whole. This may be a point for further serious engagement both with biblical scholarship (does it propose more unity than is present in the writings?) and with other observers tuned to the postmodern objections to metanarrative. Reference is made in several of these proposals, especially Colin Yuckman's,[19] to

15. Michael Goheen, "The Urgency of Reading the Bible as One Story," *Theology Today* 64 (2008): 469–83.

16. Goheen, "Notes toward a Framework."

17. Wright, "Mission as a Matrix," 104.

18. Michael Goheen, *"As the Father Has Sent Me, I Am Sending You": J. E. Lesslie Newbigin's Missionary Ecclesiology* (Utrecht: Boekencentrum, 2000).

19. Yuckman, "Ulterior Gospel."

Richard Bauckham's important book *The Bible and Mission*.[20] Bauckham owns the sense that the Bible presents a metanarrative of a sort. But, he contends, it is one that privileges the poor and the "least" and expects multicultural expressions to thrive—working against the grain, therefore, of the socially and culturally coercive and oppressive effects observable in other metanarratives.

Second, a certain circularity in this line of argument needs to be frankly acknowledged and owned: from the Scriptures is discerned the core narrative that becomes the key or clue for understanding the Scriptures. This circularity needs to be continuously attended to, in part by frankly acknowledging it, in part by noting the same circularity in every proposal (even the one that finds little or no unity in the midst of the diversity), and in part by recourse to the sense of a progressive, spiraling hermeneutical circle and with it the kinds of practices that will enable a missional hermeneutic to be self-critical and self-correcting. Some of James Brownson's suggestions along this line may help.[21] He asserts that the shared identity the Bible imparts to the community "cannot be fully grasped and embodied apart from the actual *practice* of participating in God's mission to the world." While such practice will not erase that community's given cultural identity, it "transforms it in pervasive ways, so that the quality and character of the life of the people of God becomes, in itself, an embodiment of the good news they are called to proclaim." This transformation produces a kind of "dislocation" that, Brownson says, "accompanies the experience of being called and sent" and "generates the critical principle by which a missional hermeneutic becomes self-correcting." Bauckham's book has much to contribute along these lines as well.

The Missional Purpose of the Writings

Here, the *aim* of biblical interpretation is to fulfill the equipping purpose of the biblical writings. If the first stream of emphasis regarding a missional hermeneutic lies within the arena of biblical theology, this second one pertains to the character of the biblical literature itself. If the first had to do with the canonical narrative, drawn from texts reckoned to be "the products

20. Richard Bauckham, *Bible and Mission: Christian Witness in a Postmodern World* (Grand Rapids: Baker Academic, 2003).

21. James V. Brownson, "Speaking the Truth in Love," expanded in *Speaking the Truth in Love: New Testament Resources for a Missional Hermeneutic* (Harrisburg, PA: Trinity, 1998).

of, and witnesses to, the mission of God," the second has to do with the purpose and aim of the biblical writings, and the canonical authority by virtue of their formative effect.

Darrell Guder most forcefully makes this case. "Jesus personally formed the first generation of Christians for his mission," he argues. "After that, their testimony became the tool for continuing formation."[22] Thus, "the apostolic strategy of continuing formation of missional communities became the motivation of their writings." The New Testament writings have as their purpose to equip the churches for witness.[23]

This purpose of equipping or forming the churches for mission is particularly evident in the Epistles. They "carry out this formation through direct engagement with the challenges arising out of the contexts of the addressed communities." But it is no less true of the Gospels. They are about "the same fundamental task." They invite the churches into "the process of discipleship that consists of their joining Jesus's disciples and accompanying him through his earthly ministry on the path to the cross. . . . In this preparation of disciples to become apostles, missional formation is happening in the Gospels."[24] Guder concludes that "the purpose of this 'Word of God written' was and is the continuing formation of the missional church. This formation happens as the biblical word works powerfully within the community."[25]

While Guder's display of the importance of scriptural purpose leans most heavily on the character of the New Testament writings, others suggest a similar thing with respect to the earlier testament. Goheen, for example, affirms that "the Old Testament scriptures were written to 'equip' God's people for their missional purposes." The New Testament, he goes on to say, was also written in order to "form, equip, renew the church for their mission in the world."[26]

So, for Guder, the basic question that guides interpretation and "concretely opens up the Bible for us as the written testimony that God uses to shape us for our faithful witness and service" is this: "How did this text

22. Darrell Guder, "Biblical Formation and Discipleship," in *Treasure in Clay Jars: Patterns in Missional Faithfulness*, ed. Lois Barrett (Grand Rapids: Eerdmans, 2004), 62.

23. Guder, "Missional Hermeneutics," 107–8.

24. Guder, "Missional Hermeneutics," 108.

25. Guder, "Biblical Formation," 62.

26. Goheen, "Notes toward a Framework"; see also Goheen, "Continuing Steps towards a Missional Hermeneutic," *Fideles: A Journal of Redeemer Pacific College* 3 (2008): 49–99.

equip and shape God's people for their missional witness then, and how does it shape us today?"[27] To put it another way, "How did this particular text continue the formation of witnessing communities then, and how does it do that today?"[28]

Guder's strong assertion about the equipping purpose of the biblical literature raises important questions that will require careful attention as the field of missional hermeneutics moves forward. I suggest that, across the canon, the authors of the biblical materials are more or less clear and conscious about such a set of equipping and formative intentions. Continuing work is needed in order to discern and elaborate the way in which each of the biblical writings can be understood in light of this divine purpose to form the people of God in and for their witness. This would mean engaging the relationship between the overall and constantly focusing intentions of God in and by this literature, and the specific, contextual sense of an author and his or her intentions in writing. Different genres, different epochs, different personalities are all at play here. Imaginative appreciation for this facet in each of the writings—even where it otherwise may at first glance seem muted or less consciously so—may be one of the fruits of this sort of exploration.

It may help in this regard, to soften or widen the way the missional purpose of biblical materials is characterized. Brownson, for example, makes a similar point about the Bible's purpose, but casts that purpose in a wider frame than the idea of equipping: "The basic purpose of scripture, then, is to impart a shared identity to the people of God as a body called to participate in God's mission. This identity is grounded most centrally in the gospel, the good news that in the life, death, and resurrection of Jesus, we see the culmination of God's saving purpose for the world."[29]

The Missional Locatedness of the Readers

The *approach* required for a faithful reading of the Bible is from the missional location of the Christian community.

Concurring with the assessment that it is the purpose of the Scrip-

27. Darrell Guder, *Unlikely Ambassadors: Clay Jar Christians in God's Service* (Louisville: Office of the General Assembly, Presbyterian Church USA, 2002), 5.

28. Guder, "Missional Hermeneutics," 109.

29. James V. Brownson, "An Adequate Missional Hermeneutic," unpublished presentation notes, AAR/SBL meeting, Toronto, November 2002.

tures to form the people of God, Michael Barram shifts the perspective by looking at the character of a missional hermeneutic from the other side of the coin: from the position of the community being thus formed. He defines a missional hermeneutic as more than interpretive methodology or even "broad, meta-narrative sketches of the missio Dei in Scripture," much as these lay essential groundwork. Rather, he defines a missional hermeneutic as "an approach to the biblical text rooted in the basic conviction that God has a mission in the world and that we read Scripture as a community called into and caught up by those divine purposes." He makes the claim that "Christian congregations caught up in the missio Dei read the Bible from a social location characterized by mission."[30]

For this kind of reading, a particular approach is needed, Barram says, one characterized by a "relentless commitment to articulating critical questions aimed at faithfully articulating the missio Dei and the community's role within the purposes of God." It is his fundamental thesis "that a missional hermeneutic should be understood as an approach to Scripture that self-consciously, intentionally, and persistently bring[s] to the biblical text a range of focused, critical, and located questions regarding [the] church's purpose in order to discern the faith community's calling and task within the missio Dei. Such questions," he says, "will be inherently contextual."[31]

There are several important features here. First, Barram takes seriously the believing community's ownership of the Scriptures being "for our equipping." He is not waiting for the scholars and pastors to decide how this or that text equips us in the community. He positions himself with the community itself to ask, "How shall the church read the Bible faithfully today?"[32] In doing so, he shifts the vantage point from the subject of the equipping (biblical authors and their interpreters) to the community being equipped. He envisions the community as the active subject of interpretation, not merely a passive recipient of it. In this, Barram warns our academic and pastoral selves not to presume that *we* provide interpretation *for* them. Even our own legitimate work in service to the community's *reading* of the word is called to be done in community, as part of the community.

James Miller, from the vantage point of his teaching in Kenya, moves with the same fundamental instinct. He affirms that a missional herme-

30. Barram, "Located Questions"; cf. Barram, "The Bible, Mission, and Social Location: Toward a Missional Hermeneutic," *Interpretation* 61.1 (January 2007): 42–58.

31. Barram, "Located Questions."

32. Barram, "Bible, Mission, and Social Location," 52.

neutic "belongs primarily in the context of the local church." It is there that "habits of reading, practice, praying, and thinking within a missional understanding of the church *must* take root, grow and bear fruit." A missional hermeneutic arises both from and for shared ecclesial identity and vocation, discernment and practice.[33]

Here it may prove helpful to keep listening to the experience of the base ecclesial communities in Latin America and their pastors and theologians. Pablo Richard, one of those theologians close to the ground, offers fascinating suggestions about the notion of "hermeneutical space," which he defines as "that institutional *place* where a specific interpretive *subject* gets its identity, proper to that place and different from any other subject. This space makes a certain *interpretation* of the Bible proper to that place and different from those other interpretations made in other hermeneutic *places*. Our interpretation of the Bible depends on the place where we find ourselves."[34]

Traditionally accepted hermeneutical spaces include the academic space, where "the subject of the Bible's interpretation is the expert, the exegete, the biblical professor, the graduate of biblical sciences and other related sciences." Another is liturgical space, in which the ordained priest or authorized layman reads and interprets the Bible "in the context of the ordinary teaching and magisterial function of the church." Both of these, Richard says, remain legitimate, useful, and necessary. But he claims that "the reading of the Bible in community is beginning to provide a third new and just as legitimate and necessary space for the experience of and the correct interpretation of God's Word." This he calls "communitary space."

Richard does not intend to drive a wedge between these spaces. Rather, he wants to open the church to this third and largely overlooked space, because it is here that the "spiritual, mystical, prophetic and apocalyptic creativity" of the People of God flourishes.

Barram moves one step farther. He emphasizes "an approach to biblical texts that privileges the missiological 'location' of the Christian community in the world as a hermeneutical key."[35] His accent is not only on the approach to the text, and on the community that approaches it, but it is precisely on the community's locatedness, as a sent community, in the world. He is convinced that "the 'social location' of the people of God is at the very

33. Miller, "Missional Hermeneutics."

34. Pablo Richard, "Word of God—Source of Life and Hope for the New Millennium" (manuscript), available at sedosmission.org/old/eng/richard.html (accessed November 2008).

35. Barram, "Bible, Mission, and Social Location," 42–43.

heart of a missional hermeneutic."[36] In other words, the sent community as location immediately implicates other layers of location. The community was sent to be the people of God "at this time, in this place," to borrow the title of an excellent book by Michael Warren.[37] "Located" questions, then, are those that arise out of that tangible place and time in which the sent community lives and in terms of which it seeks to discern its particular charism and vocation. The community's mission itself is the proper location from which the Bible is interpreted.

Barram illustrates the kinds of questions he is imagining as those that arise from a community's missional location. He affirms GOCN's five missional Bible study questions[38] and the use Guder made of them in his Presbyterian Church (USA) General Assembly Bible Studies several years ago.[39] But he presses for sharper specificity and locatedness, as the following examples[40] demonstrate:

- Does our reading of the text challenge or baptize our assumptions and blind spots?
- How does the text help to clarify appropriate Christian behavior—not only in terms of conduct but also in terms of intentionality and motive?
- Does our reading emphasize the triumph of Christ's resurrection to the exclusion of the kenotic, cruciform character of his ministry?
- In what ways does this text proclaim good news to the poor and release to the captives, and how might our own social locations make it difficult to hear that news as good?
- Does our reading of this text acknowledge and confess our complicity and culpability in personal as well as structural sin?
- How does this text clarify what God is doing in our world, in our nation, in our cities, and in our neighborhoods—and how may we be called to be involved in those purposes?

36. Barram, "Located Questions."

37. Michael Warren, *At This Time in This Place: The Spirit Embodied in the Local Assembly* (Harrisburg, PA: Trinity, 1999).

38. Hunsberger, "Missional Bible Study."

39. Guder, *Unlikely Ambassadors*. The five questions are: How does this text read us and our world? How does this text evangelize us with good news? How does this text convert us in personal and corporate life? How does this text orient us to the coming reign of God? How does this text send us and equip our witness? See Hunsberger, "Missional Bible Study."

40. Barram, "Located Questions."

Something very interesting is going on in the form of these questions. There is an interplay between questions about the text and questions about our reading of it. The questions are not only about what the text is getting at, but about what "our reading(s)" of the text are doing with it! In that way, the questions are, Barram says, "precisely the kinds of critically important missional questions that my social location has conditioned me to overlook or avoid."[41] The questions then provide a kind of critical criteria by which not only our questions but also our conclusions are continuously tested. The accent on "our reading" serves to underscore the community's full responsibility for its readings and to remind the community that its readings are always open to being tested. As the community reads, it is being read!

To speak about the locatedness of the community's efforts to faithfully read the biblical texts today sets in place the bridging that is proper to a hermeneutic. The community engages the texts, knowing that they bore particular meanings in the time and place of their original hearers and readers. They come with questions located in their own time and place, and that puts in motion the conversation between former times and places and current ones. A fourth stream in our conversations focuses on the dynamic this sets in motion.

The Missional Engagement with Cultures

Here the gospel functions as the interpretive *matrix* within which the received biblical tradition is brought into critical conversation with a particular human context. Brownson in many ways pioneers the terms of this conversation. So far as I am able to determine, he was the first to use the phrase "missional hermeneutic."[42] His address at the first breakfast meeting in this series in many ways structured the paths along which the conversation moved.

By proposing in his earlier work what he calls "elements of a missional hermeneutic," Brownson brings together his pastoral experience, his deep resonance with matters of missiology, and his area of formal training and work in New Testament studies. Working from these locations, his model

41. Barram, "Located Questions."

42. Brownson used the phrase in a workshop at a GOCN gathering in 1992 and again in a major presentation at a GOCN consultation in 1994. That presentation was published as Brownson's "Speaking the Truth in Love" and expanded in *Speaking the Truth in Love.*

focuses on what is taking place in the missional moment as biblical writers address the people of their own times and places in terms of the received religious tradition. How do we interpret the dynamic of the way they draw on elements of prior tradition and bring them into critical relationship with the current moment? While this dynamic was present within the Old Testament period, Brownson is drawn especially to ask the question about what is happening in the New Testament when authors appropriate Old Testament materials and with them engage the moments of the new circumstance of living "in Christ." How are they doing that, and what is at stake?

This feature is important to watch, Brownson assumes, because what we can observe New Testament authors doing in this regard has a parallel with what Christ followers in every place and culture are doing when they give witness to the good news. In such cases, the fruit of what the New Testament authors did has come to be part of the received canonical tradition. But the way they functioned, in addition to where it led them, is important for the formation of our own missional hermeneutic. What happens in the New Testament, in other words, is paradigmatic for the daily engagement of the gospel with our own culture or cultures today. This encounter is the stuff of the church's calling and mission.

Brownson finds a great deal of help in the work of his mentor J. Christiaan Beker, a Pauline scholar who engaged this dynamic in terms of the relationship between coherence and contingency in Paul's work. Brownson, however, wonders whether something else was going on for which those categories do not yet account. Investigating this question leads him ultimately to posit a third, perhaps less tangible but nonetheless critical element in what New Testament writers were doing. That is, there was some inner guidance system, an inner gyroscope, that guided these writers with respect to which parts of the tradition were brought to bear upon which dimensions of the presenting context, and in what particular ways. This third element was the gospel. Taken together, the dynamic interaction between tradition and context, "regulated by the gospel," comprises what Brownson calls the "interpretive matrix."[43]

Brownson lays out his argument in this way. His foundational theological mooring place, or "discrimen" (to use David Kelsey's term),[44] is that

43. Brownson, *Speaking the Truth in Love*, 42–43. It is important to note that Brownson's use of the term "matrix" is different from the way Wright uses it in "Mission as a Matrix."

44. David Kelsey, *The Uses of Scripture in Recent Theology* (Philadelphia: Fortress, 1975).

"the mode in which God is present among the faithful is irreducibly *multicultural*."[45] In the dynamic of expressing the tradition in each unique place, the gospel functions as the interpretive matrix, "the implicit set of rules that govern the way tradition is brought to bear in a particular context."[46] The gospel, Brownson takes it, is most fundamentally the good news that "in the life, death, and resurrection of Jesus, God has revealed the completion of a saving purpose for the world, to be received by faith."[47] As told to us in the New Testament, the gospel exhibits the following structural features: it summons to allegiance and decision (it makes a claim); it presupposes a public horizon and universal scope (it presents itself as world news); it regards death and resurrection as paradigmatic (it opens up a way). These function as criteria that must guide every fresh interpretation of biblical message anywhere and at any time.[48]

Ross Wagner provides an important example of the dynamic of which Brownson speaks. Wagner, in his book *Heralds of the Good News*, says that "from the opening words of his letter to the Roman churches, Paul reveals himself to be both a 'missionary theologian' and a 'hermeneutic theologian.' That is, Paul presents his apostolic mission as one that proclaims and interprets the gospel and Israel's scriptural traditions in the service of creating and sustaining communities called into existence by God's grace and love in Jesus Christ."[49] He notes that, "given the crucial role of Paul's gospel and mission at play in his reading of scripture, we should not be surprised if Paul's particular interpretations, while based on methods widely in use in his cultural context, do not find close parallels in the writings of other Jewish groups."[50] Wagner concludes that the "complex and dynamic interrelationship of scripture, theology, and mission within a particular cultural and historical context is nowhere more evident than in Paul's re-telling of Israel's story in Romans 9–11. . . . Paul revises the scriptural story to give Gentiles a prominent part in the drama of Israel's restoration. In so doing, he even goes so far as to cast Gentiles in a role originally written for Israel."[51] Paul provides an example of "a bold and sweepingly revisionary rereading

45. Brownson, *Speaking the Truth*, 22.

46. Brownson, *Speaking the Truth*, 39.

47. Brownson, *Speaking the Truth*, 49.

48. Brownson, *Speaking the Truth*, 50–51.

49. Ross Wagner, *Heralds of the Good News: Isaiah and Paul "in Concert" in the Letter to the Romans* (Leiden: Brill, 2002), 1.

50. Wagner, *Heralds of the Good News*, 348n22.

51. Wagner, *Heralds of the Good News*, 357.

of scripture."[52] Any enculturated witness to the gospel in our own time and place bears family resemblance to that!

Brownson's view and Wagner's example have correspondence with some of the most important missiological models developed in recent years by Lesslie Newbigin, Andrew Walls, Robert Schreiter, Lamin Sanneh, David Bosch, Stephen Bevans, and Kwame Bediako, to name a few. Newbigin's way of bringing into focus the dynamic involved in missional life and witness is to speak of a "three-cornered relationship . . . between the traditional culture, the 'Christianity' of the missionary, and the Bible."[53] The dynamic he identifies is relevant not only when the culture in view is that of another, important though that may be. It is the dynamic of the daily life and witness of every local Christian community, with respect to its own culture. As I argue elsewhere, the church always finds itself "sitting on both sides" in the encounter of the gospel with its culture.[54] Because the culture is never merely "out there" somewhere but is one in terms of which Christians—like others—imagine and navigate their world, the church sits very much on the culture side in the encounter. It is involved in what Newbigin called the "inner dialogue" as the gospel continually approaches it with life-altering good news. In this dialogue, by reading the Scriptures faithfully and welcoming its own "continuing conversion," the church is being shaped day by day to be a faithful expression of the gospel in its social setting, in life, word, and deed. Because of that, the church finds itself sitting on the gospel side in the encounter as well as the culture side. It was in this sense that Newbigin spoke often of the congregation as "the hermeneutic of the gospel." Yuckman notes how essential a component this is for a missional hermeneutic: "While traditional biblical criticism asks, 'which hermeneutic is most qualified to understand the Scriptures?' missional hermeneutics asks instead, 'what kind of community does a faithful hermeneutic foster?'"[55]

52. Wagner, *Heralds of the Good News*, 357.

53. Lesslie Newbigin, *Proper Confidence: Faith, Doubt, and Certainty in Christian Discipleship* (Grand Rapids: Eerdmans, 1995), 147.

54. George R. Hunsberger, "Acquiring the Posture of a Missionary Church," in *The Church between Gospel and Culture: The Emerging Mission in North America*, ed. George R. Hunsberger and Craig Van Gelder (Grand Rapids: Eerdmans, 1996), 289–97; cf. Hunsberger, *The Story That Chooses Us: A Tapestry of Missional Vision* (Grand Rapids: Eerdmans, 2015), 101–19.

55. Yuckman, "Ulterior Gospel."

Confluence and Synergy

Teasing out these four streams of emphasis for grounding a missional hermeneutic runs the risk of suggesting that they are mutually exclusive, perhaps even competing, visions. Certainly, each emphasis makes a somewhat discrete contribution toward a faithful missional hermeneutic. But "somewhat" may be the operative word. None of them is so independent of the others that it can stand alone. Each depends on and begs for the other accents. A certain kind of synergy begins to exhibit itself, and that is what makes this ongoing conversation promising. In addition, there is an interesting way these accents spread across matters to which any hermeneutical proposal must attend. These accents make proposals regarding the *framework* for a missional hermeneutic (the narrative of the *missio Dei*), the *aim* of a missional hermeneutic (ecclesial formation for witness), the *approach* of a missional hermeneutic (socially located questions), and the interpretive *matrix* of a missional hermeneutic (the gospel as the interpretive key). In substance and girth, these conversations have provided foundations for the continuing development of a robust missional hermeneutic.

The GOCN Forum on Missional Hermeneutics continues to build on these foundations. In its self-definition and in its annual call for papers, the forum identifies these four contributing and converging streams of emphasis as a working hypothesis of sorts, inviting work in specific biblical materials in order to test their adequacy and give further development to the field. In fact, the forum's current purpose statement shows with the addition of a fifth point of accent the kind of maturation that is underway. It is also an invitation to the conversation!

> The Gospel and Our Culture Network Forum on Missional Hermeneutics . . . explores the intersections of missiology, ecclesiology, and biblical interpretation, focusing on hermeneutical issues that arise in view of the Church's missional character. In particular, presenters and participants at the Forum explore how faithful interpretation of Scripture needs to pay attention to a number of interlocking realities in the text: (1) the ways in which the biblical text renders the identity of the *missio Dei*, the God who is engaged in mission to the whole creation; (2) the ways in which the biblical text is shaped for the purpose of forming a people of God who are called to participate in God's mission to the creation; (3) the ways in which the biblical text evokes and challenges a missionally located community's interpretive readings and questions; (4) the ways in

which the biblical text relates the received tradition to a particular context in light of the good news of the reign of God in Jesus Christ; and (5) the ways in which the biblical text discloses its fullest meaning only when read together with the culturally and socially "other."[56]

Epilogue: Six Years on—A Fellow Traveler's Response to the Journey Thus Far

The 2002–7 presentations in this conversation attempted to answer a definitional question: What *is* a missional hermeneutic? Following the development of the rubric described above, the 2009–14 meetings of the forum addressed the question: How does a missional hermeneutic play out in the actual engagement of texts? That is to say, the forum was testing the thesis that the rubric hammered out in the earlier period is sufficiently robust to lead to fruitful and faithful interpretations of texts, rooted in a sense of God's purposes and the missional nature of the church. This it did by engaging particular scriptural texts—either texts related to a particular theme (exile, for example) or texts within a particular portion of the biblical corpus (Gen. 1–11, for example). The process included peer selection of proposed paper topics, prepared formal responses, and, many times, small cluster conversations around particular texts. On several occasions, a book of importance to the field was explored in conversation with its author, in particular, C. Kavin Rowe's *World Upside Down*, Michael Gorman's *Reading Revelation Responsibly*, and N. T. Wright's *Paul and the Faithfulness of God.*[57]

A review of the forum's body of work since 2009, in this participant's estimation, leads to the conclusion that the fivefold rubric in the forum's self-definition (as stated above) stands the test of time. It proves to be generative and sustains a vigorous conversation among scholars of various fields. By its continued use, a significant degree of reception is presumed.

In addition to that general note, several characteristics of the recent conversation are worth noting and reflecting upon. They also may serve to focus areas in which further, deliberate work would be useful.

56. GOCN 2011 Forum on Missional Hermeneutics.

57. C. Kavin Rowe, *World Upside Down: Reading Acts in the Graeco-Roman Age* (Oxford: Oxford University Press, 2009); Michael Gorman, *Reading Revelation Responsibly: Uncivil Worship and Witness: Following the Lamb into the New Creation* (Eugene, OR: Cascade, 2011); and N. T. Wright, *Paul and the Faithfulness of God* (Minneapolis: Fortress, 2013).

Subtle but Important Shift in Language

Is there any significance to be attached to the forum's shift from the phrase "missional hermeneutic," the focus of conversation in the early period, to the phrase "missional hermeneutics," which has been embedded in the forum's self-description since 2009? I think there is, and it was the fruit of conscious reflection by the steering committee (of which Michael Barram is the chair). In one sense, the shift reflects a sense that the forum was not claiming or pursuing one particular *missional hermeneutic*. Rather, while seeking what might be said in common, it did not want to foreclose dialogue among different, even competing, *missional hermeneutics* (in its true plural sense).

But that is only one side of the added "s"—its pluralizing sense. More important is the "plural but singular in construction" sense of *hermeneutics*. It is a singular thing, as much as a hermeneutic is a singular thing. But they are different kinds of thing. The Merriam-Webster online dictionary puts it this way. A hermeneutic is "a method or principle of interpretation." Hermeneutics is "the study of methodological principles of interpretation." (Compare ethic, ethics, etc.) On the one hand, this seemed to be more conducive to the forum's location within SBL. But that aside, it seemed to represent better the ongoing enterprise with which the forum was engaged, not to establish *a* missional hermeneutic but to explore *the kind of* hermeneutics that is informed by a missional sense.

I believe this is an important shift in the stated purpose of the forum. For one thing, it cautions us against treating "mission" as a kind of hermeneutical key, riding roughshod over a whole range of hermeneutical matters that are equally at stake in biblical interpretation, missional as well as otherwise. The circularity that at one level must be frankly acknowledged carries with it the danger that the meanings of texts may be prejudged and therefore not heard in their fullness.

Elasticity of the Phrase "Missional Hermeneutics"

Richard Hays called our attention to this in the course of his response to a paper presented by Michael Barram in one of the forum's sessions in 2012. Hays asked what the meaning of "hermeneutic" might be if not in regard to "Paul's interpretation of scripture." As I understood it, Barram was discerning in Paul a kind of hermeneutic operating in his conversation with the church in Corinth that provides for us a *hermeneutic for embodying the gospel* in our own day. This broadening of the use of the term was evident in many ways from the beginning, and the rubric itself hints at that. Barram's earlier proposal about "located questions" envisions the way the Bible is to be understood and also the way the present day community and context are to be understood. This elasticity shows up in the range of corollary conversations that intersect with the missional hermeneutics (proper) conversation—missional theology, missional construals of church history, missional practical theology, and so on. In these and other aspects of the theological curriculum, hermeneutics is at stake (see Darrell Guder's and Michael Goheen's last two chapters in this volume). Barram saw Paul as an interpreter not only of scriptural texts but of being-gospeled communities as well. The forum's conversation has, as Hays noted, opened up an expanded range of meaning for the phrase "missional hermeneutic." This I believe is an advantage, not a detriment.

Disproportionate Attention to the First Two Streams

It becomes clearer to me as I reflect on our experiences in the forum that among the four streams of definition identified above, the accents of the first two are more located in the text (the spaces behind and within the text, as Lois Barrett suggests), and the accents of the latter two are more located in the readers (the spaces before the text). This, of course, highlights the "two horizons" in biblical interpretation: then and there—here and now. The first pair focuses on the missional dimensions of the text (direction and intent), and the second pair focuses on the missional dynamics of the church's life and social situation into which those texts are speaking (context-probing, and gospel as matrix). South African New Testament scholar Elna Mouton notes something similar in her book *Reading the New Testament Ethically*, in which she is calling for "an ongoing dialogue" between biblical scholarship and Christian ethics.[58] She describes what she calls "the creative dimensions of reception" in which the reader community is accountable both to the "free imaginative role of readers and their contexts" and the "inherent nature and constraints of the biblical texts."[59]

58. Elna Mouton, *Reading the New Testament Ethically* (Atlanta: SBL, 2002). Dan Beeby's work bringing together the hermeneutical implications of both canonical reading and missional reading lends support for this emphasis. See Beeby, *Canon and Mission* (Harrisburg, PA: Trinity, 1999).

59. Mouton, *Reading the New Testament Ethically*, 251.

As I reflect back over our work of the last six years, it is my growing sense that our work was more directly attentive to the first pair (behind and within the text) and far less directly attentive to the second (before the text). To be sure, the latter pair is not entirely absent. But it seems that in the manner in which we crafted our sessions, and by the fact of our vocations (mostly in academe) and our location as a forum in the context of the SBL, attending to the latter in such a setting proved difficult. After all, the latter two streams are by nature local and communal practices that fall more naturally elsewhere than in the academy.

Even more disturbing, though, is the observation that, in much of the popular literature and conversation touching on missional hermeneutics, the same is true. The weight falls on the side of the first pair. Perhaps it feels safer. Perhaps people are more confident there. There are more helps on the shelf; there is more to rely on. Whatever the reasons, there are consequences regarding notions of leadership, teaching, and preaching when this is the case. The resources for a more complete missional hermeneutic appear to be unavailable to stir imagination for the Christian community's routines and practices of its theological calling. If a missional hermeneutic provides the fruit of an overall vision of the Bible's message (discerned and passed on) without the fruit of a robust set of habits of receiving the Scriptures and being formed by them in local missional responses, the project will have failed to achieve its full potential.

I believe that the forum needs to set as a priority a more thorough attention to the second pair of streams (the locatedness of the readers and the engagement with culture) along with the added feature: reading with the other. This might implicate specific forms of collaborative work between (or in) annual sessions. But by their nature, the second pair are located in particular contexts, and they implicate local congregations as the theologians, the acting subject that theologizes and interprets. The work that is required must involve close companionship, therefore, between academy and parish, between scholars who care about local reception of the Scriptures and local missional communities who are reading and learning to read texts in, with, and for their contexts and their missional callings.

CHAPTER 4

Theological Interpretation and a Missional Hermeneutic

Craig G. Bartholomew

Two stars in the firmament of biblical interpretation today are theological interpretation and a missional hermeneutic. Both hold real promise for a recovery of biblical teaching that is directed toward the life of the church, the flourishing of the world, and the glory of God. Alas, both of these movements are "broad churches" with considerable diversity of opinion as to what precisely they entail. Theological interpretation has gained traction in the academy, but what precisely is it? Is it . . .

- academic reading of Scripture for doctrine?
- the application of a canonical hermeneutic in academic interpretation?
- ecclesial reception and interpretation of Scripture?
- a theological hermeneutic for academic biblical interpretation?
- a dialogue between theology and biblical studies?

There are, similarly, many different views about what a missional hermeneutic might look like. George R. Hunsberger, for example, distinguishes four major streams:[1]

- The framework for hermeneutics is the biblical story of the mission of God and of the people of God who are sent to participate in that mission.

1. George R. Hunsberger, "Proposals for a Missional Hermeneutic," *Missiology: An International Review* 39.3 (2011): 309–21.

- The goal of hermeneutics is to fulfill the Scriptures' function of equipping God's people to engage in the mission of God.
- Christian communities read Scripture from a particular social location. Out of this context, they bring questions to the text, in service of the mission of God. Here the focus is on the community and what it means for the people of God to read Scripture faithfully in light of their missional context.
- The gospel functions as an interpretive matrix, which enables the canonical tradition of Scripture to engage our various cultural and social contexts.

Dean Flemming proposes that the first two of Hunsberger's approaches are foundational for missional interpretation. He suggests we think of two essential dimensions: the first approach concerns what Scripture *is about*, the second what Scripture *does*:

> We will read Scripture more faithfully if we read it with an ear tuned to the music of God's mission. This does not mean that a missional hermeneutic will explain *everything* in our interpretation of Scripture. Nor is a missional reading exclusive of other ways of approaching biblical texts. For example, Wright affirms that we can properly speak of a messianic/christological reading that sees Christ as a hermeneutical key for our understanding of both Testaments.[2]

Flemming's approach suggests that a missional hermeneutic is comprehensive. It deals with what Scripture *is about* and what Scripture *does*. It is hard to imagine a more comprehensive perspective! And yet Flemming asserts, "This does not mean that a missional hermeneutic will explain *everything* in our interpretation of Scripture. Nor is a missional reading exclusive of other ways of approaching biblical texts."

Similarly, Michael Goheen and Christopher Wright assert that

> On the one hand, mission is an essential hermeneutical key to reading the whole of Scripture. Mission is not just one of the many subjects that the Bible talks about. Rather it is a way of reading the whole of Scripture with mission as a central concern. On the other hand, it is not the only

2. Dean Flemming, "Exploring a Missional Reading of Scripture: Philippians as a Case Study," *Evangelical Quarterly* 83.1 (2011): 3–18 at 7.

> lens we employ to read the entire canon of Scripture since mission does not constitute the comprehensive subject matter of the biblical narrative.[3]

From Flemming's comment the questions arise: if a missional hermeneutic is as comprehensive as Flemming suggests, what precisely is it that such a hermeneutic *does not* explain in Scripture? What are the other ways of reading Scripture that Flemming has in mind, and how would they relate to a missional hermeneutic? Flemming mentions a messianic/christological reading, but is not a missional reading a messianic/christological one? From Goheen and Wright's perspective the questions arise: What other lenses should we employ to read Scripture? If mission is not the comprehensive subject matter of Scripture, then what is? And what elements does a missional hermeneutic *not* address?

Although a theological and a missional hermeneutic are in fact ancient ways of reading Scripture, both are recent in their current renaissance.[4] Thus a lack of conceptual clarity is not surprising. My hope in this chapter is to tease out some of the differences between the two and suggest ways in which we need both.

David Bosch and the Centrality of Mission to Biblical Interpretation

My fellow South African David Bosch was certainly one of the major missiologists of the twentieth century. I am not aware that he ever used the expression "missional hermeneutic," although, of course, he does make mission central to biblical interpretation. He asserts, for example, that because the New Testament is "essentially a missionary document . . . it is incumbent upon us to reclaim it as such."[5] Bosch's biblical hermeneutic is complex and I will return to it below. For now I draw attention to some of his early comments in *Witness to the World*, which provide at least *one* answer to the questions I raise above.

Bosch notes the tendency toward a more comprehensive view of mis-

3. Michael W. Goheen and Christopher J. H. Wright, "Mission and Theological Interpretation," in *A Manifesto for Theological Interpretation*, ed. Craig G. Bartholomew and Heath A. Thomas (Grand Rapids: Baker Academic, 2016), 15.

4. This is probably more true of theological interpretation than of a missional hermeneutic.

5. David J. Bosch, "The Scope of the BISAM Project," *Mission Studies* 6.1 (1989): 61–69 at 63.

sion. Like many others he refers to Stephen Neill's reminder of the danger in this, that "if everything is mission, nothing is mission."[6] If it excludes nothing, "mission" becomes a term for everything God does as well as everything Christians should be doing, and thus loses precision and usefulness. Bosch is, of course, rightly sympathetic to the recovery of the comprehensive dimensions of mission and suggests a way forward by distinguishing mission and evangelism as having to do with "that aspect of the Church's life where she crosses frontiers towards the world."[7] Bosch notes that there are other aspects to the life of the church, and he refers to worship and the building up of her members through liturgy, fellowship, and teaching. He concludes that we "may therefore not call everything that the Church does 'mission' or 'evangelism.'"[8] This is helpful, but everything hinges on defining mission by the metaphor "crossing frontiers" and on just what Bosch means by "the Church."

What Is Mission?

Bosch affirms mission as comprehensive although *not all inclusive.* He approvingly quotes the Mexico City conference with its description of mission as "the common witness of the whole Church, bringing the whole Gospel to the whole world."[9] According to Bosch, "mission takes place where the Church, in her total involvement with the world and the comprehensiveness of her message, bears her testimony in word and deed in the form of a servant, with reference to unbelief, exploitation, discrimination and violence, but also with reference to salvation, healing, liberation, reconciliation and righteousness."[10] Bosch argues that mission is the traditional and scriptural symbol which answers the question as to how the church relates to the world in a dynamic and functional way.[11]

Bosch's theology of the church recently came under scrutiny, and in *Witness to the World* it is not always clear what he means by "the Church" (always with a capital "C"). Early on, he invokes the contrast between "event" and "institution," noting that historically the church tended to

6. Stephen Neill, *Creative Tension* (London: Edinburgh House, 1959), 81.

7. David J. Bosch, *Witness to the World: The Christian Mission in Theological Perspective* (London: Marshall, Morgan & Scott, 1980).

8. Bosch, *Witness to the World*, 17.

9. Bosch, *Witness to the World*, 17.

10. Bosch, *Witness to the World*, 18.

11. Bosch, *Witness to the World*, 10.

come down on one or the other of these, rather than maintaining both. In this context, "event" refers to the dynamic missional dimension of the institutional church. Later, like H.-W. Gensichen,[12] Bosch makes positive use of Lesslie Newbigin's distinction between missional *dimension* and missional *intention*.[13] According to this distinction, everything the church does should have a missionary dimension but not everything will have a missionary intention. Bosch criticizes Hoekendijk for tending to subsume the work of the church almost entirely under "intention." The Orthodox church might seem to be in danger of absolutizing "dimension." Bosch says the church needs to embody *both*: "The Church is, to use an expression of Zinzendorf, both '*Asyl*' and '*Pfeilschmide*'—both 'asylum' and 'forger of arrows.'"[14] A similar emphasis is found in Bonhoeffer:

> It is essential to the revelation of God in Jesus Christ that it occupies space within the world. . . . If God in Jesus Christ claims space in the world, even though it be only a stable "because there was no room in the inn" (Luke 2.7), then in this narrow space He comprises together the whole reality of the world at once and reveals the ultimate basis of this reality. And so, too, the Church of Jesus Christ is the place, in other words the space in the world, at which the reign of Jesus Christ over the whole world is evidenced and proclaimed. This space of the Church, then, is not something which exists on its own account. It is from the outset something which reaches far beyond itself, for indeed . . . it is the place where testimony is given to the foundation of all reality in Jesus Christ. . . . The space of the Church is not there in order to deprive the world of a piece of its territory, but precisely in order to prove to the world that it is still the world, the world which is loved by God and reconciled with Him.[15]

Bosch notes that "the Church's entire nature is missionary but she is not, in all her activities, explicitly aimed at the world. The Church must in all

12. H.-W. Gensichen, *Glaube für die Welt* (Gütersloh: Gerd Mohn, 1971), 80–96. Cf. Bosch, *Witness to the World*, 199–201.

13. Lesslie Newbigin, *One Body, One Gospel, One World* (London: International Missionary Council, 1958), 21, 155.

14. Bosch, *Witness to the World*, 200.

15. Dietrich Bonhoeffer, *Ethics*, ed. E. Bethge (London: SCM, 1955), 68. Cf. Bosch, *Witness to the World*, 221–22. He notes that "the world has no faith to confess. It can neither pray nor believe. . . . The Church is that segment of the world which submits consciously to Christ" (222).

circumstances be 'missionary,' but she is not in every moment 'missionising.'"[16] In this context Bosch seems to define "the Church" institutionally. He asserts that "the Church" is missional when it welcomes outsiders, when it is no mere object of pastoral care, when the laity are involved in congregational activities, when the congregation is pliable structurally, and when it is not defending the privileges of one group.

All of these aspects of a missional church have in view the institutional church. But what is lacking here is a sense of the church as *the people of God* who can be considered under the aspects of "gathered" as institutional church and "scattered" in the world, with the concept of the church as organism underlying both.[17] Bosch takes these characteristics from Gensichen but remarkably omits Gensichen's third point, namely, that a church is missional when "its members are equipped for involvement in society and are, in fact, actively involved in it."[18] This may be just an oversight but, if so, it is an important one.

The point is that our theology of the church *will* affect our view of mission and of a missional hermeneutic. To provide one example: Bosch's use of the metaphor "crossing frontiers" to define mission seems to depend on an excessive focus on the church as institution or as alternative community. Most of the life of the people of God is not spent in the institutional church: Christians are *always already* immersed in the world and have no need to "cross frontiers" for engagement with the world to take place. It is always already taking place.[19]

As we move on to a discussion of ecclesiology it is worth noting that in both *Witness to the World* and *Transforming Mission* Bosch avoids defining mission precisely. In *Witness to the World* he asserts that "it is, in fact, theologically far more correct and practically far more realistic to regard the Church's missionary enterprise as something that, because of its very

16. Bosch, *Witness to the World*, 199–200.

17. Cf. the ecclesiology of Abraham Kuyper. Cf. Craig G. Bartholomew, *Contours of the Kuyperian Tradition* (Downers Grove, IL: IVP Academic, forthcoming).

18. This point and the others *are* all mentioned in David J. Bosch, "Theological Education in Missionary Perspective," *Missiology* 10.1 (1982): 13–34 at 25.

19. Lesslie Newbigin makes a similar point: "When men say, 'The Church should go into educational work,' they mean that the Church as an organized body should employ and pay teachers. But if thousands of Church members are teaching in the schools of the nation but that is not regarded as 'Church work,' we have largely lost the great Biblical conception of the Church as the Body of Christ through whose *entire* membership the Lord wills to do His will in the world"; cf. "The Christian Layman in the World and in the Church," *National Christian Council Review* 72 (1952): 185.

nature and being, will always be in dispute."[20] Even more strongly, in *Transforming Mission* he says, "Ultimately mission remains undefinable; it should never be incarcerated in our own predilections."[21]

What Is Church?

Just how central ecclesiology is to these issues is apparent in Bosch's comment: "The meaning of mission is another form of the question about the Church's faith and message."[22] It remained vital to Bosch that the church be seen as fundamentally missional. He endorses Barth's view of the church as gathered, built up, and sent out,[23] as he also did of Barth's view of the interaction of the church and mission as mutually life-giving.[24] In *Transforming Mission*, Bosch invokes multiple voices to make the point with Schumacher that "the inverse of the thesis 'the church is essentially missionary' is 'Mission is essentially ecclesial.'"[25]

However, in *Witness to the World* he never defines the church clearly, and there is consequently some ambiguity about his view of it. In his penultimate chapter, entitled "The Church and the World," he articulates a far more helpful vision of the church. Here he rightly notes that most Christians spend the largest part of their time in the world and not in "the Church as institution."[26] Christ is head of both church and cosmos (cf. Col. 1:15–20), and the church is the *community of believers* living in the world under the lordship of Christ. The church is a stranger, a foreign body in the world, but it is "precisely as stranger that the Church is God's experimental garden in the world."[27] As such the church is the church-for-others, and here Bosch quotes Bonhoeffer with approval.[28] He also refers to Karl Barth who in *Church Dogmatics* IV/3 expounds the theme "The Community for

20. Bosch, *Witness to the World*, 9.

21. Bosch, *Transforming Mission: Paradigm Shifts in Theology of Mission* (Maryknoll, NY: Orbis, 2003), 9.

22. Bosch, *Witness to the World*, 25.

23. These actions, respectively, in Karl Barth, *Church Dogmatics*, ed. G. W. Bromiley and T. F. Torrance; trans. G. W. Bromiley et al. (Edinburgh: T&T Clark, 2004), IV/2.643–739; IV/1.614–726; IV/3.681–901.

24. Bosch, *Witness to the World*, 164–67, 201.

25. Bosch, *Witness to the World*, 372.

26. Bosch, *Witness to the World*, 221.

27. Bosch, *Witness to the World*, 225.

28. Bosch, *Witness to the World*, 225.

the World": "Community and worship lead to mission, mission leads to community and worship."[29]

Here Bosch comes closer to a view of the church as the people of God with a gathered (institutional) and a scattered focus. He is well aware historically of the importance missionally of the manifestation of kingdom life in the daily lives of believers.[30] And yet even in this penultimate chapter something of the tension remains between church as institution and church as organism. Bosch refers to A. A. van Ruler's engagement with Abraham Kuyper on common grace and approves van Ruler's statement that particular grace penetrates the entire world. Van Ruler uses the image of common grace being fertilized by particular grace. Bosch's conclusion from this is, "There is thus an essential difference in the 'density of grace' between Church and world but both partake of grace. The Church has therefore to be upheld as a distinctive community."[31]

There is much in Bosch's ecclesiology that is helpful. With J. H. Oldham and Lesslie Newbigin he rightly stressed the importance of the local church: "The church-in-mission is, primarily, the *local* church everywhere in the world."[32] He endorsed Newbigin's view that the local congregation of men and women who believe in and live the gospel is the only hermeneutic of the gospel[33]—and this is a deeply missional perspective. A dynamic, worshiping community is central to mission: mission is "moored in the Church's worship, to its gathering around the Word and the sacraments."[34] Bosch also places a strong emphasis on the church as an *alternative community*, and this is a helpful emphasis in many ways. However, it may also be the source of the tension in his ecclesiology identified above. Timothy Yates makes an important observation in this respect.

W. Nicol accused Bosch of a Docetic ecclesiology: his exposure to the kind of *Heilsgeschichte* views of a theologian like Oscar Cullmann, where

29. Bosch, *Witness to the World*, 225.

30. Bosch, *Witness to the World*, 98. Cf. idem, "The Kingdom of God and the Kingdoms of This World," *Journal of Theology for Southern Africa* 29 (1979): 3–13.

31. Bosch, *Witness to the World*, 226. Note that Kuyper's view of common and particular or special grace was critiqued by S. U. Zuidema, "Common Grace and Christian Action in Abraham Kuyper," in Zuidema's *Communication and Confrontation* (Toronto: Wedge, 1972), 52–105. Zuidema argues that Kuyper in his *Common Grace* corrects his earlier, more dualistic view found in his *Pro Rege*. According to Zuidema, van Ruler fails to take this correction into account.

32. Bosch, *Transforming Mission*, 378.

33. Lesslie Newbigin, *Gospel in a Pluralist Society* (Grand Rapids: Eerdmans, 1989), 222–33.

34. Bosch, *Transforming Mission*, 385.

salvation is contained within the church and sacred history is detached from the general historical continuum, allied to his espousal of the church as an "alternative community," a tendency that owed much to J. H. Yoder and Mennonite/Anabaptist views of the church, could on this view lead to a church withdrawn from the world. Even his frequent use of the term "the Church" could be seen as a retreat into universals from the more messy business of dealing with actual ecclesial entities like the Dutch Reformed Church. Against this criticism must be set Bosch's actual record of "prophetic solidarity" as outlined above.[35]

Yates is helpful in identifying Bosch's indebtedness to John Howard Yoder and Stanley Hauerwas in his ecclesiology. Their Anabaptist ecclesiology has an overemphasis on the institutional church and a corresponding weakness in their doctrine of creation. The result is the "institutional church" becomes dominant, and rigorous Christian engagement in the different spheres of life is lost sight of. There is indeed much to be learned from contemporary Anabaptist ecclesiology. But the deficiency in a doctrine of creation, and of redemption as *creation* regained, is damaging to one's view of mission and of biblical interpretation. Something of a nature/grace dichotomy is allowed to squeeze into the picture, which becomes evident, I suggest, in Bosch's view of biblical and missional interpretation. It is to this that we will turn after an examination of theological interpretation.

Theological Interpretation as Ecclesial

Theological interpretation is the attempt to recover a reading of the Bible as Christian Scripture for the church today. Until the Enlightenment, virtually everyone in the West read the Bible as Scripture. In the modern period that changed radically, and under the aegis of the historical critical method many sought to read Scripture in "objective," "scientific" ways, divorced from tradition and from theological presuppositions. The recovery of the Bible as literature in the 1970s challenged the hegemony of historical criticism, but before it could be fully appropriated, postmodernism had penetrated every aspect of biblical interpretation, ushered in a wild pluralism in methods of reading the Bible, and shattered any idea of objective interpreta-

35. Timothy Yates, "David Bosch: South African Context, Universal Missiology—Ecclesiology in the Emerging Missionary Paradigm," *International Bulletin of Missionary Research* 33.2 (2009): 72–78 at 73.

tion. Amidst that pluralism, theological interpretation found an uneasy seat at the table of biblical interpretation.

As noted above, theological interpretation today is in vogue, but is definitely a "broad church," as it were. In my view, theological interpretation should include at least the following four characteristics: reading the Bible as the word of God, with the aim of enabling us to hear God's address through Scripture today; presenting the Bible as God's word for the church (its primary recipient); grounding interpretation in the Trinity, as the God who has spoken and continues to speak; and observing that biblical meaning emerges from the economy of the Trinitarian God as revealed in the grand story of Scripture.

Each of these characteristics needs detailed unpacking.[36] For now it is important to note that the first characteristic makes the *telos* of interpreting Scripture the *kerygma* of the text, its message. Sometimes this can be read straight into our situation. Often, however, one will need to work out what the text under consideration meant at its stage in the economy of God and then see what it means in our stage. Analysis of the Bible as a drama in multiple acts (following Tom Wright's proposal) has proved fertile in this regard. When we read a text from an earlier act in the drama of Scripture we need to employ all its clues in the context of the grand story of Scripture to improvise today in our particular context as we seek to indwell the story of the Bible.

Just as a missional hermeneutic was recovered through the concept of the *missio Dei* grounded in the Trinity,[37] so too theological interpretation comes alive when the canon of Scripture is read as *the place* through which God chooses to speak authoritatively in the gathered community (institutional church). God spoke his final and full word in his Son, who affirmed the authority of the Old Testament, and who is witnessed to authoritatively in the New Testament. Thus I like to think of Scripture as the field in which is hid the pearl of great price so that as we dig in this field we are drawn ever more deeply into the very life of God.

36. Suffice it here to refer to other places where I have expanded on these aspects at some length. Craig G. Bartholomew, "Theological Interpretation," in *The Oxford Encyclopedia for Biblical Interpretation*, ed. Steven L. McKenzie (New York: Oxford University Press, 2013); Craig G. Bartholomew and Heath A. Thomas, eds., *A Manifesto for Theological Interpretation* (Grand Rapids: Baker, 2016); Craig G. Bartholomew, *Introducing Biblical Hermeneutics: A Comprehensive Guide for Hearing God in Scripture* (Grand Rapids: Baker Academic, 2015).

37. Cf. John G. Flett, *The Witness of God: The Trinity, Missio Dei, Karl Barth, and the Nature of Christian Community* (Grand Rapids: Eerdmans, 2010).

Scripture came into existence through the life of Israel, in the Christ event, and amidst the life of the early church. Its literary diversity alerts us to God's speech not being monotone: he speaks in a whole variety of genres. A helpful instrument in this respect is speech-act theory. Speech-act theory distinguishes between the locution of a speech act, the illocutionary force, and the perlocutionary effect. For our purposes the second element is the most important. The *illocutionary force* of biblical texts varies tremendously. Parts of the Bible instruct, others admonish, others invite, others tell stories, others teach us how to respond to God in prayer, others command, others send us out, and so we could continue.

Amid the diverse genres of Scripture we should not forget *tota scriptura*: as a whole, Scripture is God's unified voice, and one vital thing that it does as a whole is to tell us the true story of the world. In this sense Scripture itself functions as a hermeneutic, interpreting ourselves to ourselves, and teaching us how to see and live in the world as the theater of God's glory.

Scripture is God's word to God's people, and thus it is best received when the community gathers to hear Scripture read and preached, and to celebrate the sacraments. Such reading of the Bible proceeds from faith and listening to listening and faith. Theological interpretation is also committed to God's word being *for all of life*. By this I do not mean to assert that every answer we need or desire is found in Scripture, but to insist with Newbigin that "Jesus is the clue to understanding all that is."[38] Theological interpretation will be attentive to what Scripture *is* designed to do and what it *is not* intended to do, and will navigate the river's channel between the damaging shoals of biblicism and dualism. For example, the Bible does not provide us with a philosophical anthropology, but it does *orient us authoritatively* toward how to view humankind, and philosophy that takes theological interpretation seriously will need to employ all such insights in its quest for a philosophical anthropology.

Theological Interpretation and a Missional Hermeneutic

How does such a hermeneutic relate to a missional hermeneutic? To begin defining mission is a complicated matter. If, as a minimum, we take the idea of "sending" as central to mission, embrace the fertile emphasis of the *missio*

38. Lesslie Newbigin, *The Light Has Come: An Exposition of the Fourth Gospel* (Grand Rapids: Eerdmans, 1982), 3; cf. also Newbigin's *Gospel in a Pluralist Society*, 103–15.

Dei, and adopt a definition like that of the Lausanne Covenant, by which mission is seen as "the whole church taking the whole gospel to the whole world,"[39] then we have a basis to work from. First, it is clear that the grand story of the Bible deals with far more than mission. Mission in the sense of the *missio Dei* begins in the biblical story after the fall, in Genesis 3:15 at the earliest. It is thus unhelpful to speak of creation as missional. Mission flows out of God's great work of *redemption*, and there will thus come a time when the *missio Dei* will cease. Thus, I do not think that God is "eternally missional."[40]

Missiologists are right to ground the *missio Dei* in the Trinity: as the Father sends the Son, and as the Son sends the Spirit, so the Trinitarian God sends the church out into the world. Such sending has strong grounds in John's Gospel: "As the Father has sent me, so I send you" (20:21). However, the sending of the Son and the sending of the Spirit are both related to redemption, albeit redemption as a recovery of God's purposes for creation. And the sendings of both the Son and the Spirit are New Testament phenomena, as a result of which mission begins in earnest. This is not for a moment to deny the missional dimension of the Old Testament, but it is undoubtedly far more muted than post-Pentecost. Bosch defends his neglect of the Old Testament in *Transforming Mission* by noting that "there is, in the Old Testament, no indication of the believers of the old covenant being sent by God to cross geographical, religious, and social frontiers in order to win others to faith in Yahweh."[41] There is indeed a missional dimension to the life of Israel; as a royal priesthood it is called to be a light to the nations. However, its mission is understood almost wholly in centripetal terms whereas in the New Testament it is understood largely in centrifugal terms.

Post-Pentecost mission is central to the life and existence of the church in a way that it never was before. As a dimension of church life it is front and center, but it nevertheless remains *a* dimension. The church is also, for example, a worshiping community, a community of fellowship, a community made up of full-time servants of the Lord Christ who are

39. Lausanne Covenant §6 (1974). Affirmed in Manila Manifesto affirmation 21 (1989) and The Cape Town Commitment preamble (2010). These are the three main gatherings of the Lausanne Movement, a movement of global evangelicalism.

40. Bosch makes a similar point in his critique of DuBose's approach to mission. He rightly asks, "Is it justifiable to arrogate G. Ernest Wright's study, *God Who Acts*, for one's own purposes by admitting that the God of the Bible is the God who acts, and then to add, 'the way he acts is through his sending' (pp. 63–64)?" Bosch, "Book Reviews: Mission in Biblical Perspective," *International Review of Mission* 74 (1985): 531–38 at 533.

41. Bosch, *Transforming Mission*, 17.

at work in his world, seeking to resist evil and to develop it to his glory. The *ekklēsia* is first called, then sent; and even once sent it remains called. While it is true that healthy worship, rich family life, deep fellowship among Christians, and the practice of work as vocation are profoundly missional, this dimension is more a spinoff of their practice than of their intent. They are good in and of themselves, by their being part of God's good creation. Indeed, as an overstress on evangelism has taught us, such activities become denatured when they are made intentionally missional.

In this respect it is worth reflecting more closely on the "as" in "as the Father has sent me, so I am sending you." This is metaphorical language, which often works by juxtaposing two unlike things in order to spark insight into a reality and to draw an analogy between them. Jesus's statement certainly does this, drawing attention to the profound ways in which the life of the church is connected to and illuminated by the mission of the Son and of the Father. However, central to metaphor is also *dissimilarity*: it is also true that we are *not* sent as Jesus was sent. We are not *the* Son, and the implications and content of our sending are different in many ways from those associated with the sending of *the* Son.

My conclusion is that a missional hermeneutic has been and is being wonderfully helpful in drawing attention to the missional motif or dimension in Scripture, a motif ignored for far too long. But, just as God cannot be "reduced" to being missional, so too Scripture should not be read solely through the lens of mission. I suggest that a missional hermeneutic be seen as a subset of a theological hermeneutic or of theological interpretation.

Why Biblical Interpretation Needs a Missional Hermeneutic

But what of academic biblical interpretation? How does it relate to a missional hermeneutic? It is here that a missional hermeneutic has an indispensable role to play *today*. Ironically, the limitations of Bosch's view of biblical hermeneutics illustrate this very point.[42]

Bosch advocates a "critical hermeneutic" for missiology. Both biblical studies and missiology are necessary for biblical interpretation:

42. This is not for a moment to deny Bosch's major contribution to missional hermeneutics. See, e.g., Michael W. Goheen, "A Critical Examination of David Bosch's Missional Reading of Luke," in *Reading Luke: Interpretation, Reflection, Formation*, ed. Craig G. Bartholomew, Joel B. Green, Anthony C. Thiselton (Grand Rapids: Zondervan, 2005), 229–64.

> The reticence of biblical scholars thus indeed helps us to come to a fuller understanding of the text in its original historical setting. At the same time, however, they frequently fail to show whether, and, if so, how, the Bible can be of significance to the church-in-mission and how, if at all, a connection between the biblical evidence and the contemporary missionary scene can be made. The church thus feels left in the lurch, at least to a degree.[43]

For Bosch, biblical studies protects us from reading our own presuppositions into the biblical text, while missiology resists biblical studies' fixation with the original meaning and pushes toward what the Bible means for us today. Bosch speaks of biblical (specifically, New Testament) interpretation as making clear early Christian self-definitions. He proposes that what we need is to build on these by opening up dialogue between these and subsequent ones including our own. Self-definitions may be inadequate or wrong—Bosch seems to include biblical ones in this—and so may require correction and re-formation. Philosophically, Bosch articulates a strong antirealism: there is no objective reality out there; reality is intersubjective, and it changes if one's self-definition changes. But we cannot and should not try to avoid articulating the self-definition of Jesus, which, for Bosch, remains normative.

In an almost direct quotation from Brueggemann, to whom Bosch appeals,[44] Bosch asserts that there is no simplistic or obvious line to be drawn from the Bible to our missional practices. Instead there may be a range of alternative hermeneutical moves, which remain in deep tension with each other but may nevertheless all be valid. Evangelicals have tended to adopt a deductive hermeneutic; ecumenicals an inductive one. Bosch resists this dichotomy and asserts that in the real world there is "no such thing as a purely deductive method. Evangelicals are deceiving themselves for . . . [one] reads the Bible in terms of [one's] own context."[45] He likewise criticizes the inductive method favored by ecumenicals, because "context can become more than just a 'hermeneutical key.' It could come to determine everything, to such an extent that Scriptures ultimately can do little other than simply accede to the demands of the context." Bosch remains

43. Bosch, "Book Reviews: Mission in Biblical Perspective," 532.

44. Bosch, *Transforming Mission*, 24.

45. Quoted in Girma Bekele, "The Biblical Narrative of the *Missio Dei*: Analysis of the Interpretive Framework of David Bosch's Missional Hermeneutic," *International Bulletin of Missionary Research* 35.3 (July 2011): 152–59 at 155.

confident that through such a critical hermeneutical approach we can move toward an accurate understanding of the text on its own terms that also addresses our context.

Bosch's hermeneutic was subjected to criticism. Bekele notes his lack of attention to the Old Testament, for example.[46] J. G. Du Plessis probes his doctrine of Scripture and finds it wanting in key areas. Bosch's hermeneutic does attempt to hold together the historical-critical theological approaches with the inspired thrust of the biblical message. However, he weakens the latter by promoting a view of the Bible as the authors' interpretation of divine revelation, as opposed to the Bible itself being a revelatory record. As Du Plessis puts it, "To speak of the Bible as interpretation of revelation and not a recording of it only suspends the question of its status."[47] Bekele points out that critics such as Du Plessis are correct that Bosch cannot sustain his conviction that all subsequent missions should be assessed on the basis of the model of the Scriptures, and particularly of the New Testament, while at the same time diminishing the revelatory essence of Scriptures. Bosch, as we have seen, endeavors to retain a commitment to historical criticism, while also critiquing it for its entrapment within the negative forces of the Enlightenment. His alternative approach, the creative missional hermeneutic, thus contains unresolved—indeed unresolvable—tensions within it.

An example of these tensions is Bosch's assertion that there is no simplistic or obvious move from the Bible to our missionary practices. At face value this sounds acceptable and appears to be pointing to the hermeneutic ecology in missional interpretation. However, Bosch appeals to Brueggemann at this point, and one needs to read Brueggemann's article in order to understand what Bosch means. In "The Bible and Mission: Some Interdisciplinary Implications for Teaching,"[48] Brueggemann tells us that we must stress a *diversity* of approaches in teaching the Bible. In terms of mission, if we attend to the faith-culture lens of texts we will find in Scripture many different models, "each of which implies a different missional posture."[49] Thus we need a hermeneutic of diversity and of *suspicion*, since there are simply no disinterested texts. "Every text serves an interest and proposes a

46. Bekele, "Biblical Narrative of the *Missio Dei*," 154–55.

47. J. G. Du Plessis, "For Reasons of the Heart: A Critical Appraisal of David J. Bosch's Use of Scripture in the Foundation of Christian Mission," *Missionalia* 18.1 (1990): 75–85 at 83.

48. Walter A. Brueggemann, "The Bible and Mission: Some Interdisciplinary Implications for Teaching," *Missiology: An International Review* 10.4 (1982): 397–412.

49. Brueggemann, "Bible and Mission," 398.

missional settlement of faith and culture."[50] Brueggemann invokes Ricoeur with his double act of abolishing idols and wanting again to be called. According to Brueggemann, "These four assumptions must inform our teaching: diversity of range which rejects reductionism, articulation of faith/culture models as an intention of the text, social criticism which sees every text as interested, and literary criticism which sees language as linked to social criticism and serving social models."[51] As always, Brueggemann provides examples of such readings.

Thus 1 Kings 4:20–28 proposes that "the system is the solution" and does not allow for any elements of reality excluded or resisted by the royal system. But Deuteronomy 19:1–10, which legislates for cities of refuge, contrasts with the Solomonic vision of 1 Kings 4 (in which the royal ideology absolutizes the established order). Instead, Deuteronomy casts a vision in which every social form is a construct that can be reshaped and transformed. In 1 Samuel 2:10 Brueggemann discerns a theology from below in which we hear the voices from the margins. At the end of his article we find the sentence that is almost identical to Bosch's: "There are no simplistic or obvious moves to contemporary missional practice, for the Bible does not function in such a direct way. Rather it can open a field of metaphors for a fresh perception of social reality and social possibility."[52] Clearly, if this is what Bosch has in mind with his critical hermeneutic then it is far from integrated and allows large swaths of modern and postmodern thought to impact biblical interpretation uncritically. As Brueggemann's article reveals, this has major implications for the use of the Bible in the theological disciplines and in other subjects.

Bosch thus underestimates the extent to which modern biblical study is enmeshed in the ideologies of modernity. Like Barth and Brevard Childs, Bosch seeks to hold on to historical criticism while moving beyond it. Childs, however, would never have been as open to Brueggemann's social type of criticism as is Bosch. Newbigin, by comparison, saw more clearly the need for a missional encounter with biblical studies and sought to facilitate such a move.[53] Modern biblical studies are quintessentially, for bet-

50. Brueggemann, "Bible and Mission," 398.

51. Brueggemann, "Bible and Mission," 399.

52. Brueggemann, "Bible and Mission," 408.

53. See Craig G. Bartholomew and Michael W. Goheen, "Story and Biblical Theology," in *Out of Egypt: Biblical Theology and Biblical Interpretation*, ed. C. G. Bartholomew, M. Healy, K. Möller, and R. Parry; Scripture and Hermeneutics Series 5 (Carlisle: Paternoster; Grand Rapids: Zondervan, 2004), 172–84.

ter and for worse, a product of the Enlightenment, as their indebtedness to Spinoza, Kant, and others demonstrates.[54] Under the guise of neutrality they continue to obscure their own ideological underpinnings, a supposed neutrality affirmed by far too many Christian practitioners of biblical study in the West.

When Newbigin retired from his missionary work in India and returned to the West, he spent the remaining years of his life trying to alert us to the West being *the* major missional field today. To put it simply, the West is built on and tells a radically different story or stories of the world than the story told by the Bible. And to a very large extent modern biblical study operates within the Western metanarrative(s).

Biblical study thus urgently requires *a missional encounter with the gospel.* Only thus can a missional hermeneutic perform the task Bosch assigns to missiology: "Missiology has in the first place a critical function and operates as a leaven in theology—sometimes as a gadfly."[55] As with any healthy missional encounter, this would not obscure or neglect the many contributions of historical criticism and postmodern interpretation, but would, to use Kraemer's expression, reconfigure them within a different paradigm as a type of *subversive fulfillment.*[56] If theological interpretation is to mature and to fulfill its potential, such a missional encounter is essential. Only such an encounter will alert us to the thick contours of a healthy biblical hermeneutic and enable Christian interpretation of Scripture to move forward proactively. In biblical studies N. T. Wright's major series, *Christian Origins and the Question of God*, stands out as *the* example of what such work might look like today.[57]

Such a robust theological hermeneutic will need to have its ear finely tuned to the music of God's mission. It will, I suspect, with the help of a missional hermeneutic, also alert us to other neglected themes in Scripture, such as that worship requires a *liturgical hermeneutic*, opening us up to the role of worship in the Bible and how to read for and from worship.[58] A sim-

54. See Craig G. Bartholomew, "Uncharted Waters: Philosophy, Theology, and the Crisis in Biblical Interpretation," in *Renewing Biblical Interpretation*, ed. C. Bartholomew et al.; Scripture and Hermeneutics Series 1 (Grand Rapids: Zondervan, 2000), 1–39.

55. Bosch, "Theological Education in Missionary Perspective," 27.

56. Hendrik Kraemer, "Continuity and Discontinuity," in *The Authority of Faith*, Madras Series 1 (New York: International Missionary Council, 1939), 4.

57. Cf. Bartholomew and Goheen, "Story and Biblical Theology."

58. Scott Hahn did important work in this area. See, e.g., "Scripture and the Liturgy:

ilarly neglected theme is that spirituality requires a *hermeneutic of spirituality*, enabling us to read so as to live ever more deeply into the life of God.

When one thinks of the sheer potential of a theological and a missional hermeneutic working together, one is reminded of Neuhaus's perceptive comment:

> More and more "young fogeys" like Oden are discovering the truth that is "ever ancient, ever new" (Augustine). It is called the catholic feast and it is a feast to which he invites us. It is a moveable feast, still developing under the guidance of the Spirit. Oden is like cinema's "Auntie Mame," who observed that life is a banquet and most poor slobs are starving to death. Origen, Irenaeus, Cyril of Alexandria, Thomas Aquinas, Teresa of Avila, Martin Luther, John Calvin, John Wesley—the names fall trippingly from Oden's tongue like a gourmet surveying a most spectacular table. Here are arguments you can sink your teeth into, conceptual flights of intoxicating complexity, and truths to die for. Far from the table, over there, *way* over there, is American theological education, where prodigal academics feed starving students on the dry husks of their clever unbelief.[59]

Theological and missional interpretation have already achieved a great deal. But much more work remains to be done if biblical interpretation is truly to set a feast for today. An important element in the renaissance of theological interpretation has been the retrieval of "precritical" interpretation for today. Missional interpretation is a more recent phenomenon but it too has a rich tradition, and we need to retrieve the works of luminaries such as Karl Hartenstein, H.-W. Gensichen, Georg Friedrich Vicedom, and so many others. At the same time, even as missiology helps theological interpretation open up its multiple dimensions, we will need to work together to develop an integrated biblical hermeneutic for today.

Inseparably United," *Origins* 35.39 (2006): 648–53; "Worship in the Word: Toward a Liturgical Hermeneutic," *Letter and Spirit: A Journal of Catholic Biblical Theology* 1 (2005): 101–36.

59. Richard John Neuhaus, "An Invitation to the Feast," preface in Thomas C. Oden, *Requiem: A Lament in Three Movements* (Nashville: Abingdon, 1995), 10.

CHAPTER 5

Intercultural Hermeneutics and the Shape of Missional Theology

John R. Franke

Missionary theologian Lesslie Newbigin envisions a mission-shaped theology emerging from the ongoing interactions among the gospel, culture, and the church.[1] The dynamic and situated nature of such interaction is a reminder of the contextual and local character of a properly missional theology.[2] Taking the local character of theology seriously nurtures an appreciation for the dynamic relationships among gospel, culture, and church, and for the theological and interpretive diversity that is the result of such interaction. This raises a serious challenge for the catholicity of theology, the intention to bear witness to the one faith of the whole church. If all theology is local, how can any of us develop a theology that reflects the one faith of the church rather than one that merely accommodates our own assumptions, aspirations, and desires? Newbigin addresses this question by observing that though the ultimate commitment of a Christian theologian is to the biblical story, all would-be theologians are also participants in a particular social setting. As such, their whole outlook and way of thinking is shaped, consciously or not, by the cultural model of the society in which they participate. These cultural models should not be allowed to obscure the teachings and implications of the biblical narrative for us. But, immersed as we are in particular cultures,

1. On the development of this Newbigin triad, see George R. Hunsberger, "The Newbigin Gauntlet: Developing a Domestic Missiology for North America," in *The Church between Gospel and Culture: The Emerging Mission in North America*, ed. George R. Hunsberger and Craig Van Gelder (Grand Rapids: Eerdmans, 1996), 3–25.

2. For a detailed discussion on the significance of situatedness for the work of theology, see John R. Franke, *The Character of Theology: An Introduction to Its Nature, Task, and Purpose* (Grand Rapids: Baker Academic, 2005), 83–118.

we are often not able to see how they do cloud our vision, for it is perilously easy to absolutize our own socially constructed cultural models.

Newbigin reminds us to be wholly open to the biblical narrative in such a way that the assumptions and aspirations of our own cultures are viewed in the light of Scripture. We may then find ways of expressing the biblical story in terms that make use of particular cultural models—but without being controlled by them. We are particularly vulnerable to the undetected shaping influence of cultural assumptions on our theology; Newbigin counsels us to guard against such parochial influence by being "continuously open to the witness of Christians in other cultures who are seeking to practice the same kind of theology."[3]

If we seek to be open to the witness of Christians in other cultures, we may need to amend the standard approach to Bible reading in the West, in which hermeneutics is an interaction simply between a reader and a text. Newbigin's comment suggests that hermeneutics should involve a third group of interlocutors: Christians from other cultures who read and engage the biblical texts in different ways. Such an approach will significantly alter the standard assumptions of the hermeneutical process as well as the contours of a theology that emerges from that process. This chapter examines the idea of intercultural hermeneutics before reflecting on the contours of a mission-shaped approach to theology. Such a theology places mission at the very core of its nature, task, and purpose and thus develops forms of interpretation and practice that help shape the church as a social community embodying the gospel of Jesus Christ, living out and bearing witness to the good news of God's love for all creation.

Intercultural Hermeneutics

The task of reading the Bible with others and developing an intercultural approach to hermeneutics emerges from one of the most basic assumptions of Christian faith: that the gospel of Jesus Christ is good news for all people. This truth is at the heart of the revelation of God's love for the world in Jesus Christ, just as the angel announced it to the shepherds in Luke 2:8–11 (New International Version): "Do not be afraid. I bring you good news that will cause great joy for all the people."

3. Lesslie Newbigin, "Theological Education in a World Perspective," *Churchman* 93 (1979): 114–15.

It is one of the great failures of the Christian tradition that all too often the proclamation and living out of the Christian message has not been good news for many of the people of the world. It has frequently been the cause not of great joy but rather of pain and suffering. Too often, people have been subjugated, enslaved, and exterminated in the name of Christianity. The expansion of the church in history has often been closely connected with the extension of empire, and colonization justified by a self-serving reading of biblical texts. While all of the texts that would eventually make up the Christian canon were produced at the margins of empire, the young church was too soon and too often complicit with Rome, and the most influential location for the interpretation of these biblical texts shifted from the margins to the center. This shift led to a change in the interpretive strategies of many readers, who were as much interested in the health of the empire as they were in the health of the church. Stephen Moore observes that, in the hands of imperial powers, "the primary function of the biblical texts became that of legitimizing the imperial status quo, a function that, covertly when not overtly, continued into the modern period."[4]

Missiologists observe that much of the theological activity in Europe and North America over the past two hundred years was grounded in the intuitions and assumptions of those cultures. The Christian message and its implications were passed on in the social and cultural shape given them by the Western church. As the authors of *Missional Church* remark, "The subtle assumption of much Western mission was that the church's missionary mandate lay not only in forming the church of Jesus Christ, but in shaping the Christian communities that it birthed in the image of the church of western European culture."[5] This resulted in the colonization and oppression of numerous communities in the name of God, of Jesus, and of the Bible.

Commenting on the early encounter between Christianity and the indigenous people of North America, Richard Twiss, a member of the Rosebud Lakota/Sioux tribe, puts the matter succinctly: "Christian mission among the tribes of North America has not been very good news. What worldview influences allowed the Creator's story of creation and redemption to morph into a hegemonic colonial myth justifying the genocide and exploitation of America's First Nations people?"[6] Speaking of his own ex-

4. Stephen D. Moore, "Paul after Empire," in *The Colonized Apostle: Paul through Postcolonial Eyes*, ed. Christopher D. Stanley (Minneapolis: Fortress, 2011), 22.

5. Darrell L. Guder, ed., *Missional Church: A Vision for the Sending of the Church in North America* (Grand Rapids: Eerdmans, 1998), 4.

6. Richard Twiss, "Living in Transition, Embracing Community, and Envisioning

perience, he explains the pressure imposed by white Christians to regard the music, dance, drumming, and ceremony of his culture as "unclean" and inappropriate for followers of Jesus. The implicit message was that the old and familiar rituals and experiences had passed away and all things had "become white." To Twiss, "This meant I needed to leave my Indian ways behind me, because I had a new identity in Christ, and it WAS NOT Indian! The Bible was used to demonize just about everything important to our cultural sense of being one with God and creation."[7] He concludes that the prevailing worldview assumptions latent in Western approaches to Bible reading and theology not only linger today, but have been retained as a distinct "bias against Native culture and ways."[8] Other people groups who do not share traditional Western assumptions concerning the hegemonic forms of hermeneutics and theology may suffer from similar biases. As a corrective, intercultural hermeneutics and missional theology seek to be faithful to the central vision of the gospel as good news for *all* people.

Intercultural hermeneutics is the result of an interdisciplinary conversation among biblical studies, theology, cultural anthropology, and missiology.[9] A key insight of this hermeneutics is radical contextuality: the idea that all human discourse is embedded in and thoroughly shaped by the social setting from which it emerges. There are no noncontextual, or contextually neutral, forms of communication. Intercultural hermeneutics challenges older notions of contextuality that focus on communication rather than interpretation. In the communication model, the gospel message itself is thought to be fully established and timeless, with the challenge residing in the proper communication of that message in a culturally appropriate form. The difficulty with this model is its failure to recognize that the gospel message and all of its forms are, already, thoroughly contextual. Lesslie Newbigin notes that a cross-cultural Christian missionary does not come "with the pure gospel and then adapt it to the culture where she serves: she comes with a gospel which is already embodied in the culture by which the

---

God's Mission as Trinitarian Mutuality: Reflections from a Native-American Follower of Jesus," in *Remembering Jamestown: Hard Questions about Christian Mission*, ed. Amos Yong and Barbara Brown Zikmund (Eugene, OR: Pickwick, 2010), 93.

7. Twiss, "Living in Transition," 94.

8. Twiss, "Living in Transition," 94.

9. For early examples of this interaction in evangelical theology, see Charles H. Kraft, *Christianity in Culture: A Study in Biblical Theologizing in Cross-Cultural Perspective* (Maryknoll, NY: Orbis, 1979); and Harvie M. Conn, *Eternal Word and Changing Worlds: Theology, Anthropology, and Mission in Trialogue* (Phillipsburg, NJ: Presbyterian & Reformed, 1992).

missionary was formed." He asserts that this is the situation even with respect to Scripture: "The Bible is a book which is very obviously in a specific cultural setting. Its language is Hebrew and Greek, not Chinese or Sanskrit. All the events it records, all the teachings it embodies, are shaped by specific human cultures."[10] He concludes that "the idea that one can or could at any time separate out by some process of distillation a pure gospel unadulterated by any cultural accretions is an illusion."[11]

In other words, the process of contextualization is not something that takes place after the biblical texts, and their interpretations and corresponding doctrines, have been established. Rather, contextualization is fully present in all of these forms of witness and cannot be removed from them. Contextuality is inherent in the process of understanding and communicating. From this perspective, biblical interpretation, meaning, and communication always involve the recontextualization of texts and their particular appropriations in a variety of social and historical settings. This ongoing activity of recontextualization in and for a diversity of cultural settings is the essence of intercultural hermeneutics. Hence, intercultural hermeneutics has an inherently relational dimension that involves seeking to understand the social contexts of other interpreters. This relational dimension challenges common notions of Christian witness, and particularly of cross-cultural missionary activity. In the intercultural model, witness is not the delivery of preestablished conceptions of the gospel and Christian teaching, treating the recipients of the message as objects. (These recipients-as-objects are expected to receive the message as presented if they are to benefit from its promises.) Such an approach leads to the situation described by Twiss: the "message" comes packed in an alien ideology that, if accepted, will subvert the ecosystem of the existing culture. But truly intercultural understanding involves genuine and loving concern for others and for the cultural settings that have shaped their identity. When this approach is applied to hermeneutics, the discipline becomes an enterprise in mutual understanding in which all of the partners contribute to the conversation.

One way of understanding this process is to think of each of the participants in a conversation as a missionary to the others. Justo González reminds us that the church needs not only to speak to the world, but also

10. Lesslie Newbigin, *The Gospel in a Pluralist Society* (Grand Rapids: Eerdmans, 1989), 144–45.

11. Lesslie Newbigin, *Foolishness to the Greeks: The Gospel and Western Culture* (Grand Rapids: Eerdmans, 1986), 4.

to *hear* the world in all the diversity of its nations, cultures, and ethnicities. Listening in this way, the church will have a fuller understanding of the gospel, as Christians from all the earth bring the richness of their varied experience to its proclamation and witness: "The church needs the 'nations' in order to be fully 'catholic.' If 'catholic' means 'according to the whole,' as long as part of the whole remains outside, or is brought in without being allowed to speak from its own perspective, catholicity itself is truncated."[12]

This brings us back to Newbigin: if we are to comprehend the fullness of the gospel and the witness of Scripture, we must remain continually open to the witness of Christians in other cultures, resisting the temptation to absolutize our own culturally shaped theological models. Hence, intercultural hermeneutics poses two broad interpretive tasks that give shape to missional theology, one positive and one negative: positively, it proposes the development of theological models and convictions that emerge from the engagement of intercultural encounter; negatively, it stands in opposition to theological approaches and conclusions that absolutize particular models and systems, thus equating the gospel and Christian faith with a particular cultural setting.

The Shape of Missional Theology

Intercultural hermeneutics calls forth alternative approaches to theology and mission that share many of the concerns of postmodern cultural and philosophical thought. I suggest that missional theology emerges from the interactions among intercultural hermeneutics, missiology, and postmodern thought, and thus missional theology is (1) open and committed to the other, (2) beyond foundations, and (3) against totality. Before turning our attention to each of these aspects of missional theology, let us first briefly consider the conviction that drives a missional approach to theology.

God Is a Missionary God

A missional approach to theology arises from the conviction that the triune God is a missionary God and that his church is thus missionary by its

12. Justo González, *Out of Every Tribe and Nation: Christian Theology at the Ethnic Roundtable* (Nashville: Abingdon, 1992), 28–29.

very nature.[13] The idea of mission is at the heart of the biblical narratives concerning the work of God in human history.[14] The missional call to the church is captured in the words of Jesus recorded in the Gospel of John: "As the Father has sent me, so I send you" (John 20:21). As David Bosch observes, mission is derived from the very nature of God; thus the classical doctrine of the *missio Dei*, expressed as God the Father sending the Son, and the Father and the Son sending the Spirit, may be expanded to include another movement: "Father, Son, and Spirit sending the church into the world."[15] The church is an instrument and witness of God's mission to the world, not its end. The various historical, cultural, global, and contemporary embodiments of the church may be viewed as a series of local iterations of God's universal mission to all of creation.

While the mission of God expressed in the created order is complex and multifaceted, its unifying motivation is love. The biblical affirmation that "God is love" (1 John 4:8) points not simply to the love of God for the world, but also to the eternal life of God lived in the ongoing relationship of love that constitutes God's being in and for Godself. This is the eternal Trinitarian fellowship in which Father, Son, and Holy Spirit participate together in the giving, receiving, and sharing of love. Throughout eternity, the life of the triune God is characterized by love. This divine love is found in the reciprocal interdependence and self-dedication of the Trinitarian members to each other. Indeed, there is no God other than the Father, Son, and Spirit bound together in the active relations of love throughout eternity.

This love provides a profound conception of the reality of God as understood by the Christian tradition. Love expressed and received by the Trinitarian persons among themselves provides a description of the inner life of God throughout eternity apart from any reference to creation. In addition to enjoying the support of the biblical witness and the tradition of the church, love is an especially fruitful term for comprehending the life of God since it is an inherently relational concept. Love requires both subject and object, and the life of God comprehends both love's subject and love's object. For this reason, when viewed theologically, the statement "God is

13. See John G. Flett, *The Witness of God: The Trinity, Missio Dei, Karl Barth, and the Nature of Christian Community* (Grand Rapids: Eerdmans, 2010).

14. On the centrality of mission in Scripture, see Christopher J. H. Wright, *The Mission of God: Unlocking the Bible's Grand Narrative* (Downers Grove, IL: IVP Academic, 2006).

15. David Bosch, *Transforming Mission: Paradigm Shifts in Theology of Mission*, 20th anniversary ed. (Maryknoll, NY: Orbis, 1991), 399.

love" refers primarily to the eternal, relational intra-Trinitarian fellowship among Father, Son, and Holy Spirit, who together are the one God.

The plurality-in-unity and unity-in-plurality that characterize the life of the triune God add an important dimension to this fellowship of divine love. This means that difference and otherness are part of the divine life. The love of God is not an assimilating love, seeking to make that which is different the same; rather, God lives in harmonious fellowship with the other through the active relations of self-sacrificing, self-giving love. The Father, Son, and Spirit are indeed one God, but this unity does not make them the same. They are one in the very midst of their difference. And this is the quality of that love that characterizes the mission of God from all eternity. Hence, missional theology is open and committed to the other, in keeping with the centrality of love and relationality in the divine life and the mission of God in the world.

Missional Theology Is Open and Committed to the Other

As with intercultural hermeneutics and postmodern theory, missional theology asserts that meaning and truth are not static entities that can easily be grasped and assimilated by situated human beings. Truth is an event. It is not something that can be taken to the bank, deposited, and secured forevermore. In attempts to make truth absolute, it is reified as though it were a commodity to be accessed and controlled by human beings, with the danger that it will then be put to use in ways that empower its holders at the expense of others. Instead, truth is a reality to which we must continually aspire. From the perspective of missional theology, this aspiration involves the commitment of our entire beings to the love of God revealed in Jesus Christ through the power of the Spirit. Such love compels us to privilege others above ourselves in accordance with the teaching and example of Jesus. God's love reminds us that we are always in a position of dependence and in need of grace with respect to our knowledge of God, the source of all truth. The failure of humans to acknowledge our dependence on God and the ways in which we are prone to error have been common throughout history and inevitably lead to oppression and conceptual idolatry.

In the Christian tradition, we are invited to see Jesus in the faces of others, particularly the poor and marginalized, and also to see God in Jesus. Thus Jesus becomes the focal point for a theological orientation toward the other. The emphasis on the other and the complementary notion of hybridity are particularly promising aspects of postmodern thought for the practice of intercultural hermeneutics and missional theology. In broadest terms, the "other" is viewed as anything or anyone that falls outside of one's own categories. Here the realm and context of a person's own particular self, or what is called the "same," is constantly confronted and pierced by that which is other, that which cannot be confined in the categories of the same.

The challenge is to respect the "other" for its otherness and not to seek to eliminate its distinctive difference.[16] This has significance for the knowledge of God made known in the face of the other, which knowledge cannot be thematized or conceptualized, suppressed or possessed. Instead, in the face of the other, in the very difference and strangeness of the other, the ultimate irreducibility of the other to sameness, we glimpse something of the epiphany of transcendence.[17] A related concept is that of hybridity, which represents the persistence of difference in unity. This is not the same as syncretism, which entails the attempt to unite opposing principles. Hybridity stands for resistance to hardened differences based on binary oppositions and the refusal to absorb all difference into a hegemonic notion of sameness.

At its core, postmodernity is a movement that resists the totalizing power of reason in order to celebrate difference and diversity, and missional theology shares this commitment. The agenda of openness to the other leads to a commitment to plurality. This is what accounts for the wide array of discourses that share a commitment to postmodern thought. Reformed theologian James Olthuis summarizes this commitment admirably:

> Ethically, postmodern discourses share an alertness to plurality and a vigilance on behalf of the other. Modernist rational ethics, in its Enlightenment dream of a world increasingly controlled by a pure rationality, has shown itself not only blind and indifferent to those who are other and different, those who fall outside the dominant discourse, but violent and oppressive to them.[18]

16. For a seminal treatment of these ideas see Edward Said, *Orientalism* (New York: Vintage, 1978).

17. For an extended treatment of the concepts of otherness and transcendence see Emmanuel Levinas, *Alterity and Transcendence*, trans. M. Smith (New York: Columbia University Press, 1999).

18. James Olthuis, "Face-to-Face: Ethical Asymmetry or the Symmetry of Mutuality?" in *Knowing Other-wise: Philosophy at the Threshold of Spirituality*, ed. James Olthuis (New York: Fordham University Press, 1997), 135.

Following the concerns of postmodern discourse, intercultural hermeneutics and missional theology seek to resist the totalizing power of reason in order to celebrate difference and diversity, to remain open and committed to the witness of others. Forms of theology that are properly shaped by the mission of God will continually be characterized by openness and commitment to voices of others in the task of Christian witness. This is consistent with the rule of love that governs all forms of Christian discourse that would be faithful to the triune God, whose love does not seek to assimilate the other. The emphasis on otherness in the life of the triune God as extended into the world through the revelation of God in Jesus Christ has great significance for the practice of theology. If we are to resist the dangers of cultural accommodation and come to know and bear witness to the fullness of the gospel, we must be open to the witness of others.

Cultural imperialism is one of the great dangers in theology and easily leads to the suppression of voices that do not fit the accepted cultural norms for the practice of theology. When a particular set of social and cultural assumptions attempt to stamp the Bible and theology in their own image (as in the situation described by Twiss), then those who do not participate in the assumptions and presuppositions of the majority find themselves marginalized or eclipsed. It is often claimed that they—the others—are not being faithful to Scripture or to the Christian tradition, that they are seeking to import a particular, alien, cultural agenda into the discipline of theology. But openness to plurality and the difference of others calls us to recognize the limitations of our own perspectives and experiences. If our lives are lived for the sake of others, we can be delivered from the prison of our own imaginations and begin to experience something of the reality made known by God in Jesus Christ. This reality exceeds our particular language, thought forms, and experiences but it has come near to us in the person of Jesus Christ, who is the embodiment of the way, the truth, and the life. Openness and commitment to others, the companion notion of hybridity, and the corresponding commitment to plurality for the sake of faithful Christian witness form the positive agenda of missional theology.

Missional Theology Is beyond Foundations

In keeping with its commitment to otherness, contextuality, and plurality, missional theology affirms the postmodern critique of strong or classic foundationalism. The Enlightenment quest for epistemological certitude deeply shaped the modern era through the rejection of premodern notions of authority and replacing them with the notion of indubitable beliefs that are accessible to all individuals. Philosophically, foundationalism is a theory concerned with the justification of knowledge. It maintains that beliefs must be justified by their relationship to other beliefs and that the chain of justifications that results from this procedure must not be circular or endless, but must have a terminus in foundational beliefs that are immune from criticism and cannot be called into question. The goal is a universal knowledge that transcends time and context. In keeping with this pursuit, the ideals of human knowledge since the Enlightenment tended to focus on the universal, the general, and the theoretical rather than on the local, the particular, and the practical.

This conception of knowledge came to dominate the discipline of theology as theologians reshaped their conceptions of the Christian faith in accordance with its dictates. In the nineteenth and twentieth centuries, the foundationalist impulse produced a theological division between the left and the right. Liberals constructed theology upon the foundation of an unassailable religious experience, while conservatives looked to an error-free Bible as the incontrovertible foundation of their theology.[19] But for all their differences, both groups were drawing from foundationalist conceptions of knowledge. In other words, liberal and conservative theologians can often be viewed as working out theological details from two different sides of the same modernist, foundationalist coin.

Postmodern thought raises two related but distinct questions to the modern foundationalist enterprise. First, is such an approach to knowledge *possible*? And second, is it *desirable*? These questions are connected with what may be viewed as the two major branches of postmodern hermeneutical philosophy: the hermeneutics of finitude and the hermeneutics of suspicion. However, the challenges to foundationalism are not only philosophical, but also emerge from the context of Christian theology. Merold Westphal suggests that postmodern theory, with respect to hermeneutical philosophy, may be properly appropriated for the task of explicitly Christian thought on theological grounds: "The hermeneutics of finitude is a meditation on the meaning of human createdness, and the hermeneutics of suspicion is a meditation on the meaning of human fallenness."[20]

19. On the liberal-conservative divide concerning the proper foundation for theology, see Nancey Murphy, *Beyond Liberalism and Fundamentalism: How Modern and Postmodern Philosophy Set the Theological Agenda* (Valley Forge, PA: Trinity, 1996), 11–35.

20. Merold Westphal, *Overcoming Onto-theology: Toward a Postmodern Christian Faith* (New York: Fordham University Press, 2001), xx.

Viewed from this perspective, the questions that are raised by postmodern thought concerning the possibility and desirability of foundationalism are also questions that emerge from the material content of Christian theology.

Modern foundationalism is an impossible dream for finite human beings whose outlooks are always limited and shaped by their particular contexts, and the modern foundationalist emphasis on the inherent goodness of knowledge is shattered by the fallen and sinful nature of human beings who desire to seize control of the epistemic process in order to empower themselves and further their own ends, often at the expense of others. The limitations of finitude and the flawed condition of human nature mean that epistemic foundationalism is neither possible nor desirable for created and sinful persons. This double critique of foundationalism, emerging as it does from the perspectives of both postmodern philosophy and Christian theology, suggests the appropriateness and suitability of the language of nonfoundationalism for the task of theology that is both postmodern and missional.

One of the most significant elements of nonfoundationalism for missional theology is its commitment to contextuality, which requires the opening of theological conversation to the voices of persons and communities who are often excluded from the discourse of Western theology. Nonfoundational epistemology, intercultural hermeneutics, and missional theology all maintain without reservation that no single human perspective, be it that of an individual or a particular community or theological tradition, is adequate to do full justice to the truth of God's revelation in Christ. Richard Mouw points to this issue as one of his own motivations for reflecting seriously about postmodern themes: "As many Christians from other parts of the world challenge our 'North Atlantic' theologies, they too ask us to think critically about our own cultural location, as well as about how we have sometimes blurred the boundaries between what is essential to the Christian message and the doctrine and frameworks we have borrowed from various Western philosophical traditions."[21] The adoption of a nonfoundationalist, intercultural, and missional approach to theology mandates a critical awareness of the role of culture and social location in the process of theological interpretation and construction.

This nonfoundational approach to hermeneutics and theology places emphasis on the local, the particular, and the practical, rather than on the universal, the general, and the theoretical. According to William Stacy

21. Richard Mouw, "Delete the 'Post' from 'Postconservative,'" *Books and Culture* 7.3 (May/June 2001): 22.

Johnson, nonfoundationalist theologies "share a common goal of putting aside all appeals to presumed self-evident, non-inferential, or incorrigible grounds for their intellectual claims."[22] They reject the notion that among the many beliefs that make up a particular theology there must be a single irrefutable foundation that is immune to criticism and provides the certain basis upon which all other assertions are founded. In nonfoundationalist theology all beliefs are open to criticism and reconstruction. This does not mean, as is sometimes alleged, that nonfoundational theology cannot make assertions or maintain strong convictions that may be vigorously defended. As Francis Schüssler Fiorenza notes, to engage in nonfoundationalist theology is to accept that "it is a self-correcting enterprise that examines all claims, all relevant background theories."[23] Nonfoundationalist theology does not eschew convictions: it simply maintains that such convictions, even the most longstanding and dear, are subject to critical scrutiny and potentially to revision, reconstruction, or even rejection.

A missional theology beyond foundations seeks to respond positively and appropriately to the situatedness of all human thought and therefore to embrace a principled theological pluralism. It also attempts to affirm that the ultimate authority in the church is not a particular source, be it Scripture, tradition, or culture, but only the living God revealed in Jesus Christ. This means that human beings are always in a position of dependence and in need of grace with respect to epistemic relations with God. Attempts on the part of humans to seize control of these relations are all too common throughout the history of the church and, no matter how well intentioned, inevitably lead to forms of conceptual idolatry and oppression. Missional theology seeks to nurture an open and flexible approach that is in keeping with the local and contextual character of human knowledge.

Missional Theology Is against Totality

A third aspect of missional theology is closely related to the second. The commitment to resist foundationalism leads to a posture that is against totality. Because missional theology is positively committed to the radi-

22. William Stacy Johnson, *The Mystery of God: Karl Barth and the Postmodern Foundations of Theology* (Louisville: Westminster John Knox, 1997), 3.

23. Francis Schüssler Fiorenza, *Foundational Theology: Jesus and the Church* (New York: Crossroad, 1986), 287.

cal contextuality of intercultural hermeneutics, it stands in opposition to claims that any particular theology is universal for all times and places. This commitment arises from both cultural-anthropological and missiological considerations. From the perspective of cultural anthropology, this stance against totality is connected to the sociology of knowledge and the linguistic turn. Anthropologists maintain that humans do not view the world from an objective vantage point, but structure their world through the concepts they bring to it, particularly in language. Human languages function as social conventions that describe the world in a variety of ways depending on the context of the speaker. No simple, one-to-one relationship exists between language and the world, and thus no single linguistic description can serve to provide an objective conception of the so-called real world. Language structures our perceptions of reality and constitutes the world in which we live.

Anthropologists have discarded the older assumption that culture is a preexisting social-ordering force transmitted externally to members of a cultural group who then passively internalize it. They maintain that this view is mistaken in that it isolates culture from the ongoing social processes that produce and continually alter it. Culture is not an entity standing above or beyond human products and learned mental structures. In short, culture is not a thing.[24] The modernist understanding of culture saw it as that which integrates the various institutional expressions of social life and binds the individual to society. But this focus on the integrative role of culture faces serious challenges. According to Anthony Cohen, it became one of the casualties of the demise of "modernistic grand theories and the advent of 'the interpretive turn' in its various guises."[25]

In the postmodern view of culture, rather than exercising determinative power over people, culture is the outcome and product of social interaction, and human beings are seen as the active creators of culture.[26] Clifford Geertz provides the impetus for this through his description of cultures as comprising "webs of significance" that people spin and in which they are then suspended.[27] Geertz defines culture as a "historically transmitted pattern of meanings embodied in symbols, a system of inherited conceptions expressed

24. Roy G. D'Andrade, *The Development of Cognitive Anthropology* (Cambridge: Cambridge University Press, 1995), 250.

25. Anthony P. Cohen, *Self Consciousness: An Alternative Anthropology of Identity* (London: Routledge, 1994), 118.

26. Cohen, *Self Consciousness*, 118–19.

27. Clifford Geertz, *The Interpretation of Cultures* (New York: Basic Books, 1973), 5.

in symbolic forms by means of which people communicate, perpetuate, and develop their knowledge about and attitudes toward life."[28] According to Cohen, Geertz is responsible for "shifting the anthropological view of culture from its supposedly objective manifestations in social structures, towards its subjective realisation by members who compose those structures."[29]

Culture resides in a set of meaningful forms and symbols that, from the point of view of any particular individual, appear as "given."[30] Yet these forms are meaningful only because human minds have the ability to interpret them.[31] This leads anthropologists to look at the interplay of cultural artifacts and human interpretation in the formation of meaning. They suggest that, contrary to the belief that meaning lies in signs or in the relations between them, meanings are bestowed by the users of signs.[32] However, this does not mean that individuals simply discover or make up cultural meanings on their own. Even the mental structures by which they interpret the world are developed through explicit teaching and implicit observation of others. Consequently, cultural meanings are both psychological states and social constructions.[33] The thrust of contemporary cultural anthropology leads to the conclusion that its primary concern lies in understanding the creation of cultural meaning as connected to world construction and identity formation.

This approach leads to an understanding of culture as socially constructed. The thesis of social constructionists such as Peter Berger is that, rather than inhabiting a prefabricated, given world, we live in a linguistically construed sociocultural world of our own creation.[34] At the heart of the process whereby we construct our world is the imposition of some semblance of a meaningful order upon our variegated experiences. For the interpretive framework we employ in this task, we are dependent on the society in which we participate.[35] In this manner, society mediates to us the cultural tools necessary for constructing our world.

28. Geertz, *Interpretation of Cultures*, 89.

29. Cohen, *Self Consciousness*, 135.

30. Geertz, *Interpretation of Cultures*, 45.

31. Ulf Hannerz, *Cultural Complexity: Studies in the Social Organization of Meaning* (New York: Columbia University Press, 1992), 3–4.

32. Claudia Strauss and Naomi Quinn, *A Cognitive Theory of Cultural Meaning* (Cambridge: Cambridge University Press, 1997), 253.

33. Strauss and Quinn, *Cognitive Theory*, 16.

34. Peter L. Berger, *The Sacred Canopy: Elements of a Sociological Theory of Religion* (Garden City, NY: Doubleday, 1969), 3–13.

35. Berger, *Sacred Canopy*, 20. See also Peter L. Berger and Thomas Luckmann, "Sociology of Religion and Sociology of Knowledge," *Sociology and Social Research* 47 (1963): 417–27.

Although this constructed world gives the semblance of being a given, universal, and objective reality, it is actually, in the words of David Morgan, "an unstable edifice that generations constantly labor to build, raze, rebuild, and redesign."[36] We inhabit linguistically and socially constructed worlds to which our personal identities are intricately bound. The construction of these worlds, as well as the formation of personal identity, is an ongoing, dynamic, and fluid process, in which the forming and reforming of shared cultural meanings play a crucial role. To be human is to be embedded in culture and to participate in the process of interpretation and the creation of meaning as we reflect on and internalize the cultural symbols that we share with others in numerous conversations that shape our ever-shifting contexts.

The situated and contextual character of all human discourse leads missiologist Andrew Walls to affirm what he calls the indigenization principle as a central element of the very substance of the gospel.[37] The indigenization principle is rooted in the core gospel affirmation that God comes to us where we are and accepts us as such through the work of Christ and not on the basis of what we have been, are, or are trying to become. This acceptance of us as we are points to the notion that God does not relate to us as isolated, self-sufficient individuals, but rather as people who are conditioned by the particular times, places, families, societies, groups, and cultures in which we live. In Christ we are accepted by God in the midst of all the relations, experiences, and cultural conditioning that make us who we are.

In light of this, Walls asserts that no particular group of Christians "has therefore any right to impose in the name of Christ upon another group of Christians a set of assumptions about life determined by another time and place."[38] The notion of being a new creation in Christ is not intended to suggest that a convert to the way of Jesus starts a new life in a vacuum with a mind that has become a blank slate. We are all formed by our social, cultural, and historical circumstances. The affirmation that God accepted us as we are means that our lives and minds will continue to be influenced by ways in which they have developed, along with the assumptions and presuppositions that we learned. These are not somehow eliminated

36. David Morgan, *Visual Piety: A History and Theory of Popular Images* (Berkeley: University of California Press, 1998), 9.

37. Andrew F. Walls, *The Missionary Movement in Christian History: Studies in the Transmission of Faith* (Maryknoll, NY: Orbis, 1996), 3–9.

38. Walls, *Missionary Movement*, 8.

from our consciousness, but continue to shape the ways in which we view the world. It is also worth noting that this reality is "as true for groups as for persons. All churches are culture churches—including our own."[39]

Conclusion: Missional Plurality

Reading the Bible with others demands our commitment to radical contextuality. Without this commitment, such reading will generally devolve into the practices of coercive persuasion and assimilation that are part of colonization. From the perspective of intercultural hermeneutics and missional theology, Christian faith is inherently pluralistic and therefore committed to the affirmation and flourishing of plurality through an openness and commitment to the other as well as a nonfoundational posture that resists totality.[40]

Some critics will see this as a surrender of biblical authority. In response I suggest that Scripture itself points in the direction of multiplicity and plurality; the biblical witness is both the result of the diverse community from which the texts of Scripture emerged as well as that which is envisioned for its future. Attempts to suppress the plurality of the biblical witness by means of overarching, universalistic accounts of theology and Christian faith have led and will continue to lead to serious distortions of both gospel and the community that is called to bear witness to it. Rather than resisting plurality or viewing it as a problem to be solved, missional theology embraces plurality as the intention and design of God. It is the good news of the missional love of God for the world and all of its citizens. As Lamin Sanneh observes, "For most of us it is difficult enough to respect those with whom we might disagree, to say nothing of those who might be different from us in culture, language, and tradition. For all of us pluralism can be a rock of stumbling, but for God it is the cornerstone of the universal design."[41]

As the word of God and normative witness to the revelation of God, the texts of Scripture contain irreducible plurality. They cannot be codified into a universal system of doctrine or teaching without doing violence to

39. Walls, *Missionary Movement*, 8.

40. For the development of plurality as a central component of Christian faith, see John R. Franke, *Manifold Witness: The Plurality of Truth* (Nashville: Abingdon, 2009).

41. Lamin Sanneh, *Translating the Message: The Missionary Impact on Culture* (Maryknoll, NY: Orbis, 1989), 27.

their contents. The result of such a practice is a cultural and theological imperialism that is contrary to the gospel. As the word of God and paradigmatic witness to the revelation of God, the texts of Scripture also invite greater plurality than that contained in its pages, in order that the witness of the church to the gospel might be continually expanded to all the nations in keeping with the mission of God. To do this we must learn to read with others in such a way that we are able not only to listen to their words but also to hear what they are saying. In this way the fullness of the gospel of Jesus Christ and the love of God will be made known on the earth. This is the task of missional theology.

A Missional Reading of the Old Testament

CHAPTER 6

Reading the Old Testament Missionally

Christopher J. H. Wright

A Day in the Life of a Prophet

"A winter's day, in a deep and dark December." But this is not Simon and Garfunkel in New York, in the winter of 1965; it is Jeremiah and Baruch in Jerusalem, in the winter of 605 BCE. Jeremiah 36 tells the story of how King Jehoiakim burns the scroll of the word of God that had been delivered through Jeremiah and then painstakingly recorded in writing by Baruch at Jeremiah's dictation. It is a tense story, describing an event that the book clearly sees as the point of no return for Judah: after this act of mutiny against their God, Israel's descent into the abyss of exile in 587 BCE became inevitable.[1]

The primary significance of Jeremiah 36 for our present purpose is that it records one of the earliest instances of the production of scriptural texts. The word of God, which had formerly come only through the living voice of Jeremiah's preaching, now is to be made available to all who will read the written word or hear it read to them in other times, locations, and generations. A number of missional elements in the production of Baruch's scroll—that is, in the emergence of this piece of Scripture-in-the-making—are relevant to other parts of the whole biblical canon.

Baruch's scroll emerged *out of a story*. Almost certainly Baruch's scroll

1. Much of this chapter was developed in other places, especially *Mission of God: Unlocking the Bible's Grand Narrative* (Downers Grove, IL: InterVarsity, 2006); and "Mission and Old Testament Interpretation," in *Hearing the Old Testament: Listening for God's Address*, ed. Craig G. Bartholomew and David J. H. Beldman (Grand Rapids: Eerdmans, 2012), 180–203.

consisted of most of what we now know as Jeremiah 1–25. In those chapters it is clear that Jeremiah knew the story Israel was in and what the outcome of that story would be. He was painfully aware of the great tradition of Israel's long history of election, redemption, covenant, land-gift, kingship, and temple. I say "painfully" because, though that story was the foundation of Israel's identity and mission, Jeremiah saw that (by their incorrigible and unrepentant rejection of God's word and will) Israel was in danger of losing its unique identity and of frustrating God's purpose for it and for the rest of the world through it. Missional reading takes the shape of the biblical story seriously.

Second, Baruch's scroll emerged *into a context*. Missional reading also pays attention to the locatedness of the hearers of Scripture. In the case of Baruch's scroll, there are three "hearers," each being called by the word to a purposeful response within their own particular context:

1. The original audience on that fateful day in the winter of 605 BCE—the people, the political leaders, the king—were being challenged over their failure to respond to God's word, preached to them for a quarter century.
2. The exiles (including some survivors of the first group) would read these words in the place of their exile as a "Jeremiah scroll" and would be challenged as to whether they would respond differently now to God's word, so that their story could move forward in a new direction.
3. All future readers of the scroll, including ourselves, are challenged in our response to the written word of God in our own "missional locatedness."

Third, Baruch's scroll was produced *with a specific goal* in view. God's intention—his longing for his people—was that they might repent and so allow him to spare the threatened judgment. "Perhaps when [they] hear . . . they will each turn from their wicked ways . . . then I will forgive" (Jer. 36:3). So the purpose of this writing down—this inscripturation—of Jeremiah's words, was redemptive: it was written with the hope of provoking repentance and forgiveness. Again, this can be applied to all Scripture. A missional reading of the Bible looks for the redemptive purpose behind all of God's doings and sayings: What is God's ultimate purpose in causing these things to be written down?

Fourth, Baruch's scroll came *at a price*. The writing and reading of the scroll were costly for both Baruch and Jeremiah (Jer. 37–38; 45). A missional reading of Scripture will pay attention to the cost for the messenger of God's word. Ultimately, the full cost of God's mission would be borne by the incarnate Word himself. But many of the messengers before and after Christ had their personal share in that cost.

With this dynamic case in mind, we may survey several dimensions of a missional reading of the Old Testament.

The Missional Origin of the Texts

The processes by which biblical texts came to be written were often profoundly missional in nature. Many of these texts emerged out of conflicts, struggles, or crises, in which the people of God were engaged with the constantly changing and challenging task of articulating and living out their understanding of God's revelation and redemptive action in the world. Sometimes these events occurred among the people of God themselves, and sometimes as God's people they contended with the competing religious claims and worldviews that surrounded them. Biblical texts often have their origin in some issue, need, controversy, or threat that the people of God needed to address in the context of their mission of simply *being* the people of God in the world. The text in itself is thus a product of mission in action.

I was first awakened to this fact while teaching at All Nations Christian College, a missionary training institution in England, as long ago as 1982. An older colleague and experienced missionary on the faculty, Martin Goldsmith, used to insist that when students did their required study of some key christological texts in the New Testament, they must not imagine that they could do a simple exegesis (what the text really meant) and then add some "missiological implications," as a postexegetical afterthought. No, he insisted, they must see that the texts themselves arose out of mission and addressed missional issues. Mission was in the origin of the text, not just something added later.

This missional origin of the text is easily seen in the New Testament. Most of Paul's letters were written in the heat of his missionary efforts: wrestling with the theological basis of the inclusion of the gentiles; affirming the need for Jew and gentile to accept one another in Christ and in the church; tackling the baffling range of new problems that assailed young churches as the gospel took root in the world of Greek polytheism; confronting incipient heresies with clear affirmations of the supremacy and sufficiency of Jesus Christ, and so on. Similarly, the Gospels were written to explain the significance of the good news about Jesus of Nazareth, especially his death and resurrection. Confidence in these things was essential to the missionary task of the expanding church.

But Goldsmith's admonition led me to ask whether the same thing might be said about the missional origin of Old Testament texts. Provided we do not limit our understanding of "mission" to "sending out cross-cultural missionaries," I believe that it can. Many of these texts emerged out of the engagement of Israel with the surrounding world in the light of what they knew of God in their history and in covenantal relationship. People produced texts in relation to what they believed God had done, was doing, or would do in their world. Thus the Torah presents a theology of creation that stands in sharp contrast to the polytheistic creation myths of Mesopotamia and implies a very different relationship between its hearers and the natural world around us. It also records the exodus as an act of YHWH that comprehensively confronted and defeated the power of pharaoh and gave the lie to all his rival claims of deity and the right to allegiance. The historical narratives portray the long and sorry story of Israel's struggle with the culture and religion of Canaan, a struggle reflected also in the preexilic prophets. The mission of God through Israel for the world was at its most threatened when Israel itself succumbed to the idolatry of the surrounding nations. Exilic and postexilic texts emerge out of the task that the small remnant community of Israel faced as it struggled to define its continuing identity as a community of faith in successive empires of varying hostility or tolerance. Wisdom texts interact with international wisdom traditions in the surrounding cultures, but do so with staunch monotheistic disinfectant. And in their texts of worship and prophecy, Israelites reflect on the relationship between their God, YHWH, and the rest of the nations—sometimes negatively, sometimes positively—and on the nature of their own role as YHWH's elect priesthood in their midst.

This observation—that the canon of Scripture, including the Old Testament, is missional in its origin (in the purpose of God) and in its formation (in the multiple contexts of cultural engagement)—means that so-called contextualization is not something we add to "the real meaning" of biblical texts, but is a quality intrinsic to them. The task of recontextualizing the word of God is a missional project that has its basis in Scripture itself and has been part of the mission of God's people all through the centuries of their existence. When we speak of the finality of the canon, we mean that the scriptural witness to God's finished work of revelation and redemption has itself been completed with the apostolic witness to Christ. But the closure of the canonical witness to Christ does not end the necessary ongoing enculturation of witness to that completed work in every generation and culture.

In short, a missional hermeneutic proceeds from the assumption that the whole Bible renders to us the story of God's mission through God's people in their engagement with God's world for the sake of God's purpose for the whole of God's creation.

The Missional Revelation of God

Israel made remarkable affirmations about YHWH, affirmations that had a polemical edge in their own historical context and still stand as distinctive claims today. Among them was the monotheistic declaration that YHWH alone is God and there is no other (Deut. 4:35, 39). As sole deity, it is YHWH, therefore, who owns the world and runs the world (Deut. 10:14, 27; Ps. 24:1; Jer. 27:1–12; 1 Chron. 29:11). This ultimately means the radical displacement of all other rival gods: YHWH alone must be acknowledged as God over the whole earth and all nations (Ps. 96; Jer. 10:1–16; Isa. 43:9–13; 44:6–20). The impact of these claims is felt in such widely varying contexts as Israel's struggle against idolatry, the language of its worship, and its response to other nations both in its own contemporary international history and in eschatological vision.

The monotheism of Old Testament Israel is missional, not philosophical. That is to say, the bold affirmation that YHWH is transcendently unique and universal—the only occupant of the category "deity"—was not something to be placed on a table for philosophical comparison as a matter of polite debate among people adhering to differing religious insights. Rather, it was a truth that not only claimed Israel, to whom it was entrusted as revelation, but also claimed all nations who heard it. All nations must and would come to acknowledge YHWH's supremacy, for good or ill, depending on their response to it. "Then they will know that I am YHWH" (Ezekiel's signature). Israel knew YHWH alone as God, and confessed that knowledge ultimately for the sake of the nations that did not yet know him. That was a missional posture in principle and potential.

There is no doubt that the strength of such Old Testament affirmations about the uniqueness and universality of YHWH underlie, and indeed provide some of the vocabulary for, New Testament affirmations about the uniqueness and universality of Jesus (cf. Phil. 2:9–11 based on

Isa. 45:23; and 1 Cor. 8:5–6 based on Deut. 6:4). In fact, the New Testament amazingly affirms about Jesus four of the greatest "functions" of YHWH through which the Old Testament affirms his uniqueness. YHWH alone, in the faith of Israel, is creator of the heaven and earth, ruler of history, judge of all nations, and savior of those from any nation who turn to him. The same cosmic truths are calmly affirmed about Jesus in the New Testament.[2] And these early Christian affirmations about Jesus were just as polemical in their own historical context as those of ancient Israel about YHWH were in their context and in turn provided the primary rationale and motivation for Christian mission. We are dealing here with the missiological implications of biblical monotheism. If YHWH alone is God, and if Jesus of Nazareth alone is Lord, and if it is God's will (as it manifestly is in the Bible) that these truths be known throughout the whole creation, then there is a missional mandate intrinsic to such convictions.

A fully biblical understanding of the universality and uniqueness of YHWH and of Jesus Christ undergirds a missional response to the relativism at the heart of religious pluralism and some forms of postmodernist philosophy.

The Missional Task of Humanity

On the day of their creation, human beings were given their mission on the planet so purposefully prepared for their arrival: to fill the earth and subdue it, and to rule over the rest of creation (Gen. 1:28). This delegated authority within the created order is moderated by the parallel commands in the complementary account: "to serve and to keep" the garden (2:15). The care and keeping of creation is our human mission. We are on the planet with a purpose that flows from the creative purpose of God himself. Out of this understanding of our humanity (which is also teleological, like our doctrine of God) flows our ecological responsibility, our economic activity involving work, productivity, exchange and trade, and the whole cultural mandate.

To be human is to have a purposeful role in God's creation. In relation to that creational mission, Christians need to be reminded that God holds us accountable to himself for our humanity as much as for our Christianity. There is, therefore, a legitimate place for ecological concern and action, for biblical earth-keeping, within our understanding of Christian mission

2. Cf. Wright, *Mission of God*, chap. 4.

responsibility—since Christians too are humans made in the image of God (indeed, we are being restored even more fully to that humanity in Christ), we have not been given some privileged exemption from the mission God entrusted to our whole species. This ecological dimension of our mission not only flows from our understanding of creation, but also reflects an eschatological perspective. The biblical vision is of a new creation, of which Christ is the heir. Our care for the earth is an expression of our understanding of its future as well as its origin and thus is similar in character, origin, and purpose to our concern for the human person.

The Missional Thrust of the Story

The Old Testament begins on the stage of universal history. After the biblical accounts of creation we read the story of God's dealings with fallen humanity and the problem and challenge of the world of the nations (Gen. 1–11). After the stories of the fall and of the Tower of Babel, could there be any future for the nations in relation to God? Or would judgment have to be God's final word?

The story of Abraham, beginning in Genesis 12, gives a clear answer. God's declared commitment is to bring blessing to the nations through Abraham: "All the families of the earth will be blessed through you" (12:3). Repeated six times in Genesis alone, this affirmation is the foundation of biblical mission, for it declares the mission of God. The creator God's mission is nothing less than to bless the nations of humanity. So fundamental is this divine agenda that Paul defines the Genesis declaration as "the gospel in advance" (Gal. 3:8). And the concluding vision of the whole Bible signifies the fulfillment of the Abrahamic promise, as people from every nation, tribe, language, and people are gathered among the redeemed in the new creation (Rev. 7:9). Thus both the gospel and mission begin in Genesis, and both are located in the redemptive intention of the creator to bless the nations. Mission is God's address to the problem of fractured humanity and is universal in its ultimate goal and scope.

The same Genesis texts that affirm the *universality* of God's mission to bless the nations also, and with equal strength, affirm the *particularity* of God's election of Abraham and his descendants to be the vehicle of that mission. The election of Israel is one of the most fundamental pillars of the biblical worldview and of Israel's historical sense of identity. It is vital to insist that although the belief in their election could be (and was) distorted into a narrow doctrine of national superiority, that distortion was resisted in Israel's own literature (e.g., Deut. 7:7–11). The biblical affirmation is that YHWH, the God who has chosen Israel, is also the creator, owner, and lord of the whole world (10:14–22, cf. Exod. 19:4–6). That is, YHWH was not just the God of Israel: he was God of all (as Paul insists in Rom. 4). YHWH chose Israel in relation to his purpose for the world, not just for Israel's own sake. The election of Israel was not tantamount to a rejection of the nations; rather, it was explicitly for their ultimate benefit. Election is not an exclusive privilege, but an inclusive responsibility. If we might paraphrase John, "God so loved the world that he chose Israel."

Thus, rather than asking if Israel itself "had a mission," in the sense of being "sent" anywhere (anachronistically injecting our "sending missionaries" paradigm again), we need to see the missional position of Israel in relation to the mission of God in the world. Israel's mission was to be something, not to go somewhere. This perspective is clearly focused in the person of the servant of YHWH in Isaiah 40–55, who both embodies the election of Israel (identical things are said about Israel and the servant) and also is charged with the mission (like Israel's) of bringing the blessing of YHWH's justice, salvation, and glory to the ends of the earth.

Which brings us to Jesus, of course. At which point we might be accused of reading the whole Old Testament retrospectively and anachronistically in order to make it fit into a Christian presumptive and preemptive worldview (to which is sometimes added more sinister accusations of adopting a supercessionist rejection of the Jews in general—which I robustly repudiate). However, I am content to derive this Christotelic reading (as it has been called) of the Hebrew Scriptures from an impeccable source—the Lord Jesus Christ himself.

It seems to me that this is precisely the thrust of Jesus's second lecture in Old Testament hermeneutics in a single day (resurrection day) with his disciples, in Luke 24. He adjusts their whole understanding of "the Scriptures" by focusing their thrust and point on himself as Messiah and on the consequent mission of their bringing the good news of repentance and forgiveness, in his name, to all nations. "This is what is written," he said. By which he was not indicating a single quotation (or even several) from particular texts, but rather affirming that the whole canon of what we now call the Old Testament should be read with a messianic and a missional thrust. It all leads up to Christ, his death, and resurrection. And it all leads on beyond that to the ends of the earth. Messianic *and* missional reading of the Old Testament—that's what Jesus instructed his disciples to do. We have been fairly good at the first, but pretty lamentable at the second. Which is deeply puzzling since it could be said that the very essence of the apostle Paul's theology and practice (as apostle to the gentiles) consisted of a missional reading of the Old Testament Scriptures in the light of his encounter with Jesus as messiah. For Paul, the one followed inevitably from the other.

From this we can see much more clearly the dynamic theology that underpinned Paul's understanding and practice of mission. He saw his task as taking the gospel to the gentile nations and assuring them that, by trusting in the Messiah Jesus (who embodied the identity and mission of Israel but had been faithful where Israel had been rebellious, and had died to take upon himself their sin and the sin of the world), they were included in the family of God, members of the covenant people of God. Thus the gentiles too are called (as he put it twice in Romans) to "faith's obedience" (Rom. 1:5; 16:26): that is, to the status and the responsibility of covenant membership. In other words, through Christ, God solved the problems of Genesis 3 and Genesis 11—the root problem of sin and the consequent dividedness of humanity, seen most sharply in the separation of Jew and gentile.

The necessity of messianic and missional reading of the Old Testament carries two other implications that may be briefly mentioned. First, it indicates that in biblical theology, election is fundamentally missional, not merely soteriological. That is to say, God's choice of Abraham and Israel was instrumental, not preferential. The election of Israel was not into some saved status from which all other nations would be excluded and rejected. Rather, Israel was elected into servant status, to be the means by which God would enable all other nations to have the opportunity of being included and accepted—as so many Old Testament texts point out (which I sketch in the final point below).

And second, such a reading highlights the very close connection between missiology and ecclesiology. God's redemptive mission began by creating a community of blessing to *be* a blessing, so that all nations would come to praise the living God (cf. Ps. 67's universalizing of the Aaronic blessing). Salvation would not be a matter of whisking individual souls out of the earth and up to heaven. Rather, it would be a long-term project of creating a people for God, initially the descendants of one man, Abraham, but with the intention (emphatically built in from the very beginning) of becoming a multinational community (cf. Ps. 87). Not only, then, is it correct to say that mission is the primary reason for the church's existence in history, it is also true that the church itself—the people of God from Abraham to the "great multitude whom no one could count from every nation, tribe, people, and language" (Rev. 7:9)—is the creation of the mission of God and the demonstration of the gospel (Eph. 3:6–10).

The vogue phrase "missional church" is therefore virtually tautologous. What other kind of church is there? As a friend said to me recently, "Talk about 'missional church' sounds to me like talking about 'female women.' If it's not missional, it's not church."

The Missional Dimensions of Redemption

Mission (from a human point of view) might be defined as sharing the good news of God's redemptive work with all nations. But what is our understanding of redemption? The temptation in some Christian traditions is to confine it to the spiritual dimension of ourselves—forgiveness of personal sin and release from its bondage. While this is undoubtedly a precious biblical truth, it fails to grasp the comprehensiveness of the biblical understanding of God's redeeming work, as portrayed in the Old Testament (which of course provided the foundational source of meaning for the metaphor in the New Testament also).

The primary model of redemption in the Old Testament (primary both chronologically and theologically) is of course the exodus. It is the event to which the language of redemption is first applied. It is therefore vitally important to attend to all the dimensions of what God actually accomplished in that event. At least four such dimensions are clearly highlighted in the key narratives at the beginning of Exodus and in the later texts that celebrate the event (e.g., the Psalms and prophets).

- *Political.* The Hebrews were not a free people. They found themselves in Egypt as the descendants of people who had migrated there as famine refugees and found a welcome (a fact that was not forgotten: Deut. 23:7–8). But under the current government, they were being oppressed as an ethnic minority and viewed with suspicion and state-generated fear.
- *Economic.* The Hebrews were being exploited as a source of cheap labor in construction projects and agriculture for the economic benefit of the host nation. (Things haven't changed much.) They were not enjoying the fruit of their own work, but suffering the harsh slavery of working for a hostile state.
- *Social.* The policy of that state progressed from economic exploita-

tion to outright genocidal fury. The interference in the family life of the Hebrews by the government mandate to all the citizens of Egypt to make sure that newborn Hebrew boys were killed at birth must have inspired fear in every pregnant mother and despair among the whole community, whose very survival into the next generation was threatened.

- *Spiritual.* The play on the word *ʿaboda* highlights this point. The word can mean slavery, but also worship. While the Hebrews were under slavery to pharaoh (the self-asserting member of the gods of Egypt) they were not free to worship their true God and Lord. This explains Yahweh's insistence, "Let my people go that they may serve/worship *me*" (not pharaoh). Israel's problem in Egypt was not that they were in slavery and needed to be liberated, but that they were being forced to serve the wrong master. The point of the exodus was not merely to free an enslaved people, but to bring Israel back to its true Lord and that it might enter into covenant relationship with him.

As we reflect on all these dimensions of the great redemptive event of the Old Testament, and the first great model of God's acting as redeemer in the Bible, we need to see the whole of what was accomplished in it. It is missiologically deficient *either* to use the exodus only as biblical support for political, economic, or social action for liberation (without reference to the spiritual dimensions of redemption usually included in the work of evangelism) *or* to spiritualize the exodus into nothing more than a picture story of which the *real* message is to do with forgiveness of personal sin and release from the personal bondage to sin.[3]

The Missional Conflict with Idolatry

Deuteronomy 6:4–5 expresses the essence of Old Testament Israel's faith: one God, one Lord, one love. As seen above, monotheism undergirds the Bible, not as a philosophical abstract, but as a dynamic missionary conviction. Throughout the Bible, but especially in the Old Testament, the one living God is in conflict with the gods and idols of humanity. This conflict is close to the heart of mission (cf. Paul in Acts 26:17–18). In the

3. Cf. a fuller discussion in Wright, *Mission of God*, chap. 8.

Old Testament we may note three major historical contexts of conflict with gods/idols.

Egypt

The context here is the state idolatry in which pharaoh was deified. And the result was the politics of arrogance and oppression. The perversion of human authority into idolatry leads to injustice, oppression, and abuse. In the face of this idolatry of power, the story of exodus reads as a "power encounter" in which the crucial conflict is one of authority. Exodus 5:2 sets the issue: "Who is Yahweh? I do not acknowledge Yahweh." This leads to the subplot: "Then you *will* know" (7:5, 16; 8:10, 19, 22; 9:15–16, 29; 10:2; 14:18, 25). The climax comes in Exodus 15, in which liberation leads to celebration of the uniqueness of Yahweh as God (15:11) and the sovereignty of Yahweh as King (15:18). "Yahweh reigns!" (and not pharaoh!) is the cry of victory and joy when God confronts and destroys idolatrous, usurped power.

Canaan

The context here is the Baal cult with its desire for life, success, and wealth through fertility in crops, herds, and women. It included ritual prostitution and child sacrifice. Baalism sacralized sex and sacrificed babies—which means that "baalism" is still very much present in the modern Western world. Canaanite idolatry promised life but delivered death, not only through child sacrifice, but through the structural injustice and oppression of Canaanite society. This is graphically illustrated in the fate of Naboth. In the face of this idolatrous worship of nature, life, and fertility, the Old Testament response included rejection and warning (Deut. 7), challenge to renunciation (1 Kings 18), and call to repentance (e.g., Hosea's bold use of sexual imagery in calling Israel back to faithfulness in light of God's "husband-love").

Babylon

The context here is the great imperial power again, with exalted claims to control the destinies of nations. Mesopotamian religion attributed particular power to the astral deities (star gods) who controlled the future. In the face of this idolatry of security and control of events, Isaiah 40–55 unmasks the gods, exposing their futility and powerlessness. The stars are created and controlled by Yahweh (for they are not gods; Isa. 40:26). Alleged gods are powerless to speak or to act (41:21–24). Idolatry is blindness and delusion (44:6–20). The gods are helpless to save their own idols or their worshipers (46:1–7). Babylon's state idolatry is unmasked and exposed, and its attempts at security and control are shattered (Isa. 47). Yahweh alone controls history and therefore alone can give security (44:6–8; 45:24). In the light of all this, Israel is summoned to *witness* to Yahweh's supremacy in history (43:9–13; 44:8).

Biblical missiology needs to give more attention to identifying and addressing modern equivalents to these ancient gods and idolatries, for they are undoubtedly alive and active as much today as they were in the days of Moses, Elijah, Hosea, or Isaiah.[4]

The Missional Shaping of the Community

Our main concern here is ethical. This is the missiological dimension of Israel's holiness. Israel was called to be distinctive from the surrounding world in ways that were not merely religious but also ethical. In Genesis 18:19 this is expressed as the very purpose of Israel's election in relation to God's promise to bless the nations. In stark contrast to the world of Sodom and Gomorrah, YHWH says of Abraham: "I have chosen him so that he will direct his children and his household after him to keep the way of the Lord by doing what is right and just, so that the Lord will bring about for Abraham what he has promised him." This verse, in a remarkably tight syntax, binds together election, ethics, and mission as three interlocking aspects of God's purpose. His choice of Abraham is for the sake of his promise to bless the nations, but the accomplishment of God's mission demands the ethical obedience of God's community—the fulcrum in the middle of the verse.

In Exodus 19:4–6, Israel's ethical distinctiveness is also linked to its identity and role as a priestly and holy people in the midst of the nations. As YHWH's *priesthood*, Israel would be the means by which God would

4. I explored the Old Testament theme of idolatry in relation to mission theology in *Mission of God*, chap. 5.

be known to the nations and the means of bringing the nations to God (performing a function analogous to the role of Israel's own priests between God and the rest of the people). As a *holy* people, they would be ethically (as well as ritually) distinctive from the practices of surrounding nations. The moral and practical dimensions of such holy distinctiveness are spelled out in Leviticus 18–19.

In Deuteronomy 4:6–8, we find that such visibility would be a matter of observation and comment among the nations. This expectation in itself was a strong motivation for keeping the law—a point that I expanded in seeking a missional hermeneutic of Deuteronomy.[5] The question of Israel's ethical obedience or ethical failure was not merely a matter between Israel and Yahweh, but was of major significance in relation to Yahweh's agenda for the nations (cf. Jer. 4:1–2) and indeed of Yahweh's reputation ("name") among the nations (Ezek. 36). And that means that Old Testament ethics is inseparably linked to God's mission as the Old Testament declares it.

This missiological perspective on Old Testament ethics seems to me a fruitful approach to the age-old hermeneutical debate over whether and how the moral teaching given to Israel in the Old Testament (especially the law) has any authority or relevance to Christians. If the law was given in order to shape Israel to be what it was called to be—a light to the nations, a holy priesthood—then it has a paradigmatic relevance to those who, in Christ, inherited the same role in relation to the nations. In the Old as well as the New Testament, the ethical demand on those who claim to be God's people is determined by the mission with which they have been entrusted. There is no biblical mission without biblical ethics.

The Missional Vision of the Future

Israel saw the nations (including itself) as being subject to the sovereign rule of God in history—whether in judgment or in mercy (cf. Jer. 18:1–10; Jonah). But Israel also thought of the nations as "spectators" of all God's dealings with Israel: whether Israel was on the receiving end of God's deliverance or of God's judgment, it lived on an open stage, and the nations would draw their conclusions accordingly (Exod. 15:15; Deut. 9:28; Ezek. 36:16–23).

5. Christopher J. H. Wright, *Deuteronomy*, Understanding the Bible Series (Grand Rapids: Baker, 1994), 47–49.

Eventually, however, and in a rather mysterious way, the nations could be portrayed as the beneficiaries of all that God had done in and for Israel, and even invited to rejoice, applaud, and praise YHWH the God of Israel (Ps. 47; 1 Kings 8:41–43; Ps. 67). And, most remarkable of all, Israel came to entertain the eschatological vision that there would be those of the nations who would not merely be *joined to* Israel, but would come to be *identified as* Israel, with the same names, privileges, and responsibilities before God (Ps. 47:9; Isa. 19:19–25; 56:2–8; 66:19–21; Zech. 2:10–11; Amos 9:11–12). Psalmists and prophets envisaged a future in which the nations could be

- registered in God's city (Ps. 87)
- blessed with God's salvation (Isa. 19:19–25—with its clear echoes of exodus and of Abraham)
- called by God's name (Amos 9:11–12)
- accepted in God's house (Isa. 56:2–8)
- joined with God's people (Zech. 2:10–11)

These texts are breathtaking in their universal scope. This is the dimension of Israel's prophetic heritage that most profoundly influenced the theological explanation and motivation of the gentile mission in the New Testament. It certainly underlies James's interpretation of the Christ event and the success of the gentile mission in Acts 15:16–18 (where he is quoting Amos 9:12). It clearly inspired Paul's efforts as a practitioner and theologian of mission (Rom. 15:7–16; Eph. 2:11–3:6). And it provided the theological shape for the Gospels, each of which concludes with its own form of the great commission: the sending of Jesus's disciples into the world of nations.

And finally, we cannot omit the (even wider) vision: that not only the nations, but also the whole creation will be included in God's purposes of redemption. For this God of Israel, of the nations, and of the world declares himself to be creating a new heavens and a new earth, in which redeemed humanity will live in safety, harmony, and environmental peace within a renewed creation. Again, this is a portrait enthusiastically endorsed in the New Testament (Ps. 96:11–13; Isa. 65:17–25; Rom. 8:18–21; 2 Pet. 3:13; Rev. 21:1–5) and so not only sustains our hope today, but also enables us to see Christian concern and action in relation to the environment and care of creation as an essential part of our biblical mission as a whole.

Conclusion

What questions, then, should we be asking if we choose to engage in a missional reading of any Old Testament text? Here are some that occur to me:

1. What do we know of the context and origin of this text that involves God, or the people of God, engaging in missional issues, such as the challenge of other gods and idolatry, matters of ethical integrity, conflicting cultural worldviews and allegiances, issues facing humanity universally, the conflict with sin, evil and suffering, and so on. What can we say about *why* this text was produced and for what purpose, and what parallels could we suggest in relation to the missional contexts of the church today?
2. What does this text contribute to our understanding of God's purpose as revealed in the Bible as a whole? How does its portrayal of God's uniqueness, character, actions, thoughts, words, and intentions connect with the wider purpose of God for Israel, the nations, and creation? How does the God revealed in this text connect with the God revealed in Jesus Christ and the New Testament?
3. Where does this text fit in the whole Bible story of the mission of God? In what ways is this text *affected* or *informed by* that wider story, and in what ways does this text *contribute to* that wider story?
4. What kind of people does this text assume in reality, or envisage in hope or ideal, and does the text connect its portrayal of God's people to the reason for their election and redemption? Does the text indicate any sense of the responsibility of God's people in relation to the rest of the nations? And where the text describes or denounces only the *failure* of God's people, what ideals or goals are presupposed by that recognition of failure?
5. Does this text point toward the future in any way, particularly in relation to the realities of, and reasons for, God's judgment and the hope and basis of God's redemption? How many horizons are in the text? If there is a future dimension, what are the connections between the particular future envisaged in this text and the broader themes of biblical eschatology in Old and New Testaments? How does that eschatological dimension affect our concept and practice of mission?
6. What happens if you read this Old Testament text with Luke 24 in mind? (And what might happen if you don't?!)

7. What questions do we want to *address to this text* in the light of our own involvement in mission or awareness of issues and problems in world mission?
8. Reciprocally, and perhaps more importantly, *what questions does this text address to our present concept and practice of mission*, by way of affirmation and encouragement, or critique and correction?

CHAPTER 7

A Missional Reading of Deuteronomy

Mark Glanville

A Missional Hermeneutic and Deuteronomy

Deuteronomy is the covenant charter of ancient Israel, their call to communal transformation, not merely for their own sake as God's people but also for the sake of their (often hostile) neighbors. The people of Israel, transformed by their obedience to God's law, are to bear witness to the character of the one true God in a communal life characterized by justice and grace. They are to celebrate his generosity with joyful feasts to which all are invited, especially the stranger, the widow, and the orphan.

This ancient text from half a world away became immediate, local, and personal for me while I was pastoring a church in a poor government-housing area of Australia. Our church community regularly invited our neighbors to gather, spreading out on the green grass in the churchyard and feasting together while a blues band played the songs of Muddy Waters. We wanted to bring joy and celebration into a neighborhood that had experienced much suffering and brokenness, and our mission there was full and joyful.

This chapter is all about community, about how in Deuteronomy the good news of God's kingdom transformed one small, ancient Near Eastern community for the sake of the nations. It explores questions that missional leaders must wrestle with. What should a community of faith in the modern Western world, seeking to live out the biblical story authentically in our own place and time, look like? How might such a community immerse itself in the joys and griefs of its neighbors without losing its own distinctiveness? What does it mean today to be a community of faith, of celebration, and of justice?

A missional reading of Scripture begins by considering what kind of community the text is seeking to form. And Deuteronomy richly rewards this approach, as this text is explicitly the covenant charter for a contrast society and thus unique among Old Testament documents. The community being shaped by Deuteronomy is itself to be unique. Together its people are to stand for justice, in stark contrast to Egypt's oppression, and to celebrate the life and joy of the one true God in community, utterly separating themselves from the idolatry of the surrounding nations.

Israel had been called out from its life of slavery in Egypt and now stands at last at the end of its physical journey, poised on the very threshold of the promised land. But here, in the text of Deuteronomy, the people of Israel are called to an ongoing spiritual and ethical journey, to become the true community of God's eschatological people. Every person within this new community is to experience the freshness, the genuineness, the graciousness that flourishes when people are knit together as sisters and brothers through the redeeming activity and the loving rule of God.

The goal of this chapter is to unfold Deuteronomy's inherent missiology on its own terms and from within its location in the canon of Scripture. Along the way we will see how Yahweh, who has graciously redeemed Israel and become its king, now gives it the charter by which the redeemed slaves of Egypt are to be shaped into a new community of mutuality and grace. We'll consider four elements of Israel's story in Deuteronomy: (1) the exodus: the beginning of Yahweh's community; (2) feasting: the motivation for Yahweh's community; (3) the law: the shape of Yahweh's community; and (4) Israel and the nations: the scope of Yahweh's community.

A Missional Hermeneutic

This chapter examines Deuteronomy through the lens of a missional hermeneutic. From the perspective of the whole biblical story, mission is the encounter with the world of a community gathered by Christ to be caught up in the Father's reconciling purpose for all of his creation, living by the Spirit as a sign, instrument, and foretaste of Christ's restorative reign.[1] A

1. "Sign," "instrument," and "foretaste" are Lesslie Newbigin's characteristic images of the church, first articulated in *The Household of God: Lectures on the Nature of the Church* (London: SCM, 1954), 166. See further Michael Goheen, *"As the Father Has Sent Me, I Am Sending You": J. E. Lesslie Newbigin's Missionary Ecclesiology* (Zoetermeer: Boekencentrum, 2000), 33.

missional hermeneutic discerns that the story of God's mission encompasses all of Scripture, beginning with ancient Israel.

God's promises to Abraham are to bless both Abraham's household and all nations through Abraham (Gen. 12:1–3). In the Genesis text, the narrative of the call of Abraham follows the table of seventy nations, which are symbolic of every nation on the earth. "Abraham is singled out precisely so that blessing may come to all the nations, to all those seventy nations God had scattered over the face of the whole earth."[2] The nation of Israel is then chosen from among Abraham's descendants to be the mediator of divine blessing to all other nations. Throughout the remainder of the biblical narrative, from Genesis 12 to Revelation 22, God is forming a people to live as a foretaste of his restoring rule in the world for the sake of the nations. So for the church today, mission is not simply one task among many; rather, mission is the very hallmark of our identity as a community of Christ followers.

By "missional hermeneutic" I do not mean merely that Deuteronomy has motifs and themes that validate the missional activity of the church. I am saying much more than that. Deuteronomy is the record of the mission of God's people at a particular time and place, as they wrestled to bring good news to their unique situation in the ancient world. Deuteronomy was made to nourish and shape God's people to live as a contrast society in their own time and place. It is therefore much more than a document to be mined for missionary resources. In the context of the whole biblical story this book summons us, in *our* time and place, to enter the story of God's mission for the world in which all things are reconciled in Christ.

George Hunsberger helpfully outlines four characteristics of a missional hermeneutic:[3]

- *Missional direction*—a missional reading of Scripture rightly assumes that Scripture has a missional narrative arc. Following that arc, we find the story of God's mission to recover his purposes for all of his creation, forming a community of people who call attention to his restorative reign.

2. Richard Bauckham, *The Bible and Mission: Christian Witness in a Postmodern World* (Grand Rapids: Baker Academic, 2003), 28.

3. George R. Hunsberger, "Proposals for a Missional Hermeneutic: Mapping the Conversation" (paper presented at the 2008 American Academy of Religion/Society of Biblical Literature annual meeting); available at gocn.org/resources/articles/proposals-missional-hermeneutic-mapping-conversation.

- *Missional purpose*—a missional reading of Scripture inquires into how a particular text originally functioned to leaven its community of recipients with the yeast of the gospel so that God's people could play a particular role in the biblical story as leaven for the world.
- *Missional locatedness of the readers*—we ourselves read Scripture as a community that is caught up in God's story for his world. A missional hermeneutic relentlessly inquires, "What kind of community does this text foster today?"
- *Received tradition in new context*—how did the biblical writers appropriate elements of previous revelation and bring them to bear in new missional contexts? What contextual approaches do we learn from the biblical writer's process of appropriating older traditions for our process of bringing the gospel to bear in new settings?

To these four characteristics of a missional hermeneutic, I propose the addition of one more:

- *Prophetic challenge to every society*—we will see in what follows that Yahweh's authoritative Torah, while delivered to Israel, is nonetheless a declaration for the nations. Through Torah, Yahweh lays claim to every corner of the world. Torah makes explicit Yahweh's creational intention for the world, which he will pursue despite Israel's unfaithfulness.

Deuteronomy as a Charter for a Contrast Community

Deuteronomy seeks to shape Israel to be a display community living in the sight of the nations. While Israel pauses in Moab on the brink of entering the promised land, it is faced with a decision: either to worship the one true God or to worship other gods and so abandon the life of justice and generosity that Yahweh set out in his law. Deuteronomy doesn't so much address the individual as it offers a vision for a whole society. It doesn't merely challenge injustice (though it does that); rather, it brings the whole of human life within the scope of the covenant life. As God's people learn to love Yahweh, embracing his life-giving rule in Torah, they will live as family in thanksgiving, joy, justice, and generosity.

Torah takes a prominent place at the center of Deuteronomy both theologically and structurally. Chapters 12–26 contain the Deuteronomic law code, and the surrounding chapters (1–11, 27–34) operate as a narrative and theological frame for the law.

A missional reading of Scripture inquires into the ways that a biblical text speaks into a specific missional context. Deuteronomy addresses challenges, both internal and external, that Israel will face once it is in the land, particularly during the monarchic period.[4] Israel's future will probably include increasing social stratification and thousands being forced off their land due to invasion and economic pressures—and so Deuteronomy devotes much attention to "the stranger." Religious syncretism will pose another threat (13:1–18). External pressures will include the enticing invitations (or threats) of the great kings of Egypt and Mesopotamia, military invasions, and the allure of foreign deities. Deuteronomy calls the people of God into a missional encounter with these powerful forces and ideologies.

Many scholarly studies consider the genre and form of Deuteronomy. The two most enlightening paradigms highlight the communal dimension of the text. First, Deuteronomy adopts the ancient Near Eastern suzerain-vassal treaty form to describe the relationship between Yahweh and Israel. Second, Deuteronomy serves as a national constitution: "Something quite distinctive seems to have been crafted, a comprehensive social charter, perhaps uniquely appropriate to the peculiar covenantal identity that Israel claimed for itself."[5] Deuteronomy's democratic ethos is aimed to "empower a broad constituency of the community whose integrity and political independence it seeks to protect."[6] As a charter, Deuteronomy limits the ability of central institutions to accumulate wealth and power, carefully delimiting the responsibilities of various offices (17:14–18:22) and subordinating office bearers to the authority of the Torah.[7] While Deuteronomy permits kingship in Israel, this is "only so long as the election and prerogatives of the king are strictly delimited" (17:14–17).[8] These details remind us that Deuter-

4. There are many indicators that Deuteronomy is addressing a period in Israel with established state structures. See, e.g., 12:1–28; 17:8–20.

5. S. Dean McBride Jr., "Polity of the Covenant People: The Book of Deuteronomy," *Interpretation* 41 (1987): 229–44 at 237; repr. in *A Song of Power and the Power of Song: Essays on the Book of Deuteronomy*, ed. Duane L. Christensen (Winona Lake, IN: Eisenbrauns, 1993), 62–71.

6. McBride, "Polity of the Covenant People," 237.

7. McBride, "Polity of the Covenant People," 241–42; see also Bernard Levinson, "The First Constitution: Rethinking the Origins of the Rule of Law and Separation of Powers in Light of Deuteronomy," *Cardozo Law Review* 27 (2006): 1853–88.

8. So McBride, "Polity of the Covenant People," 241 (the king has responsibility to protect the *Begriff Jahwefamilie*); Gerhard Lohfink, "Gottesvolk: Alttestamentliches zu einem

onomy is explicitly written with community in view. One of Deuteronomy's distinctive contributions to the missional discussion is that it does not address isolated individuals, "for isolated individuals are simply not in a position to exemplify and to live the social dimension of the reign of God."[9] And the social dynamic of the community it describes is decidedly egalitarian.

Four Distinctives of Yahweh's Community

Four distinctive characteristics of Yahweh's community are at the heart of Deuteronomy:

- the exodus is presented as the founding event of Yahweh's community
- grateful feasting is the motivation for the community
- the law shapes the community
- Yahweh's lordship has implications for *every* community

The Exodus: The Beginning of Yahweh's Community

Deuteronomy seeks to shape a community in the spiritual and ethical context of the exodus. The exodus is mentioned some fifty times in Deuteronomy: this motif is the hermeneutical key to understanding the law code and Yahweh's covenant with his people. The exodus motif presents Yahweh as the liberating king who is forming a society of mutuality and justice in sharp contrast to the culture of Egypt from which he has emancipated his people.

Within Deuteronomy's theology of the exodus, Israel is not only "brought out" but also "brought in." The so-called catechetical credo states:

> We were pharaoh's slaves in Egypt. And the LORD brought us out of Egypt with a mighty hand. And the LORD showed signs and wonders, great and grievous, against Egypt and against pharaoh and all his household, before our eyes. And he brought us out from there, that he might bring us in and give us the land that he swore to give to our fathers. And the LORD

Zentralbegriff im konziliaren Wortfeuerwerk," in *Unsere großen Wörter: Das Alte Testament zu Themen dieser Jahre* (Freiburg: Herder, 1977), 111–26 at 124.

9. Gerhard Lohfink, *Jesus and Community: The Social Dimension of the Christian Faith*, trans. John P. Galvin (Philadelphia: Fortress, 1982), 72. Lohfink is referring to Jesus's kingdom ethics as expressed in the Gospels.

> commanded us to do all these statutes, to fear the LORD our God, for our good always, that he might preserve us alive, as we are this day. And it will be righteousness for us, if we are careful to do all this commandment before the LORD our God, as he has commanded us. (Deut. 6:21–25)

Three distinguishing marks of the new community that Deuteronomy is shaping are in view here. First, Israel does not simply leave Egypt; rather, it was "brought out" by Yahweh its God. The verb "to bring out" is in this context a legal term for release. Israel was "brought out," legally freed, from the ownership and rule of pharaoh, king of Egypt (e.g., Deut. 15:16).[10] In the ancient Near East a ruler who redeemed a debt slave by canceling his or her debts would maintain a claim over the redeemed person's labor.[11] Yahweh is Israel's king, in part by virtue of his having redeemed them. Deuteronomy signals this change of rule by juxtaposing Israel's former identity (*'ebed*) as pharaoh's slaves, with its new identity (*'abad*) as servants of Yahweh (Deut. 6:12–13).

Second, Deuteronomy emphasizes the injustice of Israel's former enslavement in Egypt. Pharaoh is presented as an unjust, wicked ruler whom Yahweh called to account (e.g., 26:5–9). This motif is foundational for Deuteronomy's ethics and politics (e.g., 17:14–16).

Third, Deuteronomy emphasizes that Yahweh "brought out" Israel in order to form it into a new society. The laws of Israel's new king are consistent with the ethical trajectory of the exodus itself, securing justice in the legal code for vulnerable and oppressed groups, just as redemption from Egypt brought freedom to the oppressed nation of slaves. The exodus event commonly appears in motivation clauses in Deuteronomy: "You shall remember that you were a slave in Egypt; and you shall be careful to observe these statutes" (14:12). Variations upon this clause explicitly undergird legal provisions for a Sabbath rest for animals, slaves, and strangers (5:14–15), love for the stranger (10:18–19), release for slaves (15:12–15), feasting with the vulnerable (16:11–12), prohibition against royal prestige (17:16), justice

10. Georg Braulik, "Deuteronomy and Human Rights," in *Theology of Deuteronomy: Collected Essays of Georg Braulik*, trans. U. Lindblad (North Richland Hills, TX: Bibal, 1994), 131–50 at 135.

11. Raymond Westbrook, "Slave and Master in Ancient Near Eastern Law," in *Law from the Tigris to the Tiber: The Writings of Raymond Westbrook*, ed. Bruce Wells and Rachel Magdalene (Winona Lake, IN: Eisenbrauns, 2009), 1.186–87; repr. from *Chicago-Kent Law Review* 70 (1995): 1631–75 at 1648–51.

for the vulnerable (24:17–18), and the gleanings of the harvest for the vulnerable (24:19–22).

The figure of the exodus operates as an appeal to the people's experience of Yahweh's prior activity. Those released by the exodus must not tolerate among themselves the kinds of oppression associated with Egypt. Thus Deuteronomy's law code not only stipulates provision for especially vulnerable people but also prevents one person from accumulating wealth excessively at the expense of others. More than this: it calls God's people into a shared life together. The exodus in Deuteronomy is, in part, an "experiential component to doing theology."[12] Through the exodus, Israel has learned something new about Yahweh and about the world. We see a similar dynamic in the monumental theological shift that the conversion of the gentiles precipitated in the first century CE.[13]

Feasting: The Motivation for Yahweh's Community

> You shall count seven weeks. From the time the sickle is first put to the standing grain, begin to count seven weeks. Then you will keep the feast of weeks to the LORD your God, with a proportionate freewill offering from your hand, which you give according to the measure with which the LORD your God blesses you. Feast before the LORD your God, you, your son, your daughter, your slave, your female slave, the Levite within your settlements, the stranger, the fatherless and the widow who are among you, at the place the LORD your God chooses as a dwelling for his name. Remember that you were slaves in Egypt. Observe and keep these statutes. (Deut. 16:9–12, my translation)

The festival calendar of Deuteronomy (16:1–17) offers a radical vision for a community of thankfulness, generosity, and inclusion for vulnerable people. Along with the exodus itself, Yahweh's generosity in giving the land and the harvest in its season is the grounds for the community's response in feasts of thanksgiving. Deuteronomy's festival calendar gives instructions for three feasts. In early spring, immediately before the grain harvest, the

12. Dean Flemming, *Contextualization in the New Testament: Patterns for Theology and Mission* (Downers Grove, IL: InterVarsity, 2005), 49.

13. Flemming uses this phrase in describing the Council of Jerusalem (*Contextualization in the New Testament*, 49).

community is to gather in Jerusalem for the Passover, the most solemn of these feasts, for this is the time for the people to remember their exodus from slavery in Egypt (16:1–8). Next comes the spring grain harvest, a time for celebration of God's provision in the Feast of Weeks (16:9–12). In the fall, when grapes, olives, and figs are picked, there is time for resting and joyful feasting; the call to the Feast of Booths is most emphatic: "feast!" and "you will surely feast!"

A three-part movement characterizes Deuteronomy 16:1–17: (1) Yahweh gives the land and its produce; (2) the people respond in thanksgiving with celebration; (3) which in turn produces generosity and inclusion for vulnerable people: the stranger, the fatherless, and the widow. "The concept of Israel rejoicing together 'before Yahweh' is the supreme expression of its election as Yahweh's people and the culmination of deliverance from Egypt."[14] These rituals and feasts had one main purpose: *to forge an inclusive and celebrative community, in light of the generosity of God*. Significantly then, the feasts are in themselves an eloquent expression of what it means to *be the community of Israel*. We will now trace the three-part movement that characterizes Deuteronomy's feasting texts: gift, thanksgiving, and justice.

The God Who Gives

In her book *Radical Gratitude*, Mary Jo Leddy, a Catholic nun and advocate for refugees, tells the story of a period in her life when she found it difficult to be grateful. God jolted her out of her dissatisfaction through a refugee family who was staying with her. A young girl in the family was peering out of Mary's kitchen window. The girl saw the garage through the window. She asked, "Who lives there?" Mary's world suddenly inverted as she recognized that someone *could* live there—a number of people, in fact. As Mary answered, "the car," her world was opened up to the abundance, even overabundance, that she had been gifted with.[15] This story introduces a key theme of Deuteronomy's festival calendar: thankfulness. And it touches upon a key question for missional leaders: How may we nourish worshiping communities whose shared life begins with a gift?

The theme of the divine gift of land and its abundance is central to

14. Gordon J. McConville, *Deuteronomy*, Apollos Old Testament Commentary 5 (Leicester, England: Inter-Varsity, 2002), 277.

15. Mary Jo Leddy, *Radical Gratitude* (Maryknoll, NY: Orbis, 2002).

Deuteronomy. A phrase that is often referred to as the "land-gift formula" occurs over sixty times in various configurations, such as the repeated reference "the land that Yahweh your God is giving you" (e.g., 16:1). Blessing (*barak*) is a related motif: "The LORD your God will bless you in all your produce and in all the work of your hands, so that you will be altogether joyful" (16:15). Blessing in Deuteronomy refers specifically to the fertility of animals, the soil, and the human womb, which comes as a result of the gracious attention of God (7:13–14; 12:7; 14:29; 16:10, 15). Feasting and eating are prominent (8:1–20; 11:8–17; 14:22–29; 16:1–17; 26:1–15), highlighting the flow of divine blessing that is at the heart of the book. The point of all these is that Yahweh, the giver, is giving his people all they need to flourish. A missional hermeneutic highlights for us that Deuteronomy is forming a community that lives with an awareness that at the heart of reality is a God of limitless generosity.

Deuteronomy's theology of blessing challenged ancient Near Eastern royal ideology in which the (human) king was the conduit of divine blessing to the nation. "Virtually every Mesopotamian ruler who left royal inscriptions has at some point declared himself to be the provider of 'abundance' for the land . . . thanks to the privileged relationship he enjoys with a god or the gods."[16] Deuteronomy breaks this pattern decisively in its insistence that Yahweh's gifts are for the whole community, even those without land or means (e.g., 14:28–29; 16:11, 14; 26:11). "As long as the weakest member of the community does not also participate in the fullness of God's blessing, the promise remains unfulfilled."[17]

Feast!

Grateful feasting is the natural response to the divine blessing of land and its abundance. Twice in the festival calendar we read:

16. Irene J. Winter, "'Ornament and the Rhetoric of Abundance' in Assyria," in *On Art in the Ancient Near East*, Culture and History of the Ancient Near East 34 (Leiden: Brill, 2010), 1.1163–83, 1163. See especially Peter Altmann, "Feast and Famine: Lack as a Backdrop for Plenty," in *Feasting in the Archaeology and Texts of the Hebrew Bible and Ancient Near East*, ed. Peter Altmann and Janling Fu (Winona Lake, IN: Eisenbrauns, 2004), 161. This motif is present in the Old Testament, e.g., 2 Kings 6:28–31; Ps. 72:12–16.

17. G. Wehmeier, "ברך," in *Theological Lexicon of the Old Testament*, ed. Ernst Jenni and Claus Westermann, trans. Mark E. Biddle (Peabody, MA: Hendrickson, 1994), 1:265–82 at 278–79.

> And you shall rejoice before the LORD your God, you and your son and your daughter, your male servant and your female servant, the Levite who is within your towns, the sojourner, the fatherless, and the widow who are among you, at the place that the LORD your God will choose, to make his name dwell there. (Deut. 16:11, 14)

The Hebrew word translated "rejoice" (*shmh*) in this context means simply: Feast! Kill the lamb! Share the wine![18] For much of the year, meat was rarely eaten in Israel, as it was an expensive luxury, but for the feasts a goat or a calf was to be slaughtered, and a household was to celebrate the goodness of God with wine and other delicacies. The extended household feasted together with joy, relationships were forged, and kinship confirmed. God invited his people to a life of joy, gratefully to receive his gifts with inclusive feasting.

The closest I have come to experiencing the joy of Israel's ancient feast is in my previous life as a jazz pianist. I would often play keyboard in Latino bands at huge Latino festivals. Thousands from the Latin American community would gather together to dance and to eat. When our band began to play, the whole arena would move. Every generation knew the traditional dances, and everyone, it seemed, could dance with ease and with joy. These cultural experiences can give us a sense of what Israel's ancient festivals must have felt like. The whole community, rich and poor, young and old, feasted together before the Lord with music and dancing. Gratefully and joyfully receiving the good gifts of Yahweh is at the heart of a covenant response in Deuteronomy. Yet there was provision also for serious and deeply thoughtful thanksgiving: worshipers were to come before Yahweh "with the tribute of a freewill offering from your hand" (16:10). Gratitude, both solemn and celebratory, is at the heart of a covenant response throughout Scripture.[19]

Living gratefully today in the West is a particularly difficult task, for

18. For the interpretation of *shmh* as "feast" see Peter Altmann, *Festive Meals in Ancient Israel: Deuteronomy's Identity Politics in Their Ancient Near Eastern Context*, Beihefte zur Zeitschrift für die alttestamentliche Wissenschaft 424 (Berlin: de Gruyter, 2011), 205, 180–85. Jeffrey H. Tigay says that in Jewish tradition the feast came to be called "the time of our rejoicing"; *Deuteronomy* (Philadelphia: Jewish Publication Society, 1996), 158.

19. For example, this theme of thanksgiving spills over into Pauline theology. R. P. Meye writes that gratitude is the "heartbeat of Pauline spirituality"; "Spirituality," in *Dictionary of Paul and His Letters*, ed. Gerald F. Hawthorne, Ralph P. Martin, and Daniel G. Reid (Downers Grove IL: InterVarsity, 1993), 906–16 at 915.

we Westerners are immersed in the culture of consumerism. "To increase their capacity for consumption, consumers must never be left to rest. They need to be constantly exposed to new temptations to keep them in the state of perpetual suspicion and steady disaffection."[20] Walter Brueggemann reflects, "The contemporary American church is so largely enculturated to the American ethos of consumerism that it has little power to believe or act."[21]

I suggest that it is impossible as individuals to withstand consumerism and to live gratefully; but for a community indwelt by the Spirit, this *is* possible. Some Christian communities are finding creative ways to challenge consumerism; our church in Vancouver is experimenting with sharing possessions, including vehicles, as a way of reducing our consumption. As strange as it may sound, I suggest that *feasting* is the best antidote to consumerism. Traditionally, a whole community shares in a feast. In feasting, a community may share together in the deep joy of being gifted by God and of being knit together as kindred. Such rich warmth easily trumps the shallow thrills of consumerism. We need to teach our communities how to feast with gratitude.

The festal call to thanksgiving with inclusive celebration highlights the importance of the distinctive *life* of a missional congregation. As Peskett and Ramachandra write: "Mission is not primarily about *going*. Nor is mission primarily about *doing* anything. Mission is about *being*. It is about being a distinctive kind of people, a countercultural . . . community among the nations."[22]

A Community of Generosity and Inclusivity

As a goal in and of itself, celebrative thanksgiving could turn toward self-indulgence. So it is important that generous inclusion of otherwise excluded people is the third of the three movements that characterizes the festival calendar: gift, thanksgiving with celebration, justice. We might say that justice is the corollary of thanksgiving. Twice annually an Israelite household journeys to Jerusalem for feasting, and *everybody* participates,

20. Zygmunt Bauman, "The Self in a Consumer Society," *Hedgehog Review* 1 (1999): 35–40 at 38.

21. Walter Brueggemann, *The Prophetic Imagination*, 2nd ed. (Minneapolis: Fortress, 2001), 11.

22. Howard Peskett and Vinoth Ramachandra, *The Message of Mission* (Downers Grove, IL: InterVarsity, 2003), 123.

including the stranger, fatherless, and widow. The "stranger" is a person (or family) displaced from his or her own land because of indebtedness or warfare. The "fatherless and widow" are those made particularly vulnerable due to the death of the adult male in the family. These people lived and worked within rural settlements that were owned and managed by landed families. They would have labored in agricultural work for small pay and so were always in danger of indebtedness and enslavement. Deuteronomy's vision is that, in the prescribed feasts, the most vulnerable people of the land were to be included within Israelite households; they were to be included as family. The stranger, the fatherless, and the widow were not to be used merely as cheap labor but were to be included within the work, life, and relationships of the family—and they were explicitly to share in the celebrations of God's goodness. Israel was called to something much more than charity for the poor; they were called to share their new life richly, engaging those less fortunate in relationships that could be mutually transformative.

We learn here that where Yahweh reigns, his restoring influence not only extends to individuals who suffer, but also reaches deeply into social groups and heals through rearrangement. Bauckham argues rightly that God has given vulnerable people priority in the kingdom:

> God's love has to reach the strong via the weak, because the strong can receive the love of God only by abandoning their pretensions to status above others. . . . As well as the outward movement of the church's mission in geographical extension and numerical increase, there must also be this (in the Bible's imagery) downward movement of solidarity with the people at the bottom of the social scale of importance and wealth.[23]

How may we nurture our communities into this downward movement? Deuteronomy's feasting passages provide us with a crucial clue: we must remind one another constantly that at the heart of reality is a God of limitless generosity. The first step toward "solidarity with the people at the bottom of the social scale" is thanksgiving.

Israel's feasts are an evocative image for the life and mission of a worshiping community today. As the Old Covenant community feasted before the Lord, outsiders were caught up in the joyful relationship of the worshiping community with their God. Through this rich shared life, lived out

23. Bauckham, *Bible and Mission*, 50, 53–54.

before the Lord, outsiders too would come to know and to love Yahweh, the God of Israel. For worshiping communities today mission begins with a shared life of celebration, inclusion, kinship, worship, and justice. As we live in this way, being a contrast community, our neighborhoods will notice and get caught up in the joy and healing of the kingdom of God.

The Law: The Shape of Yahweh's Community

> Israel was the Lord's garden, a small oasis of cleanness and beauty in the midst of a . . . desert of idolatry and the chaos of wickedness. And the hedge which protected this garden, was the Law.[24]

A New Order for Life

Far from the nomism with which the Old Testament law is commonly accused, the Deuteronomic law *frees* the people of God for participation in a new community. Unlike Egypt, Israel is not to be a society where economic production comes at terrible human cost. Every person is to be accorded dignity—especially the vulnerable. And idolatry with all its dehumanizing implications is to be shunned. What Gerhard Lohfink says of Jesus's miracles is true of the Deuteronomic law: it "liberate[s] from the isolating and destroying demons of a sick society."[25] Israel was uniquely privileged to receive the law, as through the law something entirely new was happening. The law was an outbreak of a new order for life, the beginning of a new epoch, wherein the future overran the present.

What are we to make of the supposed law-gospel dichotomy in light of these claims? To put the question differently: can the Deuteronomic law be fulfilled? To be sure, as Martin Luther wrote, the law brings us "to a knowledge of our impotence" (e.g., 31:29).[26] First and foremost, however, the Deuteronomic law is the great king's blueprint for the communal life of his people Israel. Israel is to put the law into practice. It is "for our good always" (6:24). The law is "rest," that deep Sabbath that humanity and all of

24. Lesslie Newbigin, *Set Free to Be a Servant: Studies in Paul's Letter to the Galatians* (Madras: Christian Literature Society, 1969), 2.

25. Lohfink, *Jesus and Community*, 83.

26. Martin Luther, *The Bondage of the Will*.

creation is longing for. A missional hermeneutic rightly draws attention to the central function of the law, which is to shape a contrast community that lives in the sight of the nations.

Deuteronomy's law code, given in chapters 12–26, forms the center of the book.[27] The law was to infuse the life of the covenant community. The written law was to be treated with the greatest reverence (31:24–29). Many in the community would have memorized the law (Ps. 1:2). The law was to be taught to the next generation (Deut. 6:7), and it was to be read every seven years (31:10).

Deuteronomy's law is unique among the law codes of the Pentateuch and of the ancient Near East in its focus on care for vulnerable people. Norbert Lohfink argues convincingly that Deuteronomy's social laws operate as a system with the goal of doing away with poverty altogether.[28] Deuteronomy's law code provides for this by decreasing the likelihood that the vulnerable will fall into debt (e.g., 14:28–29; 24:6, 10–15; 26:12–15) and by providing means of recovery when debt does occur (e.g., 15:1–3, 12–18). "It will never be possible to eliminate the existence of strangers, orphans, and widows. But it is possible, according to Deuteronomy, to create a world in which one can be a stranger, an orphan, or a widow without being poor."[29] "There shall be no poor among you," Yahweh himself demands (15:4). The societies of Israel's neighbors in Mesopotamia were characterized by the increasing alienation of a people from their land, by the erosion of ties within kinship groups, and by increasing indebtedness leading to forms of slavery.[30] None of these were to be true of Israel: she was to be the great contrast society of the ancient Near East.

One figure that features prominently in Deuteronomy's social laws is the "stranger" (e.g., 1:16; 16:11, 14; 26:11). Strangers were persons separated from their inherited land and from the traditional kinship ties that would grant them identity, belonging, and security. Therefore, they were especially vulnerable to exploitation. In other cultures, such as that reflected in the Nuzi *ḫabiru* service contracts for example, impoverished immigrants en-

27. For an analysis of the content of the Deuteronomic law code, see Stephen A. Kaufman, "The Structure of the Deuteronomic Law," *Maraav* 1 (1979): 105–58; and McBride, "Polity of the Covenant People."

28. Norbert S. J. Lohfink, "Poverty in the Laws of the Ancient Near East and of the Bible," *Theological Studies* 52 (1991): 34–50 at 43, 44, 47.

29. Lohfink, "Poverty," 44.

30. Gregory C. Chirichigno, *Debt-Slavery in Israel and the Ancient Near East*, Journal for the Study of the Old Testament Supplement 14 (Sheffield: JSOT Press, 1993), 49–53.

tered a lifelong contract "of their own free will" but from which they were unlikely ever to achieve release. Their status was little better than slavery.[31] In contrast, Deuteronomy insists upon relationships of care where displaced people are protected from exploitation by being included within a landed household and as full participants within a village.

Deuteronomy's social laws display the radically restorative ethic of the reign of God. When we read with a missional hermeneutic, we read Deuteronomy as an ancient example of the kind of community that God desires, as a paradigm for communities at any time and any place.[32] Missional leaders must then inquire: How can worshiping communities embody the kind of mutuality displayed here, living as a foretaste of the kingdom of God and as an instrument of this kingdom?

Contextualization and Normativity

A missional hermeneutic invites us to consider Deuteronomic law in terms of both contextualization and normativity. First, Deuteronomic law is highly contextualized, addressing the missional circumstances that Israel would encounter in the land, particularly during the monarchic period. The law displays for us how the yeast of the good news of God's reign might leaven the communal life of one small ancient Near Eastern kingdom in the midst of the great empires. Dean Flemming's exploration of the tension between "at-homeness" and "prophetic transformation" in the texts of the New Testament may be helpful here:[33] Deuteronomy is *at home* in the ancient Near East, and we can therefore expect, for example, the reality of slavery to be visible in its laws. For example, in the Middle Babylonian Laws of Hammurabi, harboring a fleeing slave is a capital offense (Laws of Hammurabi §§15–20). And yet *prophetic transformation* may be seen in the Deuteronomic provision that, in Israel, fleeing slaves are *not* to be returned to their masters but must be accepted within the settlements into which they have fled. This legal provision unsettles the boundary between slave

31. Isaac Mendelsohn, *Slavery in the Ancient Near East* (Westport, CT: Greenwood, 1949), 18. See also Barry L. Eichler, *Indenture at Nuzi: The Personal Tidennutu Contract and Its Mesopotamian Analogues*, Yale Near Eastern Research 5 (New Haven: Yale University Press, 1973), 23–32, 65–70.

32. See further Christopher J. H. Wright, *Old Testament Ethics for the People of God* (Downers Grove, IL: InterVarsity, 2004), 183–84.

33. Flemming, *Contextualization in the New Testament*, 23.

and free (23:16–17). Truly, "the authors [of Deuteronomy] are on the verge of undermining the slave society."[34]

It is illuminating to consider the Decalogue in the light of Israel's particular context. Though Abraham Kuyper spoke for many when he described the Decalogue as "the authentic summary of that original moral law which God wrote in the heart of man, at his creation,"[35] this does not do justice to the special significance of these commandments for Israel in her context. The Decalogue reflects those facets of God's moral, creational law that are particularly relevant for achieving Deuteronomy's narrow goals, in a way that has been highly contextualized for a small, agriculture-based, ancient Near Eastern kingdom located in the buffer zone between two great empires (Egypt and Mesopotamia) on the western end of the fertile crescent. All of these contextual elements are crucial to the final shape of the Deuteronomic code and its Decalogue. Considering the Decalogue in light of Israel's particular context demonstrates the creativity required for a community to be both at home and prophetically transformative.

A second balancing observation is that Deuteronomy's laws express normative ethics grounded in the created order *in culturally recognizable ways*. There is an "underlying and often tacit presupposition of a 'carved' creation order" in Deuteronomy.[36] For example normative principles regarding hospitality seem to be behind the judgment upon Moab and Ammon for their lack of hospitality to Israel (23:3–4). And Deuteronomy's theology of blessing draws upon a normative principle that the blessing belongs to every person within a community (e.g., 14:29). This concept of a "carved creation order" is highly relevant for the Western missional context today. We learn here that no one can dodge biblical ethics. These laws reflect the truth about the world. They are etched into the very structure of the world, and to violate them is to wreak havoc upon us, upon our communities, and upon the creation itself.

If we can agree that Deuteronomy's social laws are paradigmatic for human society, the question remains, how do we contextualize this norma-

34. Georg Braulik, "The Joy of the Feast," in *Theology of Deuteronomy: Collected Essays of Georg Braulik*, trans. U. Lindblad (North Richland Hills, TX: Bibal, 1994), 27–66 at 53.

35. Abraham Kuyper writes, "Hence it is that, for the Calvinist, all ethical study is based on the Law of Sinai"; *Lectures on Calvinism* (repr. Grand Rapids: Eerdmans, 1999), 72.

36. Craig G. Bartholomew, *Ecclesiastes*, Baker Commentary on the Old Testament (Grand Rapids: Baker Academic, 2009), 91. Bartholomew is referring to both biblical law and wisdom. See further Terence E. Fretheim, *God and the World in the Old Testament: A Relational Theology of Creation* (Nashville: Abingdon, 2005), 133–56.

tivity to contemporary situations? Christopher Wright's helpful distinction between the *function* and *objective* of Old Testament laws is one way of parsing the text for contemporary relevance. *Function* refers to what a particular law would have entailed within the culture for which it was written, and *objective* refers to the broader goals of a law that applies across times and cultures, including principles for communities, for state structures, and for individual behavior.[37] We may consider by way of example Deuteronomy's laws concerning the stranger, mentioned above. One function of these laws was that the stranger was included within an ancient Israelite family as kindred. The broader objective was that vulnerable and displaced persons might live and thrive and belong within a people. And these objectives speak forcefully to the responsibility of Western nations to offer hospitality to the world's refugee populations, which total over thirty million people at the time of writing.

Israel and the Nations: The Scope of Yahweh's Community

> The countries of the world were full of abominations, violence, falsehood. Here was one land, one people, cherished and chosen for the purpose of transforming the world. This people's failure was most serious.[38]

On the face of it, the election of *one* nation, Israel, from among the nations might seem in tension with the mission of God to *every* nation. Yet Deuteronomy offers a clear vision of how the election of one nation was to be for the sake of the whole world and, in fact, becomes the grounds for mission in Scripture.

God of Gods

Much of the vision for the mission of God to every nation can be found in the character of Yahweh, as it is contrasted to the character of the gods of the other nations. Deuteronomy's monotheism does not entail the denial of other

37. Christopher J. H. Wright, *Deuteronomy*, New International Bible Commentary (Peabody, MA: Hendrickson, 1996), 13–14.

38. Abraham J. Heschel, *The Prophets: An Introduction* (New York: Harper & Row, 1955), 2:15.

spiritual beings; rather, it asserts that Yahweh is the only god who demonstrated his surpassing power and justice in redeeming Israel and is thus the only god that may be worshiped. Yahweh is utterly transcendent over all other gods in his capacity to act in history. He is the "God of gods, Lord of lords, the great, the mighty, and the awesome God" (10:17). Such a phrase is a claim to universal lordship; Yahweh is the God over all other gods, and he is also the God over the lands and the peoples that these other gods claim to rule over. Yahweh is the great king who redeems slaves from the grip of the nongods (4:5–8). "The tragedy of polytheism and idolatry is not the arithmetic (many gods instead of one), but that [polytheists] exchange the only true source of salvation for lifeless and powerless substitutes, and in doing so, introduce injustice, bondage, and cruelty into human life (cf. Rom. 1:21–32)."[39]

The unique joy and freedom in the service of Yahweh may be seen clearly in contrast to three characteristics of other ancient Near Eastern cosmologies. First, in the ancient Near East the gods were dependent upon humankind for their sustenance: three daily sacrifices provided their food. But Yahweh is not dependent upon his creation in this or any other way. Instead, he is the one who lovingly provides for, sustains, and blesses the world (8:7–10). Second, in the ancient Near East the gods are often unpredictable, volatile, and vengeful, and as a result their world is also unpredictable. Yahweh, however, reveals himself as morally consistent in his redemptive activity and in his law, suggesting that under the loving rule of this God the world is ordered and safe. Finally, the gods of the surrounding empires were patron deities of the royal palaces; in Israel, Yahweh is the patron of the least, the defender of the poor and the powerless.

Israel is chosen to be a steward of the revelation of the one true God. The worship of this God offers unparalleled blessing, as well as the radical challenge to live as a transformed community, and he provides this not only for Israel, but through Israel to the rest of the world.

Torah and the "Prophetic Openness" of Deuteronomy

In Deuteronomy, Yahweh's actions and his word for Israel demonstrate his purposes for every nation and every time, in that they reveal Yahweh's definitive acts, character, and intentions. God demonstrates his loving concern for *every* nation by displaying it in the life of this *one* nation. "Always im-

39. Wright, *Deuteronomy*, 10.

plied in the hope of a new national life for Israel was the hope of a restored world order."[40] The oppression of Egypt is an image of the entire "creation in thrall to evil."[41] Egypt's oppression is described in ancient vocabulary for oppression with clear universal implications.[42] The account of the exodus compels attention beyond its own time and place, for here Yahweh displays his character as the God who may bring freedom out of slavery "in many places, perhaps everywhere."[43] The divine giving of land is portrayed as a renewal of creation,[44] and here again we may discern implications for the renewal of all lands.

The universal scope of Yahweh's intentions is especially visible in his giving Torah to Israel. Deuteronomy's laws are not an arbitrary set of rules for one nation, "they are a paradigm of God's re-creative initiative to bring righteousness, justice and wisdom into this world."[45] Israel is to steward the Torah, Yahweh's divine word, for the sake of every nation, for it is the will and wisdom of the "God of gods, Lord of lords" (4:5–8; 10:17):

> See, I have taught you statutes and rules, as the LORD my God commanded me, that you should do them in the land that you are entering to take possession of it. Keep them and do them, for that will be your wisdom and your understanding in the sight of the peoples, who, when they hear all these statutes, will say, "Surely this great nation is a wise and understanding people." (4:6–7)[46]

Gordon McConville describes the universal significance of Torah, which is a more central concern even than Israel's status as the elect nation: "The priority of Torah over election is expressed in Deuteronomy when Torah is made the focus of the nations' perspective on Israel (4:6–8), and when the main

40. Oliver O'Donovan, *The Desire of Nations: Rediscovering the Roots of Political Theology* (Cambridge: Cambridge University Press, 1996), 23.

41. Colin Gunton uses this phrase in regards to Jesus's miracles; *Christ and Creation* (Eugene, OR: Wipf & Stock, 1992), 18.

42. David Daube, *The Exodus Pattern in the Bible* (London: Faber & Faber, 1963).

43. Walter Brueggemann, *Theology of the Old Testament* (Minneapolis: Fortress, 1997), 178.

44. J. Gordon McConville, *God and Earthly Power: An Old Testament Political Theology*, Library of Hebrew Bible/Old Testament Studies 454 (London: T&T Clark, 2006), 78–79.

45. Ryan O'Dowd, *The Wisdom of Torah: Epistemology in Deuteronomy and the Wisdom Literature*, Forschungen zur Religion und Literatur des Alten und Neuen Testaments 225 (Göttingen: Vandenhoeck & Ruprecht, 2009), 40–41.

46. Translations are from the English Standard Version unless otherwise indicated.

expositions of the place of Torah in Israel's life (chs. 4–6) preceded the main exposition of its election (ch. 7)."[47] God's self-revelation in Torah is given preeminence because, inevitably, his witness through the people whom he chose to live as a contrast community will be clouded by their failure. Because Israel is "stubborn" and "rebellious" (9:6), its future failure to keep the covenant is seen as inevitable. Significantly, Israel's own election is contingent in Deuteronomy. Deuteronomy is a covenant document between Yahweh and one particular kingdom, Israel, which discloses Yahweh's desire for every kingdom.

The Invention of Mission

To demonstrate Deuteronomy's vision of Yahweh's universal lordship, we may compare the description of the divine patron at the beginning of two different ancient Near East law codes: the Deuteronomic code and the Laws of Hammurabi. Deuteronomy says, "For Yahweh your God is God of gods and Lord of lords" (Deut. 10:17), whereas the Hammurabi code invokes "the god Enlil, lord of heaven and earth."[48] Both texts make a universal claim. Enlil is the divine sponsor of Hammurabi, the great king of the Middle Babylonian Empire. The royal ideology expressed in this phrase justified a rapid military expansion of the empire during Hammurabi's lifetime—an aggressive centrifugal (outward) movement.[49] In dramatic contrast, Yahweh, the God of gods, chose and transformed an insignificant, henpecked kingdom (7:7) in order to create a community where the insignificant are lifted up to significance (15:4; 17:16–17).

The nature of mission in these two ancient Near Eastern nations differs according to their differing religious orientations. Whereas the religious ideology of Babylon was designed to support expansionism, the actions of Yahweh in freeing and providing for his people inspired Israel's radical social program undertaken for the sake of the "least." In Deuteronomy,

47. McConville, *Deuteronomy*, 163.

48. Laws of Hammurabi §1.1–26, in Martha T. Roth, *Law Collections from Mesopotamia and Asia Minor*, 2nd ed., Society of Biblical Literature Writings from the Ancient World 6 (Atlanta: Scholars, 1995).

49. Johannes Blauw distinguishes between the nature of mission in the New and Old Testaments, referring to a centripetal movement (from the periphery to the center) in the Old Testament and a centrifugal movement (from the center to the periphery) in the New Testament; *The Missionary Nature of the Church: A Survey of the Biblical Theology of Mission* (New York: McGraw Hill, 1962), 38–41, 54, 66.

Yahweh desires transformation rather than military expansion, and the law expresses Yahweh's desire for every nation. This vision of the kingdom of God could not be clearer. The new order of God breaks into the present by being embodied in a particular community, a humble people, honoring those without honor. The power of God's community is not reflected in its size, but in its God-given beauty (Isa. 60:9).

Literary parallels between the mission of Hammurabi and the mission of Israel abound. Hammurabi will enjoy an "eternal kingship" (Laws of Hammurabi §1.1–26). He brings blessing to the land of Babylon and to every kingdom that he conquers (Laws of Hammurabi §1.50–5.13). The language of election is used of both the king and his nation: Enlil "selected" Hammurabi, and he "made Babylon supreme" (Laws of Hammurabi §1.1–26). The most characteristic and cherished expressions of mission used in Scripture emerged from an ancient missional encounter with ancient Near Eastern culture. The military power of the Neo-Assyrian and Neo-Babylonian kings was immense, and the glamor, charm, and security that the empires offered had enormous appeal for the Israelite elite. Thus Israel's story of election by Yahweh was expressed in borrowed language explicitly to challenge these powerful forces and ideologies.

One important implication is that there is no neutral expression of mission, neither in vocabulary nor in the lived life of the church. Mission has always been, and should always be, contextualized. At their best, mission and theology are, in a sense, always being renewed and reinvented.[50] A missional encounter with culture, whether of the past and recorded in Scripture or of the present and lived out in our own communities, is both grounded in the traditions that came before and also daringly imaginative, ready to embrace new paradigms for community and fresh articulations of the story.[51] Wise missional leaders will be sensitive to the reality that authentic expressions of mission may appear highly unusual and may be found on the margins of the traditional structures of the church. They will nonetheless be rooted within the biblical story. As Lesslie Newbigin states: "No verbal statement can be produced which relieves the Church of the responsibility continually to re-think and re-state its message."[52]

50. Flemming refers to "Spirit-guided theological reflection for new situations" in the early church; *Contextualization in the New Testament*, 54.

51. See further George R. Hunsberger, *Bearing the Witness of the Spirit: Lesslie Newbigin's Theology of Cultural Plurality* (Grand Rapids: Eerdmans, 1998).

52. Lesslie Newbigin, *The Reunion of the Church: A Defence of the South India Scheme* (London: SCM, 1948), 138.

For the World and against the World

The theme of judgment in Deuteronomy focuses our view of a worshiping community's missional encounter with culture: God's people exist both *for* and *against* the world.[53] Two great sins are condemned in Deuteronomy: apostasy and injustice. For tolerating these two great sins, Israel would ultimately be exiled, as Deuteronomy predicted. Of course, these two themes are dependent on one another, for it is precisely Yahweh's good rule that forges a society in which every person and all of creation can flourish.

Judgment upon the Canaanites

The Deuteronomic texts that command the utter destruction of the Canaanite populations (7:2, 5, 23; 12:30; 20:15–16) require some discussion at this point.[54] These texts raise important questions about grace, violence, ethnicity, judgment, and the character of God. In order to clear the ground for our discussion, allow me to address the major objections to the ethics of these texts. First, Yahweh's judgment upon the Canaanites is not arbitrary, but is the divine response to their injustice and wickedness (12:31). Second, God's judgment also fell on Israel itself for the same reasons, demonstrating that judgment upon "the nations" was not ethnically motivated. Third, there is no inherent incongruity between Yahweh's judgment upon a nation at a particular point on the journey of salvation history and Yahweh's blessing all nations through Abraham at the destination of the journey. God acts in power throughout history in order to restrain evil and injustice so that blessing may flourish.

Nonetheless there are good reasons for thinking that Deuteronomy does not have in view the entire destruction of the Canaanite populations. Brueggemann asserts that this theme "requires a class reading, this rhetoric is on the lips of those who have no weapons."[55] Insofar as Deuteronomy was

53. "The Church is for the world against the world. The Church is against the world for the world. The Church is for the human community in that place, that village, that city, that nation, in the sense that Christ is for the world. And that must be the determining criterion at every point"; Lesslie Newbigin, *A Word in Season: Perspectives on Christian World Missions* (Grand Rapids: Eerdmans, 1994), 54.

54. See further, McConville, *Deuteronomy*, 90, 161; Wright, *Old Testament Ethics*, 472–80.

55. Brueggemann, *Theology*, 243.

allowed to shape the community during the monarchic period, it was a text in solidarity with those on the margins of society, those without economic power or military capacity. Lawson Younger, among others, investigates the literary techniques of ancient conquest accounts, focusing on Assyrian, Hittite, Egyptian, and Israelite texts. Younger demonstrates that expressions of annihilation in ancient conquest accounts have a highly figurative and an ideological aspect that is commonly communicated through hyperbole. These accounts use stereotyped phrases that overstate the historical reality, expressing the ideology of the text's sponsor.[56] Younger's argument is perhaps most easily demonstrated in the well-known Mesha Inscription (the Moabite Stone), wherein King Mesha of Moab claims: "Israel has gone to ruin, yes, it has gone to ruin for ever";[57] and claims that every resident in the vicinity of Nebo has been killed.[58] Of course in fact neither Israel nor Nebo were annihilated: the text is hyperbolic and ideological.[59] This observation does not mean that the Mesha Inscription is historically void and that these battles never occurred. It does show that this genre of ancient writing communicates through literary conventions that exaggerate elements of annihilation in order to make an ideological or theological point.[60] Younger demonstrates that "Joshua 9–12 shares a similar transmission code with its [ancient Near Eastern] counterparts."[61]

In Deuteronomy *herem* signifies the total loyalty that Yahweh demands and that deep human flourishing requires. Other societies were shaped by a different kind of rule and were therefore in many ways an aberration of Yahweh's intention for society. Israel is meant to reject utterly the false worship of these kingdoms. *Herem* amounts to a kind of spiritual map, distinguishing between the kingdoms of darkness and of light. The lens of

56. K. Lawson Younger Jr., *Ancient Conquest Accounts: A Study in Ancient Near Eastern and Biblical History Writing*, Journal for the Study of the Old Testament Supplement 98 (Sheffield: JSOT Press, 1990), 123.

57. "The Inscription of King Mesha," trans. K. A. D. Smelik in *The Context of Scripture*, ed. William W. Hallo and K. Lawson Younger (Leiden: Brill, 2000), 2.23.

58. The Hebrew/Moabite word *hrm* is used here, the same word employed in Deuteronomy.

59. Bruce E. Routledge argues that the significance of Mesha devoting the Canaanites to Kemosh was that the deity then stood between the two social groups, preventing exchange of any kind and therefore of any kind of human sociability; *Moab in the Iron Age: Hegemony, Polity, Archaeology* (Philadelphia: University of Pennsylvania Press, 2004), 150.

60. Similarly Wright writes, "We do need to allow for the exaggerated language of warfare"; *Old Testament Ethics*, 474.

61. Younger, *Ancient Conquest Accounts*, 241.

a missional hermeneutic highlights for us that Deuteronomy's theology of judgment is preparing a people for a wholesale confrontation with the dehumanizing idols of culture.

Canaanite Destruction and a Missional Encounter with Culture

Deuteronomy's stipulations regarding foreign participation in the covenant community demonstrate a certain tension. On the one hand, the pagan practices of the Canaanite people established in the land posed a clear threat of syncretism for Israel. Intermarriage in particular would have spelled the end of Israel's distinctive life and missional identity (7:3–4). On the other hand, Deuteronomy also insists upon the full inclusion of the stranger and the chattel slave in the life of the nation, and many of those included would have been from other kingdoms and would have worshiped other deities. Seemingly because of their vulnerability, these latter groups did not present the same threat to the community's faithfulness. Israel was to keep these principles in tension, taking steps to exclude threats to its own faithful allegiance to Yahweh but also striving to be a radically inclusive community (in line with the exodus motif). The command to separate from the Canaanites is as dependent upon the missional context of the community as the command to radical inclusivity.

This same tension of being both for and against the world faces any missional community, because a missional community must immerse itself in the world's grief and joys, its structures and sociality, and yet not drown in its whelming idolatry. As G. Lohfink puts it: "Precisely because the church does not exist for itself, but completely and exclusively for the world, it is necessary that the church not become the world, that it retain its own countenance."[62] Missional leaders must persistently ask: "What does it mean to love our neighborhood? And what are the idols that threaten our particular community in this particular place?"

I suggest that one strategy for the Western church to live faithfully amidst cultural idolatry is to relocate itself at the margins of society, with the marginalized. Scholars and laypeople reading the New Testament notice that Christ ate his way through the Gospels and that he had a reputation for eating with all the wrong people: tax collectors, prostitutes, sinners. But this social rearrangement through kingdom feasting didn't begin altogether with Christ. As we have seen in Deuteronomy, Israel was always supposed to live

62. Lohfink, *Jesus and Community*, 146.

this way, sharing the festal table—indeed all of life—with the vulnerable, with gratitude to God. Certainly, the church is called into every sphere of culture, into education, health, business, politics, and the arts. Some of us are called to influence the very center of culture. Yet no matter what our calling or sphere of influence, we cannot neglect to make our home also at the margins, with "sinners." This is how we set our table; this is where we feast.

Conclusion: There Is a Lot to Talk About!

As with all biblical books, Deuteronomy is a record of the mission of God's people at a particular time and place, struggling to leaven their unique situation with the yeast of the good news of God's rule. Deuteronomy seeks to shape a contrastive community in the spiritual and ethical pattern of the exodus and summons us to enter the story of God's mission for the world. Yahweh graciously redeemed Israel, becoming its king and giving laws to shape the community toward mutuality and generosity, away from Egypt's oppression.

The exodus from slavery to freedom provided the pattern for Israel's new life, and festivals were deliberate reminders of the need for God's people to respond with gratitude, joy, generosity, and inclusivity. The law freed the people of God to participate in a new community without the burdens of royal privilege, land alienation, and enslavement. Yahweh's law and life-giving invitation to the whole world is shown in the Torah to be more significant in Israel even than its own election.

We need to allow Deuteronomy's vision for community and for society to disrupt our settled conceptions of the biblical story. In order to hear afresh the radical call of the kingdom of God, consider what we have observed through this imaginative lens. Let's suppose that Deuteronomy's vision was deeply seeded within the nation of Israel. And let's imagine that a thoughtful member of the community who had Deuteronomy soundly memorized was to write a reflection upon what was occurring in the community. They might describe the story of Deuteronomy by writing a bullet point list something along these lines:

- This is the story of our community.
- Yahweh's redemption of a group of slaves and his kingship by virtue of that redemption stands behind the whole show.
- We are left wondering which slaves Yahweh is going to redeem next, since that is what he likes to do.

- Our community is transformed, in line with the ethical and religious trajectory of Yahweh's redeeming slaves.
- Yahweh is reliable and generous, and so the world is well ordered and blessed. We are free to be generous in return.
- Salvation and community are woven together. This is all about what Yahweh is doing for and within the community of God's people.
- This really is great news.
- There is a lot to talk about with those who are outside of our community, and people will likely ask lots of questions.
- Pharaoh doesn't think it is great news, and anybody who wants to live like pharaoh won't like it.

In sum, the exodus event opened wide the imagination of this community for what a society can look like.

Our ancient friend's reflections resound with Lohfink's summary of Jesus's ministry: "The *sole* meaning of the entire activity of Jesus is the gathering of God's eschatological people."[63] The communal dimension of salvation in Deuteronomy and throughout Scripture should inform our speaking for the kingdom. Speaking for the kingdom cannot be separated from the shared life of a community that is living distinctively within culture. Presently I work as a pastor and scholar in a kind of worshiping justice community that is embedded in one of the most post-Christian contexts in North America: Vancouver. Here, the gospel sounds ludicrous unless it is visible in the life of a particular community that is consciously playing its part within the biblical drama. As our unchurched friends are drawn into our shared life, as they witness our practices of love and justice—for example, refugee claimant housing and support, a social enterprise that offers work to our underemployed neighbors, or a weekly meal based in solidarity rather than charity—they encounter Christ. They learn to trust Christ's word and to honor him as redeemer.

There are many different aspects of the biblical story that we may draw upon when we speak for the kingdom. I sometimes find myself simply explaining our community in this way to our neighbors: "We are diverse: rich, poor, lots of ethnicities," or "We are trying to resist the individualism of our culture." People in our neighborhood often value these characteristics. And as the conversation progresses, I speak of Christ, who is the clue to our community, even as he is the clue to all of his creation.

63. Lohfink, *Jesus and Community*, 26 (emphasis original).

CHAPTER 8

A Missional Reading of Psalms 67 and 96

Carl J. Bosma

This chapter argues for a missional reading of the Psalms, a reading that deals with "God's mission that involves God's people living in God's ways in the sight of the nations."[1] To that end, I provide a New Testament basis for a missional reading of the Psalter and briefly consider objections to the proposed reading. Then I stipulate two basic assumptions for a missional reading of the Psalter and illustrate a missional reading of Psalm 67 and Psalm 96, two key missional psalms, in order to garner key missional themes.

New Testament Basis

Since the publication of William Carey's *An Enquiry into the Obligations of Christians to Use Means for the Conversion of the Heathen* in 1792, Matthew 28:18–20 has been a key text for Christians reflecting on the biblical basis for the practice of Christian missions. However, we should also give attention to another important resurrection text that, like Matthew 28:16–20, reaches its climax in a vitally important dominical pronouncement about the church's mission to the nations. In Luke 24:44–48 Jesus informs his disciples: "This is what I told you while I was still with you: Everything must be fulfilled that is written about me in the Law of Moses, the Prophets and the Psalms" (24:44).[2] According to 24:45, Jesus opens their minds so that the disciples

1. Christopher J. H. Wright, *The Mission of God: Unlocking the Bible's Grand Narrative* (Downers Grove, IL: InterVarsity, 2006), 51.

2. Herman A. Wiersinga, *Zendingsperspectief in het Oude Testament* (Baarn: Bosch &

could understand the Scriptures, after which he says: "This is what is written: The Christ will suffer and rise from the dead on the third day, and repentance and forgiveness of sins will be preached in his name to all nations, beginning at Jerusalem. You are witnesses of these things" (24:46–48).

Two features of Jesus's explanation in 24:46–48 should be considered. First, in 24:46, Jesus openly claims to be the Christ (Messiah). This claim clearly links Jesus to the messianic expectations in the Old Testament, especially God's promise to David in 2 Samuel 7:11–16. Moreover, this messianic claim also links Jesus's ministry with the vitally important theme of the kingdom of God that, according to Walter Eichrodt,[3] unites the Old and the New Testaments.

Second, Jesus explains that the Scriptures predicted not only that, according to God's plan (δεῖ),[4] the Christ must suffer and rise on the third day, but also "that repentance and forgiveness of sins will be preached in his name to all nations, beginning in Jerusalem." Jesus had already warned his disciples that the Christ must suffer (Luke 9:22, 44; 18:31–34; 24:7; cf. also 12:50; 17:25; 22:22). But here in 24:47 he adds "that repentance and forgiveness of sins will be preached in his name to all nations, beginning in Jerusalem." This significant addition argues for a missional reading of the Psalms.

In addition, it is also imperative to note that in 24:44 Jesus adds "and the Psalms" to the standard phrase "the Law and the Prophets" (16:16; cf. Acts 26:23). Clearly, therefore, the Psalms not only contain the messianic expectation of a suffering Messiah (Ps. 22) but also predict the scriptural necessity (*dei*) of preaching repentance and forgiveness of sins (Acts 11:14; 20:21; 26:20) to the nations. This unique addition, then, also argues for a missional reading of the Psalter.

Additional New Testament support for the proposed missional reading of the Psalter comes from Romans 15:7–22, where Paul defends, with quotations from the Psalter, his priestly duty to preach the gospel to the

---

Keuning, 1954), 8–9; Wright, *Mission of God*, 29–30; Mark J. Boda, "'Declare His Glory among the Nations': The Psalter as Missional Collection," in *Christian Mission: Old Testament Foundations and New Testament Developments*, ed. Stanley E. Porter and Cynthia Long Westfall (Eugene, OR: Wipf & Stock, 2010), 13.

3. Cf. Walter Eichrodt, *Theology of the Old Testament*, trans. J. A. Baker, Old Testament Library (Philadelphia: Westminster, 1961), 1:26.

4. Cf. Walter Grundmann, s.v. "δεῖ," in *Theological Dictionary of the New Testament*, ed. Gerhard Kittel and Gerhard Friedrich, trans. Geoffrey W. Bromiley (Grand Rapids: Eerdmans, 1964–76), 2:22; Joel B. Green, *The Gospel of Luke*, New International Commentary on the New Testament (Grand Rapids: Eerdmans, 1997), 856n16; Peter Doble, "Luke 24.26, 44—Songs of God's Servant: David and His Psalms in Luke-Acts," *Journal for the Study of the New Testament* 28 (2006): 267–83.

gentiles. In Romans 15:9 Paul quotes Psalm 18:49 (cf. 2 Sam. 22:50), a declarative psalm of praise in which David vows to praise God among the nations, which may be considered to be an "O.T. anticipation of N.T. evangelism."[5] Moreover, together with Psalm 18:49, Paul also quotes Psalm 117:1 in Romans 15:11: "Rejoice, O gentiles, with his people," in order to support his claim (in 15:8–9) that "Christ has become a servant of the Jews on behalf of God's truth, to confirm the promises made to the patriarchs so that the gentiles may glorify God for his mercy."[6]

Luke 24:44–48 and Paul's quotation of Psalm 18:49 and 117:1 demonstrate clearly that the Psalter is an important source for both writers' understanding of the church's mission to the nations. Consequently, the Psalter should be read not only christologically but also missionally.[7] Such a reading is vitally important for a theology of missions, first of all, because the Psalter is the longest book in the Old Testament.[8] Moreover, the Psalter is one of the most often quoted Old Testament books in the New Testament.[9] Furthermore, the Psalter contains "more direct statements about God than any other book in the two testaments of the Christian canon."[10] Finally, as H. A. Wiersinga notes, the psalms are from various periods of Israel's history, and throughout that history Israel used psalms in its cult that clearly communicate its realization that God's plan of salvation included the nations.[11]

Objections and Defense

Although the contributors to this book would heartily agree with the claim that the Psalms should be read missionally, not everyone else agrees with

5. John H. Stek, *Zondervan NIV Study Bible*, rev. ed. (Grand Rapids: Zondervan, 2002), 795. Stek also refers to Ps. 22:22–31; 56:12–13; 61:8; 65:1; and 69:30–33.

6. According to Jannie du Preez, "The Missionary Significance of Psalm 117 in the Book of Psalms and in the New Testament," *Missionalia* 27 (1999): 374, the use of the nouns "truth" and "grace" in Rom. 15:8–9 is an allusion to Ps. 117:2. Cf. Wright, *Mission of God*, 483.

7. Ps. 72, for example, is traditionally read christologically. However, in light of the clear allusion to Gen. 12:3 in Ps. 72:17, this psalm should also be read missionally.

8. W. Creighton Marlowe, "Music of Missions: Themes of Cross-Cultural Outreach in the Psalms," *Missiology: An International Review* 26 (1998): 445.

9. S. Moyise and M. J. J. Menken, eds., *The Psalms in the New Testament*, The New Testament and the Scriptures of Israel (London: T&T Clark, 2004), 2.

10. James Luther Mays, *Preaching and Teaching the Psalms*, ed. Patrick D. Miller and Gene M. Tucker (Louisville: Westminster John Knox, 2006), 69–70.

11. Wiersinga, *Zendingsperspectief in het Oude Testament*, 73.

this approach.[12] Already in 1896, for example, Max Löhr rejects the idea that Israel had a mission to the nations,[13] while in 1959 Robert Martin-Achard defends the same position.[14] Concerning the Psalms he writes: "The major preoccupation of the psalmist was not with propaganda for Yahweh directed to the heathen. . . . The Psalmist is not proclaiming that the nations will be radically transformed."[15]

George Peters takes a contrary position, asserting that "the hymn of praise is missionary preaching par excellence."[16] In support of this claim, Peters counts 175 universal references to the peoples and nations of the world in the Psalter.[17] In fact, if one were to highlight the words "peoples" and "nations" in the Psalter, beginning with Psalm 2, one would discover an ariadnic red line running through the Psalter.[18] For this reason Peters declares that "the Psalter is one of the greatest missionary books in the world," though he admits that it is "seldom seen from this point of view."[19] Peters also lists whole psalms that clearly express Yahweh's concern for the nations and expect the nations to worship and praise Yahweh (Ps. 2, 33, 66, 72, 98, 117, 145).[20]

Like Peters, but independently, Patrick D. Miller Jr. highlights the missional perspective of the psalms of praise:

12. At issue for some is whether Israel was actually sent to the nations. One of the few Old Testament texts that probably expresses this idea is Isa. 66:19. Cf. J. Alec Motyer, *The Prophecy of Isaiah: An Introduction and Commentary* (Downers Grove, IL: InterVarsity, 1993), 541.

13. Max Löhr, *Der Missionsgedanke im Alten Testament: Ein beitrag zur altestamentlichen religionsgeschichte* (Freiburg im Breisgau: Möhr, 1959).

14. Robert Martin-Achard, *Israel et les Nations: La Perspective Missionnaire de l'Ancien Testament = A Light to the Nations: A Study of the Old Testament Conception of Israel's Mission to the World*, trans. John P. Smith (London: Oliver & Boyd, 1962).

15. Martin-Achard, *Light to the Nations*, 58.

16. George Peters, *A Biblical Theology of Missions* (Chicago: Moody, 1972), 116.

17. Peters, *Biblical Theology of Missions*, 116.

18. Cf. Wiersinga, *Zendingsperspectief in het Oude Testament*, 73. For a succinct treatment of the nations in the Psalms from a canonical perspective see Gordon Wenham, "The Nations in the Psalms," in *The Psalter Reclaimed: Praying and Praising with the Psalms* (Wheaton, IL: Crossway, 2013), 161–86. For a more detailed treatment see Petrus Johannes Nicolaas Smal, *Die Universalisme in die Psalms*, ThD thesis, Vrije Universiteit (Kampen: Kok, 1956).

19. Peters, *Biblical Theology of Missions*, 116.

20. Peters, *Biblical Theology of Missions*, 116. Curiously, he omits Ps. 67 and Ps. 96 from this list. Michael Landon, "The Psalms as Mission," *Restoration Quarterly* 44 (2002): 166, expands this list to include Pss. 1; 22; 24; 40; 45; 46; 47; 49; 50; 58; 67; 68; 82; 86; 87; 95; 96; 97; 102; 105; 108; 115; 135; and 138.

> That is the purpose of praise—to respond to the experience of God's grace and power, to exalt the one who is seen and known to be that way, and to bear witness to all who hear that God is God. In that sense the praise of God in the Old Testament is always devotion that tells about God, that is, *theology*, and proclamation that seeks to draw others into the circle of those who worship this God, that is, *testimony for conversion*. . . . Perhaps less clear in the minds of many readers of the Old Testament is the fact that praise of God is the most prominent and extended formulation of the *universal* and *conversionary* dimension of the theology of the Old Testament.[21]

Others argue convincingly for a missional message of the Psalter. Christopher J. H. Wright, for example, quotes Miller's words with approval;[22] Creighton Marlowe calls the Psalter the "music of missions;"[23] Theodore Mascarenhas writes a thesis on *The Missionary Function of Israel in Psalms 67, 96, and 117*;[24] and Mark Boda describes the Psalter as a "missional collection."[25] Even more recently, Michael W. Goheen argues for a missional reading of the Psalter.[26]

Basic Methodological Assumptions

A primary assumption of the proposed missional reading of the Psalter is that, as Luke 24:44 clearly indicates, the Psalter must be read in the canonical context of the Law and the Prophets.[27] The introductory psalm, Psalm 1, clearly shows that the Psalter must be read in the light of the Torah. Psalm 1:2 encourages the reader to meditate on the Torah as a delightful key to success. Together 1:2 and the final clause of 1:3 recall Joshua 1:7, and the

21. Patrick D. Miller Jr., *Interpreting the Psalms* (Philadelphia: Fortress, 1986), 68.

22. Wright, *Mission of God*, 132–35, 478–84.

23. W. Creighton Marlowe, "Music of Missions: Themes of Cross-Cultural Outreach in the Psalms," *Missiology* 26 (1998): 445–56.

24. Theodore Mascarenhas, *The Missionary Function of Israel in Psalms 67, 96, and 117* (Lanham, MD: University Press of America, 2005).

25. Boda, "Declare His Glory among the Nations," 38.

26. Michael W. Goheen, *A Light to the Nations: The Missional Church and the Biblical Story* (Grand Rapids: Baker Academic, 2011), 58; idem, "Nourishing Our Missional Identity: Worship and the Mission of God's People," in *In Praise of Worship: An Exploration of Text and Practice*, ed. David J. Cohen and Michael Parsons (Eugene, OR: Pickwick, 2010), 32–53.

27. For this preference see also, Wenham, *Psalter Reclaimed*, 162.

simile in Psalm 1:3 recalls Jeremiah 17:8. The taproot text for mission from the Torah is Genesis 12:1–3, which belongs to the *toledoth* of Terah and is God's powerful antidote to the rebellion of the nations recorded in Genesis 11:1–9. Genesis 12:3 is a hermeneutical lens for examining, for example, the confident claim in Psalm 72:17 that all nations will be blessed through the Davidic king and that they will call him blessed. As we will note below, it is also crucial for understanding Psalm 67:1, 7 and Psalm 96:7. A second assumption is that the reader should respect the arrangement of the individual psalms in the final canonical shape of the Psalter as espoused by Brevard S. Childs and others.[28]

On the basis of these two basic methodological assumptions, we will now proceed to a deeper exegesis of Psalms 67 and 96 to illustrate the Psalter's missional intent.

Psalm 67

I chose Psalm 67, a communal prayer for blessing after a successful harvest[29]—perhaps in the postexilic period (Zech. 8:12–13)[30]—because it does not specifically refer to Israel and, as the multiple repetition of the nouns "nations" and "peoples" shows, because this is a radiant universal psalm.[31] Moreover, many commentators and missional readers of Psalm 67 recognize the missional character of the first two verses because 67:1 echoes the Aaronic blessing in Numbers 6:24–26.[32] However, many do not read these

28. Brevard S. Childs, *Introduction to the Old Testament as Scripture* (Philadelphia: Fortress, 1979), 5, 11, 523. For a discussion of this method see Wenham, *Psalter Reclaimed*, 57–79.

29. As W. S. Prinsloo, "Psalm 67: Harvest Thanksgiving Psalm, (Eschatological) Hymn, Communal Prayer, Communal Lament, Or . . . ?" *Old Testament Essays* 7 (1994): 232–34, demonstrates, the classification of the literary genre of Ps. 67 is debated. At issue is the translation of the verbs in the poem. Cf. Eep Talstra and Carl J. Bosma, "Psalm 67: Blessing, Harvest, and History: A Proposal for Exegetical Method," *Calvin Theological Journal* 36 (2001): 290–313.

30. Talstra and Bosma, "Psalm 67," 308–9, 313.

31. Ps. 67 shares this features with Pss. 65–68, with which it forms a group in Book 2 of the Psalter and shares other important themes. Cf. Stek, *Zondervan NIV Study Bible*, 855, 858; Smal, *Die Universalisme in die Psalms*, 108; J. P. M. van der Ploeg, *Psalmen I*, De boeken van het Oude Testament 7 (Roermond: Romein & Zonen, 1971), 386; Mascarenhas, *Missionary Function of Israel*, 91–93.

32. Goheen, *Light to the Nations*, 58; Wright, *Mission of God*, 475–78.

verses in terms of the psalm as a whole. But when one reads the poem in its entirety, other salient missional features besides the echo of Numbers 6:24–26 become evident.

To discover them, the reader must recognize that Psalm 67 has a symmetrical concentric structure with 67:4 at the center, framed by the refrain of 67:3 and 67:5.[33]

A God, may he be gracious to us and bless us
and make his face shine with us,
that your way may be known on earth,
. . . your salvation among all nations.
B May the peoples praise you, O God; ←
may all the peoples praise you.
C May the nations be glad and sing for joy,
for you judge (= govern) the peoples justly;
and as for the nations on the earth, you guide them.
B′ May the peoples praise you, O God; ←
may all the peoples praise you.
A′ The land has yielded its harvest.
May God, our God, bless us.
May God bless us,
so that all the ends of the earth will fear him.

Recognition of this concentric structure reveals, first of all, that 67:1–2 and 67:6–7 are symmetrical in length and contain the key word "blessing." Second, 67:3 and 67:5 mirror each other literally and frame 67:4, the only tricolon in the poem, which, as the longest poetic line in the poem, constitutes the thematic center of this chiastic structure.[34] Psalm 67:4 is also theologically significant because it affirms God's beneficent reign over the nations. Third, 67:1 and 67:6–7 speak about God in the third person, while 67:2–5 addresses God directly in the second person. For this reason this psalm lends itself to antiphonal singing. Significantly, the verses that talk about

33. Talstra and Bosma, "Psalm 67," 302. For a detailed stylistic analysis of Ps. 67 see Prinsloo, "Psalm 67"; and Mascarenhas, *Missionary Function of Israel*, 85–91.

34. Alexander Maclaren, "The Psalms," in *Expositor's Bible* (New York: Armstrong, 1903), 8.265. In concentric chiastic structures, the central element is normally the thematic center developed at the extremes. Cf. Nils W. Lund, *Chiasmus in the New Testament: A Study in the Form and Function of Chiastic Structures* (repr. Peabody, MA: Hendrickson, 1992), 40–41, 97–98.

God in the third person (67:1, 6–7) reveal a clear affinity with priestly material in the Old Testament (cf. Num. 6:24–26; Lev. 26:4; Ezek. 34:27; Zech. 8:12–13).

As noted above, the jussive prayer in Psalm 67:1 recalls the Aaronic blessing in Numbers 6:24–26. However, the synoptic comparison below shows that this prayer is not a verbatim quotation; it has been modified and parts have been omitted:

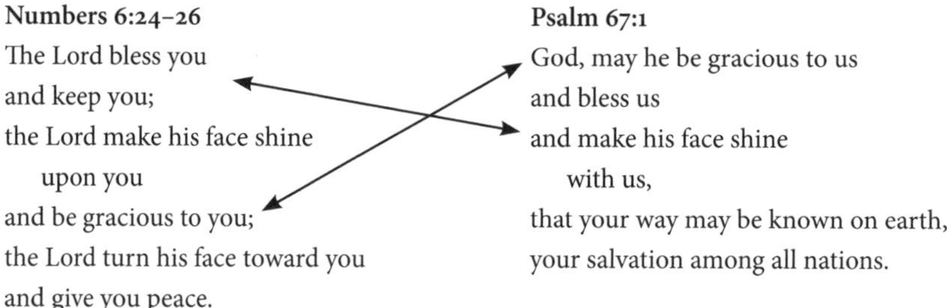

Numbers 6:24–26
The Lord bless you
and keep you;
the Lord make his face shine
upon you
and be gracious to you;
the Lord turn his face toward you
and give you peace.
Psalm 67:1
God, may he be gracious to us
and bless us
and make his face shine
with us,
that your way may be known on earth,
your salvation among all nations.

The comparison shows, first of all, that the order of the wishes in Psalm 67 has been changed. The wish that God be gracious is placed first and is followed by the wish for blessing. This strategic inversion emphasizes God's grace. Second, whereas in Numbers 6 the priest addresses the individual Israelite, in Psalm 67 the anonymous speaker uses the plural pronoun "us" and identifies himself with his audience, presumably Israel. Third, whereas in Numbers 6:25 the priest wishes that Yahweh's face may shine *upon* the individual Israelite, in Psalm 67:1 the prepositional phrase is "with us" instead of "upon us." This suggests that the recipients of God's blessing will themselves shine.[35] Fourth, according to Numbers 6:27, by pronouncing the blessing the priest will put Yahweh's name on Israel and so Yahweh will bless them. This explanation is missing in Psalm 67 and in its place there is a purpose clause in 67:2 that "interprets the Aaronic blessing for themselves in terms of Abrahamic hope [Gen. 12:3] to be a blessing to all the nations of the world."[36] The lack of this purpose clause in Numbers 6:24–26 might lead one to conclude that the priestly blessing is for Israel alone. However, the innovative addition in Psalm 67:2 shows clearly that

35. Craig C. Broyles, *Psalms*, New International Biblical Commentary (Peabody, MA: Hendrickson, 1999), 279.

36. Jannie du Preez, "Mission in Israel's Worship: Psalm 67," *Mission Bulletin* 19 (1999): 14. Cf. Tremper Longman III, *Psalms*, Tyndale Old Testament Commentary (Downers Grove, IL: IVP Academic, 2014), 214.

the wish for God's gracious blessing is not self-centered. On the contrary, in 67:1–2 Israel prays that God's abundant blessing of his people will be so obvious to all the nations that it will bring universal recognition of his deliverance as the desired outcome.

Psalm 67:3–5 elaborates on the purpose clause of 67:2. As noted above, in these verses God is addressed directly, which suggests that the congregation is speaking. In its form, 67:3–5 is a jussive wish for international praise.[37] Rhetorically, it serves to motivate the opening prayer in 67:1–2. In these jussive calls for praise, Israel prays that God's gracious blessing of his people will result in the nations' adding their praise to that of Israel.[38]

Significantly, the primary motivation for this anticipated international praise is found in 67:4, the theological centerpiece of the poem. In this pivotal verse Israel wishes that the nations will praise God eventually because of his just, benevolent, and sovereign cosmic rule. The causal *ki* clause in this verse emphasizes, first of all, that as king of the universe God characteristically judges the nations fairly.[39] Second, he leads them like a shepherd,[40] an image that is more typically reserved for Israel's own relationship with God (Ps. 77:20; 78:14, 53, 72; cf. Exod. 15:13, 18) but remarkably is used here to describe God's sovereign rule over the nations: *all* nations are under God's providential rule (cf. Amos 9:7).

What is the proof of this bold theological claim? That, according to Psalm 67:6a, "the earth has given its fruit." Conspicuously, the clause has no parallel clause, as one would expect in Hebrew poetry. This striking omission highlights its uniqueness. This single clause is vitally significant because it represents the fulfillment of God's promised covenant blessing in Leviticus 26:4 (26:20 is the curse): "Then I will give you your rains in their season, *and the land shall yield its harvest*, and the trees of the field shall yield their fruit," a promise that also occurs in Psalm 85:12; Ezekiel 34:27; and Zechariah 8:12.[41] As is evident from Psalm 85:10–13, there is an important connection between God's just international rule and his providential maintenance of the created

37. Significantly, the Hebrew verb *yada* is used four times in 67:3, 5. The basic meaning of this verb is "confess."

38. Stek, *Zondervan NIV Study Bible*, 858.

39. I read the *yqtl* verbs *tishpoṭ* and *taneham* as presents, not futures. If they are read as futures, then the *ki* clause refers to Yahweh's eschatological actions. Cf. Ps. 9:8–9; 96:10, 13; 98:9.

40. Shepherd is another important metaphor for kings in the ancient Near East. Cf. Stek, *Zondervan NIV Study Bible*, 810.

41. Talstra and Bosma, "Psalm 67," 306.

order as promised to Noah in Genesis 8:22 and to Israel in Leviticus 26:4. As Claus Westermann argues compellingly, God's blessing activity is connected to his providential upholding of the good created order.[42]

After the unique statement that God's original promise in Leviticus 26:4 has been fulfilled, Psalm 67:6b–7a reverts to 67:1b and repeats twice the wish for God's blessing on the congregation. Significantly, this double wish is concluded by a purpose statement in 67:7b that parallels the purpose statement in 67:2: "that all the ends of the earth may fear him" (cf. 65:9). This concluding clause shows that the ultimate purpose of God's blessing Israel is that the remotest nations will become "fearers of God" (cf. 65:8). These nations will recognize God's just rule not because of a magnificent military defeat but by a bountiful harvest.[43] Consequently, like 67:2, this concluding verse illustrates the truth that the nations are beneficiaries of God's blessing of Israel and that Israel understands Genesis 12:3 as the overarching purpose of its being God's elect nation.[44]

In summary, Israel's prayer for continued blessing on the occasion of a harvest has a clear missional edge to it.[45] In fact, Mascarenhas calls Psalm 67 "a daring missionary prayer,"[46] and Gerald Henry Wilson calls it a missionary pamphlet.[47] Read in the light of Genesis 12:3, Israel's prayer for continued blessing in Psalm 67 shows that it was taught to be conscious of its election being in part so that it might be a channel of blessings to the nations.[48]

Psalm 96

I selected Psalm 96 because this hymn of praise is thoroughly universalistic.[49] From the beginning to the end, the hymn concerns the implications of Yahweh's kingship for the earth (*'ereṣ*; 96:1, 9, 11, 13), nations (*goyim*; 96:3,

42. Claus Westermann, *Blessing in the Bible and the Life of the Church*, trans. Keith Crim, Overtures to Biblical Theology (Philadelphia: Fortress, 1978).

43. Broyles, *Psalms*, 279.

44. Wiersinga, *Zendingsperspectief in het Oude Testament*, 76.

45. Cf. Maclaren, "Psalms," 268; W. Stewart McCullough, "Psalms," in *The Interpreter's Bible*, ed. George A. Buttrick et al. (Nashville: Abingdon, 1955), 4:351.

46. Mascarenhas, *Missionary Function of Israel*, 121.

47. Gerald Henry Wilson, *Psalms*, NIV Application Commentary (Grand Rapids: Zondervan, 2002), 1:929.

48. Broyles, *Psalms*, 280.

49. Thijs Booij, *Psalmen*, Prediking van het Oude Testament (Nijkerk: Callenbach, 1994), 3:154.

10), peoples (*'amim*; 96:3, 5, 7, 10, 13), families of the earth (96:7), and even all inanimate elements of creation (96:11–12). Unlike Psalm 67, there is not even a pronominal reference ("us") to Israel. Moreover, references to Judah, David, Jerusalem, and the temple on Mount Zion are conspicuously absent in this psalm.[50] Instead, the focus is completely on all the earth, peoples, nations, and the families of the nations. In this psalm, they are not passive witnesses but active participants. Furthermore, this well-known hymn is, as I will demonstrate, a clear example of what Miller calls the conversionary nature of Old Testament praise. Walter Kaiser rightly classifies this psalm as another great missionary psalm,[51] and Rudolf Kittel correctly observes that in this psalm Israel sees itself obliged to fulfill its missionary vocation.[52] In fact, John H. Stek describes this psalm as a "call to all nations to praise the Lord as the only God and to proclaim the glory of his reign throughout the world—an OT anticipation of the world mission of the NT people of God (see Mt 28:16–20)."[53]

In support of this claim, we must consider, first of all, the canonical position of Psalm 96. This psalm is located in Book 4 and belongs to a series of psalms (Pss. 93–99) that proclaim Yahweh's universal and eternal reign, which theme is the heartbeat of the Psalter. This core theme reverberates clearly in 96:10, which echoes 93:1 and which, according to Beth Tanner, is the theological center of the psalm.[54] Canonically the persistent proclamation of Yahweh's kingship in these psalms functions as a hopeful response to the crisis of the exile articulated in the communal lament in Psalm 89 at the conclusion of Book 3. Although Israel no longer has a Davidic king on the throne, Yahweh still reigns.[55]

In this series of psalms, Psalm 96 is preceded by Psalm 95, which stands at the center of Psalms 90–100 and forms a frame with Psalm 100 around Psalms 96–99. Moreover, Psalm 96 is paired with its near cousin, Psalm 98, with which it shares much in form, language, and theme (espe-

50. Robert L. Foster, "A Plea for New Songs: A Missional/Theological Reflection on Psalm 96," *Currents in Theology and Missions* 33 (2006): 289.

51. Walter C. Kaiser Jr., *Mission in the Old Testament* (Grand Rapids: Baker, 2000), 34.

52. Rudolf Kittel, *Die Psalmen*, Kommentar zum Alten Testament (Leipzig: Deichert, 1914), 350.

53. Stek, *Zondervan NIV Study Bible*, 896.

54. Nancy deClaissé-Walford, Rolf A. Jacobson, and Beth LaNeel Tanner, *The Book of Psalms*, New International Commentary on the Old Testament (Grand Rapids: Eerdmans, 2014), 719.

55. J. Clinton McCann Jr., "Psalm 96," in *Psalms for Preaching and Worship: A Lectionary Commentary*, ed. Roger E. Van Harn and Brent A. Strawn (Grand Rapids: Eerdmans, 2009), 250.

cially in their opening and closing stanzas),[56] while Psalm 97 forms a pair with Psalm 99, both of which begin with the acclamation "Yahweh reigns." The relationship between these psalms may be diagrammed as follows:[57]

Psalm 95 (to Israel)		
	Psalm 96 (New Song)	+ Psalm 97 (*Yahweh malak*)
	Psalm 98 (New Song)	+ Psalm 99 (*Yahweh malak*)
Psalm 100 (to all the earth)		

Psalm 96 is preceded by Psalm 95. Although Psalms 95 and 96 share important lexical and thematic links,[58] there is a vitally significant difference between them. Psalm 95 is an exhortation to praise (95:1–5) and a call to worship (95:6–7) *addressed to Israel* assembled in the temple; Psalm 96 is a call to praise spoken by an anonymous person or persons and *addressed to all the earth* (96:1) and to the families of the nations (96:7). In view of their canonical sequence, I suggest that Psalm 95 exhorts Israel to acclaim Yahweh and that in Psalm 96, "a fitting follow up on Psalm 95,"[59] Israel "goes out," as it were, and exhorts all the earth (96:1–6) and all the families of the earth (96:7–10) to praise Yahweh and to come to join Israel in their worship of him.[60]

Psalm 96 is a remix of quotations and allusions to other texts from the Psalter and from Isaiah 40–55:

Ps. 96:1a Sing to the Lord a new song,	**Ps. 98:1a; 149:1; Isa. 42:10** Sing to the Lord a new song,
Ps. 96:2b Bless his name	**Ps. 145:1, 21** I will bless your name for ever and ever.

56. Stek, *Zondervan NIV Study Bible*, 896.

57. Marvin E. Tate, *Psalms 51–100*, Word Biblical Commentary (Dallas: Word, 1990), 535. Cf. P. Auffrett, "Essai sur la Structure Littéraire du Psaume 94," *Biblische Notizen* 24 (1984): 71–72.

58. Konrad Schaefer, *Psalms*, Berit Olam (Collegeville, MN: Glazier, 2001), 238.

59. DeClaissé-Walford, Jacobson, and LaNeel Tanner, *Book of Psalms*, 719.

60. Solomon's petition in 1 Kings 8:41–43 shows that he expected the nations to come to the temple he had constructed for Yahweh's name.

Ps. 96:2c tell of his salvation from day to day.	**Isa. 52:7** announces salvation
Ps. 96:3a Declare his glory among the nations	**Isa. 66:19** They will proclaim my glory among the nations.
Ps. 96:4a Great is the Lord, and most worthy of praise.	**Ps. 48:2a; 145:3a** Great is the Lord, and most worthy of praise.
Ps. 96:7–8a Ascribe to the Lord, O families of nations, ascribe to the Lord glory and strength. Ascribe to the Lord the glory due his name;	**Ps. 29:1–2a** Ascribe to the Lord, sons of the gods, ascribe to the Lord glory and strength. Ascribe to the Lord the glory due his name;
Ps. 96:8c Come into his courts	**Ps. 100:4** Enter his courts with praise
Ps. 96:9a Worship the Lord in the splendor of his holiness.	**Ps. 29:2b** Worship the Lord in the splendor of his holiness.
Ps. 96:10a Yahweh reigns.	**Ps. 93:1; 97:1; 99:1; Isa. 52:7** Yahweh reigns.
Ps. 96:10cd The world is firmly established, it cannot be moved.	**Ps. 93:1b** The world is firmly established, it cannot be moved.
Ps. 96:10e He will govern the peoples with equity.	**Ps. 9:8b** He will govern the peoples with equity.
Ps. 96:11ab Let the heavens rejoice,	**Isa. 44:23** Sing for joy, O heavens, for the Lord has done this; shout aloud, O earth beneath.
Ps. 96:11b And let the earth be glad.	**Ps. 97:1b** Let the earth be glad.
Ps. 96:11c let the sea resound, and all that is in it;	**Ps. 98:7a** let the sea resound, and everything in it
Ps. 96:12b then all the trees of the forest will sing for joy.	**Isa. 55:12** and all the trees of the field will clap their hands.
Ps. 96:13 They will sing before the Lord, for he comes,	**Ps. 98:9** Let them sing before the Lord, for he comes to judge the earth.

he comes to judge the earth. He will judge the world in righteousness and the peoples in his truth.	He will judge the world in righteousness and the peoples with equity.
Ps. 96:13de He will judge the world in righteousness and the peoples in his truth.	**Ps. 9:8ab** He will judge the world in righteousness he will govern the peoples with equity.

The presence of the quotations and allusions leads to the plausible suggestion that Psalm 96 was composed somewhat later and that its theology is similar to Isaiah 40–55.[61] According to Konrad Schaefer, for example, "this beautiful poem breathes the religious universalism which Isaiah announces."[62] Like Isaiah 40–55, therefore, Psalm 96 aims to inspire hope for God's people in the diaspora.

In its literary genre, Psalm 96 is a descriptive psalm of praise.[63] Thematically, this dynamic psalm belongs to the "Yahweh as King" hymns (Pss. 47; 93; 96; 97; 98; 99),[64] also known as "enthronement psalms."[65] According to Hans-Joachim Kraus, "these psalms were sung at the proskynesis of the worshipping community before 'King' Yahweh."[66]

Structurally, the psalm consists of three unequal parts: (1) a lengthy imperatival call to praise, addressed to all the earth (96:1–3), that is supported by two motivational *ki* clauses (96:4–6); (2) a second call to praise, addressed to the families of the nations (96:7–10),[67] without a motivational

61. Franz Delitzsch, *Psalms*, trans. Francis Bolton (repr. Grand Rapids: Eerdmans, 1976), 5:90, was the first to emphasize this similarity.

62. Schaefer, *Psalms*, 239.

63. For this classification see Claus Westermann, *Praise and Lament in the Psalms*, trans. Keith R. Crim and Richard N. Soulen (Atlanta: John Knox, 1965), 116–51.

64. J. Ridderbos, *De Psalmen* (Kampen: Kok, 1958), 2:440; Hans-Joachim Kraus, *Psalms 60–150: A Continental Commentary*, trans. Hilton C. Oswald (Minneapolis: Fortress, 1993), 251.

65. For theological objections to Sigmund Mowinckel's influential classification "enthronement psalm," see Hans-Joachim Kraus, *Psalms 1–59: A Continental Commentary*, trans. Hilton C. Oswald (Minneapolis: Augsburg, 1988), 45–46. Cf. Tate, *Psalms 51–100*, 504–9.

66. Kraus, *Psalms 1–59*, 45.

67. In view of the pivotal importance of the acclamation "Yahweh reigns" in 96:10, many commentators introduce a major break at this verse so that 96:10–13 forms the third unit. However, as David Morris Howard Jr. correctly notes (*The Structure of Psalms 93–100* [Ann Arbor: University Microfilms, 1986], 91), 96:10 belongs to the series of imperatives in 96:7–9. Moreover, there is neither a change in subject nor addressee. In view of the similarity between 96:10a and 96:3a and between 96:10c and 96:13, Howard suggests that 96:10 serves as a bridge between 96:7–9 and 96:11–13.

ki clause; and, surprisingly, (3) a jussive call to praise (96:11–13a), also with two motivational *ki* clauses (96:13).[68]

In the initial call to praise (96:1–3) the anonymous liturgist(s) rallies the whole earth to sing a new song[69] to the Lord (96:1–2a). The impressive triple repetition of the divine name Yahweh in 96:1–2a (and also in 96:7–8) implicitly debunks and dismisses the name of any other god or gods. According to Brueggemann, this invitation to the exclusive celebration of the divine name constitutes a necessary dismissal of the gods.[70] Following Brueggemann's example, one might read the persistent triple repetition as follows:[71]

> Sing to the Lord [not Marduk];
> Sing to the Lord [not Shemesh];
> Sing to the Lord [not Baal].

This implicit assault on the gods comes to clear expression in the double motivational *ki* clauses in 96:4–6 (cf. 95:3–5) that follow the lengthy call to praise in 96:1–3 and provides the reason why "all the earth" is to sing a new song and declare his mighty deeds among the nations.

> For (*ki*) great is the LORD and most worthy of praise;
> he is to be feared above all gods.
> For (*ki*) all the gods of the nations are idols,
> but the LORD made the heavens.
> Splendor and majesty are before him;
> strength and beauty are in his sanctuary.

These motivational *ki* clauses represent a clear example of what J. H. Bavinck calls elenctics,[72] the purpose of which is to unmask the gods and

68. Westermann, *Praise and Lament*, 148; John Goldingay, *Psalms*, vol. 3: *Psalms 90–150*, Baker Commentary on the Old Testament Wisdom and Psalms (Grand Rapids: Baker Academic, 2008), 101; deClaissé-Walford, Jacobson, and LaNeel Tanner, *Book of Psalms*, 719.

69. The meaning of the phrase "new song" is debated. According to Tremper E. Longman, "Psalm 98," *Journal of the Evangelical Theological Society* 27 (1984): 269, it denotes a victory song.

70. Walter Brueggemann, *Psalms and the Life of Faith* (Minneapolis: Fortress, 1995), 118.

71. Brueggemann, *Psalms and the Life of Faith*, 118, 127.

72. J. H. Bavinck, *Introduction to the Science of Missions*, trans. David Hugh Freeman (Philadelphia: Presbyterian & Reformed, 1960), 221–72.

demonstrate that Yahweh alone is the true God.[73] This important section begins with a quotation of 48:2a and 145:3a in 96:4a, which is followed by the resolute claim that Yahweh is to be feared above all gods. This bold claim is supported by a scathing and devastating Hebrew pun in 96:5a that consists of the nouns *'elohim* ("god[s]") and *'elilim* ("idols, worthless"). This pun and parody reduce the rival gods to absolutely nothing.[74] The basis for this bold claim is the Lord's making the heavens. In the ancient Near East the heavens represented the abode of the gods. The sun (*shemesh*), for example, was one of those deities.[75] But because the Lord made the heavens, Shemesh is, according to Genesis 1:14, just a big light, not a real god. This frontal attack on the gods continues in Psalm 96:6. In this verse the Lord's entourage does not consist of lesser gods (who in reality are no gods);[76] instead, divine royal attributes "are personified as his escorts and courtiers (89:14, 24)."[77] J. Clinton McCann calls this phenomenon a de-divination of the gods.[78]

After the exuberant triple summons to sing to Yahweh (96:1–2a), there follows a call to bless Yahweh's name (96:2b). In view of the parallelism between the verbs "extol" and "bless," and "bless" and "praise" in 145:1–2 (cf. 145:21), blessing Yahweh's name is an act of praise (cf. 63:5), the specific content of which is spelled out in 96:2c–3. In this double imperative section, the peoples of all the earth[79] are enrolled as missionary preachers of the gospel and exhorted to proclaim the gospel of Yahweh's victory day after day (96:2c).[80]

73. According to Brueggemann for this reason praise is "inevitably *a polemical act*"; *Psalms and the Life of Faith*, 118.

74. Broyles, *Psalms*, 239. Cf. Kaiser, *Mission in the Old Testament*, 34.

75. Cf. E. Lipiński, "Shemesh," in *Dictionary of Deities and Demons in the Bible*, ed. Karel van der Toorn, Bob Becking, and Pieter W. van der Horst (Grand Rapids: Eerdmans, 1999), 766.

76. Tate, *Psalms 51–100*, 514. Cf. Wright, *Mission of God*, 167.

77. Schaefer, *Psalms*, 239. Cf. Ps. 85:14. Cf. Kraus, *Psalms 60–150*, 253.

78. J. Clinton McCann, "The Book of Psalms," in *The New Interpreter's Bible*, ed. L. E. Keck (Nashville: Abingdon, 2000), 4:1066.

79. According to Delitzsch (*Psalms*, 91), Kraus (*Psalms 60–150*, 253), Kaiser (*Mission in the Old Testament*, 34), Mascarenhas (*Missionary Function of Israel*, 174), Leonard P. Maré ("Israel's Praise as an Enactment of the Gospel: Psalm 96 in Missiological Context," *Missionalia* 34 [2006]: 398), and others, the subject of the imperatives in 96:2b–3a is Israel. For Mascarenhas, 96:2b–3 constitutes Israel's missionary mandate. On this basis he claims that Ps. 96 "imposes a missionary function on Israel" (187) However, as Booij (*De Psalmen*, 3:155) notes correctly, there is no clear change in subject in 96:1–3. For a similar position see Ridderbos, *Psalmen*, 2:444.

80. True to the style of descriptive hymns of praise, the specific nature of this victory and the marvelous deeds in 96:3 are not specified.

Significantly, the relatively rare Hebrew verb *basar*[81] in this clause "is the verb for the duty of the herald who precedes a victor to bring a report to those who wait for the good news from the battle."[82] The use of this verb gives the psalm "a definite evangelical cast."[83] Consequently, Brueggemann rightly notes that genuine praise in the Old Testament is evangelical.[84]

Finally, all the earth is commanded to tell[85] Yahweh's glory and marvelous deeds among the nations and peoples (96:3). This exhortation shows that praise is a declarative act that aims to elicit the praise of all. This inference is clearly evident from the second imperatival call to praise (96:7–10) that follows the motivational clauses of 96:4–6.

This arresting call to praise (cf. 1 Chron. 16:28–29) is a modified version of the call to praise in Psalm 29:1–2.

Psalm 29:1–2	**Psalm 96:7–10**
Ascribe to the LORD, O sons of the gods,	Ascribe to the LORD, O families of nations,
ascribe to the LORD glory and strength.	ascribe to the LORD glory and strength.
Ascribe to the LORD the glory due his name;	Ascribe to the LORD the glory due his name;
	bring an offering
	and come into his courts.
worship the LORD in the splendor of his holiness.	Worship the LORD in the splendor of his holiness;
	tremble in his presence,[86] all the earth.
	Say among the nations,
	"The LORD reigns."
	The world is firmly established,
	it cannot be moved;
	he judges the peoples with equity.

Instead of being addressed to the heavenly beings, the sweeping invitation of eight imperatives in Psalm 96:7–10 is addressed to the families of nations, a phrase that recalls the phrase "families of the earth" from

81. Cf. Marlowe, "Music of Missions," 448. The second-person masculine plural imperative form of the verb *basar* occurs only here in Ps. 96:2 and in its parallel in 1 Chron. 16:23.

82. James Luther Mays, *Psalms,* Interpretation (Louisville: John Knox, 1994), 308.

83. Mays, *Psalms*, 308.

84. Brueggemann, *Psalms and the Life of Faith*, 121.

85. Surprisingly, the second-person masculine plural imperative form of the Hebrew verb *sapar* is used in the Psalter only here. It also occurs in its parallel in 1 Chron. 16:24. Cf. Marlowe, "Music of Missions," 448.

86. For the missional significance of presence see Goheen, "Nourishing Our Missional Identity," 39–40n30.

Genesis 12:3 (cf. Ps. 22:28).[87] This subtle substitution represents another striking example of de-divination in this psalm. In this summons, the families of the nations are first called upon to ascribe to the LORD the glory and strength that is due his name. That means, of course, that they cannot ascribe these attributes to their gods. Moreover, unlike 29:1–2, the families of the nations are next summoned to bring the gift of a political tribute to him (cf. 72:10; 2 Sam. 8:2, 6; 2 Kings 17:3–4) and to come into his courts in order to pay homage to him as the great king (Ps. 96:8b–9a). Remarkably, they are even exhorted to proclaim Yahweh's universal rule among the nations (96:10). These exhortations envision an international procession to the temple.

With respect to this pivotal call to praise, I make four observations. First, as in Psalms 95 and 100, all of these acts are an expression of fealty to Yahweh[88] and clearly demonstrate the conversionary character of this psalm. Moreover, like Psalms 95 and 100, the calls to praise in 96:1–6 and 96:7–10 move from enthusiasm to submission.[89]

Second, in connection with this powerful summons to praise, Christopher J. H. Wright writes:

> This is not an invitation to the nations to make room for YHWH among the pantheon of their own gods and give him some shared respect. The psalmist is not inviting the nations to move their gods along the shelf a little to make room for YHWH among their number. No, this is a call for the radical displacement of all other gods before the sole, unique, transcendent Godness of YHWH, such that all honor, glory, worship and praise goes to him, as it rightfully should. As long as other gods are worshiped, the living God is to that extent denied what is rightfully his—the total worship of his total creation. This is what makes the struggle with idolatry a major dimension of the mission of God in which he commands our cooperation.[90]

Like 96:1–6, therefore, 96:7–10 also have an elenctic function.

Third, one would have expected a motivational *ki* clause after the seven imperatives in 96:7–9. In fact, some commentators treat 96:10 as if

87. Longman, *Psalms*, 144.
88. Mays, *Psalms*, 308.
89. Goldingay, *Psalms*, 3:101.
90. Wright, *Mission of God*, 172.

it were (cf. 100:3). But it is not! Instead, in 96:10 the families of the nations are commanded to say among the nations that Yahweh reigns,[91] a claim that constitutes the highlight of the fealty ritual and the heart and gravitational center of the Psalter.[92] According to James L. Mays, "to say that the Lord reigns is to say that the gods whom other nations worship do not. The claim to kingship for a god was per se universal and preemptive of the claims for the rule of other gods."[93] In comparison with Yahweh, the gods of the nations are ineffective and (as is evident from Ps. 82) incompetent idols.[94] The purpose of this climactic command is, as Mays notes, "to turn the nations from their gods to the God whose reign means stability for the world and equity for its peoples (v. 10)."[95]

Fourth, echoing 93:1, the significance of the acclamation "Yahweh reigns" is connected with the establishment of a stable world order. Moreover, the stable world order is evidence of the present fact that Yahweh rules the peoples justly, a hallmark of his reign that is the underlying conviction of psalms of lament (cf. 9:7–10).

In view of the above, Brueggemann rightly underscores that genuine praise of Yahweh is also inevitably a political act.[96] As such, it challenges the gods, who, according to Psalm 82, fail to establish justice with the terrible negative result that the cosmos is unstable (82:5). Moreover, it also confronts the nations and governments that oppose Yahweh's righteous rule.

Because of the stability of the cosmos and of Yahweh's "setting things right," the pivotal imperatival call to praise (96:7–10) is followed by a jussive call to praise to the great personified components of creation: heavens, earth, sea, fields, and trees of the forest (96:11–13). Praise is not limited to human beings: all of creation is expected to join the swelling chorus in exuberant praise in the presence of the Lord. This thematic sequence from

91. Cf. Goldingay, *Psalms*, 3:101. According to A. A. Anderson (*The Book of Psalms*, New Century Bible [London: Oliphants, 1972], 2:685) and Mascarenhas (*Missionary Function of Israel*, 145), Israel is the subject of the imperative "say." However, there is no clear shift in subject and, according to Booij (*Psalmen*, 3:156–57), 96:10 follows logically from 96:7–9. Cf. Ridderbos, *Psalmen*, 2:445.

92. James Luther Mays, *The Lord Reigns: A Theological Handbook to the Psalms* (Louisville: Westminster John Knox, 1994), 13. According to Mays, "the liveliness and actuality of the language of the reign of God supply an organizing milieu for all the principal topics of the Christian faith" (11).

93. Mays, *Lord Reigns*, 308.

94. Mays, *Lord Reigns*, 308.

95. Mays, *Lord Reigns*, 308.

96. Brueggemann, *Psalms and the Life of Faith*, 119.

96:10 to 96:11–13 shows that "social order and creation order are inevitably intertwined."[97]

The change from a second person address to "all the earth" in 96:1–3 to a unique third person formulation in 96:11–12 suggests that if the families of the earth respond positively then there is hope for the elements of creation. This hope is based on Yahweh's coming to judge the cosmos and the peoples.

The jussive call to praise in 96:11–12a is followed by a double set of *ki* motivational clauses. These double *ki* clauses pick up the word pair cosmos/peoples from 96:10, as well as the verb "to judge," which, as Brueggemann underscores, has a positive meaning.[98] For emphasis, the *ki* clause "for he comes" is repeated, creating a terrace pattern.[99] Unfortunately, the tense of the Hebrew verbal form *ba'* is ambiguous. It could be read as past tense (Young's Literal Translation), present tense (New Revised Standard Version, Tanakh, New Living Translation), or future tense. In light of the preceding clauses (that *then* the trees of the field will rejoice), I parse the verbal form *ba'* as a participle that emphasizes Yahweh's imminent arrival to set things straight. In 96:10 I opted for a present reading of the imperfect verb to denote Yahweh's current righteous rule, grounded on his eternal kingship (93:2).[100] Here I opt for a future reading so that we have an "already" and "not yet" tension similar to Romans 8:22–23. Like Romans 8, therefore, the concluding verses suggest that the cosmos is suffering from injustice and inequity, from ecological abuse and exploitation. According to Israel's profound hope, Yahweh, the great king, who rules over creation and history, will come to deal decisively with all wickedness among the nations and establish righteousness. From a New Testament perspective the fulfillment of this hope began with the coming of Jesus and will reach its ultimate fulfillment when he returns (according to Rev. 19) as the warrior lamb, who judges with justice and makes war (19:11) and governs the nations with an iron scepter (19:15; Ps. 2:9).

97. Broyles, *Psalms*, 377.

98. Walter Brueggemann, *The Message of the Psalms: A Theological Commentary*, Augsburg Old Testament Series (Minneapolis: Augsburg, 1984), 145.

99. For the function of this terrace pattern see Wilfred G. E. Watson, *Classical Hebrew Poetry: A Guide to Its Technique*, Journal for the Study of the Old Testament Supplement 26 (Sheffield: JSOT Press, 1984), 208–11. It is not repeated in 1 Chron. 16:33. According to Goldingay (*Psalms*, 3:107), this pattern creates tension.

100. The New English Translation and Goldingay (*Psalms*, 3:107) read the imperfect verb as a present.

Summary

This brief analysis of Psalm 96 shows that this dynamic hymn has a striking missional thrust.[101] Although Psalm 96 does not contain a direct mandate to Israel to proclaim its praise of Yahweh among the nations (cf. 105:1), like 47:1; 66:1; 94:8; and 100:8, this liturgical poem itself enacts Israel's mission by calling insistently upon all the earth, its inhabitants, and all inanimate elements of creation to solemnly praise Yahweh as the only true God, to come into his courts with tribute, and to practice obeisance in recognition of his righteous rule over everything. In so doing, this psalm is, to use Miller's phrase, genuinely a "testimony for conversion."

The addition of the phrase "and the Psalms" in Luke 24:44, the reference to the preaching of repentance and forgiveness of sins in Luke 24:47, and Paul's quotation of Psalms 18:49 and 117:1 in Romans 15:9, 11 in defense of his mission to the gentiles, constitute a New Testament basis for a missional reading of the Psalter. Both Psalm 67 and Psalm 96 exhibit important missional themes. For example, a keynote in both psalms is Yahweh's kingship (67:4; 96:10) over all creation, its inhabitants, and nations. An inevitable corollary of this emphasis is a radiant inclusivism in both psalms. Beginning with Psalm 2, the peoples and nations of the earth are frequently portrayed as enemies. Not so in these psalms![102] This positive attitude toward the peoples and nations was probably inspired by Genesis 12:3, to which both psalms allude (Ps. 67:2, 7; 96:6). Both psalms strike a clear missional note and as liturgical texts fueled Israel's missional consciousness. This shows that worship and mission are not two separate activities of God's people, but are integrally related.[103] For this reason it is imperative that the church recover the use of the psalms in its worship[104] so that Psalm 67, Psalm 96, and other missional psalms may fuel and nourish its missional identity. In the case of Psalm 67 and Psalm 96 this is relatively easy because neither is specific to Israel. This striking feature facilitates a contemporary application of their message in worship and preaching.

101. James H. Waltner, *Psalms*, Believers Church Bible Commentaries (Scottsdale, PA: Herald, 2006), 470.

102. Foster, "Plea for New Songs," 288.

103. Cf. J. G. Davies, *Worship and Mission* (London: SCM, 1966), 9–21; Orlando E. Costas, *The Integrity of Mission: The Inner Life and Outreach of the Church* (San Francisco: Harper & Row, 1979), 90–91; Goheen, "Nourishing Our Missional Identity."

104. Cf. N. T. Wright, *The Case for the Psalms: Why They Are Essential* (New York: Harper One, 2013), 1–6.

A Missional Reading of the New Testament

CHAPTER 9

Reading the New Testament Missionally

N. T. Wright

When I was a young scholar, the big books in my discipline were New Testament theologies. They were being written in Germany by Rudolf Bultmann, Hans Conzelmann, and others, and in America by people like George Eldon Ladd. I went to Jerusalem on sabbatical in 1989 with the aim of writing what eventually turned into the *Christian Origins and the Question of God* series. At the time, I thought I was going to write a book on Jesus and a book on Paul and that these would form the heart of a "New Testament theology." But as I began writing about Jesus, twenty-six years ago, I quickly became aware that what people had done in New Testament theology did not align with what I was finding in the New Testament itself. New Testament theologies were basically arranging and rearranging the various theological ideas that the New Testament writers had expressed, argued out, and so on. It was as though the whole task of a New Testament scholar was to produce a beautiful synthesis of these theological ideas and to see the coherence in their relationships to one another, either for enjoyment or as a resource for our preaching. Now, some years on, I do not believe the New Testament was written in order to give people a coherent set of ideas. It does that, but not as its main purpose. Rather, the New Testament was written in order to sustain and direct the missional life of the early church.

The early church was conscious of being (and the writers of the New Testament wanted them to be conscious of being) a people through whom the love and power and new creational energy of the one God of Jewish monotheism had been let loose on the world. These writings were meant to guide and sustain, to direct and energize—to shape the early church, and to warn it about possible wrong paths. To put it basically: *the purpose of the New Testament emerges from the entire missional agenda of the early church.*

In *Scripture and the Authority of God* I sought to understand the great narrative of Scripture and to show that, after that narrative has reached its wonderful and shocking climax in Jesus by the Spirit, the very people reading the New Testament are supposed to be the ones who carry this story forward. The great story, reading at a run from Genesis to Revelation, can be told in terms of the vocation of Abraham's family to be "the light to the nations," the people through whom the creator God would bless the whole world. Certainly this is how the early Christians understood their place in God's plan: now that Jesus had summed up Israel's vocation in himself and had poured out his own Spirit on his people, it was not only time for the world to be brought under God's wise, loving rule, but there was also the fresh, healing energy by which to do it. But such a narrative reading of Scripture has received enormous resistance, sometimes in the name of "apocalyptic" traditions and sometimes in the name of a "post-Constantinian church."

Over the last decade or so in the United Kingdom, we have talked a lot about mission-shaped church. That is to say, the church must be shaped *for* its mission and *by* its mission, rather than thinking of mission as the ancillary activity of the church. While this is a good and important development, all too often we assume that we know what mission is, and then we go on with the shaping of the church accordingly. The danger is that, culturally, the word "mission" still has somewhat dualistic connotations. For many people, mission connotes snatching people away from the world and bringing them to a momentarily safe space, against the day when they will die and go to heaven. By way of contrast, consider the opposite, more mainstream or liberal view. According to this, "mission" is basically about being a generous chaplaincy presence in society, wherever society happens to be going at the moment. Many voices in my country use the word "mission" as a way of indicating that we just have to get alongside people wherever they are, whatever they are doing, and tell them that God loves them and wants them to be happy in their pursuits. So we have these two radically different views of what mission is, neither of which, in my view, has much to do with the New Testament's vision of what mission is. In fact I see both views as symptomatic of the post-Enlightenment captivity of the Western church that we often congratulate ourselves on having escaped. We have failed to see the crisis of Enlightenment dualism and its various legacies.

Surprised by Hope argues for a vision of the new heavens and new earth, over against a vision of heaven as the Christian's ultimate destiny. As I have said many times, "heaven is important, but it's not the end of the world." If our eschatology is about new heavens and new earth, then our mission must be shaped by that eschatology as well. So we affirm the move toward a mission-shaped church, but we accompany that with eschatology-shaped mission. The creator God has promised to renew his whole creation: the resurrection of Jesus is the start of that, and the outpoured Spirit is the means by which it will happen. So, in the present, those who invoke the Spirit are entrusted with bringing about real and true signs of new creation in the present time. Of course the eschatology itself is to be shaped by Jesus, by the real Jesus. Again, when you use the phrase "the real Jesus," people in the Western world collapse the phrase's meaning to either "the Jesus who died on the cross so that I can go to heaven" or "the Jesus who goes about doing good things so that we can copy him." This is why we have had trouble reading the Gospels. Neither view holds the fullness of his significance. An integrated kingdom theology is needed. And within that integrated kingdom theology we must be very clear that even the church inspired by the Spirit will not "build the kingdom" by itself. God will bring God's kingdom in God's own way, in an event as shocking and dramatic as Jesus's resurrection itself: God will do for the whole creation what he did for Jesus at Easter. But this doesn't mean there is nothing we can do in the present time. We live in between the times, between the launching of new creation and its ultimate fulfillment. This is the time for mission: for the work of God, through the Spirit-filled life and witness of the church, to bring God's healing and hope to the nations. What is often called the "gentile mission" is one specific expression of this: the peoples whom the Jews called "sinners" are brought in, because the good news is that God has dealt with sin in the death and resurrection of Jesus.

So out of all of this, I have tried in various ways to articulate a reading of the New Testament that is about God's mission for and into the world, the focus of which is, of course, Jesus. Such a reading uncovers paradoxes in our relationship to the world: "love not the world," says 1 John, but "God so loved the world," says John 3. Somehow we have to live in that rather uncomfortable dialectic, with a missional reading of the New Testament.

The basis of it all is of course the *creational, covenantal, and eschatological monotheism* that we find throughout Scripture. When God does for Israel what he is going to do for Israel, the Scriptures see this as the moment when the rest of the world is brought into the frame. I express this in deliberately general terms because sometimes the world's participation consists of being judged, and sometimes it consists of experiencing God's salvation and welcome. Actually, those two things are held together in text after text. The fulfillment of the covenant will establish the claim of the creator God upon the whole world. The Psalms are full of this. A very interesting kind of anticipation of the Christian mission can be found in some Second Temple Jewish literature. Philo of Alexandria, for instance, sees the Jewish diaspora almost as an extended Jewish empire around the world, against the day when eventually Israel will be vindicated and those who have been trying to be a light to the world will actually have their vocation fulfilled.

Jewish texts expressed both God's purposes *for* Israel and also God's purposes being fulfilled *through* Israel. We go back again and again to those passages in Isaiah about the whole new creation (Isa. 40–55), where the servant is the light to the nations. Or we read those wonderful psalms: Psalm 2, the messianic psalm in which God says, "I will give you the nations for your possession, and the uttermost parts of the earth for your inheritance"; and Psalm 72, in which we read that the king who is going to do God's justice, especially for the poor and needy, will reign from one sea to the other, and from the river to the ends of the earth. According to Psalm 72, through the king's reign and through that work of justice, especially for the poor and needy, God's glory will fill the whole earth. Psalm 89 is a paradoxical psalm. Two-thirds of it is about God's wonderful promises to the king; one-third is asking why these things aren't happening right now, why God seems to have turned his face away. But the psalmist clings firmly to those promises: this kingdom will remain, it will be like the sun and the moon, and it will be there for the whole world. Then we read Daniel 2, 7, and 9, oracles that were especially powerful for Jewish readers in the first century. They offer a monotheistic, covenantal, eschatological vision of God. When the one God does for Israel what he is going to do for Israel, this will be some kind of new, worldwide order, and Israel's Messiah, the coming king, will be Lord of all.

The way that the New Testament retrieves Psalms 2, 8, and 110 illuminates the theme of Israel's king as the one through whom the Abrahamic promise of the inheritance of the land is extended to the whole world. This king is truly human: "What is man that you are mindful of him, the son of man that you have thought for him? You have made him a little lower than the angels, you've crowned him with glory and honor, putting all things in subjection under his feet." Yes, says Paul. Yes, says Hebrews. That is still a future hope, except that it is already true about Jesus. And then in Psalm 110, one of the most often quoted Old Testament texts in the New Testament, "the Lord said to my lord, 'sit at my right hand, until I make your enemies your footstool.'"

In all of this, we see a vision of the mission of God, Israel's God, the creator God, in and for the whole wide world—the creator reaching out to embrace that whole world. The point here is not to persuade people that we have a new and better sort of religion. If you had asked one of the early Christians, "Is your religion superior to what you find in Ephesus, or Athens, or anywhere else?" they might have said with surprise, "Well, I suppose, now that you raise that question, we actually do think our way of worshiping is a lot better than the stuff that they do down the road." But that was not their primary self-identity. Instead, the point was that the one God had done what he had always promised and had thereby upstaged all the other so-called gods and lords.

The purpose of the New Testament is not to persuade people of a better "religious" path. Neither, however, is it offering a new and easy way to "get to heaven." Because of the medieval church and its preoccupation with purgatory, and because the Reformers and their successors maintained that framework (while giving different answers to the question of how it worked), the "way to heaven" has remained a central motif in readings of the New Testament, not least in American culture. That seems to me the wrong framework. The New Testament is about the one God claiming the world through Jesus, already now, in advance of the parousia and the final coming of the final kingdom. So we find in the language of "mission" (that is, the "sending" language in the New Testament) the sending of the Son. In John "the one who sends the Son" becomes almost a title for God: "the Father who sent me" or "the one who sent me." The Son *is*, in person, the mission of God, in Israel and for the world. All other sending takes place in and through him and on the basis of what the one God has done through him.

In Galatians 4, Paul reframes the exodus narrative in terms of God's sent Son: "We were slaves, but when the time had fully come, God sent forth his Son, born of woman, born under the law, to redeem those who are under the law, that we might receive the adoption of sons." The passage is full of exodus overtones. Because we are sons (compare: "Israel is my son, my firstborn"), God has sent the Spirit of the Son into our hearts, crying "Abba, Father." So we are no longer slaves, but sons, and if sons, then heirs. So the sending of the Son leads to the sending of the Spirit of the Son, which leads to the people of God discovering that they are God's heirs. But what is the inheritance? Paul doesn't say in Galatians 4, but in the parallel passage in Romans 8 the inheritance is quite clear. While many Christians today would say their inheritance was "heaven," the inheritance is actually God's new creation, the redeemed cosmos. God made a good world, and he is going to rescue it.

Just after Paul has written that this missional theology is focused on Jesus and the Spirit, he then immediately writes: "And now that you have come to know God, or rather to be known by God, how can you turn back to the weak, beggarly elements? Do you want to be enslaved to them again? This is like the people in the wilderness wanting to go back to slavery in Egypt." Notice what Paul has said: you've got the missionary God who sends the Son and sends the Spirit of the Son; well, you've either got this Trinitarian God, or you have paganism. That's the choice, right from the start: the missionary, Trinitarian God, or the gods that enslave you in destructive, dehumanizing thought patterns, worship patterns, and life patterns.

So we find that the foundation of all Christian mission is in the resurrection of Jesus. In John 20, Jesus says, "As the Father sent me, so I send you" and breathes the Spirit on his followers. You cannot do mission unless your foundation is Jesus and unless your energy comes from the Spirit. When the New Testament addresses mission, it is always given that foundation and that energy. Jesus says in Matthew 28, "All authority in heaven and on earth has been given to me. Go therefore and make disciples." Often the Western church takes notice of the latter half of that—the command to make disciples—and simply forgets the former half—that we do this because Jesus is already in charge.

Jesus's authority does not look like the authority and power structures that we are used to in the world. In the gospel, articulated sharply in Mark and Matthew, Jesus redefined the very nature of power. In Mark 10:35–45, James and John say, "We want to sit at your right and your left in your kingdom." They want to get the top jobs in the new regime. And Jesus says, "Listen, the rulers of this age do power one way, by bullying people and lording it over them. We are going to do it the exact opposite way: let the one who wants to be great among you be a servant. The one who wants to be first must be the slave of all, because the Son of Man didn't come to be served, but to serve and to give his life as a ransom for many."

A wide spectrum of readers has interpreted Mark 10:45 (i.e., "giving his life as a ransom for many") as a detached, misplaced logion about atonement. That reading is incorrect: the point of the passage is that the cross redefines the world's mode of power. Furthermore, through that redefined mode of power, we can understand what it means to say first that Jesus already possesses all authority in heaven and on earth, and second that we, his faithful, Spirit-driven, missionary followers, will be able to go into all the world in the strangely redefined cross-shaped power of the gospel. A New Testament hermeneutic must therefore be about learning to read the New Testament, not in order to cull from it the few verses that make us feel good; rather, a faithful New Testament hermeneutic will sustain and energize the church—from every possible angle—as it goes about its God-given, Jesus-shaped, Spirit-driven missionary task.

I want to elaborate briefly on three particular loci of this, in Acts, John, and Paul.

Missionary Theology in Acts

If one were to ask the average Christian where in the New Testament you find missionary theology, they might well respond with "Acts." Acts is, after all, the story of the church going out and doing its missionary activities. But Acts offers us a clever, careful theological substructure that leads to and sustains this mission. We may be tempted to simplify biblical mission to the story of a people who have been with Jesus, who know Jesus, and who had their lives transformed by Jesus—and who are now going around telling others about him. Of course, this is the surface story that we read in the text. But underneath that story a remarkable thing is happening, related to the theme of the temple and the church's mission.[1]

The temple in the Old Testament was not a religious space into which people would escape from the rest of the world to say their prayers. The temple was a kind of bridgehead, established as a place where heaven and earth would actually meet, as they had met in the first garden. So in the great narrative arc from Genesis 1 to Exodus 40, a microcosm of what was lost in Genesis 3 is recovered. God has come back to dwell with his people. For this reason the tabernacle is decorated with cosmic motifs. Widening our vision further, the narrative arc extends to 1 Kings 8, where Solomon dedicates the temple and the glory of the Lord fills the house. That same narrative arc continues to the end of Ezekiel, where we find that when Jerusalem is restored and the people come back from exile, the new temple will be built. This restoration is described in a dreamlike sequence, and at the end of it all the *shekinah* glory will return with the whirling of wheels

1. Cf. Gregory K. Beale, *The Temple and the Church's Mission: A Biblical Theology of the Dwelling Place of God* (Downers Grove, IL: InterVarsity, 2004).

under the throne chariot. The name of that city will be *adonai shamma*, "The LORD is there." When we learn to read Scripture through those narrative arcs, we see that they are unfinished narratives—and that the New Testament has a dozen different ways of saying "this is the narrative that is fulfilled in Jesus."

How do we see that unfinished narrative arc at work in Acts? In Acts we begin with the ascension. Because it has been misunderstood, the ascension has been a source of embarrassment for many people; after all it looks as if Jesus is doing some kind of primitive spaceman trick, a vertical takeoff. We see this interpretation of the ascension in our stained glass windows depicting eleven puzzled disciples looking up at a cloud, and into that cloud two feet are just about disappearing. What is the miracle of the ascension actually about? Simply, that in Jesus—the human being who is also the living embodiment of Israel's one God—heaven and earth have come together completely and forever. A bit of earth now resides in heaven, and it is the bit that we call the human body of Jesus. That is the glory of the ascension of the resurrected Jesus. We miss this particular significance of the ascension when we collapse the resurrection and ascension into one another. The foundation of everything that happens from here on is a heaven-and-earth that have come together—not in a building of bricks, mortar, and hewn timber in Jerusalem, but in the human being Jesus of Nazareth.

Then what happens in Acts 2 is a kind of reprise of the scene in Isaiah 6 or 1 Kings 8 or the end of Ezekiel. A mighty rushing wind and tongues of fire enter and fill the house where the apostles are sitting. Here they discover that Babel is reversed; they now can speak in many languages, not in order to create confusion but in order to bring God's new pluriform order into being. If the ascension shows us that a bit of earth now resides in heaven, Pentecost shows us that we now have the breath of heaven on earth. In this way Acts 1–2 begins the story of the early church within the narrative arc of temple theology. What we read here is, therefore, missionary theology. When we read it with the significance of the temple in mind, we discover that this new, joined-up heaven-and-earth reality produces a bridgehead into the world, not an escape from the world.

This is an appropriate opening for Acts. As we continue reading, we find that nearly all the real pressure points in Acts are about temples. In Acts 3–4 the disciples camp out in Solomon's porch on the edge of the temple, which is a very dodgy thing to be doing. They are worshiping in the temple, they are saying their prayers there, they are still, as far as we know, offering sacrifices. The real point, though, is that they are starting a counter-temple movement on the very steps of the temple. They are claiming that Israel's God has already raised Jesus from the dead. The Sadducees grumble because the disciples are preaching *anastasis*, "resurrection," in Jesus. As they preach the resurrection they are saying, "This is the new community, the new place where heaven and earth come together; this is the counter-temple movement, right next to the temple itself."

So it is no surprise that in Acts 7 this is the heart of what Stephen is saying. In that long speech, the thrust of his message is, "This temple is under judgment. The temple system is corrupt, just as Moses said you would always be corrupt." The implication, then, which is conferred in Stephen's vision as he is being stoned, is that the place where heaven and earth come together is Jesus; and that Jesus is there for the benefit of his followers, his people. "I see the Son of Man, standing at the right hand of power." Stephen's words slightly redescribe the Danielic vision. Jesus is there *interceding* for his people. Heaven and earth have come together, and anyone who wants to cling to the temple in Jerusalem, either in a defensive posture or as an escape from the world, has simply missed the eschatological boat. The whole world must now be brought into the realm of this new fulfillment.

We follow the narrative on into the second half of Acts, into Paul's mission. Again and again when Paul runs into trouble or conflict, which he does often, the conflict has to do with temples and worship. In Acts 14, when the local priests think that Paul and Barnabas are two of the gods come down in human form and want to offer sacrifices to them, Paul says, "No, no. The time for that is passed. God has done a new thing. In a way, though, the gods have come down—because the true God has come down in human form. Heaven and earth have come together, but not in the way you pagans imagined."

Then in Acts 17, we find the spectacular speech on the Areopagus. Scholars rightly say that Paul's decision to quote from Greek poets and philosophers is interesting as a missional strategy. He does engage them, but notice that at the start of that speech he looks up. If you've stood on the Areopagus, you know what it looks like: you look across the valley and up there, a mile or two away, is the Acropolis with the wonderful Parthenon, one of the most spectacular pieces of architecture ever designed by any human. You see plenty of other temples. And Paul looks at them and declares that they are a category mistake. These great works of art? The Almighty does not live in houses like that. What is Paul doing? He is articulating a different vision: the Jewish monotheistic vision, in which the one God has fixed a day when he will judge the world—but this one God is not far from any of us. For in him "we live and move and have our being."

Paul's new temple theology upstages the Stoics and the Epicureans and the academics, but most of all it upstages the entire Parthenon and all the architectural glories that went with it in ancient Greece. Given this, Paul was lucky to get away with his life. Socrates had been put on trial in Athens five centuries before for misleading the young and for importing foreign divinities. When the authorities picked up Paul in the marketplace, they said, "This is . . . interesting. . . . You seem to be talking about foreign divinities here: *iēsous kai anastasis*, Jesus and resurrection." This was a very dangerous charge. Paul's exposition of new temple theology precisely *for* the world managed to get him round the corner, though the text doesn't indicate that many people took him seriously. He moved on to Corinth fairly quickly.

In Acts 19, we read about the riot in the temple of Ephesus. Paul in Ephesus confronts the temple of Diana (Greek Artemis). Right from the start, this confrontation is clearly having social and economic consequences. The reason for the riot was not just religious, but also economic. The artisans who made the little silver models of Artemis were being put out of business because, they claimed, Paul had been teaching people that these gods were not real, that there was only one God. Once again we are dealing with temple theology, missionary theology. Significantly, when Paul comes back to Jerusalem the underlying charge against him is that he has defiled the temple by bringing pagans into it. All the way through from Acts 21 to Acts 26, the whole narrative is framed by a "new temple" theology. Paul argues again and again that this is what Jesus is about, this is what Jesus means—but he is very careful not to say rude things about the temple in Jerusalem. Paul is not a Proto-Marcionite. The temple was the place where, according to Psalm 132, God said he would put his name forever and forever. Yet Paul believes, as all the early Christians believed, that the temple was a signpost pointing forward. In saying "yes" to the signpost, which is the temple, you also say "no" to anyone who wants to cling on to the signpost *as though it were the reality*. Signposts are not for cherishing, they are for pointing to something else. You do what the signpost says. The signpost was pointing forward to the time when heaven and earth would come together in Jesus, and when, by the Spirit, they would come together in his people. Importantly, they come together so that the rushing mighty wind of Pentecost would drive them out into the world. Of course that kind of thinking was dangerous. It resulted in suffering. It got people killed.

This risk and imminent suffering is what the missionary theology of

Acts is telling us when we get to Acts 27, the extraordinary shipwreck scene. For the Jews, who were not a seafaring nation, the sea was regularly used as an apocalyptic image for all that was dark, dangerous, and malevolent. The sea in Daniel is the place out of which the monsters emerge. The climax of the Acts narrative is Paul's experience on this sea voyage, and it parallels the climax of the narrative in Luke, which is of course Jesus going to the cross. In the midst of the danger to Paul, we have this repeated language of salvation. "Unless these people stay in the boat, you can't be saved." "How are we going to be saved?" "Will there be many of us that are saved?" Finally and extraordinarily, when they land dripping but alive on Malta at the end of Acts 27, we read, "We were all thoroughly saved." The word here is *diasōzō*, "we were through and through saved," landing up on the shore.

Luke begins the next chapter, the last in Acts, by emphasizing this again: "Having been saved thoroughly." What is he telling us with his placement of these events? He is outlining the missionary theology that God has planted in Jesus and by the Spirit—the new temple that is Jesus and his people. They are not static; they are going out into all the world. It is dangerous; the forces of evil will try to do their worst against it; but Paul ends up in Rome, preaching the good news of the kingdom of God and the lordship of Jesus openly and unhindered—right under Caesar's nose.

If we had only the book of Acts, we would have that complete missional theology in its narrative. Thus the challenge to anyone who read Acts in the first century or anyone who reads Acts today is to ask: if that is what the mission looks like, what are the temples in our society? How are we upstaging them in our living, in our preaching, in our thinking, in our arguing—and how are we learning to face the dangers that come as a result?

Missionary Theology in John

From Acts, though, I want to switch to John, where we also have temple theology from the start. John 1:14: the Word became flesh, *kai eskēnōsen en hēmin*. He pitched his tent "and tabernacled in our midst," and we beheld his glory. Any first-century Jew who knew the relevant texts would see at once the author's intention to communicate that the glory of YHWH has returned at last, and that it looks like Jesus. New Testament Christology is not a matter of looking at Jesus and trying to pull in bits and pieces of tradition that enable them to say: "Maybe he actually crosses the line and we have to say divine things about him." New Testament Christology is about telling the story of Israel's one God coming back, at last, and then finding that in order to tell that story you have to tell the story of Jesus.

The christological temple theology is clear again in John 2. Jesus says, "Destroy this temple, and in three days I'll build it again." They say, "What are you talking about?" John pointedly explains to his readers: "He was talking about the temple of his body." As usual, having given you the hint early on, John does not go on repeating the point, but he wants us to go on thinking it throughout. Have you ever thought of what an extraordinary literary trick John plays when you get to the end of John 12? Finally, after all Jesus's ministry, and all his coming and going to and from Jerusalem, we now arrive with a flourish of trumpets in the city once more, for the last time. Here he is: this is it, his readers think. Especially if we know the other Gospels, we expect that this will be the big confrontation. Is it Jesus or the temple, and what happens when they finally square off against one another?

Instead of giving us the drama we expect, John takes us calmly and coolly into the upper room, and we have those long chapters, John 13–17. As readers we may want to stop John and say, "This narrative was going somewhere. Why have you inserted all this material?" But he *is* continuing the narrative. In these chapters *John shows us that Jesus is the true temple.* "Welcome. Come in here," John is saying. "Be with Jesus. He's promising his Spirit so that you will be the temple people." As we read these chapters we find ourselves with Jesus, learning what it means when he says that if the world hated him it will hate us. Nevertheless we are sent into the world. The farewell discourses are not a retreat from the world into a nice, cozy, private space. They are a preparation for the mission to the world. Thus, when we find Jesus standing before Pontius Pilate, we have a sense that we have been here before. This is what it looks like when the kingdom of God meets and confronts the kingdom of Caesar.

We then discover in the farewell discourses, in John 7:37–39 and again in John 20, the promise of the Spirit. Jesus cries out in John 7, "The one who believes in me, as the Scripture says, out of that person's heart will flow rivers of living water." The puzzle that exegetes have had is determining what text is being referred to, for we have no scriptural text that says exactly that. The best answer and, it seems to me, the clear answer is: the reference is to the end of Ezekiel. Here we have the new temple out of which flows the water of life, which will make even the Dead Sea fresh.

Notice: Jesus does not say, "The one who believes in me, as the Scripture says, *into* that person's heart will flow rivers of living water." That is how we have done mission all too often: if a potential convert wants refreshing and wants the Spirit, they say a prayer, believe this doctrine, and this water of life will flow into their hearts. While new life does flow inward, Jesus is saying here that "*out* of that person's heart will flow rivers of living water." The life-giving presence of Christ does not create a static, stagnant lake. We receive in order that we may give. John 7:37–39 is the Ezekiel-shaped, temple-shaped, launching of this Spirit-given mission into the world. It is a picture of the river of the water of life flowing out into the world. We see something similar when, in the picture of the new Jerusalem at the end of Revelation, the river of the water of life flows through the city, with the tree of life growing on either bank, the tree whose leaves are for the healing of the nations.[2]

Right at the heart of the farewell discourses we find a strange passage: John 16:8–11. For years, whenever this was read out in my church, traditionally sometime between Easter and Pentecost, I found its meaning elusive. "When the Spirit comes, he will convict the world," says Jesus, "of sin and righteousness and judgment. Of sin because they don't believe in me, of righteousness because I go to the Father and you will see me no more, of judgment because the ruler of this world is judged." For years I used to wonder what the Spirit's convicting the world of these things, and for these reasons, was all about. Only comparatively recently have I realized its significance: when the Spirit comes, the Spirit will do these things *through Jesus's followers*. The convicting work of the Spirit is not solitary activity; we do not stand by and watch while the Spirit does this work. An important part of the New Testament's missional theology is the call to respond to John 16 in this way: if we pray for the Spirit, we should expect that the Spirit will be teaching us how to hold the world to account. To convict of sin because they do not believe in Jesus and are blundering off in the darkness, dehumanizing themselves and everybody else; to convict of righteousness because Jesus has gone to the Father and has been shown to be in the right, and if you want to know how the world is going to be set right at last, Jesus is the person to whom you must look; and to convict of judgment because the ruler of this world (perhaps referring to Satan, or perhaps Caesar, or perhaps both) is judged, just as in John 18–19 when Jesus held Pontius Pilate to account. In holding him to account, Jesus argued with Pilate about truth and kingdom and power; then, as part of the greatest paradox in the

2. There is a whole missional theology in Rev. 21–22 that I cannot develop here. What is going on when the leaves of the tree are for the healing of the nations? What is going on when the kings of the earth bring their treasure into the city?

world, he went to his own death as if to prove the point. "What is truth?" asks Pilate, and the next moment sends Jesus to the cross. We, with fear and trembling, look and say, "there is truth," but Pilate could not see that truth. Jesus inaugurates a different sort of kingdom, a different sort of power. He says, "If my kingdom were from this world, my servants would fight." Jesus has a different sort of kingdom, a different sort of power, which is *for* this world because there is a different sort of truth—the truth of new creation.

In John, the concept of truth does not refer simply to something that corresponds to the way things are in this present world. From the Christian point of view a new epistemology exists, as a result of a new ontology. God is renewing this present world, not creating a different world. Truth is what happens when Jesus—and also those inspired by the Spirit of Jesus—speak words of new creation into the world. These are true words about the way the world really is, now that Jesus is installed and enthroned as its rightful Lord. These words call to account all the forms of truth that have been spoken or have taken place in the old world. The Spirit-led, new-temple missiology of the church calls the world to account, not least in speaking the truth to power. Words of truth do not only describe what we see in the world, but also speak a new sort of truth: the truth of new creation, of a new sort of justice, of a new sort of beauty, of a new Lord, of a new kind of power. These words of truth show up the old world as the shabby, power-hungry thing that it is.

Speaking truth is, in John's Gospel, linked with the unity of the church, and the focus on this connection is highlighted at the end of the farewell discourse in John 17. In fact, this chapter gives us the lens through which to view the rest of the text. It is no accident that in the missionary movements at the start of the twentieth century the mission and unity of the church were held firmly together. As Christians from many traditions know, if the world looks at the church and sees that it is riven with factions, arguments, squabbles, and disunity, the church has lost its authority to speak with integrity. The newspapers in my country love it every time there is a squabble in the church, because that disunity proves the church does not need to be taken seriously. In fact, when our disunity prevails, the newspapers can all the more easily do what they want to do anyway, which is to usurp the church's role of speaking truth to power. In fact, most people—including most Christians!—have forgotten that this *is* the church's task. The media thinks of truth-telling as its prerogative; but in John we see that it is in fact the task of the church. Since the Enlightenment, our narrowing of the church's mission to personal piety and individual salvation means we have forgotten that when the Spirit comes he will convince the world of sin and righteousness and judgment. The way in which he will do it is, not least, through the community that is one in love as Jesus and the Father are one.

Missionary Theology in Paul

Let's turn now to Paul and his letter to the Ephesians. I have often said to students that the quick and cheerful way through the first half of Ephesians is with the tens—1:10; 2:10; 3:10. In Ephesians 1:10 we find this summary statement, that God's purpose is to unite all things in heaven and on earth in him. Yet we in the West have lived out of a pseudotheology that understands God's purpose as rescuing some people *away* from earth to go to heaven instead. That wasn't the plan. Then in Ephesians 2:8–10 we read, "By grace you are saved by faith, not of yourselves; it's a gift of God, not of works lest anyone should boast. We are his workmanship created in the Messiah Jesus for the good works that God prepared beforehand that we should walk in them." That is the church constituted as God's work of art, his *poiēma*. We are God's *poem*, made so that the world can sing, see, and sense the rhythms of God's love and power.

The reference to good works cannot, then, be interpreted in a primarily moralistic sense, as if every biblical reference to "good works" described Pelagians trying to earn their way to heaven. Here in Ephesians 2, the good works are the whole mission of the church, the things that the church must do that show the world a different way to be human. This understanding of good works was central to the spread of the church during the first two or three centuries, despite opposition from the Roman Empire. People came across these strange little communities and were surprised to find new ways of living together. The early church demonstrated an extraordinary love that flowed outward and became obvious in their concern for the poor, their healing of the sick, and their welcome to the outcast. We are God's workmanship, created in Christ Jesus for good works.

The second half of Ephesians 2 envisions the unity of the church as the model for the unity that God intends for heaven and earth at the end of time. Following that grand vision, we receive the missionary mandate in Ephesians 3:10. Simply put, it says that through the church the manifold, multicolored wisdom of God might be made known to the principalities and powers in the heavenly places. That is missional Scripture right there, giving purpose to the very existence of this community, which is made up of

Jews, gentiles, men, women, slaves, free, rich, poor, young, old, and on and on. Caesar would have loved to have been able to produce a kingdom like that. He wanted to bring everyone together, but the only way he could do it was by the artificial and violent means of force, taxes, and crucifixions. God, the living God, through the Messiah Jesus and by the Spirit, has created one people who, in their variegated unity, are a sign to the powers of the world that Jesus is Lord. This is why immediately in Ephesians 4 we hear the great appeal for unity; in Ephesians 5 we hear the great appeal for holiness; in Ephesians 6 we hear the great warning about the spiritual warfare in which the church will be engaged if Jesus's followers pursue unity and holiness in order to be the missionary people spoken about in the first three chapters.

When I settled down to analyze the different elements of Paul's world—the Jewish, philosophical, religious, and political worlds—it gradually dawned on me that Paul does not just envisage occasional "applications" to these worlds in the midst of talking about something else. His whole missionary work is, through the gospel, to bring about and, through his teaching, to sustain and shape communities that will be a new sort of *polis*, a new sort of community, a new sort of social reality. Although Paul's communities did not have the kinds of religious practices we find in the ancient world—temples, sacrifices, priesthoods, oracles, and so on—they nevertheless did things—baptism, Eucharist, prayers, study of Scripture—that bound them together with the God they knew in Jesus, the Messiah. That "binding together" is what the ancient Roman word *religare* is all about. So they did have a sort of "religion," even though it did not look like all the religions surrounding them. They were a special, new kind of community based in a missionary theology, going out into the world and, as Paul says, "taking captive every thought to obey the Messiah."

For Paul, the task of thinking it through well was part of the church's obedience to the Messiah. "Be transformed by the renewing of your minds that you may prove that which is the good and acceptable and perfect will of God" (Rom. 12). He says, in effect: "As you learn to be this new community, as you learn the unity of Romans 14–15, as you discover the purpose of unity in your own missionary theology and strategy, you need to think freshly into God's new world." Paul writes this as he contemplates a journey to Spain. We see in his words and in his experience that, as he thinks freshly about the world, he once more upstages the Stoics, Epicureans, academics, and cynics as he did in Acts 17. So, although it seems odd to us that Paul never actually urges church communities to get on with the work of evangelism (the only time he comes close to that is Philippians 2:16 when he refers to "holding forth/fast the word of life"), he nevertheless clearly wants his young churches to live as single, united communities, so fully shaped by the cross and the resurrection of God's missionary Messiah that they will in fact be shining like lights in a dark world. Actually, that is how Christianity spread. Some people had the specific vocation of evangelists; but the "mission" of the church consisted of people being brought together in this "new temple" reality. That community, in its very existence, demonstrated to the watching world a new way to be human, a way that came through following Jesus.

The Western church has rightly seen that Romans is a great missionary document, but the church has often narrowed the missionary implications of this letter to the so-called Romans Road: "here's how you're a sinner, here's how Jesus died, here's how you are saved, and therefore, here's how you should live." These basic truths are important, but they do not get at the heart of God's covenant purposes found in Romans. We trace this covenant from Adam, from Abraham, to the Messiah, by the Spirit, and right on to the new creation. Romans 6–8 retells God's missionary narrative. Romans 6 tells the exodus story, where we come through the waters and are freed from slavery. Romans 7 tells the story of Mount Sinai, where we are given the Torah. But the Torah is confusing and, though we want to keep it, it kills us. So in Romans 8 we are set free from the Torah, and instead the presence of God is established in our midst by the Spirit, so that the Sprit leads us to our inheritance. Paul's vision of that inheritance is rooted in the death and resurrection of Jesus, animated by the Spirit through whom we will be raised from the dead to share in the new creation, and interpreted through the Psalms, particularly the messianic Psalms 2 and 8 and the "suffering" Psalm 44. We need all these angles if we are fully to understand this great, central chapter of missionary theology.

Romans gives us, in fact, a large-scale exodus narrative, in which the mission of the church is the church's present role and in which the church's "glory," as in Psalm 8, is the renewed-human "glory" of being set in a strange, paradoxical authority over the world. The narrative horizon is the whole renewed creation, and the driving reality of the narrative is Jesus as Messiah, Lord of all, through whom the new exodus has happened and is happening. The focus is on the community of Jesus's followers, we who in our suffering and in our intercession form the new missionary reality. Then, moving into Romans 9–11, we find as it were the new missionary mandate. How will people believe unless apostles are sent to them? This comes as the retold story of Israel in Romans 9–10 reaches its climax in the Messiah and, with that, the renewal of the covenant as prophesied in Deuteronomy 30. That is a complex passage, about which I and others have written a great deal elsewhere. The point for my present purposes is that here in Romans we have perhaps the most explicit account of the way in which the Spirit-led followers of Jesus are the commissioned agents of the one God, making his name known in all the world.

In conclusion, the New Testament is the birth of what we can describe as public, missionary theology. Theology ought not to be a retreat from the world, into a private space for the magic, sacred few. Theology ought to be opening up an entirely new hermeneutical space within the world. This new hermeneutical space emerges as people live together in worship and fellowship and together function as the new *polis*, with the new sort of *religio* binding us together with our shared Lord. God's new creation is happening, and we are called to be not only its beneficiaries but also its agents. As we become agents of this new creation, we provide the social, cultural, religious, ethical, and political reality toward which the different societies and cultures of our day aspire. And we do this not by retreating into a private huddle, but by living out new creation right there in the middle of the old one.

In the academic context of our own day, study of the New Testament is seriously skewed by location within the post-Enlightenment project, particularly in Germany, in the eighteenth and nineteenth centuries. As the study of the New Testament comes to be placed within the category of religion, it is interpreted differently from the ancient world's conception of religion so that it now means "that which is *not* about society." Departments of religion today, into which study of the New Testament regularly gets pulled, ensure that the real message of the New Testament is constricted. The category of religion, as we use it today, cannot make sense of the New Testament. In fact, it would make more sense to study Paul in a department of Jewish studies, or philosophy, or political science, than to study Paul in what we mean by a department of religion. As the study of the New Testament is subsumed by this contemporary idea of religion, which is non-Jewish, nonnarrative, and apolitical, the integrity of the New Testament is deconstructed.

Even in our post-Enlightenment, secularized world, however, we Westerners still have a sense that we have some sort of mission to the world. We want to go out and do justice and peace. We are like Cain: even though the fall has happened, Cain still knows that he has to go and build a city. The trouble is that the city becomes the tower of Babel, and God has to come and put a stop to their arrogance. In the same way, we in the modern West have tried to participate in this mission to the world as if there were no God. We have again and again produced towers of Babel. The Western Enlightenment arrogance is a parody of the genuine Christian mission, which makes it harder for us to engage in the true Christian mission.

People around the world, not least in the Middle East, see Christianity and the West as synonymous. They think Christianity is about economic exploitation and violent control. What a tragedy—and a travesty. Thus some missionaries in the Middle East today cannot use words like "Christian" and "Christianity." They simply have to talk about Jesus—which in many ways may be no bad thing. In their context, Christianity has become confused with Babel-building Western arrogance, but Jesus is still exciting. How can we emerge from all this confusion? The only way forward, I suggest, is to take our courage in our hands, with John 16, Ephesians 1–3, Philippians, and not least with Romans 8. Paul knew that the path forward would mean sharing the sufferings of the Messiah. But that was the way to glory—not a kind of glory that snatches us away from earth to a distant shining heaven, but the glory spoken of in Psalm 8, the truly human authority over the world. Putting Paul and John together, we know that this is the glory revealed on the cross. For the church, mission can be credible and effective only when it is following in the path of Jesus. That is part at least of Paul's great conclusion: those he justified, he also glorified. That is how we are "conformed to the image of the Son," and that is how, reading Scripture in the power of the Spirit, we are enabled to share in his mission to the world.

CHAPTER 10

Reading James Missionally

Joel B. Green

On the face of it, the New Testament letter of James seems a poor candidate for a missional reading. For example, in their extensive study of *The Biblical Foundations for Mission*, Donald Senior and Carroll Stuhlmueller dismiss the potential contribution of James in two sentences. James urges Christians to lead lives of integrity, they say, but he does not reflect on the "witness value" of their good deeds.[1] In a more recent volume dedicated to constructing "a biblical theology of mission," Andreas Köstenberger and Peter O'Brien devote an entire chapter to the General Epistles and Revelation, but completely bypass the letter of James.[2] This is perhaps unsurprising, since we look to James in vain for such traditional mainstays of mission as a directive to carry the gospel to the nations (e.g., Luke 24:46–47; Acts 1:8). Even the letter's copious interest in caring for the have-nots is cast as a matter *internal* to the community: "Imagine *a brother or sister* who is naked and never has enough to eat" (James 2:15, emphasis added).[3]

1. Donald Senior and Carroll Stuhlmueller, *The Biblical Foundations for Mission* (Maryknoll, NY: Orbis, 1983), 309.

2. Andreas J. Köstenberger and Peter T. O'Brien, *Salvation to the Ends of the Earth: A Biblical Theology of Mission*, New Studies in Biblical Theology (Downers Grove, IL: InterVarsity, 2001), 227–50. According to their Scripture index, the only reference to James is in a footnote (242n33) listing James 1:2 as one of several uses of the Greek term *peirasmos* (which they translate as "persecution").

3. Cf. Mariam Kamell, "The Economics of Humility: The Rich and the Humble in James," in *Engaging Economics: New Testament Scenarios and Early Christian Reception*, ed. Bruce W. Longenecker and Kelly D. Liebengood (Grand Rapids: Eerdmans, 2009), 157–75; Craig L. Blomberg, *Neither Poverty nor Riches: A Biblical Theology of Material Possessions*,

From this traditional viewpoint, the pressing question is whether James urges his audience to engage in mission. In reality, this way of putting things does not take us very far, since it assumes that we know already what mission entails, even before we begin our reading of the letter. Accordingly, debates about the missional quality of James turn out to be arguments over whose definition of mission is best. We are aided, then, by the emergence in recent years of a missional hermeneutic at the interstices of biblical studies and missiology.[4] From this perspective, we are encouraged to read James within the context of the Christian Scriptures, guided by a different set of questions—especially these two: How does the letter of James locate its readers within the scriptural narrative of God's mission? How might James's letter shape its readers in their formation as participants in God's mission? My agenda in what follows is determined by these two questions.

True, each of these questions can be conceived as a heading, each with its own drop-down menu of related concerns. Nevertheless, they will be enough to guide the reading of James that follows. The gravity of the first question is recognized in its baseline assumption that Scripture shapes (or ought to shape) the patterns by which we conceptualize and experience the world, find our place in it, and deliberate on the nature of faithful response to God's gracious initiative. The second underscores the importance of how we embody the gospel as communities of God's people in the world. From this perspective, we recognize immediately that James's general interest in the internal life of certain communities of those who follow Jesus presents no deterrent to a missional reading. On the contrary, James invites reflection on what it means for the church to be a missionary outpost in a world whose patterns and conventions are out of step with God's mission.

Locating James's Audience

We turn, then, to our first question: How does the letter of James locate its readers within the narrative of God's mission? After a brief orientation

---

New Studies in Biblical Theology (Grand Rapids: Eerdmans, 1999), 148–60. Unless otherwise noted, citations from Scripture follow the Common English Bible.

4. Important milestones include, e.g., David J. Bosch, "Towards a Hermeneutic for 'Biblical Studies and Mission,'" *Mission Studies* 3.2 (1986): 65–79; Michael Barram, "The Bible, Mission, and Social Location: Toward a Missional Hermeneutic," *Interpretation* 61 (2007): 42–58; George R. Hunsberger, "Proposals for a Missional Hermeneutic: Mapping the Conversation," available at gocn.org/resources/articles/proposals-missional-hermeneutic-mapping-conversation.

to the importance of narrative for identity formation, we will explore how James tells the story.

On Narrative Identity

Who we are—our identity—is largely shaped by the stories we tell, the narratives we seek to inhabit. In identity theory, "narrative identity" refers to a person's internalized and evolving story, which provides her with a sense of unity across time and with purpose and significance. These stories may be unique at the individual level, but they tend to follow patterns shared by others within one's community of reference. Not surprisingly, research demonstrates that the life story a person relates is at least as revelatory of the world or culture within which she frames meaning as it is about her life itself.[5]

According to cognitive scientist Mark Turner, "*story* is a basic principle of mind. Most of our experience, our knowledge, and our thinking is organized as stories." Indeed, "narrative imagining is our . . . fundamental cognitive instrument for explanation."[6] Here, Turner treads a well-worn path in the cognitive sciences, a path cleared in recent years especially by those who study people suffering some form of brain damage. Individuals with lesions to the neural equipment responsible for the generation of narrative suffer from a diminished capacity to organize their experiences in terms of past, present, and future—and, consequently, suffer a loss in their grasp of their own identities. In a collaborative study, Kay Young and Jeffrey L. Saver observe that "confabulating amnestic individuals offer an unrivaled glimpse at the power of the human impulse to narrative."[7] So essential is narrative to the formation of one's identity and beliefs that humans manufacture stories in order to justify their present situations or to

5. Dan P. McAdams, "Narrative Identity," in *Handbook of Identity Theory and Research*, ed. Seth J. Schwartz, Koen Luyckx, and Vivian L. Vignoles (New York: Springer, 2011), 1:99–115; Stephen P. Reyna, *Connections: Brain, Mind, and Culture in Social Anthropology* (London: Routledge, 2002).

6. Mark Turner, *The Literary Mind: The Origins of Thought and Language* (Oxford: Oxford University Press, 1996), 5:20.

7. Kay Young and Jeffrey L. Saver, "The Neurology of Narrative," *SubStance* 30 (2001): 72–84 at 76. For examples of the lengths to which humans will go to make storied sense of what they believe to be true, see, e.g., Todd E. Feinberg, *Altered Egos: How the Brain Creates the Self* (Oxford: Oxford University Press, 2001); William Hirstein, *Brain Fiction: Self-Deception and the Riddle of Confabulation* (Cambridge: MIT Press, 2005).

wrap those circumstances in a blanket of significance. This is true not only of persons who have suffered brain damage, however. Embodied human life performs like a cultural, neuro-hermeneutical system, locating (and, thus, making sense of) current realities in relation to our grasp of the past and our expectations of the future. I use the phrase "our grasp" advisedly, since the stories we tell and live should not be confused with an empirically verifiable account of "what really happened." Perceptual data can be interpreted in various ways according to the hypotheses with which we operate, yet my mind disambiguates that data according to what I understand to be possible and true. Not surprisingly, then, when shown how to read the same data in a different way, I can do so, flipping back and forth between rival interpretations as my perception shifts (as in the famous optical illusion: is it a duck or a rabbit?). Memory, too, is not passive retrieval of objective information, but active, purposeful reconstruction, through which we seek coherence and typically attribute meaning by means of cause-effect relations. The narrative patterns by which we understand life in the world are learned; they comprise a network of default (though not static) assumptions about our environment and about "the way the world works"; with their own neuronal substrate, they come to operate at a preconscious, taken-for-granted level; and, constitutive as they are of a person's cultural hermeneutical system, they are integral to embodied human life.

Coming at the importance of narrative from the other direction, we also recognize that narratives of all kinds (for example, print novels, comics, stories told over Saturday morning coffee, and cinematic narratives) effect transformations in those who hear or read them. They shape us affectively, for example, and they influence (that is, they complicate, simplify, redirect, or sanction) the stories by which we make sense of our own lives. Indeed, research shows that when we read a book, say, about wizards or vampires, we psychologically become wizards and vampires and that the sense of belonging that comes from internalizing narratives cultivates the same feelings of contentment we would have if we actually were part of the world described.[8] If spending time with Harry Potter provokes life-altering qualities of empathy (presumably, by identifying with a fictional character who himself identifies

8. Cf. Shira Gabriel and Ariana F. Young, "Becoming a Vampire without Being Bitten: The Narrative Collective-Assimilation Hypothesis," *Psychological Science* 22.8 (2011): 990–94; Loris Vezzali, Sofia Stathi, Dino Giovannini, Dora Capozza, and Elena Trifiletti, "The Greatest Magic of Harry Potter: Reducing Prejudice," *Journal of Applied Social Psychology* 45.2 (2015): 105–21.

with marginal groups, like Muggles and Mudbloods), what of spending time with "James, a slave of God and of the Lord Jesus Christ" (James 1:1)?

If "reality" does not come to us "clean," but always through the filters of our perception, if the world is always for us already an interpreted world, then we must inquire: Conceptualized how? Within what narrative account will we interpret? If humans live story-formed lives, then what stories are shaping us? If humans go to great lengths to impose structure on sensory data, and if this structure takes the form of the narratives by which we have learned to configure the world, then which narratives pattern the ways we think, feel, believe, and behave? What stories give us identity? By what stories do we make sense of the world? The point, of course, is that the scriptural narrative provides an alternative framework within which to construe our lives so that we are reminded of and pressed to embrace the human vocation to serve God's mission in the world.[9]

These observations remind us, first, of the importance of the narrative structure of Scripture itself, including the narrative structure of the gospel. By narrative structure, I do not mean that all biblical books are narratives. I mean, rather, to draw attention to the Bible as a whole narrating God's work: from Genesis to Revelation, from creation to new creation, with God's mighty acts of redemption—the exodus from Egypt and the new exodus of Jesus's life, death, and resurrection—the center points in God's grand story. In this sense, Scripture promotes a narrative structure by which to grasp what is true and to align our lives with that truth. Second, this emphasis on narrative draws attention to the importance of the story of Jesus, whether in Matthew or Hebrews or, indeed, in the whole of the biblical canon, for making sense of God's agenda. Understanding Jesus's advent as the midpoint of the great story of God and God's mission in the world reminds us that we must interpret God's work in relation to Jesus. It is in Jesus that God's character and aims are most fully revealed. Third, this emphasis on narrative is consonant with what socioscientific investigation has long identified about conversion, including Christian conversion: that it includes a reordering of life in terms of the narrative shared with and told by the community of the converted. Conversion entails autobiographical reconstruction: I learn to tell my life's story in a new way.[10]

9. See Dan R. Stiver, *Theology after Ricoeur: New Directions in Hermeneutical Theology* (Louisville: Westminster John Knox, 2001), 52–53; Nicholas Wolterstorff, "Living within a Text," in *Faith and Narrative*, ed. Keith E. Yandell (Oxford: Oxford University Press, 2001), 202–13.

10. Peter L. Berger and Thomas Luckmann, *The Social Construction of Reality: A Treatise in the Sociology of Knowledge* (New York: Doubleday, 1966), 160: "Everything preceding

The Narrative of James's Letter

What narrative does James's letter recount? For James, God's mission has four primary kernels,[11] which we can map as follows:

creation → advent of the Lord Jesus Christ → present, exilic life → new creation

Creation

Direct references to creation in James are minimal but important. This is because images of the beginning (and the end) are lush with opportunities to shape a people's imagination, the basic patterns by which they order experience and both conceptualize and seek to live in the world. The first appears in James's reference to "the Father of lights" (1:17, my translation). Consider this phrase in its context: "Don't be misled, my dear brothers and sisters. Every good gift, every perfect gift, comes from above. These gifts come down from the Father, the creator of the heavenly lights, in whose character there is no change at all. He chose to give us birth by his true word, and here is the result: we are like the first crop from the harvest of everything he created" (1:16–18). The Common English Bible helpfully clarifies that James uses the phrase "Father of lights" to refer to God as creator and, thus, to creation (see Gen. 1:3, 14–17); and the larger context demonstrates that his interest in creation is focused especially on the nature of the creator God.[12] This God does not send temptation (James 1:13–15), but sends good things. This God does not waver between giving good and bad things, for his character is consistently oriented toward providing good things. And this God is known for his generosity. He gives "without a second thought, without keeping score" (1:5), and he gives "every good gift, every perfect gift" (1:17).[13]

---

the alternation is now apprehended as leading toward it, . . . everything following it as flowing from its new reality. This involves a reinterpretation of past biography *in toto*, following the formula 'Then I *thought* . . . now I *know*.'"

11. I borrow the term "kernel" from Seymour Chatman, for whom it refers to major narrative events: "Nodes or hinges in the structure, branching points which force a narrative into one or two (or more) possible paths"; *Story and Discourse: Narrative Structure in Fiction and Film* (Ithaca, NY: Cornell University Press, 1978), 53.

12. The whole of James 1:13–18 can be read as James's reflection on Gen. 1–3 in order to buttress his claim regarding God's character and gifts.

13. Cf. Timothy B. Cargal, *Restoring the Diaspora: Discursive Structure and Purpose in*

We hear a second echo of the creation account in Genesis when James takes up his concerns with the tongue, that "restless evil" (James 3:8). Of the tongue, he observes: "With it we both bless the Lord and Father and curse human beings made in God's likeness" (3:9). Using the rare word *homoiōsis* ("likeness"), James calls to mind the words of Genesis 1:26–27: God made humanity "according to our image and likeness [*homoiōsis*]" (Septuagint, my translation).[14] In this way, James ties the status of human beings to their godlikeness, such that to profane the one is to profane the other. He grounds his call for ethical comportment in creation and more particularly in the God who created human beings in his likeness.

At the one end of James's "narrative," then, stands creation, concerning which James stakes claims both about God and about humanity. As we continue to read the letter, we discern more and more a critical edge to James's cosmology, since he sets friendship with God in opposition to friendship with the world (4:4) and contrasts two ways of construing the world, two kinds of "wisdom" (3:15–18). The one comes from the earth, is worldly minded and diabolic, characterized by jealousy, selfish ambition, disorder, and pervasive evil. The other comes "down from above," from the creator God (compare 1:17; 3:15, 17), and is known by its purity, peacefulness, gentleness, obedience, mercy, good behavior, fairness, and genuineness. The difference between these two patterns of life is captured well by Luke Johnson: "If I forget that everything comes as a gift from God (1:17), then I identify what I have with who I am. And I can be more only if I have more. If another has more, then the other is a threat to me, makes me less. Envy, then, moves inexorably toward hostility and murder: I can be more only if I eliminate the other."[15] At work in this case would be a deformed grasp of God and God's world, which James counters by grounding the past of his theological narrative in the openhanded goodness of God on display in creation. The God of whom James speaks is no Scrooge, no demanding

---

the Epistle of James, Society of Biblical Literature Dissertation Series 144 (Atlanta: Scholars Press, 1993), 84–85.

14. Sophie Laws notes that, in the history of interpretation, a distinction was sometimes made between "image" and "likeness," as in Irenaeus's judgment that "image" referred to the human's fundamental rational nature while "likeness" referred to the human's moral potential, but observes that James seems to give no indication of such distinctions; *A Commentary on the Epistle of James*, Harper's New Testament Commentary (San Francisco: Harper & Row, 1980), 156.

15. Luke Timothy Johnson, *Brother of Jesus, Friend of God: Studies in the Letter of James* (Grand Rapids: Eerdmans, 2004), 217.

benefactor. This God is the antidote to the temptation to turn in times of need to the world's wealth, or to its wealthy, or to violence.

New Creation

Explicit references to new creation are also limited, even though the eschatological horizon of the narrative identity James wants to inculcate in his audience pervades the letter. Among the plain references to the end time, the first two stand in parallel:

1. Those who stand firm during testing are blessed. They are tried and true. They will receive the life God has promised to those who love him as their reward (1:12).
2. Hasn't God chosen those who are poor by worldly standards to be rich in terms of faith? Hasn't God chosen the poor as heirs of the kingdom he has promised to those who love him (2:5)?

Eschatological vision rests in divine promise and choice. And the parallelism between these two texts suggests that the kingdom is for James to be identified as a future life with God characterized as a reversal of fortunes.

This (future) reversal of fortune is the consequence of divine judgment, a motif that resurfaces in James's final chapter: "Therefore, brothers and sisters, you must be patient as you wait for the coming of the Lord. . . . You also must wait patiently, strengthening your resolve, because the coming of the Lord is near. Don't complain about each other, brothers and sisters, so that you won't be judged. Look! The judge is standing at the door!" (5:7–9) Here James correlates the Lord's "coming" (*parousia*; 5:7–18) with divine judgment, a motif signaled earlier in 4:12: "There is only one lawgiver and judge, and he is able to save and to destroy. But you who judge your neighbor, who are you?" Who is the coming judge? This is not altogether clear, and either case can be made—that James refers to the Lord Jesus (explicitly in 1:1; 2:1) or that he refers to God the Father (as in 3:9; 5:4, 10–11). Does Jesus return in order to judge, or does God come in judgment? Given Jesus's resurrection to glory and concomitant share in God's identity, it is unclear that a choice is necessary.

James is not concerned with end-time speculation. His focus instead falls on the existential situation of his audience, comprised as it is of trials, need, and distress. Exilic life provides the occasion for growth to maturity (1:2), not for taking matters into their own hands—which would be tantamount to usurping God's roles of provider (in the present) and judge (in the future). Their response is to be one of faithful resistance, not retaliation, as they live their lives in dependence on the God who will act to set things right. This is the God who will judge the world, reward the faithful, and punish the arrogant who oppress the needy.

With this vision of creation and new creation, James frames his narrative mural of God's character and God's aims. The beginning and the end of the story speak of God's gracious character and of the human vocation grounded in their having been made in God's likeness—a likeness shared by all humanity, a likeness that was not lost because of sin but continues to call us to reflect, in our relationships, God's holiness and integrity. With this narrative frame, James reminds us that, though we are formed in God's likeness, we are not God (to whom alone belongs judgment); that present life in the dispersion is not "home"; and that, however permanent present inequities may seem, they are not the whole story, for the Lord is coming to set things right.

Advent of the Lord Jesus Christ

The middle of James's narrative turns on Jesus's mission and message. James explicitly refers to Jesus only twice: in 1:1, where he identifies himself as a "servant of God and of the Lord Jesus Christ," and in 2:1, where he instructs his audience, "My brothers and sisters, when you show favoritism you deny the faithfulness of our Lord Jesus Christ, who has been resurrected in glory." Although I follow the Common English Bible in its translation of this second text, how best to render James's phrasing is disputed along two lines. First, should we translate James's phrase as "the faithfulness of Jesus" or as "faith in Jesus"? Either way, the primary concern is that we understand that James here indicts his readers for their inconsistency: followers of Jesus simply cannot practice favoritism, since to do so would counter Jesus's own mission.[16] Second, how should we understand the genitive phrase "of

16. I take James's phrase as a subjective genitive and thus read *pistis* as a reference to Jesus's "faithfulness"; cf. Wesley Hiram Wachob, *The Voice of Jesus in the Social Rhetoric of James*, Society of New Testament Studies Monograph Series 106 (Cambridge: Cambridge University Press, 2000), 64–65 ("faith-obedience"); Patrick J. Hartin, *James*, Sacra Pagina 14 (Collegeville, MN: Liturgical Press, 2003), 117 ("Jesus' faithfulness to his Father's will through the obedience of his life"), 129–30. Luke Timothy Johnson, *The Letter of James: A New Translation with Introduction and Commentary*, Anchor Bible 37A (New York: Doubleday, 1995), 220: "the faith of Jesus in God as reflected in his teachings." Cf. Bruce A. Lowe, "James 2:1 in

glory"? The King James Version adds the words "the Lord" in order to make sense of it: "our Lord Jesus Christ, *the Lord* of glory." Several more contemporary translations read "our glorious Lord Jesus Christ" (e.g., Today's New International Version, New Revised Standard Version, New American Bible). The translation represented by the Common English Bible works from the premise that the Lord's "glory" refers to God's exaltation of Jesus by raising him from the dead and, therefore, to Jesus's partnership in God's glory. But even the more prosaic reading represented by Today's New International Version or New Revised Standard Version coheres with the view that Jesus's glory and his impartiality are paired with the glory he shares with God grounded in his embrace of those whom God esteems—not the high and mighty, but the needy and humble. Here, christological affirmation serves James's rhetorical appeal to ethical comportment.

Although less explicit, two additional lines of evidence speak to the crucial role of Jesus's advent for the narrative by which James orders the world. The first is the way James wove Jesus's teaching into the fabric of his letter. A few examples will suffice:

I assure you that if you have faith and don't doubt . . . (Matt. 21:21)	Whoever asks shouldn't hesitate. They should ask in faith, without doubting. (James 1:6)
But whoever stands firm until the end will be saved. (Matt. 10:22)	Those who stand firm during testing are blessed. . . . They will receive the life God has promised to those who love him as their reward. (James 1:12)
Happy are you who are poor, because God's kingdom is yours. (Luke 6:20)	Hasn't God chosen those who are poor by worldly standards to be rich in terms of faith? Hasn't God chosen the poor as heirs of the kingdom he has promised to those who love him? (James 2:5)

the Πίστις Χηριστοῦ Debate: Irrelevant or Indispensable?" in *The Faith of Jesus Christ: Exegetical, Biblical, and Theological Studies*, ed. Michael F. Bird and Preston M. Sprinkle (Peabody, MA: Hendrickson, 2009), 239–57. If one prefers the translation "faith in Jesus," however, the point need not be lost, since one could still speak of the deficient faith of James's audience, who apparently, and wrongly, imagine that they can both practice partiality and confess their faith in Jesus—so, e.g., Scot McKnight, *The Letter of James*, New International Commentary on the New Testament (Grand Rapids: Eerdmans, 2011), 174–80.

But I say to you that you must not pledge at all. You must not pledge by heaven, because it's God's throne. You must not pledge by the earth, because it's God's footstool. You must not pledge by Jerusalem, because it's the city of the great king. And you must not pledge by your head, because you can't turn one hair white or black. Let your yes mean yes, and your no mean no. Anything more than this comes from the evil one. (Matt. 5:34–37)

Most important, my brothers and sisters, never make a solemn pledge—neither by heaven nor earth, nor by anything else. Instead, speak with a simple "Yes" or "No," or else you may fall under judgment. (James 5:12)

James's dependence on the Jesus tradition is much more extensive.[17] Taken together, these allusions and echoes are unambiguous markers of James's determined efforts not only at identifying Jesus as an exemplar worth emulating but also at inscribing his audience's lives into Jesus's message. Jesus's reading of Israel's Scriptures, Jesus's representation of God's mission, Jesus's assessment of faithfulness—these fill out the story James wants to tell, shaping how his audience conceptualizes the world and lives in it.

We can discern a second, less obvious witness to the importance of Jesus's advent in these two phrases: God "chose to give us birth by his true word" (1:18), and "welcome the word planted deep inside you—the very word that is able to save you" (1:21). Although, again, some ambiguity swirls around these phrases,[18] it is difficult not to hear in them a reference to God's gift of new birth by which human cravings are overcome, moral filth is set aside, people are enabled to do the word, and they receive their eschatological reward (1:14–15, 21–27). Although James does not use the term, we might

17. For a list of allusions and discussion, see Dale C. Allison Jr., *A Critical and Exegetical Commentary on the Epistle of James,* International Critical Commentary (New York: Bloomsbury, 2013), 56–62; more fully, Patrick J. Hartin, *James and the "Q" Sayings of Jesus,* Journal for the Study of the New Testament Supplement Series 47 (Sheffield: Sheffield Academic Press, 1991). Recognizing these parallels does not depend on accepting the Q-hypothesis held by some scholars.

18. This "word" could be God's work at creation, for example, or the "word planted deep inside of you" might correspond to the Stoic notion of a divinely given human reason shared by all humanity.

think in terms of the "gospel," and for Christian readers this leads inevitably to reflection on the story of Jesus.

Why James refers to Jesus so infrequently is unclear. What is clear, though, is that Jesus's advent is a necessary pivot point in the narrative James sketches. We might wish for more reflection on the nature or content of the word by which we are saved, but it is clear enough that the human problem—internal craving that leads to sin and death (1:14–15)—has as its antidote the gospel, which when internalized is powerful to save. It is also clear that Jesus's faithfulness is realized in reflecting God's own impartiality, and this marks the way for those who serve Jesus.

Present, Exilic Life

With regard to the story he spins, James devotes the lion's share of his attention to the current situation of his audience. He interprets their scattered locations with a metaphor deeply embedded in Israel's story; they are exiles: "From James, a servant of God and of the Lord Jesus Christ, to the twelve tribes in the dispersion: Greetings!" (1:1, my translation). Actually, in his letter opening, James identifies his audience with the use of paradoxical metaphors. On the one hand, they are like Israel in the diaspora, away from home, longing for their regathering and restoration. On the other, they are "the twelve tribes," an image that portends the restoration of God's people at the end of the ages.[19] For James, God acted decisively to form the eschatological people of God, yet, while awaiting the eschaton, those very people live in a world whose commitments and habits challenge those of God's faithful. The faithful are God's restored people, awaiting restoration. Reading the opening and closing of the letter, we find the narrative world that James constructs marked first by the temporal nature of the diasporic experience of God's people as a journeying, not-at-home people and then by the relentless, socioreligious threat of assimilation and defection ("if any of you wander from the truth"; 5:19–20). Their homes and gatherings are missional outposts; insofar as they practice the word (and not only listen to it), their deepest allegiances and dispositions counter what matters most in the world within which they live.

19. See Todd C. Penner, *The Epistle of James and Eschatology: Re-reading an Ancient Christian Letter*, Journal for the Study of the New Testament Supplement Series 121 (Sheffield: Sheffield Academic Press, 1996), 181–83.

Consider some of the ways James portrays exilic life: "various tests" (1:2), "the testing of your faith" (1:3), "poor" (1:9), "testing" (1:12), "difficulties" (1:27), worldly contamination (1:27), "conflicts" and "disputes" (4:1), victims of deceitful behavior (5:4), condemnation and murder (5:6), a life of wandering (5:19). Clearly, James is aware of the daily struggles of his audience. He does not deny the reality of their experiences with violence, their loss of identity, their neediness; instead, he interprets their experiences. From his vantage point, he is addressing people whose commitments to serve (as he serves) the Lord Jesus Christ have led to transformed attitudes and behaviors that locate them squarely in the dispersion (1:1). So he gives them, first, the example of Abraham, God's friend (2:23), that prototypical stranger (e.g., Gen. 11; 22:4); second, the model of Rahab (James 1:25), who assisted Israel on its journey from enslavement to promise; and third, the example of Job, that beacon of patient endurance in an unfriendly world.[20] And he locates present, exilic life in the larger narrative that runs from creation to new creation, a narrative in which Jesus's mission powerfully enables and profoundly determines the character of faithful response to God's graciousness.

This, then, is how the letter of James locates its readers within the canonical narrative of God's mission. In answering this, our first question, we have already begun to address the second: How might James's letter shape its readers in their formation as participants in God's mission?

Embodying the Gospel

According to Jacques Derrida, gift-giving is an impossibility. This is because the very act of giving inevitably participates in an exchange cycle: the gift morphs into an obligation that must be repaid.[21] Reciprocity rules. Derrida's analysis is worked out in conversation with philosophy, anthropology, and literature in the modern West, but it easily finds a home in traditional cultures as well, characterized as they are by a range of relationships—within the family, within the village, among friends, and with

20. Allison (*James*, 714–17) notes how popular interpretation and extrabiblical traditions emphasize Job's exemplary qualities, irrespective of the somewhat more complex picture we find in the Old Testament book itself.

21. Jacques Derrida, *Given Time: 1. Counterfeit Money*, trans. Peggy Kamuf (Chicago: University of Chicago Press, 1992).

outsiders—all marked by forms of reciprocity.[22] The Roman social world, too, was constructed through debt-webs that defined the nature of all sorts of personal and social alliances and that manifested themselves in status scales (who is up? who is down?) and barometers of belonging (who is in? who is out?); economics and social relationships were and are strikingly intertwined. Even a cursory reading of James leaves one with the impression that James's audience is largely made up of the down and out, but who wanted to be—indeed, strove to be—up and in. The effect of James's rhetoric is essentially to transform these deep-seated and widespread social practices and conventions—and the hopes they nurtured—by rejecting the rules of reciprocity and so redefining what it means to be up or down, in or out. As we read early on in the letter, "Brothers and sisters who are poor should find satisfaction in their high status. Those who are wealthy should find satisfaction in their low status, because they will die off like wildflowers" (1:9–10). As James makes clear, this topsy-turvy valuation scale is sanctioned by God: "My dear brothers and sisters, listen! Hasn't God chosen those who are poor by worldly standards to be rich in terms of faith? Hasn't God chosen the poor as heirs of the kingdom he has promised to those who love him?" (2:5). "God stands against the proud, but favors the humble" (4:6). The sequelae of this world transformation can be summed up with reference to Leviticus 19:18, which serves James as a précis of kingdom instruction (that is, as "the royal law"):[23] "Love your neighbor as yourself" (James 2:8).

One way to summarize James's message would be to take with utmost seriousness its christological framing: believe, think, feel, and behave like Jesus. If historical Jesus studies over the past two or three centuries teach us anything, though, it is that "Jesus" easily becomes a wax nose that can be pinched or broadened, elongated or shortened, depending on the interests of the interpreter-sculptor. The question, then, is what it would be to believe, think, feel, and behave like Jesus *as James tells the story*. We can develop what this would mean under three headings: embracing exilic life, recognizing God's gracious character, and living an integrated life.

22. Concerning traditional societies, the modern classic is Marshall Sahlins, *Stone Age Economics* (London: Routledge, 1972). See also the wide-ranging study of S. N. Eisenstadt and L. Roniger, *Patrons, Clients, and Friends: Interpersonal Relations and the Structure of Trust in Society*, Themes in the Social Sciences (Cambridge: Cambridge University Press, 1984).

23. Cf. 1:25: "the perfect law, the law of freedom"; 2:12: "the law of freedom."

Embracing Exilic Life

Just as the opening of James's letter places the whole of his instruction under a christological umbrella, so it provides his audience with their essential identity. They are diasporic, exilic, journeying people, a people who should never confuse this world with their real home. Later, James will press this point in the strongest terms, identifying as adulterers those who befriend the world. After all, "whoever wants to be the world's friend becomes God's enemy" (4:4). Throughout, his portrait of the world is unrelentingly negative (1:27; 2:5; 3:6).

As basic as this reality might seem, we should not overlook or downplay the difficult situation in which James has located his audience. Exile may provide an arena for mission, but it is hardly a place of comfort, particularly not for people oriented (as most people are) toward fitting in, belonging. Even though people may take comfort from the news that diasporic life is temporary, such a life nonetheless complicates their status in the world. Who are we? What are our characteristic practices? Who decides? When is acculturation appropriate, and when does it become a cancer that leads to loss, that is, to deconversion and defection? The constant, booming drumbeat of standard conventions, allegiances, and practices complicates the lives of those who are called to step to a different drummer. Embracing the reality of diasporic life at least introduces the possibility of hearing and following an alternative cadence, however, for it presses questions of identity, of critical discernment and engagement with pervasive social institutions, and of the commitments and dispositions that beg for faithful embodiment.

Recognizing God's Gracious Character

Anyone who needs wisdom should ask God (James 1:5). "You don't have because you don't ask" (4:2). Whoever is suffering or sick should pray (5:13–18). James's instruction assumes that what we see, taste, feel, hear, and smell is not all there is. Life is not a zero-sum game in which each gain or loss we experience is balanced by the losses or gains of others. According to that theory, the only way to have is to take from others, with craving and violence conjoined in a never-ending cycle. This is the life of hoarding and stealing (5:1–6), of strategizing business plans without reference to God (4:13–16), of boasting and violent speech (3:1–12, 14), of jealousy and selfish ambition (3:14–16), and, indeed, of sin and death (1:14–15).

James presents an alternative narrative map, one marked at each stage by God's good gifts. God created the world, God gave new birth by his true word, God gives wisdom, God gives the kingdom to those who love him, God comes to the aid of his people, God restores health, God sends rain—God's gracious provision dots the landscape of James's letter. "Every good gift, every perfect gift, comes from . . . the Father" (1:17). God's "very nature is to give to everyone without a second thought, without keeping score" (1:5). Those who embrace this version of reality, this narrative configuration of the world, are free to turn their backs on self-preservation, jealousy, and violence.

Living an Integrated Life

Two texts in James 1 bring into focus the overall aim of James's message—the one more general and abstract, the other more pointed and concrete. The first is the chain of effects that leads from "the testing of your faith," through "endurance," to maturity and completion (1:2–4). These last two terms, *teleioi* and *holoklēroi*, form a hendiadys capable of a range of translations, including maturity and completeness, but also wholeness, integrity, perfection, fully formed, and so on. Reflecting on the whole of the letter, Richard Bauckham highlights five aspects of this theme for James:[24]

1. Integration, or the harmonious wholeness of the individual and of the community.
2. Exclusion, that is, rejection of allegiances and behaviors incompatible with single-minded devotion to God.
3. Completion, which refers both to developmental maturation and to actualizing in life the whole of God's instruction.
4. Consistency, or "the consistent devotion of the whole person, the whole of life, the whole community, and ultimately the whole cosmos to God."[25]
5. Divine perfection, the standard by which wholeness can and ought to be measured.

24. Richard Bauckham, *James: Wisdom of James, Disciple of Jesus the Sage*, New Testament Readings (London: Routledge, 1999), 177–83. Very much worth consulting, too, is Patrick J. Hartin, *A Spirituality of Perfection: Faith in Acts in the Letter of James* (Collegeville, MN: Liturgical Press, 1999).

25. Bauckham, *James*, 181.

James articulates the problem of human wholeness in various ways that are situation specific and that have wider purchase. His audience tries to befriend the world rather than God, and so becomes God's enemy (4:4; cf. 2:23); this opposition depends on classical ideas of friendship, understood in terms of shared heart and mind. James censures the "double-minded" (1:7; 4:8; cf. Ps. 119:113): lacking a pure heart, they claim to be truly devoted to God, but their affections and behaviors declare the opposite. James speaks to his audience as "adulterers" (4:4, my translation), echoing the biblical tradition of Israel as God's unfaithful wife: they claim a covenant relationship with Yahweh, yet engage in idolatry.

At the beginning of the letter, James traces two competing chains of effects: trials that lead to maturity (progression: 1:2–4) and temptations that lead to death (regression: 1:14–15). Since the same Greek term, *peirasmos*, underlies both English words, "trials" and "temptations," we may ask what determines whether humans face *diabolic temptation* (which impedes and corrupts human life) or *divine test* (which refines and deepens human life). On this point, James's argument is straightforward. The challenges of exilic life provide space for the unbridled exercise of human desire, the result of which is sin and death. Although one might be tempted to fault exilic life itself, or to lay the blame for these seemingly overpowering temptations at God's feet, or the devil's, this is a wrongheaded analysis. The problem is internal to the human person: human craving, a disposition toward double-mindedness. Faithfulness in exile takes a different turn, requiring that God's true word, the gospel, be similarly internalized. Through a transformation that is itself God's gift, the divine word must be received and fully embodied so that it permeates who one is and what one does.

The second text in James 1 that brings into focus the aim of James's message is more pointed and concrete: "If those who claim devotion to God don't control what they say, they mislead themselves. Their devotion is worthless. True devotion, the kind that is pure and faultless before God the Father, is this: to care for orphans and widows in their difficulties and to keep the world from contaminating us" (1:26–27). With these words, James concludes his opening salvo regarding the importance of hearing *and* doing the word. With these words, "faith" takes on flesh; as James will later write: "I'll show you my faith by putting it into practice in faithful action" (2:18). With these words, James launches the two primary sets of behaviors constituent of "faithful action" as this is developed throughout the letter: genuine faith expresses itself in control of the tongue, that is, in personal and communal speech ethics (1:26); and genuine faith expresses itself in honoring the poor and extending hospitality to the needy (1:27).[26] We might say that, for James, "integrity" or "wholeness" is realized in controlling the tongue and in hospitality to the needy. Both, as we have seen, are expressions of Scripture's royal law ("love your neighbor as yourself"; 2:8), and both presume a Christlike rejection of showing favoritism to those judged by worldly canons to be wealthy and of high status. After all, has God not chosen the poor (2:5)? Are not all people made in God's likeness (3:9)?

Summary

How might James's letter shape its readers in their formation as participants in God's mission? This second question occupied us in this section. Our answer took us back and forth across James's writing as we focused on three important motifs: embracing exilic life, recognizing God's gracious character, and living an integrated life. It might be tempting to single out this last motif—integrity, wholeness, perfection, maturity—as the best way of summarizing James's perspective on embodying the gospel. Certainly, we have good reasons for doing so, given the way James's persuasive artistry unfolds in the letter. This could leave us with an anemic understanding of James, however. James pushes further. His audience may be scattered here and there, but for him they are a *diasporic people*; he gives them this identity by interpreting their lives within the framework of a journeying people living in exile, awaiting final restoration. Embodying the gospel entails embracing this metaphoric identity. Likewise, his understanding of wholeness requires a deep-seated conversion concerning the nature of the universe: new ways of thinking, feeling, believing, and behaving that have as their basis and guide the creator God who gives new birth and lavishly provides for his people.

26. On James's speech ethics, see William R. Baker, *Personal Speech-Ethics in the Epistle of James*, Wissenschaftliche Untersuchungen zum Neuen Testament 2/68 (Tübingen: Mohr Siebeck, 1995). The literature on James's wealth ethics is voluminous; among recent publications, see, e.g., Stephan Joubert, "*Homo reciprocus* No More: The 'Missional' Nature of Faith in James," in *Sensitivity towards Outsiders: Exploring the Dynamic Relationship between Mission and Ethics in the New Testament and Early Christianity*, ed. Jacobus (Kobus) Kok, Tobias Nicklas, Dieter T. Roth, and Christopher M. Hays, Wissenschaftliche Untersuchungen zum Neuen Testament 364 (Tübingen: Mohr Siebeck, 2014), 382–400; Kamell, "Economics of Humility"; Kamell, "James 1:27 and the Church's Call to Mission and Morals," *Crux* 46.4 (2010): 15–22.

Conclusion

If "mission" is understood with reference to God's agenda in the world, and not merely as an index of individual or churchly outreach on God's behalf, then "missional" refers more broadly to how the community of God's people comes to identify itself with, and to participate in, God's work. Accordingly, our agenda in this chapter has prioritized two questions: How does the letter of James locate its readers within the narrative of God's mission? How might James's letter shape its readers in their formation as participants in God's mission?

With the first question, we assumed that Scripture shapes (or ought to shape) the patterns by which we configure the world and seek to live in it. In addressing this question, though, I was especially interested in how the letter of James tells the grand story—or, perhaps better, how James locates and interprets his audience within that grand story. I also urged that the way James tells the story is critical to the formation of his audience's identity and, then, to the nature of their faithfulness in the world. This approach supported my claim that James invites reflection on what it means for the church to be a missionary outpost in a world whose patterns and conventions are out of step with God's mission.

With the second question, I hoped to underscore the importance of embodying the gospel as communities of God's people in the world. This led to my reiterating several key points from James's narrative map, apart from which such embodiment would be impossible and apart from which James's audience would be left with little more than humdrum abstractions. Even a so-called general epistle like James provides occasional warrants for particular forms of gospel life. Taking this route to an examination of James, we saw both that James's general interest in the internal life of certain communities of Jesus followers presented no obstacle to a missional reading and that the particular forms of embodiment counseled by James for his first-century audience continue to call for embodiment across the centuries. After all, until the Lord's coming, Jesus followers continue their diasporic existence: God's restored people awaiting restoration, their deepest allegiances and dispositions out of step with what matters most in the world within which they live, tempted to take matters into their own hands rather than trust God's goodness and leave judgment to him, called to think, feel, believe, and act like Jesus.

CHAPTER 11

A Missional Reading of Colossians

Dean Flemming

Despite a considerable interest in the missional reading of Scripture in recent years, there is still no consensus on what it looks like. Interpreters widely agree that it involves more than simply extracting "missionary texts" (e.g., Matt. 28:19–20; Acts 1:8; Rom. 10:14–15) from the biblical mine.[1] But what precisely is involved in missional interpretation is not easy to pin down. George R. Hunsberger helpfully maps four "streams" or approaches to missional hermeneutics, each representing a somewhat different emphasis.[2] The first stream reads Scripture as a witness to the gracious mission of the triune God, while the second asks how the biblical writings function to equip and energize God's people to participate in the *missio Dei.*

In contrast, the other two streams on Hunsberger's map shift the spotlight more to the reader and the context. The third shows particular interest in the missional location of the communities reading Scripture and the questions those communities bring to the text. The final stream emphasizes Scripture's missional engagement with different cultures and social contexts, in light of the Christ-centered gospel. Each of these four perspectives is relevant to a missional reading of Scripture, and they frequently overlap.

1. See David J. Bosch, "Reflections on Biblical Models of Mission," in *Toward the Twenty-First Century in Christian Mission: Essays in Honor of Gerald H. Anderson*, ed. James M. Phillips and Robert T. Coote (Grand Rapids: Eerdmans, 1993), 175–76.

2. George R. Hunsberger, "Proposals for a Missional Hermeneutic: Mapping the Conversation," *Missiology* 39 (2011): 309–21. Hunsberger's analysis emerges out of a series of annual meetings sponsored by GOCN. See also the discussion of various approaches to missional interpretation in Michael J. Gorman, *Becoming the Gospel: Paul, Participation, and Mission* (Grand Rapids: Eerdmans, 2015), 51–57.

For the purpose of this chapter, however, I am concerned primarily with the first two streams, which have to do with the missional character of the biblical text. For the most part, I reserve the question of how Scripture engages specific contexts today (streams three and four) for my concluding reflections. In this exploration, I use Paul's letter to the Colossians as a case study for reading Scripture missionally.

This chapter, then, reads Colossians first as a *witness* to the mission of God and the people who are caught up in that mission and, second, as an *instrument* of the *missio Dei*. At the same time, I want to show that a missional reading takes seriously how Paul contextualizes the gospel for his first-century audience, within their particular life circumstances.

The Missional Context

Paul writes as a missionary-pastor to a young Christian congregation in the Asian city of Colossae in the Lycus Valley.[3] Although Paul did not found this church (Col. 1:7; 2:1), he clearly situates it within the sphere of his ministry as apostle to the gentiles. His missional goal is for the Colossians to live as a mature, stable, missional community, faithful to the Christ they received (1:23–28; 2:6–7; 4:5–6).

Paul carries out that community-forming ministry in the face of a strong headwind—a deceptive teaching that bubbled up in Colossae.[4] This rival "philosophy" threatens to take captive the Colossian Christians (2:8) by offering them what Paul sees as a noxious substitute for the Christ-centered gospel. That much is clear. What is less clear is the precise nature of this alternative message and practice. Paul can assume the Colossians know full well what he is talking about, so he does not need to spell it out in detail. At most, he gives us tantalizing glimpses, primarily in the polemical section of Colossians 2:8–23.[5]

3. I take Paul as the likely author of this letter. For a recent defense of that position, see Nijay K. Gupta, *Colossians* (Macon, GA: Smith & Helwys, 2013), 3–10. In any case, Colossians is traditionally accepted as part of the Pauline writings by the church.

4. For this section, see the similar arguments in Dean Flemming, "Paul the Contextualizer," in *Local Theology for the Global Church: Principles for an Evangelical Approach to Contextualization*, ed. Matthew Cook, Robb Haskell, Ruth Julian, and Natee Tanchanpongs (Pasadena, CA: Carey, 2010), 2–3.

5. Derek Tidball, *In Christ, in Colossae: Sociological Perspectives on Colossians* (Milton Keynes: Paternoster, 2011), 60.

Not surprisingly, scholars offer a whole menu of possible backgrounds for the Colossian "philosophy."[6] It seems best, however, to understand the problem to which Paul responds as a kind of syncretistic stew combining different religious notions and practices.[7] This fits well with what is known about the local context of Phrygia in western Asia Minor. By the first century, local Phrygian culture and religion had become well integrated with Greek and Roman elements, including a medley of gods and goddesses and a thriving emperor cult. Thrown into the mix was a significant Jewish minority presence.[8] Furthermore, as Clinton Arnold shows, popular religion in Asia was thoroughly syncretistic. In particular, it featured an awareness of various spirit and astral powers that could threaten people's daily lives.[9] Added to that, ancient people felt they were at the mercy of fate, which was considered to exercise control over them, like a ship at the mercy of an unpredictable tempest.[10]

It is plausible, then, that the false teaching was offering to supplement the gospel of Christ with various means of helping people survive in an insecure world. These supplements probably included such things as observing taboos (2:21), ascetic practices (2:23), visionary experiences (2:18), and invoking angels (2:18). The philosophy also apparently borrowed certain practices from Judaism, such as rules about eating and drinking and observance of a sacred calendar (2:16), perhaps as a means to spiritual well-being. In addition, the letter's frequent references to "wisdom," "knowledge," "understanding," "mystery," and "fullness" may imply that the philosophy promised a deeper level of spiritual understanding and fulfillment than the Colossians could get through the faith they had been taught.

6. For a comprehensive treatment of the various options, see R. M. Wilson, *A Critical and Exegetical Commentary on Colossians and Philemon* (London/New York: T&T Clark, 2005), 35–78.

7. James D. G. Dunn argues that the Colossian "philosophy" was not syncretistic, but was rather a Jewish "apology" that promoted the distinctive religious practices of the Jews, such as circumcision and Sabbath observances; *The Epistles to the Colossians and to Philemon: A Commentary on the Greek Text* (Grand Rapids: Eerdmans, 1996), 29–35. The lack, however, of a polemic against law observance and circumcision such as we find in Galatians (the word "law" does not appear in Colossians) and the absence of Old Testament citations make this unlikely.

8. See Tidball, *In Christ, in Colossae*, 28–31.

9. See Clinton E. Arnold, *The Colossian Syncretism: The Interface between Christianity and Folk Belief at Colossae* (Grand Rapids: Baker, 1996), 234–44.

10. For references, see Charles H. Talbert, *Ephesians and Colossians* (Grand Rapids: Baker Academic, 2007), 18–19; cf. Walter T. Wilson, *The Hope of Glory: Education and Exhortation in the Epistle to the Colossians* (Leiden: Brill, 1997), 3–4.

Above all, Paul believes that this "human tradition" (2:8) degrades the role of Christ for his people. Perhaps the most scathing indictment in Colossians of the threat is that it is "not according to Christ" (2:8). Either directly or indirectly, the false teaching questioned the sufficiency of Christ to provide spiritual fulfillment and security in a world of unseen powers.[11]

In sum, the alternative approach that Paul counters probably represents a mixing of the Christian message with aspects of the practices, beliefs, and worldviews that inhabited the Colossians' cultural world. It is not hard to imagine such a syncretistic cocktail appealing to young converts who might have struggled to disentangle themselves fully from their former patterns of thought and behavior (2:20).

In any case, Paul's missional goals for the church in Colossae are not glued to any single interpretation of the letter's background. A more important question concerns how Paul responds to the threat of the rival teaching in Colossians. For the most part, his strategy is to reflect positively on the gospel of God's redemptive mission in Christ. He does so in language and categories that speak a fresh word for the circumstances of his audience. How, then, do Paul's targeted reflections to a church under pressure bear witness to the mission of God? And how do they contribute to Paul's missional goal of forming a mature Christian community in Colossae, a faith community that is equipped to participate in the gospel's growth and progress in the world (1:5–6)?

Colossians as a Witness to God's Mission

God's Mission and Creation

Most interpreters recognize that Christ is at the center of Paul's theological reflection in Colossians. However, Paul is not primarily interested in

11. For descriptions of the Colossian "philosophy" more or less along these basic lines, see Arnold, *Colossian Syncretism*, 228–44; Andrew T. Lincoln, "The Letter to the Colossians," in *The New Interpreter's Bible*, ed. L. E. Keck (Nashville: Abingdon, 2000), 11:560–68; Dean Flemming, *Contextualization in the New Testament: Patterns for Theology and Mission* (Downers Grove, IL: IVP Academic, 2005), 215–17; Douglas J. Moo, *The Letters to the Colossians and to Philemon* (Grand Rapids: Eerdmans, 2008), 46–60. For an alternative, highly stimulating attempt to read Colossians against a backdrop of Roman imperial ideology, see Brian J. Walsh and Sylvia C. Keesmaat, *Colossians Remixed: Subverting the Empire* (Downers Grove, IL: IVP Academic, 2004).

Christology as such, but rather in God's purpose to restore all things in Christ (Col. 1:20). To read Colossians *christologically*, one must also read it *missionally*. Colossians paints the narrative of God's mission in Christ with broad strokes on a cosmic canvas. This sweeping story "begins with God's creation of the world and aims at its final re-creation."[12] The lead character in this drama is Christ, who is supreme over all things (1:15–20; 2:9–10). This emphasis seems entirely appropriate, given that the rival teaching apparently questioned the sufficiency of Christ in regard to the worldly powers. Colossians trumpets the cosmic nature of Christ's role in creation and reconciliation in a way not seen in Paul's earlier correspondence. Whereas letters like Romans and Galatians show God's saving mission in Christ in relation to Abraham, Israel, and the Jewish law, Colossians shines a spotlight on Christ's relationship to the creation, the world, and the powers.[13]

God's purpose in Christ for creation is expressed above all in the magnificent "Christ hymn" of Colossians 1:15–20. Echoing the Wisdom traditions of the Old Testament and Hellenistic Judaism, this lyrical passage forms the theological backbone of the letter. The hymn sings praise to Christ as the supreme sovereign of both creation (1:15–18a) and redemption (1:18b–20). Paul's repeated use of the word "all" (*panta*) highlights God's comprehensive work in Christ in relation to the created order: "*all things* have been created through him" (1:16); and "through him God was pleased to reconcile to himself *all things*" (1:20). Christ is the *agent* of creation (*di' autou*, "through him"; 1:16), the sphere in which it takes place (*en autō*, "in him"; 1:16), the sustainer of God's created world ("in him all things hold together" 1:17), and creation's goal (*eis auton*, "for him"; 1:16). Christ is active in God's creative purpose from beginning to intended end.

This robust creation emphasis implies that God's mission begins with creation, not the fall. God has always had a purpose for "all things." This includes his creative and redemptive relationship to humanity, but it is certainly not limited to that. Behind the theology of the hymn stands the Old Testament understanding that God intends the whole of creation to bring him glory (e.g., Ps. 148; Isa. 6:3), and that God deeply values creation—enough to purpose in Christ not only to sustain it (Col. 1:17), but ultimately to redeem and restore it through the death of his Son (1:20).

A prominent feature of the poem in 1:15–20 is Christ's supremacy over

12. Marianne Meye Thompson, *Colossians and Philemon* (Grand Rapids: Eerdmans, 2005), 130.

13. Thompson, *Colossians and Philemon*, 148.

all of the powers that are active in the cosmos. That includes "things invisible," which Paul names as thrones, rulers, authorities, and powers (1:16). In Paul's world, these terms likely represent personal, cosmic powers.[14] Paul may be saying that Christ is sovereign over all created powers, good and bad. Colossians 1:20, however, views them as part of the "all things" that need to be reconciled, and in 2:15 Christ triumphs over them (cf. 1:13; 2:10). Consequently, Paul primarily sees these spiritual powers "as hostile and threatening to God's purposes in Christ."[15] Here Paul deflates the power of "the powers," by assuring the Colossians that such forces are simply part of the order created through and for Christ. The powers are "no match for their maker."[16]

What is more, God's purpose through Christ is "to reconcile to himself all things, whether in earth or in heaven" (1:20). God's creation is going somewhere. What God has already accomplished in the cross of Christ (1:20) will come to fulfillment in the end: God will restore his broken and alienated creation. This includes the transformation of all human relationships with God and one another; ultimately, it will include the renewal of the entire cosmos (cf. Eph. 1:10; Phil. 2:10).[17]

In Colossians, God's purpose of reconciling "all things" embraces not only the church (1:18), but even the cosmic powers that oppose it. For the latter, God's "making peace" (1:20) probably includes the thought of *pacifying* the powers by subjecting them to the lordship of Christ (cf. Phil. 2:10–11). Such an understanding surely would ring bells for inhabitants of a Roman world that teemed with the empire's notions of peace. For Rome, global peace, the *Pax Romana*, was secured by brute force, the subduing of the empire's enemies.[18] But peacemaking in Colossians subverts the claims of Rome: "Christ's way of pacifying his enemies is not with the mighty machines of imperial glory. Instead it comes by means of a lowly and shameful crucifixion—'through the blood of his cross' (1:20)."[19]

Paul also uses the language of the "image" (*eikōn*) of God to express God's re-creative purpose. The hymn announces that Christ "is the image

14. See Eph. 1:20–21; 3:10; 6:12; 1 Enoch 61:10; 2 Enoch 20:1; Testament of Levi 3:8. For these and other references, see Arnold, *Colossian Syncretism*, 253–55.

15. Lincoln, "Letter to the Colossians," 598.

16. Talbert, *Ephesians and Colossians*, 191; cf. Flemming, *Contextualization in the New Testament*, 220–21.

17. Thompson, *Colossians and Philemon*, 114.

18. See Thompson, *Colossians and Philemon*, 196–97.

19. Flemming, "Paul the Contextualizer," 6; cf. Peter T. O'Brien, *Colossians, Philemon* (Waco, TX: Word, 1982), 56.

of the invisible God" (1:15). Even as humanity was created in the "image of God" (Gen. 1:27), Christ perfectly represents God in the visible, human sphere. At the same time, Paul can picture God's people as a new humanity, "which is being renewed in knowledge according to the image of its creator" (Col. 3:10). Christ offers both the pattern for humanity's renewal into God's image and the means by which it happens. Gordon Fee summarizes well the connection between Colossians 1:15 and 3:10: "The Creator of the first creation, who himself bears the Father's image, now is seen as the Creator of the new creation, as he restores his own people back into the divine image—that is, into his own image that he alone perfectly bears."[20]

Finally, in view of God's loving mission to reconcile all things through the cross of Christ (1:20), Paul makes the breathtaking claim that the gospel "has been proclaimed in all creation [*en pasē ktisei*] under heaven" (1:23 English Standard Version). Most commentators limit this statement to something like a hyperbolic reflection on the universal preaching of the gospel "to every [human] *creature* everywhere" (cf. 1:6).[21] But given the use of the term *ktisis* ("creation") in Colossians 1:15 (cf. Rom. 1:20; 8:19–22), it is likely that Paul has in view a wider horizon. "If Christ is Lord of all creation (Col. 1:15–17), then the telling of the gospel carries transforming effects to the entire created order—from stars to starfish, from gulls to glaciers."[22] Paul assures his readers that the hope promised by the gospel is cosmic in its scope (1:23). The gospel, as Christopher J. H. Wright puts it, "is good news for *all* creation."[23]

God's Mission and Redemption

If Colossians celebrates God's mission to reclaim the whole of creation, then the focus of that work concerns what God is doing in Christ to redeem his

20. Gordon D. Fee, *Pauline Christology: An Exegetical-Theological Study* (Peabody, MA: Hendrickson, 2007), 522.

21. E.g., Jerry L. Sumney, *Colossians: A Commentary* (Louisville: Westminster John Knox, 2008), 88.

22. Dean Flemming, *Recovering the Full Mission of God: A Biblical Perspective on Being, Doing, and Telling* (Downers Grove, IL: IVP Academic, 2013), 166; cf. N. T. Wright, *Colossians and Philemon* (Grand Rapids: Eerdmans, 1986), 85; David W. Pao, *Colossians and Philemon* (Grand Rapids: Zondervan, 2012), 110.

23. Christopher J. H. Wright, *The Mission of God's People: A Biblical Theology of the Church's Mission* (Grand Rapids: Zondervan, 2010), 198.

people, the church.[24] But *how* Paul articulates God's saving work is distinctive and tailored to the context. From the perspective of the rival teaching, Christ's work on behalf of the believers in Colossae was apparently deficient and unable to provide spiritual fullness and well-being. Paul responds by assuring his audience that Christ is not only *supreme*, but also wholly *sufficient* for their present experience of salvation.

Colossians, then, gives special weight to the present fullness of salvation that God's people have received in Christ. Not surprisingly, the story of God's redeeming mission that Colossians tells centers on the death and resurrection of Christ as saving events. As he does in Romans, in Colossians Paul affirms that God's people participate in the drama of Jesus's dying and rising (Col. 2:12–13; 3:1–4; cf. Rom. 6:3–14; 8:11, 17). But the shape of that participation looks somewhat different here. Whereas Romans affirms that Christians *have* died with Christ and that they *will be* raised with him in the future (Rom. 6:7–8; 8:11; but see 6:4b), Colossians dares to claim even more for their present redemption in Christ. Not only were they buried with him in baptism (Col. 2:12), but they *already* have been raised with Christ to a new heavenly life (2:12–13; 3:1).

Has Paul, then, cut the line of tension between the "already" and the "not yet" of salvation in favor of its present realization? That does not seem to be the case. Colossians retains a robust hope in the future that awaits God's people (1:5, 22, 23, 27, 28; 3:4, 24). Nevertheless, Paul's particular emphasis on the "now" of salvation in this letter offers a word that his audience needs to hear. By presently sharing in Christ's resurrection, they also enjoy the fullness of his resurrection life and power (2:12–13; 3:3–4; cf. 2:9–10).

Paul draws on a gallery of images that unpack the present meaning of Christ's death and resurrection for the Colossians, many of which speak directly into their situation. For example, he assures them that God has already rescued them from the dominion of darkness and has transferred them into the kingdom of his beloved Son (1:13). Here Paul recontextualizes Old Testament language that describes Israel's deliverance from bondage in Egypt ("rescue" in 1:13; "redemption" in 1:14). For the Colossians, it announces God's power to liberate his people from the enslaving powers of sin and darkness through Christ (cf. 2:20: "with Christ you died to the elemental spirits of the universe").

Paul again takes up the theme of God's victory over the powers in

24. For this section, see the similar and more extensive arguments in Flemming, *Contextualization in the New Testament*, 223–27.

Christ at the climax of his theological argument in 2:8–15. Three striking images interpret the meaning of Jesus's death in 2:15. In the cross of Christ, God "disarmed the rulers and authorities," stripping them of their power; he made a public spectacle of them, exposing them as weak and worthless, for all to see; and he "triumphed over them." This final metaphor asks the readers to imagine the familiar triumphal procession, in which a victorious Roman general led his defeated captives through the city in full public view. The audacity of such images could not have been lost on Paul's audience. According to all normal standards of judgment, it was *Christ*, not the powers, who was stripped, shamed, and vanquished, when a cross was raised on Golgotha. But Colossians flips such cultural expectations on their head. As N. T. Wright memorably frames it, "The cross was not the defeat of *Christ* at the hand of the powers: it was the defeat of the powers at the hands—yes, the bleeding hands—of Christ."[25] From the perspective of Colossians, God dealt a death blow to the powers in Jesus's death and resurrection. This victory is part of the working out of God's restoration of all things in Christ, through the cross (1:20).

But liberation from the powers alone does not exhaust the present significance of God's redeeming work in Christ in Colossians. Christ's death brought them forgiveness of sins (1:14; 2:13; 3:13), the canceling of the debt incurred by their transgressions (2:14), and a "spiritual circumcision" of the heart (2:11; cf. Deut. 10:16; 30:6; Jer. 4:4; Ezek. 44:7).[26] Paul also applies the *reconciliation* language of the Christ poem directly to the church. God has already begun the work of restoring all things to himself (Col. 1:20) by reconciling the Colossians through the nailing of Christ's body to the cross (1:21–22). Once they were estranged from God and hostile in attitude; now, God has restored them to fellowship so that they might reflect God's holiness.

The army of images that Paul uses to portray the meaning of Christ's death for the Colossians carries two implications. First, it shows the breadth and richness of Paul's understanding of the cross; and, second, it demonstrates how he tailors his reading of Jesus's death to the needs and concerns of his audience.

Christ's *resurrection* plays an equally important role in Paul's witness

25. N. T. Wright, *Following Jesus: Biblical Reflections on Discipleship* (Grand Rapids: Eerdmans, 1994), 19.

26. On the meaning of Col. 2:11, see Moo, *Colossians and Philemon*, 196–200; Michael F. Bird, *Colossians, Philemon* (Eugene, OR: Cascade, 2009), 78–79.

to God's mission in Colossians. As I noted earlier, Paul accents the Colossians' present participation in God's raising Christ, more than he does the promise of resurrection in the future. At the same time, Christ's resurrection remains part of a bigger story. As Marianne Meye Thompson wisely notes, "What God did for Christ in raising him from the dead to new life, God will do for all the world."[27]

The Colossians, then, await the final act in the drama of God's mission. They can embrace a forward-looking *hope*, kept for them in heaven (1:5), promised in the gospel (1:23), and belonging to the reality of future glory (1:27; cf. 3:4). They both *participate* in the blessings of salvation now and *anticipate* the full inheritance to come, when Christ will be revealed (3:4, 24).[28] But in the shadow of that glorious hope lies the reality of judgment. Colossians issues a somber warning that those who persist in idolatry and disobedience, those who refuse to serve the creator and lord of all things, will, in the end, face God's righteous judgment (3:6, 23).

The Gospel, the Apostle, and God's Mission

For Paul, God's mission is bound up with the gospel—its proclamation and its embodiment in God's people. Paul weaves language about the gospel and the message about Christ throughout the letter like a golden thread.[29] At the outset, he reminds the Colossian believers that their hope lies in "the word of truth, the gospel" (1:5; cf. 1:23). Most likely, this phrase implies a contrast with the rival message, which, if left unchecked, would disfigure the genuine gospel of Christ like a powerful acid. Paul draws on an assortment of terms to speak about the gospel in Colossians, including "the word" (4:3); "the word of God" (1:25) and "the word of Christ" (3:16); "the faith" (1:23; 2:7); and "the truth" (1:5). All of these terms describe the message that God's people have received about what God has graciously done in Christ. But the gospel is more than a mere truth to be believed. It is a living and dynamic power that grows and produces fruit, both in the lives of the Colossians and throughout the whole world (1:5–6).

Especially striking is Paul's identification of the gospel as the "mystery" (*mystērion*) of Christ (1:26–27; 2:2; 4:3), a mystery formerly concealed,

27. Thompson, *Colossians and Philemon*, 113.

28. Thompson, *Colossians and Philemon*, 20–21.

29. Moo, *Colossians and Philemon*, 67.

but now revealed to the saints (1:26). It is widely agreed that Paul's use of this language arises from a Jewish apocalyptic context. Nevertheless, the term also held ties to the secretive pagan mystery cults of Paul's world. Gentile converts surely would have recognized that connection; it is even possible that some Christians in Colossae had a background in the cults related to local deities.[30] Even so, Paul risks taking over language that carries considerable baggage within the Greco-Roman world, and he redefines it in light of the gospel. This mystery represents God's great purpose to include the gentiles in his salvation plan, a purpose centered in the indwelling Christ, the "hope of glory" (1:26–27). The Colossians should give up the search for any form of higher spiritual truth or secret wisdom, because "all the treasures of wisdom and knowledge" are hidden in Christ, the true mystery of God (2:2–3).

As an apostle by God's will (1:1), Paul himself becomes an actor in the drama of God's saving mission in the world. Colossians 1:23–2:5 illuminates the apostle's own involvement with the gospel. Paul carries a divine commission to proclaim and teach Christ among the gentiles (1:25, 27–28). He ministers under God's authority, as a "servant" (*diakonos*) of the gospel and the church (1:23, 25). But Paul's gospel mission also involves suffering and struggle on behalf of Christ (1:24, 29; 2:1; 4:3, 18). In this regard, Paul makes the quite stunning claim in 1:24: "I am completing what is lacking in Christ's afflictions for the sake of his body, that is, the church." It is possible that this much-debated statement points to Paul's sharing in the so-called messianic birth pangs (Gal. 4:19), the sufferings that, according to Jewish texts, would precede the arrival of the messianic age (Dan. 7:21–27; 12:1; Jub. 23:13; 2 Ezra 4:36–37; 13:16–19). Thompson thus argues that "Paul's participation in these afflictions signals that as a messenger of God's decisive salvation in Christ, he suffers the afflictions that are associated with the decisive eschatological or end-time events."[31]

But if Paul makes use of a traditional Jewish expectation, he recasts it in a distinctively Christian and missional mold. Paul can rejoice in his suffering (Col. 1:24), because those afflictions become a means of participating in the sufferings of Christ (cf. Gal. 6:17; 2 Cor. 1:5; 4:10–11; Phil. 3:10). By sharing in Christ's sufferings, Paul embodies the gospel he proclaims, the gospel of Jesus crucified and risen. Paul's sufferings give that gospel a bodily, visible presence in the world. Paul's apostolic suffering, then, fills up

30. See Arnold, *Colossian Syncretism*, 272.

31. Thompson, *Colossians and Philemon*, 45.

"what is lacking," in that it becomes a means of extending Christ's redemptive work, accomplished on the cross, in the world. As a result, God uses Paul's suffering to bring spiritual life to others (Col. 1:24; 2:1; cf. 2 Cor. 1:6; 4:12; Eph. 3:13). Paul's "struggle" (Col. 1:29; 2:1) is therefore a real part of his mission as an apostle of Christ crucified.

However, it is not just that Paul sees himself and his gospel ministry to be part of God's great purpose to restore all things in Christ: he also wants the Colossians to find *their* place in the same story and so live as fruitful participants in that grand narrative. This brings us to a second key aspect of a missional reading of Colossians. How does this letter shape and equip God's people to share in the *missio Dei*?

Colossians as an Instrument of God's Mission

Mission and Christian Formation

As with all the Pauline letters, Colossians serves as an extension of Paul's God-given apostolic and gospel ministry. This assumes that Paul's missionary work as an "apostle of Christ Jesus" (1:1) is not confined to initial evangelizing and planting new communities of believers. The aim of Paul's mission in regard to the Colossians is that they remain stable and firmly established in the faith (1:23). God commissioned him on their behalf "to fulfill the word of God" (*plērōsai ton logon tou theou*; 1:25 King James Version). It is likely that this phrase refers to more than simply Paul's fulfilling the task of preaching the gospel among them. Rather, Paul desires that the word of God should accomplish the full purpose that God intends for it. The word is fulfilled when it bears fruit among the Colossians and brings about a strong and growing community of believers (cf. Rom. 15:19).[32] What Paul implies in Colossians 1:25 he states openly in 1:28: "It is [Christ] we proclaim, warning everyone and teaching everyone in all wisdom, *so that we may present everyone mature in Christ*" (emphasis added). Christian formation, then, is essential to Paul's missionary calling.[33] Indeed, this letter functions as a vital tool of Paul's mission in Colossae.

32. Moo, *Colossians and Philemon*, 154–55; cf. Paul Bowers, "'Fulfilling the Gospel': The Scope of the Pauline Mission," *Journal of the Evangelical Theological Society* 30 (1987): 193–95.

33. See Michael Barram, "The Bible, Mission, and Social Location: Toward a Missional Hermeneutic," *Interpretation* 61 (2007): 53–57; David G. Peterson, "Maturity: The Goal of

An Identity to Embody

Paul's witness, then, to the superiority and sufficiency of Christ in Colossians bears a particular focus: the forming of a faithful, mature, missional community in Colossae. Consequently, Paul seeks to shape his hearers' imaginations so that they can live into their true Christian identity. That identity is precisely what is at stake in Colossae. The syncretistic philosophy may sound attractive, but it represents a dangerous substitute for the gospel they received. It lures them into ways of thinking and acting that are "not according to Christ" (2:8).

A Community "in Christ"

Paul therefore repeatedly reminds his audience of who they are "in Christ." This begins with the letter's opening address. Paul identifies his audience as "the saints and faithful brothers and sisters in Christ in Colossae" (1:2).[34] As God's "holy ones" (*hagioi*), they are called and set apart to belong to God in a special way. At the same time, God set them apart in order to *be* a holy people, reflecting God's holiness in their distinctive character and conduct (cf. 1:21). Using similar language, Paul calls them "God's chosen ones, holy and beloved" (3:12). This is their identity: they already *are* God's holy and beloved community, by virtue of their relationship with God. But as the following verses on the Christian lifestyle make clear, they must intentionally live into that identity (3:12–17).

Paul's salutation also reminds them of *where* they are: they are both "in Christ" and "in Colossae" (1:2). To say that the Colossians are "in Christ" locates them in the sphere of Christ, the realm of God's beloved Son (1:13). Over and over in Colossians, Paul identifies the church as being "in Christ" or "in him" (1:2, 4, 14, 28; 2:5, 6, 7, 10, 11), "with Christ" (2:12; 3:1, 3), or "in the Lord" (3:18, 20; 4:7, 17; cf. 1:27: "Christ in you"). Although they live out their Christian calling "in Colossae" (1:2), their primary identity and existence is determined by their life in union with Christ and under his lordship. Later Paul describes them as "hidden with Christ in God" (3:3), a place of inti-

---

Mission," in *The Gospel to the Nations: Perspectives on Paul's Mission*, ed. Peter Bolt and Mark Thompson (Downers Grove, IL: InterVarsity, 2000), 185–204.

34. I prefer to take "saints" (*hagiois*) as a noun, rather than as an adjective ("to the holy and faithful brothers"), in light of the use of the term "saints" in other Pauline salutations (Rom. 1:7; 1 Cor. 1:2; 2 Cor. 1:1; Eph. 1:1; Phil. 1:1).

mate connection to the life of Christ. In Colossians, this astounding claim means that they "are united with the one who holds the universe together, in whom it was created, and through whom it will be redeemed."[35] And because the church is "in Christ," it is drawn into God's purpose to redeem and reconcile the world through Jesus the Messiah.

The Body of Christ

In part, Paul answers the question "who are we?" by inviting his audience to envision themselves as Christ's body (2:24). Christ is not only lord of creation (1:15–17), but he is also "head of the body, the church" (1:18). Here the church represents more than a local congregation in Asia. "Set in a cosmic context," notes Andrew Lincoln, "Christ's body in Colossians is seen as a universal phenomenon."[36] The church enjoys a unique, organic relationship with Christ, its head. As such, it stands as a sign and foretaste of God's purpose to reconcile the entire cosmos. Furthermore, Christ's headship means that Christ is both lord over the body and the one who gives it life. Christ nourishes the church and causes it to grow "with a growth that is from God" (2:19).

The growth of the church becomes a key theme in Colossians. Paul prays that his hearers might "bear fruit in every good work" and "grow in the knowledge of God" (1:10). The goal of that growth is Christian maturity (2:28; 3:14; 4:12) and a deeply rooted faith (2:7; cf. 2:5). Only a mature, growing, and stable church can, on the one hand, resist the appeal of the false philosophy and, on the other, participate in God's great restoring purpose for the world.

A Global, Multinational Community

One way that Paul energizes the church to participate in God's mission is to remind them that they are part of something much bigger than themselves. Near the beginning of the letter, he thanks God that the same gospel that continues to grow and flourish throughout the world is bearing fruit in the lives of the believers in Colossae, from the time they first received it (1:5–6).

35. Thompson, *Colossians and Philemon*, 125.
36. Lincoln, "Letter to the Colossians," 575.

They are caught up in the universal progress of a gospel that is not fenced in by geographic or ethnic barriers.

The Colossians are therefore part of a new humanity, which transcends and relativizes the distinctions that divided the old humanity. The tide of God's new creation swept away the old order of relationships: "There is no Greek and Jew, circumcised and uncircumcised, barbarian, Scythian, slave and free, but Christ is all and in all" (3:11). Jesus's reconciliation of "all things" (1:20) includes the dismantling of every barricade to genuine human community, whether racial, national, social, or cultural. Paul's audience must imagine a humanity that is stunningly different from what is normal in their social world. The categories that marked out Jewish distinctiveness and superiority—"Greek and Jew, circumcised and uncircumcised"—no longer apply. The same is true of terms like "barbarian" and "Scythian," which some gentiles used in order to look down their noses at non-Greeks.

Likewise, the social status of Christians—whether slave or free—gives way in light of the church's primary relationship to Christ (3:11). Roman legal codes insisted that slaves belonged to their human masters; but in the new humanity, slaves and slave owners are equally enslaved to the Lord Christ (3:25).[37] The church's identity, then, as a multiethnic, unified community, becomes an embodiment of the gospel, which announces God's peacemaking purpose in Christ (1:19–22; 3:15).

A Lifestyle to Practice

Christ's Lordship and Christian Conduct

In Colossians, the Christian lifestyle is anchored in both God's redemptive mission in Christ and the church's identity in Christ. The same Christ who is lord over the cosmos and the church (Col. 1:15–20; 2:19) is also lord over the Christian's daily life in the world. The new life, then, becomes a response to the lordship of Christ and his victory over the powers. Paul prays that the church would "walk in a manner worthy of the Lord" (1:10 English Standard Version). Even as they received Jesus as lord, they must "continue to live [their] lives in him" (2:6).

In particular, Jesus's death and resurrection serve as the pattern for

37. Thompson, *Colossians and Philemon*, 96.

appropriate Christian conduct in the world. Nowhere is this more visible than in Colossians 3:1–4. In these verses we find a christological foundation for Paul's instructions about Christian living in 3:5–4:6. "Paul calls the Colossians to a new moral vision, one that is determined by their solidarity with the triumphant and exalted Lord and their experience of dying and rising with him."[38] As a result, they must "seek the things above," trading in an earthly perspective for a heavenly one (3:1, 2, 5). Paul invites them to embrace a counterimagination, a new way of seeing the world. The story of Christ, his death, resurrection, exaltation, and return (3:1–4), not only grounds their salvation, but also shapes their Christian formation and conduct.

Paul's ethical instructions in Colossians 3:5–4:6 unpack what cruciform and resurrection behavior looks like in concrete settings.[39] Because they have died with Christ (3:3), they must therefore "put to death" the destructive and idolatrous patterns that characterized their old life in league with the powers of darkness (3:5–11; cf. 1:13). And since they are raised with Christ, who reigns triumphant over sin and the powers, the church embodies that victory through its obedient daily conduct. What is more, Paul's list of virtues (3:12–17) spotlights attitudes and behavior that reflect the cruciform love of Christ: compassion, kindness, humility, gentleness, patience, forgiveness, and peace. The focus throughout this section falls on interpersonal relationships within the body (e.g., 3:13, 15). However, the virtue list reaches a rousing climax in 3:17, in which Paul urges the church to do "everything," whether in word (*logos*) or deed, under the lordship of Christ. Does this include behavior toward those outside the church? That seems likely, given the parallel between what Christians say and do in 3:17 and Paul's concern for Christian speech (*logos*) and behavior in relation to outsiders in 4:5–6. The working out of Christ's lordship in the whole of life includes the church's witness—via word and deed—to unbelievers.

Christ's Lordship and the Christian Household

Colossians 3:18–4:1 explores how Christians live out their new identity within the basic relationships of their social world—as wives and husbands,

38. Flemming, *Contextualization in the New Testament*, 227.

39. On resurrection behavior, see Michael Barram, "Colossians 3:1–17," *Interpretation* 59 (2005): 188–90.

children and parents, slaves and masters.[40] Paul's instructions to members of the Christian household (a so-called household code) need to be seen against the backdrop of the wider culture. This kind of moral teaching has numerous parallels in the ancient world and would no doubt strike familiar chords with Paul's audience.[41] What's more, it advocates an ethic that has much in common with contemporary standards in Paul's world. Does this household code, then, simply fix a stamp of approval on the traditional patriarchal values of the dominant culture?

That conclusion fails to account for the internal *difference* between these instructions and conventional Greco-Roman morality. Three factors bring this to light. The first relates to the passage's function in the context of the letter. In the verses leading up to this section, Paul insists that the church represents a new humanity, which transforms all social relationships (3:10–11), and where love governs every human interaction (3:14). In particular, the household relationships in 3:18–4:1 concretely illustrate what it means to do "everything" in the name of the risen and reigning Lord (3:17).

Second, whereas instructions from Aristotle and others tended to protect the interests of the household powerbrokers—husbands, fathers, and masters—Paul's exhortations are striking in their reciprocity. Women, children, and even slaves are treated as morally responsible persons, and limitations are placed on those holding the reins of power.

Third, the passage bristles with references to "the Lord" (3:18, 20, 22, 23, 24). Especially noteworthy is Paul's assurance to slaves that, by working for their earthly masters, they are actually serving their heavenly Lord (3:23–24). This "Lord" language functions as more than an effort to affix a thin Christian veneer on a thoroughly pagan convention. Rather, Paul gives ordinary household relationships a distinctive motivation and character.[42] Thompson's conclusion is compelling: "It is simply impossible to live on the model of Jesus Christ within the structures of society and to leave the relationships within them fundamentally unchanged."[43]

Paul's strategy is not to campaign against the power structures of the

40. See the similar arguments to the following in Flemming, "Paul the Contextualizer," 14–15.

41. See Dunn, *Colossians and Philemon*, 243, for references to various ancient parallels to the New Testament household codes. Dunn rightly cautions, however, that there is no standard form of "household code" in the ancient world (243–44).

42. See James P. Hering, *The Colossian and Ephesian Haustafeln in Theological Context: An Analysis of Their Origins, Relationship, and Message* (New York: Peter Lang, 2007), 76–78.

43. Thompson, *Colossians and Philemon*, 94.

Roman world, such as slavery. Surely, as a marginalized and minority community within a dominant Roman culture, the church has no platform from which to make wholesale changes in the social structure. Instead, Paul's missional approach seeks to engage the culture in transforming ways from within. As Ben Witherington III argues, Paul envisions Christians living out their calling within social institutions like the ancient household, even as they embody a visible, internal difference. Over time, the yeast of the gospel would do its work.[44]

Unlike 1 Peter, Colossians does not explicitly address the situation of Christians who are wives or slaves of unbelievers (1 Pet. 2:18–3:6; cf. 1 Tim. 6:1–2). Nevertheless, Paul's instructions do not preclude such a scenario. Furthermore, Margaret MacDonald perceptively wonders "whether the detailed exhortation to slaves may have been inspired at least in part by the difficulties caused by the membership of slaves whose masters were nonbelievers."[45] In this case, the integrity of Christian slaves' conduct toward their human masters becomes part of their service to Christ (Col. 3:22–24) and, thereby, their wise conduct toward outsiders (4:5).

Prayer and Thanksgiving

Colossians also highlights the missional role of prayer and thanksgiving. At the outset of the letter, Paul assures the church of his unceasing prayer and thanksgiving for them (1:3, 9). In particular, he expresses gratitude for God's effective work among them (1:3–8) and prays for their continued growth and fruitfulness (1:9–14). Later, Paul reports that Epaphras, the church's founder, "is always wrestling in his prayers on your behalf, so that you may stand mature and fully assured in everything that God wills" (4:12). The prayers and thanksgiving of Paul and his coworkers serve as key instruments of God's missional purpose to form a mature and fruitful community.[46]

At the same time, Paul urges the Colossians to pray and give thanks (4:2; cf. 1:12; 3:15–17; 2:7), including as a means of sharing in his missionary

44. Ben Witherington III, *The Paul Quest: The Renewed Search for the Jew of Tarsus* (Downers Grove, IL: IVP Academic, 1998), 202.

45. Margaret Y. MacDonald, *Colossians and Philemon* (Collegeville, MN: Michael Glazier/Liturgical Press, 2000), 162. Jerry L. Sumney makes a similar suggestion, based on the sociological makeup of Pauline communities; *Colossians*, 234.

46. See Teresa Okure, "'In Him All Things Hold Together': A Missiological Reading of Colossians 1:15–20," *International Review of Mission* 91 (2002): 65.

work. By interceding, asking that God will "open a door" for Paul faithfully to declare the gospel (4:3), these Christians participate in the mission of God, in partnership with Paul (see Phil. 1:5). It is in this light that we should read Paul's closing appeal to the church: "Remember my chains" (Col. 4:18). This amounts to a final invitation to intercede on his behalf, in effect, "a call for the believers to participate with Paul for the sake of the gospel."[47]

A Message to Proclaim

Near the end of Paul's exhortations about the Christian lifestyle in 3:5–4:6, he turns explicitly to the question of how God's people should relate to unbelievers: "Conduct yourselves wisely toward outsiders, making the most of the time. Let your speech always be gracious, seasoned with salt, so that you may know how you ought to answer everyone" (4:5–6).

A number of missional implications emerge from these verses.[48] First, Paul forges a vital link between a witness of word and a witness of life. He begins by urging Christians to conduct themselves wisely (literally, "walk in wisdom") toward nonbelievers. Paul often calls God's people to live their lives in ways that are magnetic and attractive toward outsiders (e.g., Rom. 12:17; 16:19; 1 Thess. 3:12; 5:15; Titus 2:9–10). Here, walking wisely "means they are to act in a way that is cognizant of who is watching and of the impact their behavior may have for the gospel."[49]

Such engagement with unbelievers carries a sense of urgency and purpose: "Make the most of every opportunity" (literally, "buying back the time"; Col. 4:5). It follows, then, that part of what it means for Christians to walk wisely toward outsiders and to squeeze the importance out of every critical opportunity involves speaking graciously (4:6).[50] Paul envisions a mission in which word and walk are one (cf. "word or deed" in 3:17).

Second, this passage comes hard on the heels of Paul's appeal that the Colossians pray for his own missionary work (4:3–4). Paul's desire that God

47. Pao, *Colossians and Philemon*, 323.

48. See Flemming, *Recovering the Full Mission of God*, 197–98.

49. Ben Witherington III, *The Letters to Philemon, the Colossians, and the Ephesians: A Socio-Rhetorical Commentary on the Captivity Epistles* (Grand Rapids: Eerdmans, 2007), 199.

50. Although the participial phrase "buying back the time" (*ton kairon exagorazomenoi*) in 4:5 is grammatically tied to the command "conduct yourselves wisely," conceptually it relates both to the preceding command and to Paul's instructions about speech in 4:6. For the language of "squeezing the importance out of every moment," see Gupta, *Colossians*, 188.

would open the door for him to speak the "word" (*logos*; 4:3) parallels the Colossians' gracious "speech" (*logos*; 4:6) toward outsiders. In both cases, the spoken word is "necessary" (*dei*) and plays a vital role in their witness to the gospel.[51] But there is also a difference. Whereas Paul directly seeks to proclaim "the mystery of Christ" (4:3), the church's speech focuses on answering the questions or objections of unbelievers (4:6; cf. 1 Pet. 3:15–16). Here Paul pictures the congregation's witness less in terms of overt proclamation than of responding to outsiders in the course of ordinary conversations. Moreover, their reply should fit the dialogue partner and the occasion. They ought to know how to answer, literally, "each one" (*heni hekastō*; Col. 4:6).

Third, Paul assumes that Christians will engage unbelievers in the public square (cf. 1 Cor. 5:10). This passage does not picture a "navel-gazing" community, safely tucked away in pious isolation. Rather, Paul envisions a Christian community that is "expected to hold its own in the social setting of marketplace, baths, and meal table and to win attention by the attractiveness of its life and speech."[52]

What kinds of questions would believers encounter? We might imagine associates or family members asking why these Christ followers no longer participated in meals at pagan temples that honored the local deities and the emperor. Perhaps unbelieving friends probed as to why Christians' social habits and sexual practices had so dramatically changed. At times, these queries may have been unsympathetic or even hostile, prompted by Christian behavior that swam against the current of the culture.[53] Once again, word and behavior are inseparable. The passage assumes that when God's people live lives that prompt questions, opportunities for verbal witness will follow.

Fourth, whether in the form of defense or of invitation, the church's responses to unbelievers should always be gracious (literally, "with grace"; Col. 4:6). Such speech is winsome, edifying, and attractive. Moreover, it is "seasoned with salt"—lively and sprinkled with wisdom, not bland and dull. At the same time, Paul's mention of "grace" (*charis*; 4:6) contains an echo of the grace that God freely gives to the church (1:2, 6; 4:18). The same grace that opens doors for Paul to bear witness to the good news will also enable God's people to give an appropriate, gracious response to each person who questions them. In contrast to a rival teaching that promoted ascetic practices and

51. Thompson, *Colossians and Philemon*, 101.

52. Dunn, *Colossians and Philemon*, 267.

53. As Jerry L. Sumney argues, "the immediately preceding reference to Paul's imprisonment for the gospel" lends support to the unfriendly nature of at least some of the questions Paul envisions; *Colossians*, 263.

individual wisdom and experiences, Paul turns the community's focus outward, toward a gracious witness of word and life within their social world.[54]

Reading Colossians as Missional Communities

A missional reading of Colossians is concerned not only with Paul's desire to form a mature, missional congregation in Colossae, but also with how this letter can *continue* to equip Christian communities to participate in God's mission today. I conclude with some reflections on how that might begin to happen.

Understanding Our Place in the Drama of God's Mission

The breathtaking vision in Colossians of God's mission to restore all things in Christ continues to shape the church in mission today. Like the early Christians of the Lycus Valley, we too must find our part as active players in that saving drama. God has already begun his restoring work in the world in and through the church. Liberated by God from the dominion of darkness, the church bears witness to the fullness of life under the lordship of Christ and, with thanksgiving, participates in God's great purpose to reconcile all things to himself.

Unfortunately, we have often settled for a much squintier vision of God's mission and the church's role in it. If we shrink the concern of the *missio Dei* to simply a matter of saving individual souls so that they are ready for heaven, we lose the grand sweep of the story that spans from creation to new creation. We miss God's intention *fully* to renew persons and Christian communities in his loving image and to break down all barriers that divide (3:10–11). We ignore God's missional purpose for all of creation, as well as people. In short, we veer "off mission."

Practicing a Robust Mission

Colossians offers us a rich and integrated notion of the church's participation in the *missio Dei*. Paul's witness to his own mission includes gospel

54. Gupta, *Colossians*, 189.

proclamation, Christian formation, intercessory prayer, and even suffering for the sake of others. Similarly, Paul envisions a church engaged in a seamless mission of word and life (4:5–6), which flows out of who they *are* as a new humanity in Christ. At the same time, the *manner* of our mission as God's people must be consistent with the message. Cruciform love shapes the character of "whatever we do" in service to Christ (3:17; cf. 1:8; 2:2; 3:1–14). We must *become* the gospel of the crucified one, if our message hopes to ring with authenticity in our world.[55]

What is more, if God is on a mission to restore the whole of creation in Christ (1:15–20), then surely creation care becomes a vital aspect of the church's participation in that mission. As Christopher J. H. Wright points out, "Holistic mission . . . is not truly holistic if it includes only human beings (even if it includes them holistically) and excludes the rest of creation for whose reconciliation Christ shed his blood (Col. 1:20)."[56] Surely reading Colossians missionally will lead us to see the church's calling to creation-care as an indispensable witness to Christ's lordship over all creation, as well as a foretaste of the new creation to come.

Contextualizing the Gospel

Paul's message to the Christ followers in Colossae models how the gospel can speak to fresh and challenging circumstances in context-sensitive ways.[57] Paul responds to a potentially explosive situation with both firmness and flexibility. On the one hand, "the word of truth, the gospel" (1:5) cannot sit comfortably with syncretistic substitutes. Matters such as Christ's unique supremacy, his sole sufficiency for salvation, and his lordship over all of human life remain nonnegotiable. But, at the same time, Paul's articulation of the gospel and its implications shows remarkable sensitivity to his audience and their context. Colossians does not deploy the same language, images, or theological arguments as we find, say, in Galatians or 1 Corinthians. Rather, Paul enables the abiding word of the gospel to come to life in fresh ways that address the worldviews, felt needs, and misperceptions of the Colossians.

55. See Gorman, *Becoming the Gospel.*

56. Christopher J. H. Wright, *The Mission of God: Unlocking the Bible's Grand Narrative* (Downers Grove, IL: IVP Academic, 2006), 416.

57. For this section, see the similar arguments in Flemming, "Paul the Contextualizer," 15–16, 18. For a broader exploration of New Testament precedents for contextualization, see Flemming, *Contextualization in the New Testament.*

A missional reading of Scripture takes seriously *both* how the gospel and the traditions available to Paul are contextualized within the biblical text *and* how churches might follow Paul's lead within their own situations today. On the one hand, in our efforts to do theology in context we must retain a clear vision of the normative gospel. "In the theological dance between the constant gospel and changing circumstances, the gospel must take the lead."[58]

In particular, Colossians speaks to the church's ongoing engagement with syncretism.[59] We do not have to look far to find analogies to the Colossian problem in many global contexts today—places where Christianity, established religions, and traditional folk beliefs live in close quarters. But syncretism is no stranger in the West either, whether in the form of new age spiritualities, "mix and match" theologies (e.g., self-described born-again Christians who also believe in reincarnation), or a "consumer" gospel that promises uninterrupted blessings at little or no cost. Admittedly, the lines between appropriate contextualization and Christ-compromising syncretism are often difficult to draw. Nevertheless, the Spirit must help us to discern when the gospel is diluted to the point that it is no longer "according to Christ" (2:8).

On the other hand, we will do well to learn from Paul's unwillingness to impose a "one-size-fits-all" theology on his audience. Paul dares to use language that is shared by the local religious culture (e.g., "mystery"). He enlists images and ethical conventions from the world of everyday the Colossians inhabit (especially 2:11–15; 3:18–4:1). At the same time, he draws on traditional biblical language (e.g., "forgiveness," "redemption," "circumcision") and recontextualizes it for his gentile audience. If we read Colossians missionally, we will seek—guided by the Spirit—to discover ways of articulating and embodying the gospel that faithfully and appropriately encounter people within their life circumstances. We will draw upon our own stories, language, and cultural resources, without surrendering our scriptural moorings.[60]

58. Flemming, "Paul the Contextualizer," 15.

59. On the implications of Colossians for the church's encounter with syncretism, see Flemming, *Contextualization in the New Testament*, 231–33.

60. For examples of this kind of biblically grounded contextualization, see Rose Dowsett, ed., *Global Mission: Reflections and Case Studies in Local Theology for the Whole Church* (Pasadena, CA: Carey, 2011); Jackson Wu, *One Gospel for All Nations: A Practical Approach to Biblical Contextualization* (Pasadena, CA: Carey, 2015).

Reshaping Our Theological Imaginations

When Paul employs the power language of the ancient religious culture or the picture of the Roman triumphal procession (2:15), he is not simply identifying with his audience; rather, he invites them to see the world from a new vantage point. Colossians still has the power to reshape the theological imaginations of Christian communities and their participation in the mission of God. What that looks like, however, will not be the same in every place or time. Consider the language of the "rulers and powers," which plays such a critical role in Colossians (1:13, 16; 2:8, 10, 15; cf. 1:11). For Paul and his early Christian audience, it likely speaks, in the first place, to concerns about personal, cosmic powers and Christ's supremacy over them. But how should we appropriate such language in a twenty-first-century missional reading of Colossians?

Michael Barram rightly argues that missional interpretation of Scripture must take into account the social location of the interpretive community.[61] While teaching in Asia, I saw firsthand that, for numerous majority-world churches, the Colossians treatment of the powers comes as a practical word of hope and confidence. It brings the assurance that Christ is more powerful than any evil spirits or supernatural powers; they are already defeated in the cross.[62]

Many Christians in the West, however, find it far more difficult to identify with Paul's worldview in regard to "the powers" or to see the activity of personal spiritual beings in their world. Rather than flatly "demythologize" the powers, some Christian interpreters find analogies for Paul's "powers" language in the destructive forces that lie behind and are active in human institutions and systems. Thompson, for example, insists that one only need "list individual, corporate, and cosmic forces of tradition, consumerism, illness, sin, nationalism, militarism, and so on, to show that there are anti-God powers at work in the world."[63] Such a reading calls

61. Barram, "Bible, Mission, and Social Location," 42–58.

62. Unfortunately, Western missionaries sometimes either ignore or deny the reality of the New Testament power language in majority world settings. As a result, Christianity easily can be perceived as theologically irrelevant and pastorally impotent to address the forces that influence people's daily lives. See Hwa Yung, *Mangoes or Bananas? The Quest for an Authentic Asian Christian Theology* (Oxford: Regnum, 1977), 72–75.

63. Thompson, *Colossians and Philemon*, 39. See also the valuable discussion of the powers in Ephesians in Timothy G. Gombis, *The Drama of Ephesians: Participating in the Triumph of God* (Downers Grove, IL: IVP Academic, 2010), 35–58.

God's people to a prophetic counterimagination. For Timothy Gombis, this means resisting the work of the powers within cultural patterns of injustice, exploitation, and idolatry; patterns that are all the more destructive because they appear to be inevitable and normal.[64] In so doing, the church participates in Christ's victory over the powers and God's mission to restore all things.

Again, this latter reading probably does not represent Paul's first understanding of the powers in Colossians. For Paul, however, the powers can operate at various levels, including through earthly, political rulers (1 Cor. 2:8). Consequently, this second reading seems consistent with Paul's wider thought. On a *hermeneutical* level, both of these readings allow the assurance of Christ's victory over the powers in Colossians to speak in analogous ways to faith communities in widely different missional locations. Both invite God's people to reimagine their world and God's mission in it.

A missional reading of Colossians, then, seeks to understand how this Christ-exalting letter bears witness to God's all-embracing mission in the world, and how it calls Christian communities to engage in that mission in their own corners of the world. Whether in the first century or the twenty-first century, the latter task calls for Spirit-guided discernment. Like the early Christians of the Lycus Valley, we live out our missional identity simultaneously "in Christ" and "in Colossae" (1:2). We, too, must resist the temptation to let an overdose of "Colossae" cloud our Christian identity and witness. And like them, it is precisely "in Colossae" that we embody God's mission, speaking and living the gospel in the presence of a watching world (4:5–6).

64. Gombis, *Drama of Ephesians*, 54–58.

A Missional Reading of Scripture and Preaching

CHAPTER 12

A Missional Reading of Scripture and Preaching

Michael W. Goheen

A paperweight sits on my desk, just where it has been for the past fifteen years since I purchased it in Edinburgh. The words of Ephesians 3:8 encircle a portrait of John Knox, the sixteenth-century Protestant reformer: "Unto me is this grace given, that I should preach the unsearchable riches of Christ." I keep it where I will see it often, to remind me of the enormous privilege and responsibility I have of preaching the good news of Jesus Christ. I began my professional life as a church-planter and pastor. And even though I have been in the academic world for over twenty-five years, I have also been employed as a minister of preaching for most of that time and so have continued to preach regularly. Since much of my academic teaching has been in missiology and biblical theology, this paper represents a confluence of three streams of interest for me: scriptural interpretation, mission, and preaching. These three flow together always, for faithful preaching cannot be separated from a missional reading of Scripture.

Scripture as a Tool of God's Mission in and through His People

C. S. Lewis opens his *Preface to Paradise Lost* with the comment that the "first qualification for judging any piece of workmanship from a corkscrew to a cathedral is to know *what* it is—what it was intended to do and how it is meant to be used."[1] Following Lewis, we might well say that the first qualifi-

1. C. S. Lewis, *A Preface to Paradise Lost* (Oxford: Oxford University Press, 1961 [orig. 1942]), 1.

cation for preaching Scripture is to know what it is—what it was intended to do and how it is meant to be used. Of course, this would open out into the enormous fields of a doctrine of Scripture and of hermeneutics. But for our purposes in this chapter we may begin with the summary statement that the Bible is both a *record* and a *tool* of God's mission in and through his people. Both of these features are important for the preacher. But to recognize that the Bible is a tool used by God to shape his people for their missional vocation is essential to the homiletic task.

Donald Bloesch speaks of the Bible as having "an ontological as well as a functional authority."[2] That is, the Bible is not only the instrument employed by the Holy Spirit, but is itself also the word of God as breathed out by the Spirit. "The Bible not only directs us to the truth but also speaks truth. It not only points to truth but also communicates the truth. . . . Scripture could be an ongoing instrument of God's Spirit only because the Spirit was the ultimate author of Scripture. . . . The Bible is more than a tool of the Spirit—it is the very voice of the Spirit."[3] To use Herman Bavinck's terms, the Bible is both "God-breathed" (ontological) and "God-breathing" (instrumental).[4]

It has been my experience that, in their zeal to protect the Bible from liberal attack, evangelicals often stress the ontological authority of Scripture to the neglect of its instrumental power. Their concentration on inspiration, infallibility, and inerrancy has led to an exasperated response from others who find such theological reflection to be beside the point: these folk want to get on with the task of using it properly. After all, they might argue, it is what Scripture *does* that matters, not merely what it *is*. But both are important, as Bloesch contends—what Scripture is, as well as how it is meant to be used. In the theological circles I frequent, and especially among preachers, it is the instrumental authority of the Bible that needs to be stressed. As those who preach Christ we need to be deeply convinced not only that the Bible is the word of God but also that it functions as a powerful tool in the hands of the Spirit to form a people for his missional purposes.[5]

2. Donald G. Bloesch, *Holy Scripture: Revelation, Inspiration, and Interpretation*, Christian Foundations (Downers Grove, IL: InterVarsity, 2005), 133.

3. Bloesch, *Holy Scripture*, 133.

4. Herman Bavinck, *Reformed Dogmatics: Prolegomena*, ed. John Bolt, trans. John Vriend (Grand Rapids: Baker, 2003), 1:385, 439.

5. Cf. Michael W. Goheen and Michael D. Williams, "Doctrine of Scripture and Theological Interpretation," in *A Manifesto for Theological Interpretation*, ed. Craig G. Bar-

A Model of Biblical Authority

The story of the Bible is that God's ultimate purpose is to renew the entire creation. This has been described as God's mission, his great redemptive work, and he chooses a people to participate in it. The authority of Scripture must be understood in terms of its place in this story. A primary question that must be asked is: "What *role* does scripture play within God's working toward this goal?"[6] The Bible does not simply give us a reliable commentary on the work of God: it takes an active part in bringing that work to fruition. Since God employs a people for his purpose, and the Bible plays an important role in shaping this people for their mission, then biblical authority is a "sub-branch" of "the mission of the church."[7]

In post-Enlightenment interpretation, the role of Scripture is often seen as limited to conveying information, or as divine self-communication, or as a record of revelation. Surely, Scripture does do these things—but it is more: God's "self-revelation is always to be understood within the category of God's mission to the world, God's saving sovereignty let loose through Jesus and the Spirit and aimed at the healing and renewal of the creation."[8] To get hold of the authority of Scripture, then, includes attending to its formative role, how it works in power to shape a missional people. Out of the history of redemption described in the Bible, various kinds of books arose as products of God's mission, and each played a role in forming God's people for their mission in the world. For example, the apostolic writings "were not simply *about* the coming of God's Kingdom into all the world; they were, and were designed to be, part of the *means whereby that happened*."[9]

Old Testament Scriptures as the Tool of God's Missional Purposes

To dig more deeply into what it means that the Scriptures are a tool of God's missional purposes, we must be alert to the storyline of the Bible. Specifically, we must take account of the difference between the Old and New

---

tholomew and Heath Thomas (Grand Rapids: Baker, 2016), 48–71; Herman Ridderbos, *Studies in Scripture and Its Authority* (St. Catharines: Paideia, 1978), 20–36.

6. N. T. Wright, *Scripture and the Authority of God: How to Read the Bible Today* (New York: HarperCollins, 2011), 28.

7. Wright, *Scripture and the Authority of God*, 27–28.

8. Wright, *Scripture and the Authority of God*, 28–29.

9. Wright, *Scripture and the Authority of God*, 51.

Testament Scriptures, and the impact of the coming of Jesus Christ. The basic argument of N. T. Wright's *Scripture and the Authority of God* offers a helpful structure to do just this.[10] Wright reminds us that the Old Testament Scriptures were written to equip God's people for their missional calling to be a distinctive people: "A full account of the role of scripture within the life of Israel would appear as a function of Israel's election by God for the sake of the world. Through scripture, God was equipping his people to serve his purposes."[11] This equipping takes several forms. In order that Israel might fulfill its missional calling as a light to the nations, the law was given to order Israel's national, liturgical, and moral life; wisdom literature helped to shape daily conduct in conformity with God's creational order; the prophets threatened and warned Israel of the consequences of disobedience and the promised blessings of obedience; the psalms brought all of Israel's life before God's presence in worship and prayer; the historical books continued to tell the story of Israel, reminding Israel repeatedly of its missional place in God's unfolding story. In short, the Old Testament canon was shaped by and for a people called to be a community of mission, a light to the nations.

New Testament Scriptures as the Tool of God's Missional Purposes

The New Testament Scriptures also emerge in the context of the mission of God's people. The New Testament tells the story of God's mission through Israel as it climaxes in Jesus, and it brings that story to bear in various ways on the early church to form and equip it for its missional calling in the world. We can discern three stages of the emergence of the New Testament.

Jesus Fulfills the Purpose of the Old Testament Scriptures

Jesus accomplishes conclusively what the Old Testament Scriptures had been trying to do—bringing salvation to God's people and, through them, to the world.[12] Wright says that the "work which God had done through

10. Wright, *Scripture and the Authority of God*, 33–59. I use Wright's basic structure and much of his helpful articulation in what follows, but not everything I say is necessarily found in his book.

11. Wright, *Scripture and the Authority of God*, 35.

12. I am thankful to my friend and former colleague Howard McPhee who read an

scripture in the Old Testament is done by Jesus in his public career, his death and resurrection, and his sending of the Spirit. . . . Jesus thus does, climactically and decisively, what scripture had in a sense been trying to do: *bring God's fresh Kingdom order to God's people and thence to the world*."[13] In Christ, the intent of these Scriptures to shape a missional people is finally fulfilled.

Consider, for example, how this relates to preaching Exodus. The first section of that book narrates God's mighty act of redemption that liberates Israel from Egyptian idolatry to be a holy people (Exod. 1–18). This mighty deed looks forward to a more powerful redemptive act in Jesus that can accomplish true liberation for his people. Exodus continues with the record of how God binds his people to himself in covenant, calling them to be a priestly kingdom and holy nation, and then gives them the law to shape their lives (Exod. 19–23). But even though they say they will do everything the Lord said (19:8; 24:3, 7), there is need for a new and better covenant established in the work of Jesus Christ to accomplish what the former covenant alone could not do. Exodus concludes with God's coming to dwell among his people as a holy God (Exod. 25–31, 35–40) and a gracious and forgiving God (Exod. 32–34). The express purpose of his presence with his people is to make them holy (31:13). Yet the structures of tabernacle and temple that symbolized his presence amidst his people were to be fulfilled by a future reality: the intimate and powerful presence of God in Jesus (John 1:14) and his Spirit (John 14–16; 1 Cor. 3:16). Thus, our preaching of Exodus will always point to Christ, who accomplishes the purpose of forming a missional people through redemption, covenant, and presence. In the climactic work of Christ, the goal of the Old Testament to shape God's people into a missional community is decisively accomplished.

Jesus Is Powerfully Present in Apostolic Preaching and Teaching

The apostles proclaim the good news that Israel's story has been fulfilled in Jesus, that he has accomplished what the Old Testament had been trying to do. By preaching this Jesus as the fulfillment of Israel's story, God's New Testament people are shaped for their mission in the world. The New Tes-

---

earlier draft of this chapter and whose comments helped me clarify my thinking on some issues in this section.

13. Wright, *Scripture and the Authority of God*, 42 (emphasis added).

tament refers to this proclamation as "the apostles' teaching," "the gospel," "the word of God": "It was the story of Jesus (particularly his death and resurrection), told as the climax of the story of God and Israel and thus offering itself as both the true story of the world and the foundation and energizing force for the church's mission."[14]

Herman Ridderbos makes a helpful contribution here. He defines New Testament authority in terms of the redemptive-historical categories of *kerygma*, *martyria*, and *didache*.[15] *Kerygma* is the work of a herald in proclaiming the good news of the person and actions of Jesus Christ as the climax of the Old Testament story, calling urgently for a response. *Martyria* is the divinely authoritative witness of the apostles to what God has accomplished in Jesus Christ to shape a kingdom people for the sake of the world. *Kerygma* and *martyria* pertain mainly to the so-called historical books of the New Testament: they are witness to the historical events in the life of Jesus Christ. *Didache* on the other hand represents a more "advanced stage of revelation" that builds on the proclamation of and witness to Jesus Christ. *Didache* is the function of the New Testament Epistles. They build up the church by unfolding the significance of the gospel of Jesus Christ for the church's missionary calling, in all the particular contexts of the young church.

The term *didache* comes from the Jewish discipline of religious instruction that took place in the synagogue or between a rabbi and his disciples. In the context of New Testament Scriptures, it is instruction that further explains and unfolds the significance of God's mighty acts in history for the missional community. While *kerygma* and *martyria* make known the mighty act of God in Jesus Christ, *didache* works out the missional implications of Jesus's life, works, and teaching for specific communities.

Ridderbos's elaboration of New Testament authority is important for preaching because it subverts the Western propensity to see truth in terms of unchanging ideas. In fact, it is precisely here that one may see the difference between the biblical and Western cultural stories. In the Western story, ultimately reliable truth is found in eternal ideas that transcend history. In the Bible, ultimately reliable truth is found in God's mighty acts in history, especially in Jesus Christ. Many years ago, one of my university professors, a Jewish rabbi, said to me something like the following: "The difference

14. Wright, *Scripture and the Authority of God*, 48–49.

15. Herman N. Ridderbos, *Redemptive History and the New Testament Scriptures* (formerly *The Authority of the New Testament Scriptures*), trans. H. De Jongste, rev. Richard B. Gaffin Jr. (Phillipsburg, NJ: Presbyterian & Reformed, 1988), 49–76.

between Jews and Christians is a different understanding of truth. We Jews believe truth resides in historical *events* that give meaning to a *story* and shape a *community* to live in that story. You Christians believe truth resides in theological ideas around which a community forms by believing those ideas." I now see that he was articulating not merely a Jewish but in fact a biblical view of truth; however, I would argue that the central events by which to interpret the story and form the community are those events centered in Jesus Christ, rather than the exodus. Ridderbos helps us see this: it is in a witness to and proclamation of the Christ event, authoritatively interpreted in Scripture, that truth is found. The teaching of the New Testament draws out the significance of that event for various mission situations.

We can summarize the apostolic ministry as preaching Christ and teaching the significance of his work. As it was proclaimed and taught, the apostolic gospel was God's powerful word to call into existence a missional community, to shape that community to be a faithful people, and to work through them to draw others to faith.

Apostolic Preaching and Teaching Makes Christ Powerfully Present

The verbal proclamation, witness, and teaching of the apostles take literary form in the canon of the New Testament. This word of God, now written, continues to form, equip, and renew the church for their mission in the world in the way that the living word of the apostles had done. The New Testament authors, conscious of their authority and inspired by the Spirit, wrote books that would shape the church for its mission, and these books "carried the same power, the same *authority in action*, that had characterized the initial preaching of the word."[16]

Preaching Christ to Form a Distinctive Community for the Sake of the World

This model of Scripture leads me to make the following statement about preaching: *we preach Christ to form a distinctive community for the sake of the world*. I am going to open up the various parts of that statement in the remainder of this chapter.

16. Wright, *Scripture and the Authority of God*, 51.

We Preach Christ

In the first part of this chapter I considered the authority of Scripture in terms of Wright's helpful model. What is clear is that whenever one preaches from any passage in Scripture, one must preach Christ, for it is Jesus who fulfills all that the Old Testament is trying to accomplish. And so any text in the Old Testament should lead us forward to Christ (cf. John 5:39–40; Luke 24:27, 44–46). The New Testament is the witness to, proclamation of, and teaching about Jesus Christ. And so any text in the New Testament will look back and have the good news of Jesus Christ as its foundation. "The whole of revelation, summed up in Scripture, is a special revelation that comes to us in Christ. Christ is the center and content of that whole special revelation, which starts in Paradise and is completed in the Apocalypse."[17] Indeed, "without this controlling center [the gospel of Jesus Christ], the Bible is a mere encyclopedia of religion with no more plot than a telephone directory."[18] In our preaching of Scripture, then, we must preach Jesus Christ.

We might express this in terms of the model we have outlined. In fulfillment of the Old Testament, Christ is first present *bodily* to bring salvation to his people and, through them, to the world. Upon the completion of the central events of the biblical story—crucifixion, resurrection, exaltation, and Pentecost—Christ is present through *apostolic preaching and teaching* for the same purpose. In the postapostolic era, Christ is present in *New Testament writings* as the expression of apostolic preaching and teaching, again for the same purpose: to bring salvation to his people and, through them, to the world. And today, in the faithful *preaching and teaching* of Scripture, Christ is present for the same purpose.

Jesus Christ himself comes to us clothed in the very words of Scripture, as Martin Luther puts it: "Holy Scripture is the garment which our Lord Christ has put on and in which He lets Himself be seen and found."[19] John Calvin says, "This, then, is the true knowledge of Christ, if we receive him as he is offered by the Father: namely, clothed with his gospel."[20] It is not mere words of teaching or theological ideas that are conveyed in the act

17. Bavinck, *Reformed Dogmatics: Prolegomena*, 1.321.

18. Eugene Peterson, *Reversed Thunder: The Revelation of John and the Praying Imagination* (New York: HarperCollins, 1988), 27.

19. Martin Luther, quoted in Karl Barth, *Church Dogmatics* (Peabody, MA: Hendrickson, 2010), I/2, 484.

20. John Calvin, *Institutes of the Christian Religion* 3.2.6, trans. Ford Lewis Battles, ed. John T. McNeill (Philadelphia: Westminster, 1960), 548. Cf. also 2.9.3 (426).

of preaching. Rather, by the Spirit, the living Christ comes to us clad in the garment of the gospel.

We Preach Christ to Form a Distinctive Community

The biblical story shows that God chose and covenanted with a people to participate in his mission of restoring the entire creation and gathering a people from all nations. At the very heart of this elect people's identity is the call to live distinctively. Howard Peskett and Vinoth Ramachandra capture this core motif when they say that "mission is not primarily about *going*. Nor is mission primarily about *doing* anything. Mission is about *being*. It is about being a distinctive kind of people, a countercultural . . . community among the nations."[21] The role of scriptural books in this story is to form this covenant people to be a distinctive and countercultural community. And faithful preaching of the word will align itself carefully with this purpose.

This formulation speaks of the formation of a *community*. A problem with much preaching is its implicit assumption of an individualistic view of sin and salvation. In that view, preaching becomes primarily a matter of bringing salvation to individuals. But the core of the biblical covenant is, "I will be your God and you will be my people." Not individuals, but a people, a community, is being shaped for the sake of the world. This observation does not diminish the importance of individuals within that community hearing the word and responding in faith. But preaching is not about proclaiming salvation to individuals bound together merely by their common interest to be nurtured in faith. Preaching is about forming a distinctive community to play its role in God's purposes. As the community is built up by the preaching of the word, individual Christians will in turn be nurtured in their faith.

In the remainder of this section I make four points: we preach Christ (1) to liberate God's people from bondage to cultural idolatry; (2) to invite God's people into the true story of the world; (3) to proclaim Jesus as the power of God to liberate from the power of cultural idolatry, allowing us to live faithfully in the biblical story; and (4) to form a distinctive community for the sake of the world. I will use the book of Colossians as an example to illustrate these points.[22]

21. Howard Peskett and Vinoth Ramachandra, *The Message of Mission* (Downers Grove, IL: InterVarsity, 2003), 123.

22. Much of this section derives from a series I preached on Colossians along with

We Preach Christ to Liberate God's People from Bondage to Cultural Idolatry

In my early preaching ministry I operated within a couple of mistaken assumptions. First, I assumed the best categories to capture the content of Paul's letters are "theology" and "ethics": in the first part of his letters Paul reflects theologically on the gospel in a manner close to academic theology today, and then in the latter part he applies his theology in a section on ethics. (An Enlightenment model of principles and applications underlies this kind of thinking.) This assumption was wedded to another: that sin and salvation are to be understood primarily in individualistic terms. Sin is about individual disobedience, and salvation is a matter of the *ordo salutis*, of offering the benefits of salvation to individuals.

My first assumption was mistaken, I now believe, because Paul's letters are not written as abstract and timeless theology and ethics. They are highly contextualized pastoral letters written to churches in particular settings facing various kinds of dangers. They are *didache* in the sense described above by Ridderbos—they work out the implications of the Christ event for a particular community so that its people might embody the gospel more faithfully for the sake of the world. And contrary to the second assumption, Paul understands fully, as do most outside the West not deeply affected by individualistic ideology, that sin and idolatry take on structural forms and that salvation in Scripture has to be understood within the cosmic—communal—personal framework of the biblical story. Both of these points are clear in the book of Colossians.

Colossians is not an abstract theological and ethical treatise disconnected from the Roman world: it is deeply contextual and missional. The events surrounding Jesus revealed in the gospel are brought by Paul to bear on the lives of the church at Colossae so they might be faithful in the way they live before outsiders (Col. 4:5–6). The gospel is addressed to the difficult situation in which they live. Specifically, the Colossian church lives in a society *enslaved by "the powers."* What does the gospel have to say to this situation?

The Colossian church understood well the powers at work in the Ro-

---

colleagues from three churches: Andrew Beunk and David Groen at New West Christian Reformed Church, Burnaby, British Columbia; Riccardo Stewart and Jim Mullins at Redemption Church Tempe, Tempe, Arizona; and Chris Gonzalez and Nick Barker at Missio Dei Communities, Tempe, Arizona.

man Empire. There were many gods who ruled and oppressed its citizens (1 Cor. 8:5). Among them were Aphrodite (goddess of sex), Hephaestus (god of technology), Mars (god of war), Ploutos (god of wealth), and Bacchus (god of pleasure). At the top of the ladder, and unifying them all, was political power, deified in the Caesar, and nourished by the imperial theology and religious practices. The Colossian church understood the comprehensive scope and spiritual power of these gods to tyrannize their lives. The question is, how are we, today, to understand the significance of these powers?

Biblical scholars have noted the importance of "the powers" in Paul's letters and have begun a complicated discussion that we cannot enter into here in detail. Briefly, I suggest that to account for Paul's rather unsystematic teaching about evil and the powers we need to take account of three things: personal and spiritual demonic forces, structural and systematic evil, and the idolatrous human heart (fig. 1).[23]

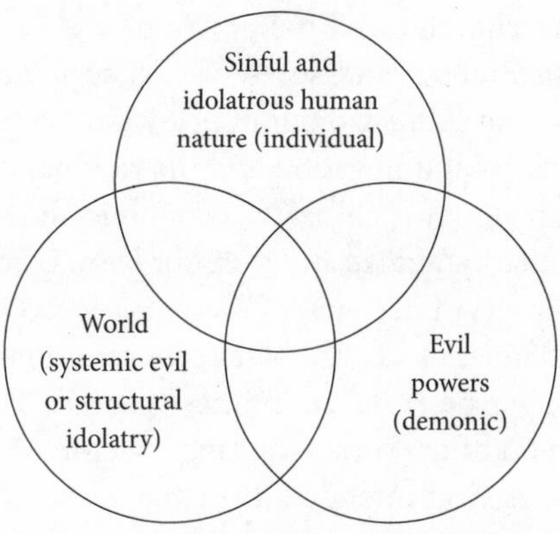

Figure 1. Paul's Understanding of Evil

These powers are real, demonic forces at work in our world. (Only a culture in bondage to a naturalistic religious secularism would deny this.) Such powers certainly tempt and ensnare individuals in our own day as they did in Paul's. But dark forces also get a foothold in human life through social structures and cultural institutions. What better way to foster greed

23. I owe this diagram to my former colleague Mariano Avila at Calvin Theological Seminary who used it in Calvin's Opening Convocation 2013 to describe Paul's view of human life under the powers of evil in Eph. 2:1–3.

than through powerful marketing in a society organized around consumption as the chief end of human life? In fact, Paul does not always sharply distinguish between the spiritual powers that are at work and the cultural powers *through which* they work.

The ways in which we structure our communal lives together are shaped by the religious direction of our hearts. If our religious allegiance is not directed toward God as he is revealed in Christ it will find another focus and will serve some aspect of the creation. The Bible calls this idolatry. Out of this idolatry we shape our political, economic, educational, and social lives together. Idolatry is not simply a matter of misdirected loyalty. It gives a foothold to demonic powers in human affairs. Anthony Thiselton rightly sees that for Paul, demonic powers working through idolatry "operate more forcefully in their *corporate, structural, or institutional effects* than any evil generated by any individual human person as such. *Evil systems* have power. Sometimes the net effect of corporate or structural evil is greater than the sum of the individuals who promote it."[24]

The Colossian church faced the power of evil in the idolatrous systems of the Roman Empire, and surely we do so today in our own culture. In the West, we have directed our lives toward material prosperity that comes from technological innovation and the rational organization of our economic lives. Many today speak of the economic and technological powers, among others, that tyrannize and ruin our lives. Our idolatry has given a foothold to the powers of darkness.

Paul has good news for the Colossian church and for us as well. God's people need no longer be enslaved by these powers: Christ has liberated us from the dominion of darkness, winning a victory over the powers and restoring us to live as God intended. Paul wants the Colossian church to realize their liberation in Christ. He wants them to live so that in everything it is Christ—and not the cosmic powers—who has supremacy (Col. 1:18).

Our preaching must follow Paul's pattern. What are the idolatrous powers of our culture? How are we enslaved to them? What damage are these powers doing? How can we preach Christ as the victor over these powers? To fail to address the pressing cultural issues of our day is to fail at a fundamental level. Martin Luther rightly said: "If you preach the gospel in all aspects with the exception of the issues which deal specifically with your time you are not preaching the gospel at all!" Karl Barth comments on

24. Anthony C. Thiselton, *1 Corinthians: A Shorter Exegetical and Pastoral Commentary* (Grand Rapids: Eerdmans, 2006), 160. He is commenting on 1 Cor. 10:14–22.

the way John Calvin preached contextually: "Calvin, having first established what stands in the text, sets himself to re-think the whole material and to wrestle with it, till the walls which separate the sixteenth century from the first become transparent! Paul speaks, and the man of the sixteenth century hears."[25] This must be the way we proclaim the good news.

We Preach Christ to Invite God's People into the True Story of the World

Lesslie Newbigin tells us that the "business of the sermon is to bring the hearers face to face with Jesus Christ *as he really is*."[26] I stress here the words "as he really is" because we have a tendency unintentionally to tailor the Jesus we proclaim to fit our cultural idolatry. For example, if individualism really does operate powerfully as a tacit framework of thought in our culture, then we will tend to present Christ simply as a personal savior who distributes the benefits of salvation to individuals. Indeed, he is Savior and does enable individuals to participate in the salvation he has accomplished. But is that Christ "as he really is"?

What kind of Christ did Paul proclaim in Colossians? A careful look at the Christ of Colossians 1:15–20 explodes our small views. It looks back to the beginning of the world where Christ created all things visible and invisible (1:16). And this includes the "thrones and powers and rulers and authorities" that held the Roman Empire in bondage. Paul also looks forward to the end or *telos* of history where Christ is reconciling to himself all things, whether things on earth or things in heaven (1:19). Paul here sees Christ as the alpha and omega of universal history. At the middle of history stand two events that enable us to interpret the meaning of cosmic history: the crucifixion, in which Christ triumphed over all the powers and authorities that hold the Roman Empire and the world in slavery (2:15), and the resurrection, in which Christ inaugurated a new world and became the firstborn of its people (1:18). Christ is nothing less than God in human flesh, the one in whom the fullness of God lives in bodily form (2:9; cf. 1:19). To believe in this Christ, then, draws us into the middle of the cosmic story of God's reconciling work.

25. Karl Barth, *The Epistle to the Romans* (London: Oxford University Press, 1953), 7.

26. Lesslie Newbigin, *The Good Shepherd* (Grand Rapids: Eerdmans, 1977), 24 (emphasis added).

The Bible tells the true story of the world, whose center is Christ, and then invites us to embrace Christ and take up our own roles in that story. But all people live in human cultures with a center other than Christ and are molded by a story other than the one narrated in the Bible. And these cultural stories have a powerfully formative effect on the lives of all who live in them. Paul warns the Roman Christians "not to be conformed by the world" (Rom. 12:2)—and by "world" here he means the idolatrous story of Roman culture. He calls his readers to be not conformed but *transformed* by the renewing of their minds. They are to find new life in Christ and the story the Bible tells. Paul understands the pull of the secular cultural story and understands well the need to form the churches within an alternative story so they can live out an alternative and distinctive way of life.

Paul is not the only one to preach an alternative narrative centered in God's redemptive work over against the dominant idolatrous narrative of his culture. This is also the way the Old Testament prophets proclaimed the word of God. Walter Brueggemann calls this "prophetic preaching" and describes it as the "staging and performance of a contest between two narrative accounts of the world in an effort to show that the YHWH account of reality is more adequate and finally more reliable than the dominant narrative account that is cast among us as though it were true and beyond critique."[27] Since "prophetic preaching is rooted in the alternative narrative of the God of Israel" then it "can take place only where the preacher is deeply embedded in the YHWH narrative."[28]

Thus it is imperative that the Bible be understood as a canonical and narrative whole. Newbigin rightly comments, "I do not believe that we can speak effectively of the Gospel as a word addressed to our culture unless we recover a sense of the Scriptures as a canonical whole, as the story which provides the true context for our understanding of the meaning of our lives—both personal and public."[29] It is only as we are transformed by the comprehensive and compelling story of Scripture that we will resist being conformed to the world. Neglecting the integrity of the Bible as a story, and instead allowing it to be absorbed piecemeal into the story of our own secular culture, may lead us to become warmly pious, morally upright, theologically orthodox idol-worshipers.

27. Walter Brueggemann, *The Practice of Prophetic Imagination: Preaching an Emancipating Word* (Minneapolis: Fortress, 2012), 3.

28. Brueggemann, *Practice of Prophetic Imagination*, 4–5.

29. Lesslie Newbigin, "Response to 'Word of God?' John Coventry, SJ," *Gospel and Our Culture Newsletter* 10.13 (1991).

Too often in our preaching we invite our hearers to take hold of the benefits of salvation accomplished by Christ in a way that allows them to be situated quite nicely within the dominant cultural narrative. But our preaching must challenge the idolatrous story being told on TV, on the internet, in schools, in popular culture, and elsewhere. Again Newbigin surely has it right: "Preaching is the announcing of news; the telling of a narrative. In a society that has a different story to tell about itself, preaching has to be firmly and unapologetically rooted in the real story."[30]

This story, the real story of our world, "creates a symbolic world which its readers can enter and thereby have their perception of the world transformed." Here Richard Bauckham is speaking specifically about the book of Revelation but what he says holds as well for the other scriptural books and for the biblical story as a whole. He tells us that the church was "constantly confronted with powerful images of the Roman vision of the world." In this context the book of Revelation provides a "set of Christian prophetic counter-images which impress on its readers a different vision of the world." Over against the pollution of idolatrous cultural images, the book of Revelation purges "the Christian imagination, refurbishing it with alternative visions of how the world is and will be."[31] This is what preaching is called to do. Set against the pervasive idolatry of our culture, preaching narrates the story of an alternative world centered in Jesus and invites hearers to live in this story.

One sociologist who makes no claim to the Christian faith observes that the "waning of Christianity as practised in the West is easy to explain. The Christian churches have comprehensively failed in their one central task—to retell their foundation story in a way that might speak to the times."[32] Note the two aspects of his sociological observation: Christians have failed to nurture their members with the foundational story, and they have not made that story speak to the times. These are precisely the first two points I am making. We preach Christ to liberate the people of God from a false and idolatrous cultural story and at the same time invite them to find freedom and life in the true story of the world centered in Jesus Christ.

It is significant to note the way Paul structures the first chapter of Colossians. He begins with the *cosmic* scope of reconciliation: the Son is the creator and reconciler of all things (1:15–20). He then moves to the *com-*

30. Lesslie Newbigin, "Missions," in *Concise Encyclopedia of Preaching*, ed. William Willimon and Richard Lischer (Louisville: Westminster John Knox, 1995), 336.

31. Richard Bauckham, *The Theology of the Book of Revelation* (Cambridge: Cambridge University Press, 1993), 17.

32. John Carroll, *The Existential Jesus* (Brunswick, Victoria: Scribe, 2008), 7.

munity that embodies that reconciliation: the Son is the beginning of the new creation and therefore the head of a new humankind (1:18). And finally comes the *individual* believer: "Once you were alienated from God and were enemies in your minds because of your evil behavior. But now he has reconciled you by Christ's physical body through death to present you holy in his sight, without blemish and free from accusation—if you continue in your faith, established and firm, and do not move from the hope held out in the gospel" (1:21–23). There is an urgent kerygmatic call to individuals to believe and remain established and firm in the gospel. However, the call to individuals is put in a bigger context—within the cosmic story of creation and the reconciliation of all things. Moreover, the believers at Colossae are part of the body and church who acknowledge the supremacy of Christ in all things by virtue of the new creation.

The logic of the biblical story, and of Paul's explanation of it here in Colossians 1, is the progression from cosmic to communal to personal. This stands in contrast to the way much preaching is done, focusing only on the individual response and the benefits received, without reference to the broader cosmic and communal frameworks of the biblical story. In a society that expects instant gratification, it is easy for a preacher to succumb to a congregation's desire to see the relevance of the ancient text quickly. This motivation can easily drive what G. C. Berkouwer calls "soteriological self-centeredness," which he says has "marginalized the cosmic scope of the biblical story." He rightly assesses what is true about much preaching: "Such an approach does not repudiate that [cosmic dimension], it simply pays it no mind."[33]

If we are to form our congregations with the gospel that stands at the center of the biblical story, then we will need to follow Paul's example and pay more attention to the cosmic and communal dimensions of Scripture. But this will not neglect the individual; for, as Paul says, "you also were included in Christ when you heard the word of truth, the gospel of your salvation" (Eph. 1:13; cf. 1:7–10).

We Preach Christ to Proclaim Jesus as the Power of God

We preach Christ as the power of God to liberate us from the power of cultural idolatry, allowing us to live faithfully in the biblical story. The Colos-

33. G. C. Berkouwer, *The Return of Christ*, Studies in Dogmatics (Grand Rapids: Eerdmans, 1972), 211–12.

sians understood well the strength of the religious powers that shaped the Roman Empire: they needed a message that was even more powerful. The question for us is whether we—living in the secular West and seduced by the myths of the neutrality of secular or pluralistic culture—can understand that we too are in the grip of religious powers. To the degree that we do *not* so believe, we will not see the need for a gospel that is powerful.

Sadly, most Christians in the West do not really believe that religion is a power at the core of culture, shaping and forming all aspects of a society. In the West, religion has been devalued to become simply another human activity alongside of others like sports, politics, business, and education. By "religion" we often mean simply what we believe about the future, about the spiritual realm, about life after death. We do not recognize that throughout history, religion has been and is today the formative power at the core of every culture. In other nations of the world this truth is still current, though we often lose sight of it in the West. African theologian Kofi Osare Opoku makes this point:

> In African culture, religion and culture are inextricably bound up. Religion derives its profound meaning to the African from it touching him in the totality of his culture. Religion touches every aspect of life and there are no blank areas in life where man is supposed to fall on other resources. Life is religion and religion is life; and religion is not restricted to certain areas of life but pervades all of life.[34]

The idolatrous religion that pervades the secular West is powerful. Bavinck says that sin "is a power that controls everyone and everything. . . . [It] organizes all the entities and forces God has created into rebellion against him."[35] Paul and the churches to which he wrote certainly understood this; idolatry gave a foothold for demonic power. The need is for a gospel with power sufficient to deliver and rescue the people of God from idolatry. That

34. Kofi Osare Opoku, "The Relevance of African Culture to Christianity," *Mid-Stream* 13.3–4 (1974): 155.

35. Herman Bavinck, *Reformed Dogmatics*, vol. 3: *Sin and Salvation in Christ*, ed. John Bolt, trans. John Vriend (Grand Rapids: Baker, 2006), 145. G. C. Berkouwer follows Bavinck in characterizing sin as a power: it is a "seductive power," a "deadening power," a "damning power which holds our lives in peril," a "deadly force," an "active, dynamic and destructive force," a "cataclysmic and disruptive power," a "power that seeks to rule and to ruin everyone and everything," a "virulent force," and a "pernicious power"; *Sin*, trans. Philip C. Holtrop (Grand Rapids: Eerdmans, 1971), 235, 239, 240, 241, 259, 261–63, 265.

is why Paul characterizes the gospel "as the power of God unto salvation" (Rom. 1:16; 1 Cor. 1:18; 2:4–5).

In a stirring chapter on preaching, C. John Miller urges the preacher to realize this call. The awesome mystery of preaching is that "Christ Himself becomes present and speaks through a feeble human being."[36] The purpose of preaching is to aim the message at people "with the purpose of bringing Christ to them and them to Christ. The goal is to change them by the power of the gospel."[37] We short-circuit the whole process when we are captured by other goals—and we have all heard and may have practiced these—such as preaching merely for the sake of delivering an eloquent message, a work of art, or a scholarly theological composition. Miller employs a military metaphor to drive home the real purpose of preaching: "The preacher should see preaching much more as a declaration of war, a conflict in which well-disciplined words march as to war to bring the hearers to surrender to Jesus Christ. We need to use the pulpit as a battle station."[38] Thus a crucial starting point for all preachers is the "deep-seated conviction that the gospel will renew anyone who receives it by faith." A virtual law of preaching is that "you get what you expect the gospel to do in lives."[39] Miller is correct: the gospel we preach is the power of salvation to anyone who believes, and this truth must form part of the preacher's mental and spiritual equipment.

We Preach Christ to Form a Distinctive Community for the Sake of the World

We preach Christ to form a distinctive community, it is true, but this formation of a people is not an end in itself. We must always keep in mind the missional thread in the biblical story: the people of God are to be a distinctive community *for the sake of the world*. This point can be well made by a brief reference to Karl Barth's discussion of *beneficia Christi* (benefits of Christ) and sacred egocentricity.[40] He asks a deceptively simple question:

36. C. John Miller, *Outgrowing the Ingrown Church* (Grand Rapids: Zondervan, 1986), 120.

37. Miller, *Outgrowing the Ingrown Church*, 123.

38. Miller, *Outgrowing the Ingrown Church*, 124.

39. Miller, *Outgrowing the Ingrown Church*, 128.

40. Karl Barth, *Church Dogmatics*, IV: *The Doctrine of Reconciliation*, part 3.2, trans. G. W. Bromiley (Peabody, MA: Hendrickson, 2010), 554–69.

What does it mean be a Christian? The classic answer is "to be a recipient and possessor of the *beneficia Christi*." Barth lists these benefits: regeneration, conversion, peace with God, reconciliation, justification, sanctification, forgiveness of sins, empowerment to live a life of liberation, beloved of God, freedom, adoption as God's children, hope of the resurrection of the body, foretaste and heirs of eternal life, and a new obedience. All these come by grace as gifts of God in Jesus Christ by the Holy Spirit in response to repentance and faith. It is this, he says, that inspires the preaching of the church. It is the way the New Testament has been read and preached and the way the means of grace have been understood.

"There can be no disputing," says Barth, "that something true and important is meant and envisaged in all this."[41] Yet if we are not alert it would be easy to make the reception, possession, and enjoyment of these benefits what is essential to being a Christian. Barth wonders: Can it really be the end of Christian vocation that I should be blessed, that I should be saved, that I should receive, possess, and enjoy all these gifts and then attain to eternal life without any regard for others? Does this not smack of a pious or sacred egocentricity? Would it not be strange and even contradictory that the selfless and self-giving work of God should issue in a self-seeking concern with our own salvation? Would not this egocentricity stand in stark contrast to the being and action of the Lord? Would this not turn the church into an institute of salvation that forgot its missional purpose in the world? Would this not make us *pure* recipients and possessors of salvation?[42] "Is not every form of egocentricity excused and even confirmed and sanctified, if egocentricity in this sacred form is the divinely willed meaning of Christian existence and the Christian song of praise consists finally only in a many-tongued but monotonous *pro me, pro me*, and similar possessive expressions?"[43]

Barth's critique pinches because this is the path that much preaching in our time follows. Preaching is a means of grace that channels blessing and salvation to God's people. But if it is left there, we betray the role and vocation to which God has called his people in the biblical story. We are blessed to be a blessing; God works first of all *in* but then *through* his people. If I can rephrase a fitting comment by N. T. Wright: "The church, believing that all the benefits of Christ were just for them, has betrayed the purpose

41. Barth, *Church Dogmatics*, IV/3.2, 563.
42. Barth, *Church Dogmatics*, IV/3.2, 568.
43. Barth, *Church Dogmatics*, IV/3.2, 567.

for which God has given them. It is as though the postman were to imagine that all the letters in his bag were intended just for him."[44]

Perhaps I can illustrate by recalling a sermon I heard years ago. It stood out in my mind because, though it was a very good sermon, it begged for a missional thrust that never came. The text was Psalm 63, and the focus was on desiring and knowing God.

> You, God, are my God,
>   earnestly I seek you;
> I thirst for you,
>   my whole being longs for you,
> in a dry and parched land
>   where there is no water.
> I have seen you in the sanctuary
>   and beheld your power and your glory.
> Because your love is better than life,
>   my lips will glorify you.
> I will praise you as long as I live,
>   and in your name I will lift up my hands.
> I will be satisfied as with the richest of foods;
>   with singing lips my mouth will praise you. (Ps. 63:1–5)

The preacher began by speaking of the new movement of spirituality in our culture. This was the reaction of humankind made in the image of God to arid secular naturalism, which suppresses anything that cannot be measured or does not find its place in the web of cause-and-effect. Human beings were made to know, desire, and love God. That is what is expressed in this psalm: the proper human longing for God. The sermon proceeded to deal properly with poetic genre and attend carefully to the text. Singing this psalm in Israel would foster a hunger to know and love God. However, such a thirst and hunger could not be fulfilled in the law. Only in Christ could this knowledge and desire of God find a place in human life. Jesus prayed: "For you [the Father] granted him [the Son] authority over all people that he might give eternal life to all those you have given him. Now this is eternal life: that they know you, the only true God, and Jesus Christ whom you

44. N. T. Wright, *What Saint Paul Really Said: Was Paul of Tarsus the Real Founder of Christianity?* (Grand Rapids: Eerdmans, 1997), 108. In the original quote he speaks of the covenant rather than the benefits of Christ.

sent" (John 17:2–3). The preacher urged us to respond to the good news, to seek Christ, and thus to know God. This, he said, is the only way our aching desire for God can be assuaged. He ended with reflection on the marvelous grace of God to fulfill that need in Christ and urged thankfulness for the blessing God had provided for us.

I was moved to reach out again to Christ. But I sat there, as it were waiting for what *must surely come next*: you have been given the knowledge of God as a preview of the knowledge of God that will one day cover the earth (Isa. 11:9; Hab. 2:14) *so that* others may view it and be incorporated into the community that knows the living God. As I sat there it struck me that the sermon had begun well, with a vivid description of the longing for God that overflowed from postmodern culture, a longing for God that had become so twisted in various kinds of spiritualities. Surely the ending must be that we as the people of God have a message, backed up by our lives, that will both confront the emptiness of postmodern spiritualities and at the same time fulfill the deepest longings. But that ending never came!

Missional preaching will not take away from the blessing and benefits we have in Christ; it will just keep clear that we betray our purpose as God's people if we think that all the blessings are just for us.

Conclusion: Devotion to the Apostles' Teaching

The last verses of Acts 2 offer us a model of what the church should be. In it we see a threefold movement. First, the church in Jerusalem devoted itself to the apostles' teaching, to fellowship, to the breaking of bread, and to prayer (2:42). These were the means of grace, the channels by which the Spirit brought the new eschatological life of the kingdom to the church. As the church devoted itself to these means, second, it manifested a life of power, communal solidarity, compassion, justice, joy, and praise (2:43–47). And finally, inevitably, this communal life was attractive: "And the Lord added to their number daily those who were being saved" (2:47).

One of the four "means of missional grace" is the apostles' teaching. Apostolic teaching is "the story of Jesus (particularly his death and resurrection), told as the climax of the story of God and Israel and thus offering itself as both the true story of the world and the foundation and energizing force for the church's mission."[45] Our preaching is to follow the model

45. N. T. Wright, *Scripture and the Authority of God*, 48–49.

of the apostles: preaching Christ (especially his death and resurrection), proclaiming that gospel as the climactic moment of the story begun in the Old Testament, and drawing out the missional orientation of the people of God to the world. In this way the people who listen to our preaching will be nourished in the new life of Christ for the sake of the world. And we may pray that the Lord will add to our number those who are being saved.

Our preaching, in the power of the Spirit, has the potential *both* to nurture new life in Christ *and* to orient God's people to the world. It would be a travesty and a betrayal of our vocation if we just left it at the first.

CHAPTER 13

Missional, Christ-Centered, or Gospel-Centered Preaching—What Is the Difference?

Timothy M. Sheridan

In a sermon delivered July 9, 1876, Charles Spurgeon boldly proclaimed, "We preach Christ and him crucified. No Christ in your sermon, sir? Then go home, and never preach again until you have something worth preaching."[1] Christ is at the heart of the gospel message, and the gospel is at the heart of the task of preaching. But what do these have to do with the mission of God and the mission of the church? The memorable statement made at the 1952 International Missionary Council meeting held at Willingen rings in my ears as a preacher of Christ: "There is no participation in Christ without participation in His mission to the world."[2] Can we preach Christ without a call to participating in Christ's mission to the world? This chapter will explore a central question: What does a missional reading of Scripture contribute to preaching Christ and the gospel? This question will be explored by putting the "Christ-centered" preaching model of Sidney Greidanus and the "gospel-centered" preaching model of Timothy Keller in conversation with a missional reading of Scripture.

1. C. H. Spurgeon, "To You," delivered at the Metropolitan Tabernacle in Newington (London) on July 9, 1876 (published Sept. 1, 1904); available at spurgeongems.org/vols49–51/chs2899.pdf.

2. Norman Goodall, ed., *Missions under the Cross: Addresses Delivered at the Enlarged Meeting of the Committee of the International Missionary Council at Willingen, in Germany, 1952, with Statements Issued by the Meeting* (London: Edinburgh House, 1953), 190.

A Missional Reading of Scripture

A missional reading of Scripture seeks to renew our understanding of the relationship between the Bible and the mission of the church today. As Richard Bauckham explains, this hermeneutical key is not simply a study of the themes of mission in the biblical writings, or a "biblical theology of missions," but "a way of reading the whole of Scripture with mission as its central interest and goal."[3] A missional reading of Scripture seeks to understand the mission of the church in the world, to inform and shape the missional praxis of the local church as it takes its place within the biblical story, the true story of the world.

To see that the entire biblical story has a missional center demands that we shift the theological priority in our understanding of mission. Mission is first and foremost the mission of God, not primarily an activity of the church but the work of the triune God to redeem and renew his creation. The church is the community of God's people called to committed participation in this *mission of God* through its proclamation and demonstration of the gospel in its words, deeds, and communal way of life. As Chris Wright puts it: "A missional hermeneutic proceeds from the assumption that the whole Bible renders to us the story of God's mission through God's people in their engagement with God's world for the sake of the whole of God's creation."[4]

Several key implications flow from such a missional reading of Scripture. The Bible tells one unfolding story of redemption. God's mission, or long-term purpose and goal, is to restore the entire creation and the whole of human life from sin. God carries out his mission by calling, gathering, and forming a community to partner with him for the sake of the world. The mission of God's people is to participate at God's calling and command, in God's own mission to the world, which centers on the historical events of the life, death, resurrection, and ascension of Jesus and all that God accomplished through them. How might a missional reading shape the practice of preaching? That is our question.

3. Richard Bauckham, "Mission as Hermeneutic for Scriptural Interpretation," *Currents in World Christianity Position Paper* 106 (1999): 1.

4. Christopher J. H. Wright, *The Mission of God* (Downers Grove, IL: InterVarsity, 2006), 51.

Christ-Centered Preaching

The first model of preaching to put into conversation with a missional reading of Scripture is that of Sidney Greidanus, professor emeritus of preaching at Calvin Theological Seminary, whose "Christ-centered" model of preaching Scripture is rooted in the Reformed redemptive-historical tradition of biblical hermeneutics. Christ-centered preaching is for Greidanus similar to, yet distinct from, a theocentric model.

For Greidanus, a key element of theocentric preaching is that the preaching text must be interpreted in light of God's complete revelation within the biblical story as a whole, the unfolding story of redemptive history.[5] Thus, an Old Testament text must be interpreted in light of its New Testament fulfillment. We can move from the Old Testament to New Testament fulfillment along many different lines, but move we must.[6] Alternatively, when we move from the New Testament to the Old Testament, we must bring with us the fullness of revelation we have in light of the entirety of redemptive history to our understanding of God's revelation in the Old Testament text.

Further, the preacher must give attention to the preaching text's purpose in the context of the whole canon and within the sweep of redemptive history.[7] For example, David's defeat of Goliath is not to be reduced to a moralistic Sunday school story about defeating the giants in our lives, for it has its own place and purpose within the unfolding story of God's redemption in the book of Samuel. The purpose and contemporary application of the preaching text must be consonant with its purpose and application within the flow of redemptive history.

Finally, our preaching must also reflect the thoroughly theocentric purpose of the biblical story as a whole: Scripture is revelation about God, his actions, his person, his will, and his plan.[8] A God-centered worldview must inform the reading of every text of Scripture.[9]

But what distinguishes Christ-centered preaching? As Greidanus points out, this term takes on a slightly different meaning within each of the

5. Sidney Greidanus, *The Modern Preacher and the Ancient Text* (Grand Rapids: Eerdmans, 1988), 113.

6. Sidney Greidanus, *Preaching Christ from the Old Testament* (Grand Rapids: Eerdmans, 1999), 234–77.

7. Greidanus, *Modern Preacher*, 113.

8. Greidanus, *Modern Preacher*, 113–14.

9. Greidanus, *Modern Preacher*, 114–16.

various Christian traditions that affirm the necessity of preaching Christ. For example, Roman Catholic homiletician Domenico Grasso writes: "The object and content of preaching is Christ."[10] Similarly, Eastern Orthodox theologian Georges Florovsky argues: "Ministers are commissioned and ordained in the church precisely to preach the Word of God. They are given some fixed terms of reference—namely, the gospel of Jesus Christ."[11] And, of course, Charles Spurgeon, quoted at the beginning of this chapter, is adamant about the necessity of preaching Christ: "No Christ in your sermon? Then go home!" Further complexity comes, suggests Greidanus, from the reality that Christ is both the eternal Logos through whom creation came into being and the incarnate Son of God revealed in the New Testament. Thus, for some, "preaching Christ" means to preach "Christ crucified," drawing a line to Christ's atonement on the cross from each text. For others, this might include drawing a line to Christ's resurrection. When it comes to the Old Testament, some link the text to the presence of the eternal Logos who is active in the Old Testament; others see all God-centered preaching as Christ-centered by default, since Christ is the second person of the Godhead.[12]

New Testament examples of preaching Christ remind us of how broad the possibilities are. For example, in 1 Corinthians 2:2, Paul writes, "For I resolved to know nothing while I was with you except Jesus Christ and him crucified." For Paul, this meant not merely attending to the event of the crucifixion, but bringing together the many biblical-theological motifs and themes of redemptive history that find their fulfillment and climax in Christ.[13] Then again in 1 Corinthians 15, Paul reminds the community in Corinth of the gospel he preached in this way: "For what I received I passed on to you as of first importance: that Christ died for our sins according to the Scriptures, that he was buried, that he was raised on the third day according to the Scriptures" (15:3–4). It was both the cross and the resurrection that formed the central content of Paul's preaching, which would include for Paul the meaning of these events and their manifold implications for the early Christian communities. As Greidanus reminds us, these central events provide insight and climactic fulfillment for many biblical

10. Domenico Grasso, *Proclaiming God's Message: A Study in the Theology of Preaching* (Notre Dame: University of Notre Dame Press, 1965), 6.

11. Georges Florovsky, *Bible, Church, Tradition: An Eastern Orthodox View* (Belmont, MS: Nordland, 1972), 9.

12. Greidanus, *Preaching Christ*, 3.

13. Greidanus, *Preaching Christ*, 5–6.

themes, including the themes of God's justice, love, final victory over evil, and salvation from sin, to name a few.[14]

Finally, it is clear from the New Testament that much early preaching centered upon the announcement that the kingdom of God was breaking into history in power.[15] The preaching of the kingdom was central both to Jesus's own teaching and also to the teaching carried on in the early community of his followers in the book of Acts. As Luke records it, the very center of Paul's ministry was "proclaiming the kingdom of God and teaching about the Lord Jesus Christ" (Acts 28:31).

Greidanus draws some conclusions from this breadth of New Testament examples of preaching Christ. To preach Christ is to preach the gospel of the kingdom, to preach that Jesus is Lord, and to consider in that preaching the massive implications of his reign and rule over all of creation. Therefore, to preach Christ is to proclaim some facet of his *person*, *work*, or *teaching* so that people might believe him, trust him, love him, or obey him more fully.[16] As Greidanus summarizes, preaching Christ means "preaching sermons which authentically integrate the message of the text with the climax of God's revelation in the person, work, and/or teaching of Jesus Christ as revealed in the New Testament."[17]

Greidanus illustrates several ways to do this, from both Old and New Testament texts and from the diverse genres represented in Scripture, in seven "pathways" to lead us from a text to this climactic revelation in Christ:

1. Redemptive-historical progression: tracing God's redemptive history from the text's historical setting to either Jesus's first or second coming.
2. Promise-fulfillment: showing how a promise of the coming Messiah found its fulfillment in Jesus's first coming.
3. Typology: moving from on Old Testament event, person, or even institution that becomes a type that prefigures or anticipates its antitype in Jesus.
4. Analogy: highlighting similarities between the teaching of a text and the teaching of Jesus, or at least demonstrating an analogy of authorial purpose with the purpose of one of Jesus's teachings.

14. Greidanus, *Preaching Christ*, 6–7.
15. Greidanus, *Preaching Christ*, 7–8.
16. Greidanus, *Preaching Christ*, 8–10.
17. Greidanus, *Preaching Christ*, 10.

5. Longitudinal themes: tracing the biblical-theological theme of a text throughout the Old Testament, up to and including its development through the person, work, or teaching of Jesus.
6. New Testament reference: moving directly from an Old Testament text to a New Testament reference or allusion or even to Jesus's teaching on a similar topic.
7. Contrast: demonstrating the contrast between an Old Testament text and the person, work, or teaching of Jesus in the New Testament.[18]

Greidanus makes a significant contribution to the practice of Christ-centered preaching both through his textbooks on preaching and through his expository commentaries on the Old Testament.[19] Before engaging Greidanus's model with a missional reading of Scripture, let's now consider Timothy Keller's "gospel-centered" model of preaching.

Gospel-Centered Preaching

Timothy Keller, pastor of Redeemer Presbyterian Church in New York City, has influenced many preachers over many years. Some of his sermons are widely available on the internet; Logos Bible Software recently released his "Sermons Archive"; he has lectured on his method of preaching; and, through the Gospel Coalition network and conferences, thousands of pastors have been shaped by Keller's call to "gospel-centered" preaching.[20]

The Aim of the Sermon

Keller argues that, every time you preach, you should preach the gospel to the *hearts* of those who hear, not just to their minds, wills, or emotions.[21] Typical evangelical preaching, Keller argues, is an exhortation of biblical

18. Greidanus, *Preaching Christ*, 227–87.

19. To date, three have been published on the books of Genesis, Ecclesiastes, and Daniel.

20. At the time of this writing, Timothy Keller's *Preaching: Communicating Faith in a Skeptical Age* (New York: Viking, 2015), had not been released. Keller generously provided a prepublication copy for use in research for this chapter.

21. Keller, "Preaching to the Heart without Being Legalistic," lecture 1, Ockenga Institute Pastors' Forum, Gordon Conwell Seminary, Hamilton, MA, April 4, 2006.

principles, or biblical information, or even biblical theology, aimed either to the will or to the emotions. The exhortation is often to live in a certain way, and the truths of the text target the will or stir the emotions in the process. Most preaching of this type assumes that the aim of the sermon is to give people information, which they then take with them and with which they seek to change their life. Keller's preaching seeks instead to bring the gospel of grace to bear on the human heart, changing the heart on the spot, during the delivery of the sermon.

Defining the "Heart"

In order to appreciate fully the distinctions Keller is making, and to grasp the nuances of his preaching method, we must probe his theological anthropology, particularly the central importance he gives to the human heart. Keller takes his cue from what he understands the Scriptures (and particularly the book of Proverbs) to mean by their description of the human heart. For Keller, the heart is the root of human nature, where we see the motivational structure of our thoughts, our emotions, and our wills: all that we are and do flows out of the heart. The heart is the control center of our lives: here we find the foundational commitments that shape every aspect of our lives. Keller asks, "What motivates you? What are you committed to? What have you set your deepest hopes on? What really gives your life purpose and meaning? What is most attractive to you?" For Keller, the answers to these questions begin to uncover what is living inside your heart.

Keller's understanding of the central role of the heart is shaped by his appropriation of Jonathan Edwards's teaching on the role of human "affections." According to Edwards, the affections are the inclinations of the soul. They are not identical to emotion, yet the affections deeply stir the emotions. Again, Keller illustrates: perhaps you get really angry when you are insulted, but your friend does not get angry when the same thing happens to him. Why this difference? Edwards would suggest that you have set the affections of your heart on your reputation, but your friend has not done that. Therefore, when your reputation is threatened, you become angry. Your emotions are stirred because of what you have set your affections upon.

Keller argues that Edwards shows us how the human heart is always looking for beauty, for excellence, for something to worship, to put hope in. This inclination of our soul is what Edwards means by affections. Therefore, what we set the affections of our hearts upon, what our hearts worship, what our hearts look to for beauty—these things will shape the motivations and reasons for doing the things we do. For Keller, this has everything to do with preaching: the main goal of the sermon is to go after this motivational structure of the heart and allow the gospel to redirect and reshape it. On the spot. During the sermon.

This happens, argues Keller, as the preacher makes truth *real*, not just clear. The preacher appeals to the heart, not just the mind, to change the affections while the sermon is being preached. This is why, Keller argues, it is not enough to lay out biblical principles or exposit the text with rich biblical theology. Sermons must bring people to Jesus so that the hearts of those who hear are stirred, moved, melted, and reconfigured by him while they listen.

Making the truth of the gospel real requires great skill on the part of the preacher to bring together the clarity of logic with the power of the imagination.[22] Moreover, to make truth real will require skillful contextualization of the gospel so that the story and language of the gospel is able to speak in a compelling way to the cultural context of the audience, particularly to those who are skeptical toward the gospel.[23] Keller highlights the six principles that are essential for contextual preaching of the gospel: the use of accessible vocabulary, the appeal to culturally respected authorities, the ability to demonstrate an understanding of doubts and objections, the need to both affirm and challenge baseline cultural narratives, the offer of the gospel that pushes on the culture's pressure points, and the call for gospel-based motivation for obedience.[24] This playful combination of logic and imagination, combined with the ability to enter, challenge, and retell the culture's stories with the story of the gospel, demonstrating how the longing of those cultural stories are met and fulfilled in Christ, is a skill Keller has developed thoroughly. His broad use of literature, film, philosophy, apologetics, science, and varied expressions of popular culture is striking and aids in his passion to make the truth of the gospel real to New Yorkers.

There are two keys a preacher must use in order to make the truth of the gospel real and to seek heart change in those who hear, argues Keller.

22. In *Preaching* (chap. 6), Keller expands this into six adverbs to describe that preaching to the heart entails preaching affectionately, imaginatively, wondrously, memorably, Christocentrically, and practically.

23. Keller, "Preaching to 'Emerging' Culture," lecture 5, Ockenga Institute Pastor's Forum, Gordon Conwell Seminary (South Hamilton, MA, April 5, 2006). Keller treats the issue of contextualization of the gospel at length in *Center Church* (Grand Rapids: Zondervan, 2012), 89–134. See also *Preaching*, chaps. 4–5.

24. Keller, *Preaching*, chap. 4.

The first is to provide a deep analysis of human sin.[25] The language Keller uses is this: the preacher needs "always [to] identify the sin underneath the sin." This "sin underneath" is rooted in the human heart, misdirecting the heart's motivations and affections away from the gospel and away from how the text calls us to live. For Keller, it is always the sin that operates at the deepest levels of the human heart, the sin that captures the heart's affections, that must be addressed by the preacher. If the preacher focuses only on the "surface sins" of thoughts, behaviors, attitudes, or words, then the motivational structures of the heart that drive those sins will remain untouched by the gospel.

For Keller, preaching must consider "why people do the things they do" and "how people change." He invites preachers to grapple with the following questions: "How do we deal with our sin problem? Our failure to live as God calls us to? How do we change and preach in a way that empowers others to change?" For Keller, whether the preaching text addresses issues of personal obedience, or character, or communal engagement in the mission of God, it is always confronting us with the reality of our own failures to live up to God's call for his people.

In order to make possible true transformation, the preacher must challenge the idolatry of the human heart that so often lies underneath the surface sins:

> Idolatry is always the reason we ever do anything wrong. Why do we ever lie, or fail to love, or break promises, or live selfishly? Of course, the general answer is "because we are weak and sinful," but the specific answer is always that there is something besides Jesus Christ that you feel you must have to be happy, something that is more important to your heart than God, something that is spinning out a delusional field and enslaving the heart through inordinate desires. So the secret to change (and even to self-understanding) is always to identify the idols of the heart.[26]

Keller's second admonition to preachers is to apply the finished work of Christ—his substitutionary life, death, resurrection, and ascension—to the human heart. As the "sin underneath the sin" is exposed, some aspect

25. Keller, "Preaching to the Heart without Being Pietistic," lecture 2, Ockenga Institute Pastor's Forum, Gordon Conwell Seminary (South Hamilton, MA, April 4, 2006).

26. Keller, "Preaching the Gospel in a Post-Modern World," chap. 5. Course Syllabus for Doctor of Ministry Program (Orlando: Reformed Theological Seminary, January 2002), 95.

of the finished work of Christ should be brought to bear upon the human heart so that its motivational structure is changed. This change comes through uprooting the idols that the human heart is worshiping and replacing them with faith in some aspect of the finished work of Christ, so that Christ and all that he has accomplished becomes the object of the heart's affections, and the heart is redirected toward worship of Christ and away from idols. This will happen, argues Keller, when Jesus becomes real and the affections of the heart are stirred by his beauty until the heart worships him and him alone.

Keller offers the following illustration to help us see the nuances of his model. Increasingly, people in Western culture are self-centered consumers. Yet Christ calls us to live selfless, generous lives. How do we preach to the human heart on this important issue? Keller responds: we must bring the work of Christ into this issue of generosity and money. Why do people fail to be generous? At one level it is simply because they are sinners. But a deeper answer can come only by probing how people's hearts relate to money. For some, money brings security—"if I just have enough money, then I am secure," some might say: security has become for them an idol of the heart. For others, money brings status—"if I just have enough money, I can live in a certain neighborhood, I can wear the right clothes, I can feel good about myself": status has become for them an idol of the heart. In either case, the problem underneath the sin of a failure to be generous is the problem the preacher must probe. This sin underneath the sin is ultimately a failure of the heart to look to Jesus instead of wealth for security or for status. Preaching to the heart on this issue will bring transformation: to the degree that you can make Jesus real to the heart, people will begin to worship and adore Christ, the affections of their hearts will begin to shift, and they will become more generous.[27] This is for Keller the goal of preaching. The focus must be not on bending the will, but rather on melting the heart, preaching toward the affections, and aiming at what the heart is truly worshiping, so that the idols underneath the sin of selfishness wither and Christ becomes more precious and beautiful. For Keller, the only way to fix the heart is to present the beauty of Jesus in the field of discourse of any particular sin, so that the heart's affections are drawn away from idols and toward Jesus.

Keller describes the narrative flow of his preaching in this way.[28] He be-

27. Keller gives this extended illustration in "Preaching to the Heart without Being Pietistic."

28. As he makes clear, this is not necessarily the outline of every sermon, but rather

gins with the text and unpacks in detail what the original author intended to communicate to the original audience. Then, he explicates what the text calls us to be like or to do: "Here is what you should be living like in light of this text," as he puts it, or what is sometimes called the "application problem" of the text. The next move is crucial for Keller: "But, guess what—you will never do it! Here is the reason why." This is where Keller talks about the sin underneath the sin, seeking to expose the idols of the human heart that prevent us from living up to what the text calls us to. Then he moves to Christ, lifting up Christ as both the solution to the application problem (as some aspect of his finished work is preached in a way that is aimed toward the affections) and as the hermeneutical resolution of the theme raised in the text.

Keller wants to do more than preach Christ as the ultimate fulfillment of the biblical theme raised in the text.[29] He seeks to lift up Christ as the only one who is able to help us respond in obedience to the call of the text. For Keller, the preacher should create a "problem" in the sermon by revealing the demands that the text makes on us. Then "the plot thickens," as he puts it, as we are not sure how we will live up to these demands. The preacher then brings in Jesus as the hero: because Jesus has already obeyed what the text calls us to—and has done so as our substitute—we too can now live this way as his Spirit is alive in us and empowering us.[30] Here is how Keller summarizes the "story he is trying to tell" in his preaching:

> In every text of Scripture there is somehow a moral principle. It may grow out of what it shows us about the character of God or Christ, or out of either the good or bad example of characters in the text, or because of explicit commands, promises, and warnings. This moral principle must be distilled clearly. But then a crisis is created in the hearers as the preacher shows that this moral principle creates insurmountable

---

the story that the sermon is telling through whatever outline is utilized. See Keller, "Preaching to the Heart: Unintentional Preaching Models," lecture 4, Ockenga Institute Pastor's Forum, Gordon Conwell Seminary (South Hamilton, MA, April 5, 2006).

29. This is how Keller would summarize much "Christ-centered" preaching; "Preaching to the Heart: Unintentional." This is not to say that Keller is not Christ-centered. In fact, Keller is adamant that preachers must preach Christ from every text of Scripture. In *Preaching* (chap. 3), Keller notes a variety of ways in which this can be done and highlights the following six basic ways of preaching Christ: preach Christ . . . from every genre of the Bible, through every theme of the Bible, in every major figure of the Bible, from every major image in the Bible, from every deliverance storyline, and through instinct.

30. Keller, "Preaching to the Heart: Unintentional."

problems. The sermon shows how this practical and moral obligation is impossible to meet. The hearers are led to a seemingly dead end. Then a hidden door opens and light comes in. The sermon moves both into worship and into Christ-application when it shows how only Jesus Christ has fulfilled this. If the text is a narrative, you can show how Christ is the ultimate example of a particular character. If the text is didactic, you can show how Christ is the ultimate embodiment of the principle. Finally, we show how our inability to live as we ought stems from our rejection of Christ as the Way, Truth, and Life (or whatever the theme is). The sermon points out how to repent and rejoice in Christ in such a way that we can live as we ought.[31]

A Missional Reading of Scripture in Conversation with These Models of Preaching

Building on this brief survey of these two models of preaching we are led to ask: What will a missional reading of Scripture contribute to preaching Christ and preaching the gospel? It is not simply a question of what a missional reading might add to either or both of these models; rather, what contributions are gained for the task of preaching when we put these models in conversation with a missional reading of Scripture? I offer six theses that seek to stimulate reflection on this important question.

We Need to Remove the Eclipse of Mission from Redemptive History

Greidanus helps us see how to preach the Bible in a Christ-centered way within the flow of redemptive history. We could locate strong grounds for such an approach in Luke 24, which records the encounter of the risen Christ with two of his followers on the road to Emmaus: "Then he opened their minds so they could understand the Scriptures. He told them, 'This is what is written: The Christ will suffer and rise from the dead on the third day, and repentance and forgiveness of sins will be preached in his name to all nations, beginning in Jerusalem'" (24:45–47). Christ is pointing us to his own life, death, and resurrection as the fulfillment of the Old Testament Scriptures. But what has been missed, as Chris Wright demonstrates

31. Keller, "Preaching the Gospel in a Post-Modern World," 78.

so well, is that we find here not only a strong clue for a christological center but also a strong clue for a *missional* center to the biblical story. Christ is pointing both to the events surrounding his life, death, and resurrection *and to* the mission to all nations that flows from those events, as the focus and fulfillment of (the whole of) Scripture: "Luke tells us that with these words Jesus 'opened their minds so they could understand the Scriptures,' or, as we might put it, he re-set their hermeneutical orientation and agenda. The proper way for disciples of the crucified and risen Jesus to read their Scriptures is from a perspective that is both *messianic* and *missional*."[32]

Wright uses this image to illustrate the value of a missional reading of Scripture: like any hermeneutical framework, it functions like a map in which not all features are highlighted, but only those most significant to the map-reader's need to see clearly and to establish direction. The hermeneutical framework of a missional reading provides "a way of 'seeing' the whole terrain, a way of navigating one's way through it, a way of observing what is most significant."[33] A missional-reading map allows us to see the fundamental orientation of the biblical story to the mission of God, allowing the major features of that story to stand out clearly and enabling us to see fruitful and surprising connections between many other features and that main story line. This refreshed seeing of the biblical landscape is essential to shaping the missional role and identity of God's people today. If the God of redemptive history is a missional God, and if the mission of this God is the central clue to the biblical story of redemption, it follows that the people of this God are missional in their own identity and purpose.

A Missional Reading of Scripture Draws Us Back into the Larger Story of God's People

Keller's "narrative flow" for preaching a text begins by moving from the preaching text to the original author's intended message.[34] And, as Greidanus reminds us, we must always embed the author's message within its larger narrative context.[35] What is that larger narrative context? A missional reading will continually remind us to see the original message of the text as

32. Wright, *Mission of God*, 107.
33. Wright, *Mission of God*, 139.
34. Keller, "Preaching to the Heart: Unintentional."
35. Greidanus, *Modern Preacher*, 112–13.

embedded in the larger story of God's mission through God's people. The larger narrative context always situates us within the story of God's mission.

Here I want to draw particular attention to the importance of a missional reading of Scripture for our understanding of the Old Testament story of God's people. N. T. Wright calls us to attend to the centrality of Israel's story for our own reading of Scripture: "For many writers . . . the long story of Israel seems to function merely as a backdrop, a source of prooftexts and types, rather than as itself the story of God's saving purposes."[36] Wright helps us to read the biblical text with real understanding of the long history of Israel and how that history shaped the missional identity of God's people to be a light to the world. This ancient story shapes our understanding of what God continues to do in the world through his people today. Wright's work resonates with the older statement made by Johannes Blauw in his important work on the mission of God's Old Testament people. Many years ago, Blauw put it this way:

> When we speak about the Church as "the people of God in the world" and enquire into the real nature of this Church, we cannot avoid speaking about the roots of the Church which are to be found in the Old Testament idea of Israel as the people of the covenant. So the question of the missionary nature of the Church, that is, the real relationship between the people of God and the world, cannot be solved until we have investigated the relation between Israel and the nations of the earth.[37]

Michael Goheen offers a helpful image of Israel's missional identity and role in the Old Testament story in his comment that Israel was a community "facing in three directions at once."[38] They were first called to look *backward* to creation, to embody God's original design and intention for human life. They were also called to look *forward* to the consummation, to bear in their corporate life God's promise of the goal of history, a restored humanity on a renewed earth. And finally they were called to look *outward* to the nations, for whose sake they were chosen, to confront the idolatry of neighboring peoples. Israel faced all of these directions so that the nations might come to know and worship the living God of Israel as the true God of the whole world.

36. N. T. Wright, *Justification: God's Plan and Paul's Vision* (Downers Grove, IL: InterVarsity, 2009), 11.

37. Johannes Blauw, "The Mission of the People of God," in *The Missionary Church in East and West*, ed. Charles C. West and David M. Paton (London: SCM, 1959), 91.

38. Michael W. Goheen, *A Light to the Nations* (Grand Rapids: Baker, 2011), 25–26.

A Missional Reading Will Call the Church to Missional Practices

Through the important work of James K. A. Smith, there is a renewed appreciation for the ways in which habitual practices have a formative effect on communities of faith, particularly on identity formation.[39] A missional reading of Scripture will direct us to missional practices that flow out of the text. By the term "practices," I am not referring simply to activities or programs of the church, but to all of the habitual rhythms of *being* and *doing* within local congregations as we engage our missional role and vocation in local contexts. As Darrell Guder argues, these practices provide "meaning, orientation, and purpose. Therefore they are essential to the formation of intentional missional communities of the Spirit."[40] These practices "aim to do nothing less than shape our identity by shaping our desire for what we envision as the kingdom—the ideal of human flourishing," as Smith puts it.[41]

Thinking in terms of the narrative flow of the sermon, to use Keller's image, the biblical text in a missional reading continually moves the people of God into missional practices in communal life. These embodied practices, to use Goheen's image, point us *backward, forward*, and *outward* to the ways of life that reflect God's intention for human life, God's promised restoration of all things, and that challenge and confront the cultural idolatry of our Western societies.

As Guder writes, there is an ethical dimension to the biblical text that preaching must capture:

> The ministry of the Word disciples God's people so that they can move out into the apostolate for which God's Spirit calls and empowers them. Gospel preaching is, therefore, always ultimately ethical in its orientation, because it addresses the shape and behavior of Christian witness in the particular place in which each community is God's sent people. Gospel preaching is the public testimony of the Lordship of Jesus Christ over all the contending idols and powers which lure the church away from faithful and obedient witness.[42]

39. James K. A. Smith, *Desiring the Kingdom* (Grand Rapids: Baker, 2009), 75–88.

40. Darrell Guder, ed., *Missional Church: A Vision for the Sending of the Church in North America* (Grand Rapids: Eerdmans, 1998), 154.

41. Smith, *Desiring the Kingdom*, 87.

42. Darrell L. Guder, "Missional Theology for a Missionary Church," *Journal for Preachers* 22.1 (1998): 3–11.

A missional reading of Scripture draws us to the communal, missional dimension of the ethical orientation of the text, or what we might call the "application" issue in preaching. A missional reading seeks to shape the way of life of a community in light of its role and identity in the biblical story, a way of life that is ultimately embodied through our habitual missional practices.

A Missional Reading Shows the Comprehensive Scope of the Church's Mission

When we make the connection between the original author's message and how the text calls us to live—the missional practices we are being called to embody—a missional reading will ground our own Christian community's mission in the cosmic scope of God's redemptive mission, as that has been unfolded in the biblical story. When the mission of the church is understood within the context of God's redemptive purposes for the creation, it becomes clear that mission involves the entirety of the church's life, deeds, and words. This will call the church to be both an incarnational presence in its local context and an *attractive* community that embodies God's renewal of all things.

If the scope of God's mission is as wide as creation, then the church's mission must reflect God's reign and rule in every area of life. The various vocational settings to which God's people are called are where the church's missional role and identity are expressed, and where missional engagement takes place, as God's people take up their vocational tasks for the life and flourishing of neighbor and world. Preaching from a missional reading of Scripture empowers and equips God's people for the various callings where they are to be missionally engaged.

We Must Attend to How Preaching Can Equip and Empower God's People for Mission

A missional reading is vital for the forming and nourishing of God's people, equipping them for their missional role in God's world. But we must ask, with George Hunsberger, "What exactly is it, in the biblical writings, that equips? Equips how, and in what manner, in which directions, in what areas of life, toward what forms of missional engagement?"[43]

43. George Hunsberger, "Proposals for a Missional Hermeneutic: Mapping the Conversation," GOCN White Paper (January 28, 2009).

Michael Goheen offers some helpful ways forward, building on N. T. Wright's work, to demonstrate how Scripture is not only a record of God's mission, but also a tool of God's mission.[44] The various books of Scripture, both Old and New Testaments, were given to nurture God's people for their missional calling in various missional contexts. Each genre in its own way plays a part in this missional activity of God. As Goheen notes, through law and instruction God seeks to order the communal way of life of his people to be a light to the nations; through wisdom literature God seeks to shape our lives in conformity with God's creational purposes; through the prophets and apostles God calls his people back to their purpose and mission; through poetry and liturgy God comes to nourish our worshiping life and shape our missional identity; through narratives that retell our story God reorients us to his purposes for and through his people; through the gospel proclamation of Christ God demonstrates how his mission brought salvation to God's people and through them to the world.[45]

As we preach various genres of Scripture and attend to the ways in which they function to equip God's people for mission, we must be careful—as Keller warns—not to fall into a "missional legalism."[46] We must recognize the subtle danger of moralism or legalistic activism expressed in missional ways. Preaching that does not root a community in the transforming power of the grace of God that we encounter in Christ will fail to provide the lasting change and motivation that can sustain missional engagement.[47] Without transformation at the heart level, there is no power for God's people to take up their mission, however broad (or narrow) that mission is conceived to be.

We Need to Move beyond Polarities of Perspective on the Gospel

Keller offers this note of concern: "Individual and corporate aspects of salvation, mission, and Christian living are often pitted against one another, and the individual aspect nearly eliminated."[48] Keller urges us to not lose

44. Michael Goheen, "Continuing Steps toward a Missional Hermeneutic," *Fideles: A Journal of Redeemer Pacific College* 3 (2008): 49–99.

45. Goheen, "Continuing Steps," 92–98.

46. Keller, "Preaching to the Heart without Being Pietistic."

47. Keller, "Preaching the Gospel in a Post-Modern World," 82.

48. Keller, *Center Church*, 268.

the individual aspects out of concern to recover the corporate aspects.[49] When "the classic doctrines regarding sin—as an offense against God's holiness that incurs his righteous wrath, as Christ propitiating God's wrath and taking our punishment as our substitute, and as the 'great exchange' of our sin being placed on Jesus and his righteousness being placed on us—are rejected as too individualistic and as contributing to the reason for the church's failure to become missional,"[50] Keller argues, we have lost balance. But from those working with a missional reading of Scripture, the larger concern seems to come from the opposite direction. As Lesslie Newbigin argues, many people in the West have grown accustomed to reading the biblical story starting with the question of individual salvation, "as if the whole cosmic drama of salvation culminated in the words, 'For me; for me.'"[51] This "soteriological self-centeredness," to borrow a phrase from G. C. Berkouwer, is a perniciously Western perversion of the gospel.[52]

Goheen suggests that a missional reading of Scripture helps reorient us to the logic of the biblical story, a logic that rescues us from our Western tendencies toward individualism. By such a reading we may be reoriented into a "cosmic-communal-individual" logic, as Goheen describes it. For example, reflecting on the cross, Goheen invites us to see that the cross is first a *cosmic* victory through which God accomplished the goal of history. Second, the cross creates a *community* that experiences God's grace and is transformed into a missional people. Third, through the cross, *individual* members of that community can share in this victory and mission through repentance and faith.[53] For Goheen, the order here is crucial: "God's goal is *cosmic*, creationwide renewal; he chooses a *community* to embody that future; and *individuals* are called to join this community and play their role in the bigger story."[54] He challenges us to begin not with the individual, but rather with the cosmic scope of what God has done in Christ. Only by seeing the cosmic and communal contexts of redemption do we understand the fitting place of individual participation.

49. Keller, *Center Church*, 268–71.

50. Keller, *Center Church*, 267.

51. Lesslie Newbigin, *The Gospel in a Pluralist Society* (Grand Rapids: Eerdmans, 1989), 179.

52. G. C. Berkouwer, *The Return of Christ*, trans. J. van Oosterom (Grand Rapids: Eerdmans, 1972), 211.

53. Goheen, *Light to the Nations*, 109–10.

54. Goheen, "The Mission of God's People and Biblical Interpretation: Exploring N. T. Wright's Missional Hermeneutic," paper presented at Scripture and Hermeneutics Seminar Meeting (San Francisco, November 18, 2011), 4.

So, as preachers, should we preach an individualistic, salvation-focused gospel? Or a cosmic and communal gospel of the kingdom? Should we ditch classic doctrines in favor of missional ones? We must move past these polarities. But how? Newbigin again is helpful here, reminding us that the gospel is first and foremost the announcement of historical events and their significance. We must realize that the meaning of these events and all that God has accomplished through them cannot be exhausted by only one image, whether that image is the (cosmic) kingdom of God or the (individual) atonement of a sinner saved by grace. This *event* character of the gospel will go a long way in helping us to overcome the false polarities emerging around the preaching of the gospel today:

> We are speaking about a happening, an event that can never be fully grasped by our intellectual powers and translated into a theory or doctrine. We are in the presence of a reality full of mystery, which challenges but exceeds our grasp. . . . Down the centuries, from the first witness until today, the church has sought and used innumerable symbols to express the inexpressible mystery of the event that is the center, the crisis of all cosmic history, the hinge upon which all happenings turn. Christ the sacrifice offered for our sin, Christ the substitute standing in our place, Christ the ransom paid for our redemption, Christ the conqueror casting out the prince of the world—these and other symbols have been used to point to the heart of the mystery. None can fully express it.[55]

Our preaching must seek to explore the richness of the many images and the comprehensive implications of all that God has accomplished through Christ. Such preaching will go a long way to form and shape churches as missional communities who participate in God's mission, engaging with God's world for the sake of the whole of God's creation.

55. Lesslie Newbigin, *The Open Secret: An Introduction to the Theology of Mission*, rev. ed. (Grand Rapids: Eerdmans, 1995), 49–50.

A Missional Reading of Scripture and Theological Education

CHAPTER 14

The Implications of a Missional Hermeneutic for Theological Education

Darrell L. Guder

The theology and practice of missional hermeneutics focus in the rigorous and comprehensive engagement with the Scriptures in which the interpretation of the text serves the formation of gathered communities so that they can be sent into the world as Christ's witnesses. The working hypothesis of the missional hermeneutics discussion of these last years, at least within the circle of the Gospel and Our Culture Network (GOCN), has been that the biblical witness is not only inbreathed by God's Spirit but also empowered by that Spirit to form and equip the gathered community for its vocation to be witnesses to Christ in Jerusalem, Judea, Samaria, and to the ends of the earth. The genesis of the missional hermeneutics discussion is much broader and more complex than any particular strand of it. We are seeing a theological grassroots movement in which complementary questions and concerns are emerging and merging into a challenging conversation that bears the marks of what Avery Dulles would call "an emerging theological consensus."

One crucial theme of this discussion must be the concern for the implications of such a hermeneutic for theological education. This concern has never been far from my mind as I have gone about the teaching of missional and ecumenical theology at Princeton Seminary. Every course I offer is a curricular investigation of what this hermeneutical discipline might really be about. It has been especially stimulating and generative to be able to offer cross-disciplinary courses in the missional interpretation of Scripture, specifically, of Pauline texts. These courses were officially listed as New Testament/theology courses, fulfilling requirements in either Greek exegesis or theological hermeneutics. In partnership with my friend and colleague Dr. Ross Wagner, we designed courses that combined basic exegetical work on the Greek text with its missional interpretation. Working our way through several epistles, we explored together some of the ways in which these texts continued the formation of their readers for missional witness *then* and how they might do so in our gathered communities *today*. Both students and faculty came away from those courses with a strong sense that the work we were doing was essential to the equipping of servant leaders of missional communities today. The focus of our discussion of the implications of a missional hermeneutic will thus be upon the scriptural formation of the congregation. Such a focus will have implications for every aspect of the theological training of the servant leaders of such congregations. What is required is an integrated theological approach, in which the doctrine of Scripture and the practices of scriptural formation function as one formative process in the local community.

For the sake of the *missio Dei* and the church's faithful service as its first fruit, instrument, and sign, both our theology of scriptural authority and our practices of scriptural formation need critical review and revision. Rather than conceptualizing that authority as a set of propositions about the Scriptures, we discover that Scriptures demonstrate their authority in the way the Spirit works through them to continue the apostolic mission through the formation of witnessing communities. They are authoritative in that they work formatively to equip communities for their vocation, their witness to Christ in the world into which God is sending them. The epistles' authors, through their writings, were continuing the formation of the congregations they had founded. The purpose of that founding was to continue the apostolic mission ignited at Pentecost, which often entailed cross-cultural translation and the forming of new expressions of apostolic mission communities. Similarly, the gospel writers provided the catechetical formation of such apostolic missionary communities, as they invited believers to join the first disciples in the process of personal and intensive formation that the rabbi Jesus conducted with them. The outcome of that discipling was their own apostolic vocation: in Peter's words, their mandate to "proclaim the wonderful deeds of him who had called them out of darkness into his marvelous light" (1 Pet. 2:11).

Our consensus about what missional hermeneutics is, how it might work, and why it is crucial for the faithful living and witnessing of equipped communities affirms the Reformation's commitment to *sola scriptura*. In the Swiss stream of the Reformation, the priority placed upon the formative power of Scripture was expressed early and repeatedly. As early as 1526 in the Disputation held at Ilanz in Graubünden, Johannes Comander framed the authority of Scripture for the vocation of the church: "The Christian church is born out of the Word of God; it shall remain in it and not listen to the voice of any stranger." Eberhard Busch describes how this summarizing statement shaped the Reformed consensus that was emerging in Switzerland. If this basic conviction is affirmed, he comments, then what follows is the conviction that "the church owes its entire existence to the Word of God." Further, "this Word is identical with the voice of the good shepherd according to John 10:3." Thus, "the church stands and falls in relation to this one thing, that it hears his voice." And then this necessary clarification: "The Word of God is authoritatively documented in the Holy Scriptures of both testaments, which, on the basis of this God's Word, bear within themselves the authority of the Holy Spirit."[1] This becomes the interpretation of the *sola scriptura* principle basic to every strand of the Reformation.

It was this conviction—that the church had been born out of the word of God—that led the Reformation pioneers to orient congregational life around scriptural formation. The preaching of the word of God became the central event of gathered worship, and it was carried out as the exposition of texts. Linked to the "audible word of God" was the "visible word of God" proclaimed in the celebration of the Lord's Supper. But the task of biblical formation was not confined to the pulpit and table for an hour on Sundays. Luther, Calvin, and Knox all made biblical teaching and formation of the community a priority for their churches. In Geneva, Calvin preached from the pulpit in St. Pierre's Cathedral. But every week he expounded Scripture in the medieval Auditoire next door to the larger church, producing a commentary on every book in the Bible except the book of Revelation. Further, reformers insisted that the Bible was to be made available to everyone in the vernacular. Catechisms were to be written and used for the formation of the congregants' faith. The Christian was encouraged to learn the faith, to engage in public discourse about the gospel and its meaning, and to translate the biblical vocation of witness into daily life. The inherited Christendom pattern that had made most Christians mere passive consumers of authoritative ministrations provided by a special caste of Christians was to be replaced with the practice of the priesthood of all believers. That basic claim—that the church is born out of the word of God—was, in effect, translated into the priority of biblical formation in congregations across

1. Eberhard Busch, *Reformiert: Profil einer Konfession* (Zürich: Theologischer Verlag Zürich, 2007), 55.

Reformation Europe. This certainly must be recognized as a great legacy of resources for missional hermeneutics today. But one of the most obvious signs of the decline of Western Christendom has been the loss of that focus upon congregational missional formation and a corresponding decline in biblical literacy.

Theological education today inherits that Reformation tradition in its curricular emphasis upon biblical studies as one of the four major areas of academic theology defined by Schleiermacher. Obviously there is a very pluralist spectrum of views about what the authority of Scripture actually means and how it should work. If, however, the basic emphases of the missional church project and the consensus regarding missional hermeneutics are the guiding convictions for our curriculum design, then we must approach the task in ways that imply a critique of current models of theological education. We would certainly advocate the traditional emphasis upon biblical studies, including biblical languages, exegesis, biblical history, and biblical theology, as the foundational studies for a servant leader of the church. The future equipper of the saints must have the basic tools for responsible biblical exegesis. But we would advocate more. One can express the concerns here with the current jargon of the academic guild, and especially its focus upon outcomes: our theological academy tends to center its attention on the competencies and skills of our graduates. That is the intentional outcome of our educational efforts. We are educating professionals to be the pastoral or ministerial leaders of our congregations. We see ourselves as parallel to law schools and medical schools. In fact, those of us teaching in universities call ourselves "divinity schools" and march very intentionally to the drum of the secular guild. But the missional mandate of the sent community requires that in this matter, as in so many, we undergo "transformation by the renewing of our minds" (Rom. 12:2).

What needs especially to be renewed is the biblical understanding and practice of the witnessing community in a particular place. The purpose of the apostolic mission was not to generate professional apostles or ordained ministers, nor was it the purpose of their proclamation merely to save souls. The apostolic mission was to form gathered and sent communities who would continue the witness to God's salvation in Christ that had brought them into existence in the first place. The original company of apostolic missionaries started out as people called by Jesus to be equipped by him for the mission that awaited them after Easter. Their process of formation, as I suggested, was that of disciples of a rabbi who formed them for their apostolic calling. Their graduation *from* the school of discipleship was *into* the work of the

Spirit at Pentecost, the apostolic mission. Its strategy was to found witnessing communities. The disciples in the first apostolic community were empowered and sent out to be community-founding missionaries. And the Spirit continues that same mission today, as God enables apostolic missionaries to form witnessing communities from generation to generation, from culture to culture, from language to language, and from polity to polity. Crucial to every generation and every cultural translation of the apostolic mandate is the biblical formation of the witnessing community. To be witnesses who belong to Jesus Christ and are his instrument for the spreading of the good news of the gospel, every such particular community needs its own version of the discipling process that prepared the first apostles. In the ancient liturgical discipline that assigns a gospel text to every Sunday and places its reading and exposition at the center of worship, we can discern that ancient commitment to the continuation of the apostolic mission.

We are not advocating any attempt to return to pre-Constantinian Christianity. But we are suggesting that the present paradigm shift, the decline of the established church structures of Western Christendom, presents us with an important opportunity. We are, in some ways, closer to the situation of pre-Constantinian Christianity. In the West, we are again becoming a marginalized minority movement, like the early church. With growing clarity, we can recognize our missional vocation as we learn to realize that we now live in a difficult mission field. As we come to terms with these changes, we begin to appreciate that they can and should have a direct impact upon our educational strategies for the preparation of servant leaders of missional communities, called to serve as Christ's witnesses in the mission field of the post-Christian West.

As the outcome of our educational efforts, we could focus upon the formation of biblical equippers of the saints, rather than professional clergy who are supposed to be experts in the organizational maintenance of denominational entities. We could orient our learning goals to the communities served by our graduates as their teaching elders, their equippers and mentors, rather than their professional ministers. The proper outcome of missional theological education, built and shaped by a missional hermeneutic, is that the community of equipped witnesses in a particular context will live out their lives intentionally as Christ's witnesses wherever and however God sends them. What that community of sent ones should experience when gathered is continuing formation and equipping, centered in the biblical word interpreted missionally. This needs to become the priority of the missional congregation, the community seeking to respond to that mandate, and therefore it must become the priority of our theological education: the biblical equipping of equippers of the saints.

One could define the purpose of the formation accomplished with a missional hermeneutic by referring to Paul's recurring formational theme in his epistles, summarized in Philippians 1:27: "This is what is important—lead your public life in ways worthy of the gospel of Jesus Christ." Or, to cite the classic text in Ephesians 4:1: "I beg you to lead a life worthy of the calling to which you have been called." The task of missional hermeneutics is to guide the community in its discovery of what conduct, what practices of witness, what demonstrations of the gospel are truly worthy of the gospel, worthy of God, worthy of our calling. It is for that worthy witness that Paul is praying when he writes to the Philippians "that their love might abound more and more, with knowledge and insight, so that that they might together approve what is truly excellent" (Phil. 1:9–10).

As heirs of centuries of Christendom, we do not confront this challenge without resources. There are diverse examples of such formation resulting from rigorous engagement with the Scriptures. We can, for instance, draw on the ancient catechetical traditions in the patristic period that prepared adult converts for incorporation into witnessing eucharistic communities through the disciplines of baptism. Central to that formation was the close attention given to witnessing practices that disclosed something of God's goodness expressed in the gospel—conduct worthy of Jesus Christ. We can discover fruitful examples of Bible-centered formation in the companies of missionaries that evangelized Ireland under St. Patrick's lead, and the continuation of that Celtic piety in the Scottish and North European mission. Disciplines of biblical formation are found in the stories of monastic mission, beginning with the public witness of early Benedictine communities and later the Franciscan and Dominican orders. Investigating the history of Western Christendom with a view to finding such resources leads us to think about the importance of a missional hermeneutic for the formal study of church history in our seminaries.

Here again, the missional vocation of the congregations our graduates serve will need to guide our setting of educational goals and the curricular design intended to implement them. David Bosch charts the way with the second third of his book *Transforming Mission*, which interrogates the role and action of mission in the major epochs of Western Christendom's history.[2]

2. David Bosch, *Transforming Mission*, 20th anniversary ed. (Maryknoll, NY: Orbis, 2011), 185–356.

This is not a history that merely needs to be learned so that our teaching elders are better informed. The basic thrust of biblical formation should permeate our historical inquiry as well. When we approach the history of Western Christendom from the perspective of the essentially missionary nature of the apostolic church, we are confronted by the strange absence of mission as a theological theme in the developing ecclesiologies of Western Christendom. The practice of mission is always present, in diverse ways, but the biblical and theological engagement with mission is largely absent. Neither the theologies of the church nor the theologies of Scripture carry forward the essentially missional character of both that characterized the apostolic and subapostolic periods. One of the reasons for this loss of a theology of mission was the so-called Christianization of Europe under Constantine. David Bosch points out that from the early medieval period on, the so-called Great Commission was not interpreted in the churches of Western Christendom as having any significance for the church's definition or purpose in its already "Christianized" context. It wasn't until William Carey's reclamation of the text as relevant to the emerging global mission in the late eighteenth century that it was read as authoritative for the church's understanding of its missionary task.[3]

The contemporary situation of the Christian movement confronts us with two contradictory facts: Western Christendom, after over fifteen centuries of privilege and dominance, is in rapid decline, while the Christian movement in the global South is thriving. While former church buildings in the West now are being "repurposed" as everything from condominiums to bookstores, growing churches in the global South are struggling to provide the buildings and organizational means to cope with their expanding numbers. A significant proportion of the theological seminaries in North America are considered to be at risk of closing, while there is urgent need in the global church outside the West for leadership and thus for leadership formation. We can no longer teach church history as primarily a Eurocentric enterprise, and we are establishing chairs of world Christianity out of the growing awareness that God's people are marching through history in different directions, and we in the West are becoming marginal to their pilgrimage.

These contradictory paradigm shifts, with their demographic implications, constitute a challenge to our inherited forms of theological education. We need to reorient our ways of learning and interpreting our history. A missional hermeneutical approach to our history is clearly essential as

3. Bosch, *Transforming Mission*, 347–49.

part of the formation of servant leaders today. Our mission field is now at our front door, and it is a difficult and challenging mission field. Not long ago, we defined mission in terms of departing Christendom, crossing the borders of Western culture and moving into what some called "the two-thirds world." We are now having to learn that we are sent ones when we leave our Christian gatherings and enter our immediate mission fields—our own neighborhoods. The task of theological education today is to prepare future servant leaders to be both missionaries and missionary equippers in resistant and even hostile contexts in the West. We have excellent resources for this task, since Christendom still hosts most of the religious research and has most of the money for such undertakings. But the lenses through which we read and interpret our history must be changed. Today, we need to interrogate and interpret our history from the perspective of Christendom's reductionisms of the gospel and its mission, its compromises with its context, the cultural captivities that define it. Such critical work on our history is the prerequisite for our ability to understand our context. The absence of mission as theologically definitive of the church's purpose and practice will constantly confront us and call for both critical and constructive work. We will have to give particular attention to the ways in which the Bible has functioned in the church of Western Christendom in order to sort out the kind of radical reorientation that must result from reading our history through a missional hermeneutic of Scripture.

I have sketched the implications of a missional hermeneutic for theological education in the areas of biblical study and formation and in the engagement and interpretation of our history as a Christian movement. Matters get much more complicated when we begin to think about the institutional history of Western theological education. We all know that the structures, institutions, offices, and content of the Western theological academy grew out of the scholarly communities that emerged in the monastic movement. It's a remarkable story from which countless blessings have flowed that have enriched Christian life and witness over the centuries. But it is an intellectual and institutional history located totally within, and shaped by, Western Christendom. The roots of our theological education even today are defined by that ancient partnership of throne and altar, by the privileging of the Christian faith and the Christian church, by the assumption that our European context represented the reign of God in Christ, which was God's intention for human history. The Christendom cradle of Western education was profoundly influenced by the church's partnership with power, wealth, property, and social prestige. Preserving the tradition and its institutions was the major emphasis. The goal was more mastery than missional service—we still educate "masters" of divinity. That historical development of theology as a cluster of academic disciplines taught by credentialed scholars was pervasively shaped by the absence of mission in our ecclesiological reflection. The implicit task of theological formation was to continue and to maintain the *corpus Christianum*, the Christian society ruled by Christ through his vicar, the bishop in Rome. The express purpose was to generate a class of lesser nobility called the clergy, who were credentialed to provide the religious ministrations their members needed. Their power and authority within society were symbolized by the trappings of their offices, expressed by titles ranging from "reverend" to "your grace" and "your holiness." The primary task of that ecclesiastical hierarchy was the maintenance of the powerful and wealthy institutional church. That maintenance did not rule out the need for theological renewal and reform, nor did it invalidate that countless ministers have served God and his people faithfully. But the practice of ordered ministry was always both implicitly and explicitly within the structures of a church that saw itself as an end in itself. The assumption that largely guided this intellectual universe was that the boundaries of European Christendom defined the reign of God intended by God and implemented in the historical project initiated with Constantine. God reigned through the divinely ordained hierarchy and clerical nobility of the church, which was the kingdom of God on earth.

Thus, when the Reformers quite rightly emphasized that the church was born out of the word of God, their understanding of the authoritative work of God's word did not include any questioning of the Christendom system that was their context. Their critique was directed toward the cleansing of the vineyard, including the problems of ecclesiastical corruption and abuse, but not toward a radical redefinition of the vineyard. The birthing of the church out of the word of God was not the birthing of a missional church, but rather a church that ultimately served the inherited structures of Western Christendom. In all of the significant theological course corrections that resulted from the Reformation, there was no reclamation of the essentially missional nature and purpose of the church. The exception was, of course, the radical Reformation, within which the rejection of Western Christendom was linked with an articulate sense of missional vocation.

The continuing development of Western theological education generates, of course, a great diversity of institutional forms, almost all of which can trace their ancestry back to the medieval faculties of theology. These diversifying strands of theological formation have interacted with the

Christendom legacy in a variety of ways. The absence of mission continues, however, to wield its influence as the story moves toward modernity. The absence of a missional hermeneutic creates a theological framework that allows the various strands of Western Christianity to rationalize their numerous reductions and distortions of the biblical gospel. All of them became especially skilled in justifying the divisions that characterize Western Christendom from the sixteenth century onward. Such patterns persist in our various theological traditions today.

Our challenge today is to remove the Christendom lenses that blur our understanding of our vocation and its practice. As we do so, however painfully, we gradually come to see that our gospel is domesticated, our ecclesial traditions are compromised, and our practice of Christian witness is challenged to define what will truly be conduct worthy of the gospel of Jesus Christ. The resolution of this theological dilemma is not going to be a matter of strategic renewal or improved programs. It cannot be treated as a problem to be solved. The impact of an authentically missional hermeneutic upon theological education, as upon the life and practice of the church in general, is going to demand repentance and conversion.

We turn, then, to the implications of a missional hermeneutic for the work of theology proper. What would be the outcome of a critical and constructive interaction between a missional hermeneutic of Scripture and the discipline of theology or doctrine or, to use the term favored by Karl Barth and Otto Weber, dogmatics?[4] We discover one approach to that issue in the way in which Reformed theologians like Barth and Weber defined the task of dogmatics. They suggested that it was the particular role of the discipline of dogmatics to scrutinize the church's exposition of God's word in its preaching and teaching to assess if it was faithful to that word. To borrow St. Paul's language, their theological endeavor was to investigate the church's message in terms of its worthiness to the gospel of Jesus Christ. Without using the term, they were creating a theological space for a missional hermeneutic to begin to shape doctrine.

When we examine how Barth restores mission to the very center of his ecclesiology, we discover that he is, in fact, working consequently with a missional hermeneutic that guides his interpretation of the church's identity, vocation, and practice. Much work remains to be done on how Barth's interpretation of Scripture can contribute to the formation of com-

4. Barth's great project is entitled *Church Dogmatics*, while Otto Weber's two-volume theology text is entitled *Foundations of Dogmatics*.

munities of witness. One could make the claim that *Church Dogmatics* is a consequently Trinitarian exposition of God's mission, to be carried out by a people gathered by his Spirit to serve his healing purposes through the practice of the vocation of witness. Barth never uses the term *missio Dei* to my knowledge, but what I would call his "Trinitarian missiocentricity" can certainly be construed as an authentically missional theological proposal that does, in fact, translate effectively into the life and practice of a gathered community.

That concern for translation into the practice of the community points us toward perhaps the most pressing implication of a missional hermeneutic for the work of theology. German systematic theologian Martin Kähler famously claimed early in the twentieth century that "mission is the mother of theology." By this he meant that theology was "an accompanying manifestation of the Christian mission" and not a "luxury of the world-dominating church." David Bosch summarizes Kähler's argument: "The New Testament writers were not scholars who had the leisure to research the evidence before they put pen to paper. Rather, they wrote in the context of an 'emergency situation' of a church which, because of its missionary encounter with the world, was *forced* to theologize."[5] One can interpret that definition of the theological enterprise as the "luxury of a world-dominating church" as an appropriate description of the way theology tended to function within Western Christendom. The urgency of the changing context as Christendom declines compels us to do our theologizing in different ways, for different reasons, and working toward different outcomes. The basic challenge is to overcome, to set aside the long-standing division between theology proper and practical theology.

The practices of the missional community should translate the missionally interpreted biblical word into its being, doing, and saying in the world. If that is to happen, the witnessing community needs the guidance of doctrinal theology formed by a missional hermeneutic and thus faithful to the Scriptures. That theological guidance will equip the community to struggle with the questions that inevitably arise when the community is sent into the world. What is conduct worthy of our calling? How does the gathered community care for its own and for its neighbors? How does it cope with the hard challenges of mortality? How does it demonstrate God's inclusive love in its hospitality? How does it argue Christianly and strug-

5. Martin Kähler, *Schriften zur Christologie und Mission* (Munich: Kaiser, 1971 [orig. 1908]), 189–90, cited in Bosch, *Transforming Mission*, 16.

gle for consensus? How does it use its resources and steward its property? How do our members engage their Muslim, Buddhist, or Hindu neighbors? These matters of praxis are, in fact, theology translated into service. This is the context for a radically missional rethinking of what we have come to call "practical theology." The biblical formation of the community for its missional vocation should consciously focus upon the public calling of the apostolic church. As Paul says, the church is to lead its public life worthy of the gospel of Jesus Christ. The imperatives addressed to the New Testament communities constitute a comprehensive curriculum for the missional formation of a community of public witness. Taken together and carefully read and interpreted, the New Testament imperatives lay out for us the "community that Jesus intended."[6]

We can no longer do abstract theologies of the church: we must instead translate the theological claims we make into the conduct that demonstrates what the gospel of God's reign in Christ means in terms of our witness before a watching world. I don't know how, institutionally, we overcome the problematic curricular separation of the study of ecclesiology from the cluster of disciplines we call practical theology. A missional hermeneutic, however, will require that this false dichotomy be addressed as our various disciplines replace their silo mentality with a commitment to holistic formation for the service of witness. A missional hermeneutic is our primary resource to do that, precisely because it originates in the purpose of the scriptural witness as witness-empowering testimony.

The church is born out of the word of God. That basic conviction of the Reformation properly continues to define our doctrine and practice of the church. But when mission is returned to the center of our calling and our missional vocation is reclaimed as the definition of what it means to be a Christian, then that birthing becomes a much more comprehensive, mobilizing, and ongoing claim. It does not just point back to roots and founders, but rather speaks to a continuing process of biblical begetting of the witnessing community. It is the power and purpose of the word of God to guide and shape the community's life, its practices, and its thinking so that it can be faithful to its calling.

The implications for theological education of a missional hermeneutic are, by any standard, radical. They constitute a profound challenge to

6. Gerhard Lohfink, *Jesus and Community: The Social Dimension of Christian Faith*, trans. J. P. Galvin (Philadelphia: Fortress, 1984). The original German book is entitled *Wie hat Jesus Gemeinde gewollt?* ("How did Jesus intend the community?").

our institutional status quo. There are no easy answers to this challenge, although there are certainly encouraging signs. The growing interest in "missional hermeneutics" is itself one such sign. The work of theologians such as Christopher Wright, Tom Wright, and Michael Goheen is a further sign. We can recognize in theological scholarship leading up to the present context that fundamental missional issues were beginning to be addressed, although the term "mission" may not have been explicitly used.[7] These endeavors are a summons to a transformation of theological education that can come only as the Spirit renews our corporate thinking and deciding. For it to happen, we shall need to repent of our conformities to the enticing captivities of Christendom. Yet, such a transformation can take place, precisely because of the power of God's word at work in the church. We can engage in this transforming work with confidence, because God is faithful.

One of the classic concerns in theological education is to integrate theological formation upon a centering vision and purpose. We have sought to demonstrate that the missional vision of the church's vocation is such a centering and integrating orientation. There is, however, an inherited tension in the theological academy that tends to separate intellectual discipline from personal spiritual formation. If the gathered community is the basic instrument of the apostolic mission, then the shared life of those who are being prepared to lead such communities needs to be accorded as much attention as the curricular disciplines of the seminary. Recent experimentation with learning cohorts is promising. When students carry out their theological formation in intentional communities that integrate academic discipline with the corporate practices of spiritual growth, then their capacity truly to be equippers of the saints for the work of service is greatly enhanced. Such missiocentric integration of theological formation needs to be pursued energetically, especially in the context of the post-Christendom West.

The missional reading and interpretation of Scripture must reshape theological education so that the community of saints may be equipped through their encounter with the written word of God. This claim is based on the more comprehensive claim that the purpose of the gathered community of believers is to continue the apostolic mission in concrete places

7. The exegetical and theological work of biblical scholars such as Leonhard Goppelt, Eduard Schweizer, Joachim Jeremias, Peter Stuhlmacher, H. H. Rowley, Markus Barth, and Alan Richardson, to mention only a very few, prepares the way for the emerging concern for biblical missional formation.

by serving as Christ's sent witnesses. Theological education serves that purpose by equipping teachers and mentors of the gospel to serve such gathered communities. The outcome of our theological educational endeavors is thus not the qualified professional graduate but the gathered community of obedient witnesses who are enabled to be about their vocation because our graduates serve them as "equippers of the saints." This recasting of the goal and purpose of theological education translates the larger reclamation of the church's essentially missional vocation into the actual practice of the theological academy. Just as the church is not an end in itself, the theological seminary is not an end in itself, but a gathered, equipped, and commissioned community that serves the church by equipping its servant leaders.

CHAPTER 15

A Missional Reading of Scripture for Theological Education and Curriculum

Michael W. Goheen

Mission and the Crisis in Theological Education

Voices from various quarters are expressing concern about the following aspects of theological education today:[1]

- Preparation for pastoral ministry: the subjects taught in seminary are highly theoretical, and such detached theological reflection alienates students from ministry, leaving them unprepared for their pastoral calling.
- Spiritual and moral formation: seminaries by their very nature are primarily interested in the cognitive side of training, the intellectual mastery of information, and so are unable to nurture, oversee, or even assess the spiritual growth of students.
- Connection to the local congregation: seminaries are academic institutions that often have little connection to local congregations they serve.
- Faculty qualifications: faculty are chosen primarily on the basis of their academic record, and so seminaries are populated by professors with little or no pastoral experience.
- Professionalization of ministry: the academic-professional model of ministry leads to the placing of inexperienced young people as

1. Of course, the degree to which each of these is true will vary from institution to institution. Nevertheless, each one of these critiques has been made many times, and I have heard most of them directly.

leaders of congregations—because of their academic qualifications, not because of their ministry experience.

- Residential requirements: students are separated from their churches and required to be resident in academic institutions for many years.
- Cost: many students, who subsequently enter pastoral ministry and thus rarely command a high salary, finish their degrees with crippling debt.
- Pedagogy: lectures and transfer of information is the primary pedagogical mode, and a final exam or research paper becomes the primary way of assessing whether the student has mastered the information presented in the course.
- Curriculum: various problems that have been raised with curriculum will be treated later in this chapter.

Several contextual factors help to bring these concerns to the fore. The first is the cultural shift against the Enlightenment worldview, a public and culturally formative vision that has held unrivalled supremacy for several centuries in the West. The postmodern ethos of the West has lately raised questions concerning some of the deeply problematic assumptions of the Enlightenment that have shaped theological education. The second is the increasingly neo-pagan environment of Western society that makes clear to many pastors that they are in the midst of a missionary setting where an institutional "maintenance mode" will no longer suffice. And for some there is a third: the critique from mission leaders and the church in the Southern hemisphere. For at least four or five decades, "Third World Christians [have been] . . . questioning the assumptions which have dominated theological education for at least the last one hundred and fifty years."[2]

In the past half century, some of those involved in the Western missionary tradition offered their own reflections on theological education, from which there is much to be learned.[3] The cross-cultural experiences of those who had gone out from the West as missionaries, and their struggle to train leaders for the burgeoning church of the non-West, has given them the gift of new eyes by which to see more clearly the assumptions of the controlling cultural story of the West that has shaped theological education.

2. J. Andrew Kirk, *Theology and the Third World Church* (Downers Grove, IL: InterVarsity, 1983), 46.

3. Cf. Harvie M. Conn, "Theological Education and the Search for Excellence," *Westminster Theological Journal* 41.2 (1979): 311–63.

This was especially evident in the middle part of the twentieth century. Many of the significant critiques that one encounters today were voiced over four decades ago by leaders in the Western missionary tradition, as well as some from the Third World. As the explosive growth of the church in the Southern hemisphere became evident, the need for ministerial training to equip leaders there became more urgent. The search was on, among those who refused to import inappropriate Western models of theological education to the global South, for new models of theological education. Their reflections remain a largely untapped resource, and those who are willing to return to this conversation now will find fresh wisdom there.

There is a second reason that midcentury mission leaders may provide insight today: they recovered the centrality of mission in the biblical story. In fact, many lived through and participated in the early struggle to articulate how this central theme of mission impacts the reading of Scripture, the nature and task of theology, and the enterprise of theological education. For the many pastors today who are awakening to the centrality of mission—and this appears to be widespread, in light of the current growth in the number of books and consulting ministries capitalizing on the word "missional"—it will be essential to return to this rich tradition that struggled with the centrality of mission for theological education.

The *Missio Dei* and the Missionary Nature of the Church

In 1952 the International Missionary Council met in Willingen, Germany, and proposed a new theological framework for mission, which was destined to have far-reaching consequences for theological education. In the decade and a half up to this time massive changes had been taking place. The growth of the church in the non-Western world, the missionary movement's self-criticism in regard to its own theological foundations, the widespread loss of confidence in the "Christian" nature of the West on the heels of demonic ideologies and rapid secularization, and the demise of colonialism—all combined to foment a crisis in understanding the nature of mission. Clearly, mission could no longer be understood as only a cross-cultural activity initiated by mission organizations in the Christian West to be carried out in the non-Christian non-West. If old definitions simply did not fit the new realities of the mid-twentieth century, what was the future for Christian mission? The task of Willingen was to draft a new theological vision for mission in the midst of this turbulent time.

The final statement adopted at Willingen, entitled "The Missionary Calling of the Church," begins: "The missionary movement of which we are a part has its source in the Triune God himself."[4] Mission is not first of all a human enterprise: it has its true source in the love of the Father who sent the Son to reconcile all things to himself. The Son sent the Spirit to gather his church and empower them for mission; the church was sent by Jesus to continue his mission: "There is no participation in Christ without participation in his mission to the world. That by which the Church receives its existence is that by which it is also given its world-mission. 'As the Father has sent Me, so send I you.'"[5]

This new framework for mission made clear that the starting point for mission was, first, the mission of God as narrated in Scripture and, second, the missionary nature of the church as it participates in God's mission. Here we see a radical shift in focus and also a remarkable widening of the implications of mission. A host of assumptions tied to colonialism and Christendom were shattered. Rooted in God's reconciling mission, the missional vocation of the church was now perceived to be no longer limited geographically to the non-West or to certain intentional activities of outreach. Mission was now recovered as defining the very identity of the church: the role it was called to play as covenant partner with God in *his* mission.

It is sometimes forgotten that this crucial moment coincided with the ascendency of biblical theology in the ecumenical movement.[6] Brevard Childs observes three major elements of consensus in the biblical theology movement: (1) theological: the main character in the Bible is God, who is acting in history; (2) narrative unity: the Bible is one unfolding story of God's redemptive work that climaxes in Jesus Christ, and all books and events must find their meaning within this narrative context; (3) history: the redemptive work of God is revealed in his mighty acts in history.[7] All three of these components are present in a World Council Report issued

4. Norman Goodall, ed., *Missions under the Cross: Addresses Delivered at the Enlarged Meeting of the Committee of the International Missionary Council at Willingen, in Germany, 1952; with Statements Issued by the Meeting* (London: Edinburgh House Press, 1953), 190.

5. Goodall, ed., *Missions under the Cross*, 190.

6. Lesslie Newbigin was the primary crafter of the Willingen statement, and he is deeply indebted to this approach to Scripture; cf. Michael W. Goheen, "*As the Father Has Sent Me, I Am Sending You*": *J. E. Lesslie Newbigin's Missionary Ecclesiology* (Zoetermeer: Boekencentrum, 2000), 122–23.

7. Brevard Childs, *Biblical Theology in Crisis* (Philadelphia: Westminster, 1970).

three years before Willingen entitled *Guiding Principles for the Interpretation of the Bible* (Oxford, 1949). The statement affirms that "the unity of the Old and the New Testaments is . . . in the ongoing redemptive activity of God in the history of one people, reaching its fulfilment in Christ."[8] Thus as Willingen spoke of the sending activity of the triune God, it had in view not a mere theological formula, but an actual historical record summarizing God's long redemptive journey in the biblical story. The participation of God's people in his mission must also be articulated in this narrative context. Their missionary identity issues from the role they play in this story of God's mission.[9]

We pause to emphasize the importance of this "Willingen moment." This was not merely a matter of articulating a new framework for mission as it was traditionally conceived. This was a radically new understanding of mission, bursting with implications far beyond the cross-cultural missionary task of the church. Willingen pointed us to a central thread in the story of the Bible: God has taken up the people of God into his mission to reconcile all things to himself. This determines our very identity, our very nature and vocation.

Implications for Scriptural Hermeneutics, Theology, and Theological Education

The effects of Willingen were far-reaching, with at least three important implications. The first is a *missional hermeneutic*: if the mission of God and the participation of the church in that mission is a central theme of the biblical story, then it is imperative to ask what a hermeneutic might look like that reads the whole of Scripture with mission as a central category. The second is a *missional theology*: if mission is a dominant motif in the biblical story, it is imperative to ask how this impacts theological reflection on Scripture. Obviously Scripture is the primary source and authority for theological reflection, and if mission is central to the Bible then theology must take account of this. Moreover, if the central identity of the church is missional, then the question arises as to how theology equips the church

8. Ellen Flesseman-van Leer, ed., *The Bible: Its Authority and Interpretation in the Ecumenical Movement*, Faith and Order Paper 99 (Geneva: World Council of Churches, 1980), 14.

9. Cf. Michael W. Goheen, *A Light to the Nations: The Missional Church in the Biblical Story* (Grand Rapids: Baker, 2011).

for its vocation. This central scriptural theme must both *inform the content* and *shape the goal* of theology. Thus, missional theology is the theological consequence of taking seriously God's mission and the church's participation in that mission. The third implication of Willingen applies to *missional theological education*: If there is a fundamentally missional quality to the church, then surely it should be reflected in the theological education meant to serve that church. Already at Willingen, the consequences of the *missio Dei* and of the missionary understanding of the church for theology and theological education were raised:

> This study has of necessity led us to consider theological education and we cannot but express our concern that theological education throughout the world should be much more radically oriented to the total missionary task of the Church. This should mean not only a study of the history of religions and of the Christian movement in other lands, but also an emphasis upon the missionary obligation of the Church in such subjects as theology, Church history and Christian ethics.[10]

What are the ramifications of a missional reading of Scripture for theology and theological education? The remainder of this chapter offers some brief reflections on missional theology and its implications for theological education, before turning finally to a proposal that sketches elements of a missional curriculum.

Mission and Theology

The early pioneers of the missionary movement were concerned primarily with the pragmatics of carrying out cross-cultural mission. Little theological reflection on mission seemed necessary in view of the confident assurance of the Western missionary movement. The crisis of mission in the mid-twentieth century raised new questions about the nature, goal, and validity of Christian mission. This produced growing theological reflection on mission—a theology of mission. However, the centrality of mission in the biblical story obstinately refused to be reduced to one more biblical theme. A growing chorus of voices called for something more radical: to move beyond a theology of mission, to a missional theology. Harvie Conn insists

10. Goodall, *Missions under the Cross*, 214.

that the "question is not simply, or only, or largely, missions and what it is. The question is also theology and what it does."[11]

"Missional" as an adjective here is not another minor subspecies of theological reflection, like liberation or feminist theology. Rather, it defines a constituent component of all theological reflection that is faithful to Scripture. Thus, we are in need, says David Bosch, of a "missiological agenda for theology rather than just a theological agenda for mission; for theology rightly understood, has no reason to exist other than critically to accompany the *missio Dei*."[12] Along the same lines, Darrell Guder urges that the "formation of the church for mission should be the motivating force that shapes and energizes our theological labors in all their diversity and distinctiveness."[13]

These authors are rightly reacting against a theology that "received its main features [during] the period in which Christianity had practically ceased to be a missionary religion."[14] Both the nature and purpose of theology and its main curricular divisions were formalized when the church lost the horizon of mission from its existence. A major problem was that "the present division of theological subjects [was] canonized in a period when the church in Europe was completely introverted."[15] It was felt that the missional theologies of the Third World church might present a challenge to the nonmissional theologies of the West at precisely this point, since they had been forged in the fire of mission. Thus, Bosch notes, "Third World theologies are *missionary* theologies, whereas First World theologies are not," and so, he hopes, "Third World theologies may become a force of renewal in the West."[16]

What is missional theology? Missional theology is a theological task that probes the implications of the church's missional vocation as it participates in the *missio Dei*. The question is, What difference does it make *for*

11. Harvie Conn, "The Missionary Task of Theology: A Love/Hate Relationship?" *Westminster Theological Journal* 45 (1983): 1–21 at 7.

12. David Bosch, *Transforming Mission: Paradigm Shifts in Theology of Mission* (Maryknoll, NY: Orbis, 1991), 494.

13. Darrell Guder, "From Mission and Theology to Missional Theology," *Princeton Seminary Bulletin* 24.1 (2003): 48.

14. Lesslie Newbigin, *Honest Religion for Secular Man* (Philadelphia: Westminster, 1966), 102.

15. David Bosch, "Theological Education in Missionary Perspective," *Missiology* 10.1 (January 1982): 26.

16. David Bosch, *Believing in the Future: Toward a Missiology of Western Culture* (Valley Forge: Trinity, 1995), 36.

theology if the mission of God and the missionary nature of the church is a constituent thread in the biblical story?

The implications of the missional nature of the church need to be worked out in at least two areas: the congregational life of the church and the theological curriculum. First: how does the missional nature of the church impact the life of the congregation—its nurturing ministry, its vocation of witness, and its structures to enable nurture and witness? Second: how does the dominant motif of mission in the biblical story shape the theological enterprise—in the content of its various disciplines (biblical studies, systematic and historical theology, church history, ethics and ecumenical studies, congregational theology), in its curricular division between theoretical theology (biblical studies, systematic theology, church history) and practical theology, in its purpose and goal, its unity, and its methodology?

Missional theology rejects the notion of a *theologia perennis*—a timeless theology valid for all times and places—and is alert to all theology taking place in particular historical and cultural contexts. There is no supracultural or metacultural theology; there is only theology that reflects on the gospel in a particular context and is directed to the particular needs of a church. While the gospel has universal validity, our particular theologies do not. While particular contextual theologies may well enrich churches in other cultural contexts—in fact, they will always do so if they are rooted in Scripture, since the gospel is universally true—they will be formed by particular historical and cultural traditions in response to the needs of the churches in those settings. The mission of God's people is highly contextual, and the church in each place and time must negotiate a way to live faithfully at the crossroads between the biblical and cultural stories.

The very nature of theology as contextual reflection on universally valid divine revelation requires at least two things. First, there is an urgent need for a threefold dialogue with Christians from other cultures, other historical eras, and other confessional traditions. If our theologies are not to become parochial and accommodated to the idolatry of our particular cultures we will need the mutually correcting and enriching voices of Christians from other settings. Second, missiology as a particular discipline[17] offers a critical voice to recall theology to its missional vocation.[18] To quote Conn's striking words: "Missiology stands by to interrupt at every

17. It is troubling to see how many seminaries have removed missiology from the required core of their curriculum under various pressures to trim curricular hours.

18. Bosch, "Theological Education in Missionary Perspective," 27.

significant moment in the theological conversation with the words 'among the nations.'"[19]

Finally, the goal and purpose of theology is to form the church for its missional calling. Richard Bauckham laments that too often "the academic guild of biblical scholars" has a "largely self-generated agenda [that] increasingly excludes the church from its context and implied audience." Biblical scholarship, he insists, must "address the church in its mission to the world" and even make the church in the West not simply its audience, but its primary dialogue partner.[20] Bauckham's observation is true not only of biblical studies but of other theological disciplines as well.

Bauckham makes his comments in passing, as he moves on to offer a missional hermeneutic. Lydia Harder gives more attention to this issue. She speaks of the center and the periphery of theology.[21] At the center of theology is the church in mission, and at the periphery are the scientific concerns of the academic guild. Too often this is reversed, and students are invited in as guests into the academic conversation, which is little concerned with the church in mission. Backed by a theory-praxis dualism and a deductivist epistemology, it is assumed that the student will then take the content he or she needs from this academic conversation and apply it to his or her own pastoral situation. This is deeply problematic on a number of levels and one of the reasons so many theological students are unable to build the bridge between "scientific" academic study and life in the local congregation. What usually happens—that is, if such a student stays in seminary (and many do not)—is that "when the exams are past, much of what has been learned is unfortunately left behind in the library and lecture room. When the student finds himself subsequently in a local church situation, he does not draw on his academic training in theology; rather he begins a new, often improvised, system of learning."[22] Often this improvised system of learning is highly pragmatic and devoid of rich biblical and theological reflection.

The "ultimate allegiance and obligation" of theology and theological education "is to the church engaged in mission and not to the educa-

19. Harvie Conn, *Eternal Word and Changing Worlds: Theology, Anthropology, and Mission in Trialogue* (Grand Rapids: Zondervan, 1984), 224.

20. Richard Bauckham, "Mission as Hermeneutic for Scriptural Interpretation," *Currents in World Christianity Position Paper* 106 (1999): 1–2.

21. Lydia Neufeld Harder, "Formal Theological Education: The Centre and the Boundaries," in *Theological Education on Five Continents: Anabaptist Perspectives*, ed. Nancy R. Heisey and Daniel S. Schipani (Strasbourg: Mennonite World Conference, 1997), 103–5.

22. Kirk, *Theology and the Third World Church*, 48.

tional institution and the world of the *academia*."[23] There is a proper and valuable place for academic dialogue among scholars, but the goal must always be theological insight that serves the church in mission. Harder's further notion of the scholar's being bilingual—able to speak the languages of both the academy and the church—is helpful.[24] But this will require that scholars be as deeply rooted in the church as they are in the academy. This will strengthen the purpose of theological study to serve the church and to equip it for its mission.

Mission, Theological Education, and Curriculum

A new understanding of mission and of the missional nature of theology has clear and manifold implications for theological education, including its purpose, pedagogy, structures, the relation between academy and church, qualifications for faculty, and many more. In the remainder of this chapter I trace some implications for curriculum. The following sketch is more than a theoretical model for a missional curriculum. It is a curricular work-in-progress that we are implementing at the Missional Training Center in Phoenix, Arizona.[25] We take as our clue the critiques of a traditional curriculum and suggestions for a way forward made by various mission leaders over the last four or five decades, the most important for us being Harvie Conn, Lesslie Newbigin, and David Bosch.[26]

23. Bernhard Ott, *Beyond Fragmentation: Integrating Mission and Theological Education: A Critical Assessment of Some Recent Developments in Evangelical Theological Education* (Eugene, OR: Wipf & Stock, 2001), 222.

24. Harder, "Formal Theological Education," 106–8, 112.

25. I emphasize work-in-progress as we are early in the process. In this experiment in theological education we are seeking to address more than just curriculum. In fact, it is quite difficult to separate some of this discussion of curriculum from pedagogy, structures, and other aspects of theological education. Cf. missionaltraining.org.

26. E.g., Bosch, "Theological Education in Missionary Perspective," 13–34; Bosch, *Transforming Mission*, 489–98; Harvie Conn and Samuel Rowan, eds., *Missions and Theological Education in World Perspective* (Farmington, MI: Associates of Urbanus, 1984); Conn, "Missionary Task of Theology"; Conn, *Eternal Word*, 211–312; Lesslie Newbigin, "Theological Education in a World Perspective," *Ministerial Formation* 4 (1978): 3–10; Newbigin, *Honest Religion for Secular Man* (London: SCM, 1966), 101–4. The work of Darrell Guder is also very helpful, especially "From Mission and Theology to Missional Theology"; and "Missio Dei: Integrating Theological Formation for Apostolic Vocation," *Missiology* 37.1 (January 2009): 63–74.

A Comprehensive Vision of Mission

If "missional" is used as an adjective to describe the kind of curriculum I am advocating, it is essential right at the start to ward off certain misunderstandings of mission. Mission cannot be reduced to describing certain intentional activities directed toward unbelieving folks to draw them to faith. This is not a curriculum whose primary purpose is to promote evangelism and church planting or to deal with subjects that arise from such intentional outreach. Rather, we are talking about an identity, an orientation to the world, a holistic vision of mission in which the church is called to embody the gospel in its whole life, public and private, as a contrast to the way the idolatrous cultural story shapes a community's life. To be sure, evangelistic activity, church planting, and deeds of justice and mercy will—must!—flow from this orientation to the world. However, the core of a missional identity is that a people are formed by the gospel for the sake of the world. Both of those phrases are important: "formed by the gospel" and "for the sake of the world." They stand together in the biblical story, yet in the history of the church the first was stressed to the neglect of the second.

Important for theological education is the imperative for God's people to live under the lordship of Christ in their various callings in the public square. For theological education this has at least two implications. On the one hand, it is important for training pastors. Unfortunately, theology is often directed to theological themes or various activities that enable a pastor to work within the institutional church. Pastors are ill equipped to empower the folks under their care to live out their vocations in light of the gospel. As bishop of Madras, Newbigin warned the pastors under his care against a clericalist conception of ministry, which would confine their ministry to the institutional church. He urged them instead to look outward and to think of their task "to train our lay members who are playing key roles in the life of government, business, and the professions to be ministers of Christ in these secular situations. All of this is involved in our calling and ordination."[27] Training pastors in a way that equips them for this task will alter the curricular choices made for theological education. There will be much more concern, for example, for courses that probe the spiritual cultural forces that shape the public square.

On the other hand, a curriculum with a reach beyond an "institu-

27. Lesslie Newbigin, *The Good Shepherd: Meditations on Christian Ministry in Today's World* (Grand Rapids: Eerdmans, 1977), 76–77.

tional church theology" will attract and equip those not called to the ministry of the word. Many folk in the church whose callings are in the public square would be well served by a good theological education that trained them to see their whole lives in light of the gospel. In fact, a mix of those training for pastoral ministry and those engaged in ministry in the public square leads to a very different kind of conversation on theological issues, to the benefit of both kinds of student.

A Unifying and Directing Core

The subtitle of Edward Farley's seminal work on theological education indicates a problem with which much writing has been concerned—"the fragmentation and unity of theological education."[28] The first task of a missional curriculum is to define the center that unifies the various disciplines (see fig. 1 on p. 311).

Some suggest that mission be that center.[29] And that goes a long way down the road I want to travel. But more needs to be said. It seems better to start with what the apostle Paul says is of first importance for the church: the gospel itself (1 Cor. 15:1–3). When starting with the gospel, however, one is led inexorably on to the biblical story revealed in the gospel, to mission as one key that unlocks that story, and finally on to a missionary encounter with the cultural story. I propose that the unifying and directing core of a missional curriculum be four threads woven together into a single cord: gospel, biblical story, mission, and missionary encounter with culture.

All theological work must begin with Jesus the Christ as he is revealed in the gospel. This stands as the unifying and interpretive center of the biblical story (Luke 24:27, 44–46; John 5:39, 46). But surprisingly, few theological curriculums take time to articulate what the gospel is. One seasoned pastor, a top student from a well-known seminary, lamented: "I got everything at seminary except the gospel." He wasn't saying it was absent; rather, it was tacitly assumed, but never explicitly discussed or connected to theological reflection. This has been confirmed to me many times since. There are many different understandings of the gospel, both articulated and as-

28. Edward Farley, *Theologia: The Fragmentation and Unity of Theological Education* (Philadelphia: Fortress, 1983).

29. E.g., Jeffrey Greenman, "Mission as the Integrating Center of Theological Education," in *The Bible in World Christian Perspective*, ed. David Baker and Ward Gasque (Vancouver: Regent College, 2009), 193–210.

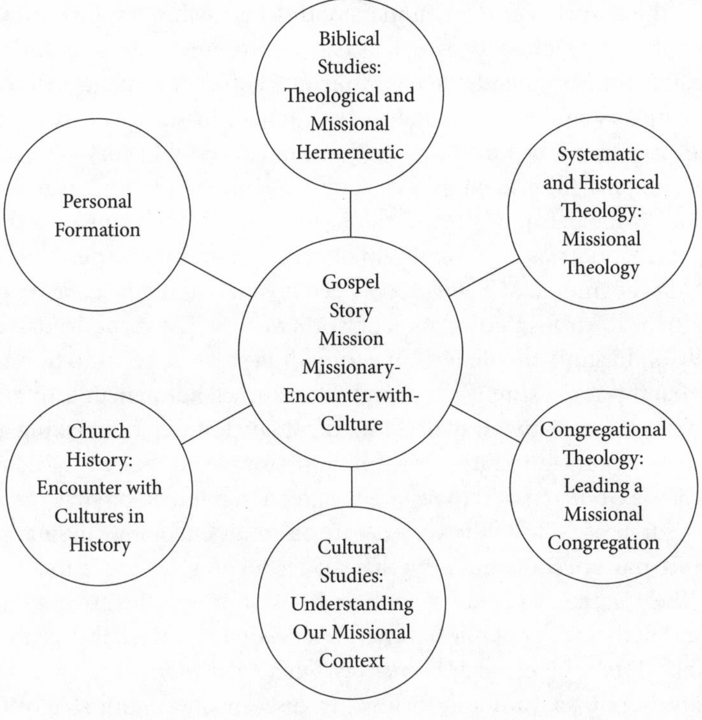

Figure 1

sumed, and these will lead to differing understandings of church, theology, and ministerial formation. Thus a conversation about the gospel should be the *first* conversation that takes place in theological education, as the basis for further theological work.

When he addressed the Lausanne Assembly in 1974, René Padilla said there is "no use in taking for granted that we all agree on the Gospel that has been entrusted to us." He believed the gospel had been truncated in various ways as it had been coopted by various idolatrous cultural spirits: "The greatest need of the church today is the recovery of the full Gospel of our Lord Jesus Christ."[30] His reference was to the mission of the church, but what he said holds equally for theological education.

30. René Padilla, "Evangelism and the World," in *Let the Earth Hear His Voice: International Congress on World Evangelization, Lausanne, Switzerland* (Minneapolis: World Wide Publications, 1975), 144.

If the gospel is properly understood then it will point forward to the climax of universal history as well as back to the creation of the world. The gospel is, on the one hand, the revelation and accomplishment of the end of cosmic history in the person and work of Jesus Christ, especially his death and resurrection. The kingdom—the *telos* of universal history—is revealed and accomplished, present and coming, in Jesus. On the other hand, the kingdom is the defeat of sin and the restoration of God's rule over the entirety of creation: it is creation regained, renewed, restored. Thus, the gospel sets us in the middle of a story—between creation and new creation—that claims to be the true interpretation of world history. The gospel leads us necessarily on to study the Bible as one unfolding story. It needs to be emphasized that this is not simply a redemptive-historical hermeneutic, or biblical theology, or a narrative way of doing theology. Rather, it is looking at the Scriptures as a metanarrative, a worldview-story. And the central theme of this story is God's mission to restore the creation polluted by sin to be again the kingdom of God. By its very nature as an all-encompassing narrative, Scripture must become the story that shapes theological education.

The grammar of Luke's account of Jesus's words to the disciples makes it clear that there are not one but two keys needed to unlock the meaning of the biblical story here: not *Messiah* only, but also *mission* (Luke 24:45–46).[31] This sends us backward and forward to discern the central role of God's people in his mission. And so the third strand of a theological core or prolegomena should be mission—the mission of God's people as they participate in God's ongoing mission.

The central nature of mission is that God's people are called to embody and make known God's creational and redemptive purposes for the sake of the world. And that missional call highlights the critical importance of the fourth thread—a missionary encounter with culture. Embodiment of God's purpose will always be in a certain cultural context; the answer to the gospel will always be shaped by a particular culture. Thus, there will always be a missionary encounter between the gospel and a cultural story—two very different ways of narrating the world—within the very life of God's people. *This is of the very essence of Christian identity and experience*. God's people necessarily live in a cultural context that is shaped around a different center than the gospel. And so there will always be a tension between the two.

31. Cf. Christopher J. H. Wright, *The Mission of God: Unlocking the Bible's Grand Narrative* (Downers Grove, IL: InterVarsity, 2006), 29–30.

A missionary encounter requires an understanding of our culture so as to discern what faithful contextualization looks like. Understanding our culture—its religious nature, its story, its current religious spirits—will be essential for theological education. But a missionary encounter will also involve probing the gospel's "yes" to creational currents and its "no" to idolatrous currents—faithful contextualization.[32]

This "gospel-biblical story/church-mission/missionary-encounter-with-culture" dynamic is essential to the Christian faith and must pervade the ongoing life and calling of the church. In fact, when this is not recognized, one is open to a syncretistic accommodation with the idols of culture that masquerades as faithfulness. This fourfold lens enables us to rightly see and study the vocation and mission of the church in its many dimensions.

While this dynamic was obscured and marginalized in the Western church because of its long relationship of accommodation to its culture, such is not the case with those who have to struggle with theological education in the Third World, where the missional tension between the gospel and culture is more evident. Significantly, the concluding statement of the Asian First Consultation on Theological Education and Ministry defined the aim and purpose of the theological school in terms of a "community that exists in encounter with the world, a witnessing community in the forefront of Christ's loving involvement and prophetic confrontation with society."[33]

This fourfold lens not only reveals the missional essence of congregational life, but also enables students to see the cultural situatedness of various theological disciplines, including the way that cultural spirits have shaped them. Telling the Western story carefully as part of the prolegomena for theological education enabled me to set many topics later in the curriculum in the context of currents within that story: for example, in hermeneutics, the way both a historical-critical method (characteristic of more liberal scholarship) and a grammatical-historical method (characteristic of evangelical churches) are deeply indebted to a Cartesian methodological approach to knowledge; in systematic theology, the way individualism has impacted our understanding of sin, salvation, and humanity; in New Testament studies, the way the gospel of the kingdom in the Gospels was neglected or misunderstood because of our various dualisms. The list could go

32. Cf. Dean Flemming, *Contextualization in the New Testament: Patterns for Theology and Mission* (Downers Grove, IL: InterVarsity, 2005).

33. *Theological Education and Ministry: Reports from the North East Asia Theological Education Consultation, Seoul, Korea* (Tainan: Presbyterian Bookroom, 1967), 297.

on indefinitely. None of these are new. But by noting the origin and development of, say, methodological reason, individualism, and dualism as they arise from within the Western story, we can equip students with a broader framework to analyze their impact on their own theology.

Missional Content and Purpose in All Disciplines

The place, role, and content of the various theological disciplines in the curriculum will derive from this center. A missional curriculum will be one in which the various subjects are formed both in content and purpose by this core, which sees mission—defined as a missionary encounter between the gospel and the cultural story—as defining the church. A missional curriculum does not mean merely adding more courses on mission or evangelism or world religions or other subjects traditionally associated with missiology. Rather, it explores how mission will reframe biblical studies, systematic theology, church history, and congregational theology to equip the church for its mission.

Two distinctions are important if we are to properly understand the word "missional" as an adjective to describe all theological disciplines. The first, introduced by Newbigin in the middle of the previous century, is between missional dimension and missional intention. (He is reflecting on the nature of mission itself rather than on theology.) There are *intentional* activities such as evangelism, church planting, and works of justice and mercy that have as their express purpose and intent the making known of the gospel in word or deed. However, most of our lives are not aimed deliberately at that goal. Yet all of our lives have a missional *dimension*. That is, every part of the life of the Christian community—individually and corporately—witnesses to the renewing power of the gospel.

This distinction may also be applied helpfully to theological education. Some—but not all—subjects in the curriculum *intentionally* deal with various issues of mission. Yet all theological subjects should have a missional *dimension*. That is, when mission is seen to be a central component of the Christian faith, it raises new questions and formulates different approaches to the same subject matter.

The second distinction important to an understanding of the adjective "missional" is between the goal and content of theology. Theology must be missional in the sense that its *goal* is to equip the church for its missional calling. Theology plays a role in the formation of leaders and a congregation to embody the gospel more faithfully for the sake of the world. Again, both phrases must be held together: formation "to embody the gospel" and to embody the gospel "for the sake of the world." But theology must also be formed in its *content* by the central theme of mission. How does the category of mission shape the various theological disciplines? For too long, biblical studies, systematic and historical theology, church history, and pastoral theology have primarily treated "to embody the gospel" and neglected "for the sake of the world." Karl Barth critiqued this kind of theology as "pious and sacred egocentricity."[34]

This call for a missional curriculum does not seek to scrap the traditional curriculum and begin over. It is not an attempt to impose a new kind of theological imperialism by making all theological disciplines branches of missiology. Rather, it seeks to transplant into the curriculum the biblical truth that mission is "not simply yet another subject but a dimension of theology as a whole."[35] It is a matter of bringing missional questions to bear on the work of the various theological disciplines, of *reframing*, not replacing, theology as it has developed historically. It is bringing new perspectives, new questions, and new light to familiar issues and themes. It is, to quote Conn again, a matter of "interrupting the theological conversation among the various disciplines with the reminder, 'among the nations.'"[36]

Biblical Studies

If we are rightly to interpret Scripture, it is essential to understand its nature and purpose.[37] Scripture is neither simply a history of Israel nor a biography of Jesus, nor a repository of theological and ethical truths. It is first and foremost a record and a tool of God's mission to restore all creation in and through his people that finds its climactic moment in Jesus Christ. The Bible is an organic narrative unity that tells the story of salvation and finds its concentrated center in Jesus Christ. If the content of Scripture is redemptive-revelation culminating in Christ, then the purpose of Scripture

34. See chap. 12 in this book. Cf. Karl Barth, *Church Dogmatics*, IV: *The Doctrine of Reconciliation*, part 3.2, trans. G. W. Bromiley (Peabody, MA: Hendrickson, 2010), 554–69.

35. Bosch, "Theological Education in Missionary Perspective," 26.

36. Conn, *Eternal Word*, 224.

37. Cf. Michael W. Goheen and Michael D. Williams, "Doctrine of Scripture and Theological Interpretation," in *A Manifesto for Theological Interpretation*, ed. Craig G. Bartholomew and Heath Thomas (Grand Rapids: Baker, 2015), 48–71.

is to lead us to faith in Jesus Christ so we can be wise unto salvation, take our place in this story, and be equipped to live more faithfully in that salvation (2 Tim. 3:15–17).

Yet being made wise unto salvation is not just about ourselves. The scriptural backdrop is always "so that": "May God be gracious to us and bless us and make his face shine on us—so that your ways may be known on earth, your salvation among all nations" (Ps. 67:1–2; cf. 67:7). The purpose of Scripture is to make us wise unto salvation so that we might manifest that renewal in the midst of the world.

And so this is where mission interrupts the conversation in biblical studies: Has biblical studies taken into account the "so that" nature of God's work in his covenant people? Has the orientation to the world shaped the questions biblical studies have put to the Scripture? "Studying God's Word," says Darrell Guder, "is always a process of posing questions to Scripture. The questions we ask will control the answers we receive." A basic question that will faithfully orient us to the nature and purpose of Scripture is: "How did this text equip and shape God's people for their missional witness then, and how does it shape us today?"[38] This question is important for biblical scholarship: "All the resources of historical, critical, and literary research on the biblical testimony can and must contribute to the church's formation by illumining all the dimensions of this fundamental question."[39] A missional understanding of biblical studies will ask whether scholarship is aimed at this goal.

This does not reduce biblical studies to a missional hermeneutic. What is needed is, rather, a robust theological hermeneutic that has an eye for mission as an essential part of the biblical story.[40] A theological hermeneutic is concerned for the theological or kerygmatic message[41] of the text that comes from careful attention to the final form of the text in its

38. Darrell Guder, *"Unlikely Ambassadors: Clay Jar Christians in God's Service": A Bible Study for the 214th General Assembly of the Presbyterian Church (U.S.A.)* (Louisville: Office of the General Assembly, Presbyterian Church, 2002), 5.

39. Darrell Guder, "From Mission and Theology to Missional Theology," *Princeton Seminary Bulletin* 24.1 (2003): 48.

40. Cf. chap. 4 in this book. Bartholomew and Thomas, eds., *A Manifesto for Theological Interpretation*, include a chapter on missional hermeneutic.

41. I prefer "kerygmatic" to "theological" since the latter word can convey simply information about God or the propositional content of the text. The question of what the text is trying to do or the response it seeks—faith or hope or repentance or wisdom or obedience and so forth—is essential.

canonical location in the context of the whole redemptive-historical story, in its location in the literary context of the theological message of the whole book, in keeping with its literary genre, its particular address in its original cultural and historical setting, and its fusion with our contemporary horizon. All of this is strengthened as one takes account of the central missional thread of Scripture.

The kerygmatic purpose comes into focus with the kinds of questions urged by homiletics scholars as they wrestle with the meaning of the biblical text for preaching. The biblical authors did not just intend to convey information, but to produce an effect, to accomplish something. "Why did the author write this? What effect did he expect it to have on its readers? . . . An expository sermon . . . finds its purpose in line with the biblical purposes."[42] "True 'biblical preaching' will want to be faithful not only to a message, but to an intention. The question, 'What is the passage trying to do?' may well mark the beginning of homiletical obedience."[43] We might say that "what is the passage trying to do?" may well mark the beginning of hermeneutical obedience. Only a theological hermeneutic that understands the kerygmatic nature and purpose of Scripture and interprets it accordingly can begin to address this question. A strong grasp of the centrality of mission will be an essential ingredient in answering the question: "What is the passage trying to do?"[44]

It is not just the goal of Scripture to form the church for its mission; it is also the content of biblical studies that must be informed by the central theme of mission. Yet it is often the case that the study of Scripture proceeds as if God were concerned only for his covenant people: the missional trajectory and horizon of the nations is often left out of the picture altogether.

A remark by Gordon Wenham offers a window on the bigger problem. He observes the way Old Testament scholars read the Abrahamic promise in Genesis 12:2–3 in terms of a threefold promise—descendants, land, bless-

42. Haddon W. Robinson, *Biblical Preaching: The Development and Delivery of Expository Messages* (Grand Rapids: Baker, 1980), 109.

43. David G. Buttrick, "Interpretation and Preaching," *Interpretation* 35.1 (January 1981): 58.

44. Speech-act theory helpfully foregrounds these kinds of questions in biblical interpretation. Cf. Nicholas Wolterstorff, *Divine Discourse: Philosophical Reflections on the Claim That God Speaks* (Cambridge: Cambridge University Press, 1995). For a simple introduction see Richard S. Briggs, "Getting Involved: Speech Acts and Biblical Interpretation," *Anvil* 20.1 (2003): 25–34; available at biblicalstudies.org.uk/pdf/anvil/20–1_025.pdf (accessed 30 May 2015).

ing. And yet the goal of that threefold promise is so that he might bless all nations—the grammar is clear. Wenham observes: "Von Rad and Cline's understanding of the promises as tripartite, descendants, land and blessing of Israel, fails to pay sufficient attention to the climax of the promise that 'in you all the families of the earth shall find blessing.'"[45] The focus of the patriarchal accounts is on what God will do for Abraham so that all nations on earth might be blessed. Unfortunately, the academic discipline of biblical studies too often does not attend to the universal horizon of God's covenant with Israel. One could multiply examples from Old and New Testament studies. Neglect of this fundamental perspective on the covenant will continue to foster leaders who read, preach, and teach the Bible with a "pious egocentricity."

Attention to mission interrupts biblical scholarship with the words "among the nations," asking if they have taken account of that central theme in their exegesis and whether their work is directed toward equipping the church for its missional role.

Systematic Theology

Kevin Vanhoozer provocatively alleges, "Laypersons in the church would perhaps have been within their rights to bring a class-action suit against systematic theologians for criminal pastoral and missiological negligence."[46] If this is so, then it is appropriate to inquire into this negligence: How should mission shape the purpose and content of systematic theology?

Perhaps a helpful way to begin is to note the crisis that systematic theology is facing in some circles. Our postmodern climate distrusts all totalizing systems constructed by human rationality. But this critique comes not only from postmodernism; Third World theologies have unmasked these "neutral" theologies as a "construction of a logically coherent system, organized around a Western historical agenda insisted upon as universal by the Western church."[47] Moreover, the narrative nature of Scripture has been

45. Gordon Wenham, "The Face at the Bottom of the Well," in *He Swore an Oath: Biblical Themes from Genesis 12–50*, ed. Richard S. Hess, Gordon J. Wenham, and Philip E. Sattherthwaite, 2nd ed. (Grand Rapids: Baker; Carlisle: Paternoster, 1994), 203.

46. Kevin Vanhoozer, "One Rule to Rule Them All? Theological Method in an Era of World Christianity," in *Globalizing Theology: Belief and Practice in an Era of World Christianity*, ed. Craig Ott and Harold A. Netland (Grand Rapids: Baker Academic, 2006), 93.

47. Conn, *Eternal Word*, 222–23.

recovered, and story has been set over against system. To view Scripture as a "data dump"[48] of theological truths, or pieces of a theological jigsaw puzzle waiting to be assembled in a systematic way,[49] or as a mass of undigested theological facts ripe for systematizing[50] is to misunderstand the very nature of Scripture.

So it may appear wise, at first blush, to write off systematic theology as the product of an earlier rationalistic age and to decide not to include it in a missional curriculum. However, that would be rash and would also miss the role that systematic theology, rightly pursued, can play in equipping a missional church. Systematic theology is a thematic and synthesizing discipline that, in the midst of scriptural diversity, assumes a certain unity about God, humanity, salvation, creation, and so on as it is revealed in Scripture. Systematic theology answers the question: What does the Bible teach about *x*?[51] Perhaps systematic theology can be compared to literary studies where one traces a character or theme through a novel. The purpose is not to replace the novel with these studies but to better understand that theme or character within the novel, and so understand the novel itself better.

How could this kind of theological discipline equip church for its missional calling? We can point to two areas of church life. First, the cultural context raises questions and issues for Christians that need clear articulation. Leaders in God's church must be equipped to answer these concerns. Here are just two examples taken from my own pastoral ministry in the past year: What does the Bible teach about God and how is that different from what my Muslim neighbor believes about Allah? Who is Jesus Christ and how do you know he is the only way? Examples like this can be multiplied in any living missional congregation. But what is behind them all is the question: What does the Bible teach about God or about Jesus Christ or about some other theme in Scripture?

The need for systematic theology may arise also as we observe the way scriptural teaching is twisted by cultural idolatry in the beliefs of the people of God. To take only one example: Has not the legitimate recovery of the personal dimensions of salvation at the Reformation capitulated to a

48. Michael Williams, "Systematic Theology as a Biblical Discipline," in *All for Jesus: A Celebration of the 50th Anniversary of Covenant Theological Seminary*, ed. Robert A. Peterson and Sean Michael Lucas (Fearn, Ross Shire: Christian Focus, 2005), 203.

49. Wayne Grudem, *Systematic Theology: An Introduction to Biblical Doctrine* (Grand Rapids: Zondervan, 1994), 29.

50. Charles Hodge, *Systematic Theology* (New York: Scribner, 1871), 1:2.

51. Cf. the excellent chapter by Williams, "Systematic Theology as a Biblical Discipline."

rampant individualism—expressed in theology itself in limiting soteriology to the *ordo salutis*—that does not take account of the cosmic (communal) personal structure of biblical revelation? Systematic theology can help to challenge and correct misunderstanding and to articulate Scripture's teaching afresh to equip the church for its mission today.

Thus, the task of systematic theology, suggests Newbigin, is "to declare to each generation what is the faith, to expose and combat errors destructive of the faith, to expel from her body doctrines which pervert the faith, and to lead her members into a full and vivid apprehension of the faith."[52] Here theology has both a positive and a negative task: to give a fresh and relevant articulation of the faith designed to lead the church into a living and vibrant faith, and to protect the Bible's teaching from the cultural idolatries that would distort the truth and lead the church astray. Thus only a theology that addresses and illumines the issues of the day can equip a church for its missional calling.

This definition of theology makes it a highly contextual discipline. I quoted Newbigin asserting that the responsibility of the church is to declare to each generation what is the faith. He continues:

> This is always a fresh task in each generation, for thought is never still. The words in which the Church states its message in one generation have changed their meaning by the time the next has grown up. No verbal statement can be produced which relieves the Church of the responsibility continually to re-think and re-state its message. No appeal to ecumenical creeds, to the universal belief of the Church, or to the Scriptures, can alter the fact that the Church has to state in every new generation how it interprets the historical faith, and how it relates it to the new thought and experience of its time. . . . Nothing can remove from the Church the responsibility for stating *now*, what is the faith.[53]

This contextual nature of theology is threatened by a "tendency to abstraction" and by dehistoricized "timeless" formulations that often characterize systematic theology.[54] But a contextual theology is also threatened by our Christendom past. For example, we articulate an understanding of baptism

52. Lesslie Newbigin, *The Reunion of the Church: A Defence of the South India Scheme* (London: SCM, 1948), 137.

53. Newbigin, *Reunion of the Church*, 138.

54. John Murray, "Systematic Theology," in *The New Testament Student and Theology*, ed. John H. Skilton (Phillipsburg, NJ: Presbyterian & Reformed, 1976), 25.

or the Lord's Supper in terms of rival interpretations between competing theological traditions. This may be of some help. However, we need urgently to ask how the sacraments can shape an identity that will equip the church to live as a faithful contrast community over against, for example, the powerful forces of consumerism.[55]

Systematic theology is not missional only in the sense of equipping the church to be faithful in its vocation; it also needs to be missional in its content, taking account of the missional thread at the center of the biblical narrative. Hendrikus Berkhof observes that "in the main dogmatical handbooks . . . mission is either entirely neglected or only touched on in passing. . . . Therefore, I regret to say that the highly necessary enrichment of systematic theology by taking in the mission as an essential element in God's mighty deeds is still ahead of us."[56]

We can illustrate this both negatively and positively. Negatively, it is common to read, for example, Reformed systematic theologies that make the covenant central to their systematic structuring. Yet somehow whole theologies can be written that manage to miss the missional intent of the covenant! Positively, Hendrikus Berkhof offers an example in his *Doctrine of the Holy Spirit* of how taking mission seriously can deepen our understanding of Scripture's teaching on the Holy Spirit. The category of mission enables us to bring together the Protestant insight that the Holy Spirit is connected to Scripture and to individual salvation, as well as the Roman Catholic insight that the Spirit works in the ministries of the gathered church.

Again, mission interrupts the conversation in systematic theology with the words "among the nations," asking if our theological work is equipping leaders to nurture a missional congregation and if the central missional theme of Scripture is shaping our theological formulations.

Church History

An African proverb says, "Until lions have their historians, the hunter will always be the hero of the story." All history writing tells a story as it selects, arranges, and interprets the "facts" of history. At least two stories are told

55. John F. Kavanaugh's *Following Christ in a Consumer Society: The Spirituality of Cultural Resistance*, 2nd ed. (Maryknoll, NY: Orbis, 2006) calls us to just this kind of theology. Cf. 155–63.

56. Hendrikus Berkhof, *The Doctrine of the Holy Spirit* (Atlanta: John Knox, 1964), 33.

in the way church history is taught. The first is the story of the institutional church. It is undeniable, says Bosch, "that church history has traditionally concerned itself only with the domestic aspect of the history of the church, concentrating on matters of interest to the church as institution."[57] A second story is a Christendom rivalry of ecclesial traditions. Thus, the christological controversies of the early centuries are told in terms of competing schools of orthodoxy and heterodoxy, and Reformation history told in terms of doctrinal disagreement on Scripture, church, sacraments, and so on. The cultural context, which is the occasion of such controversy, is left out of the picture.[58]

"We have to ask in all sincerity whether the study of the history of the church ought not to be completely redesigned."[59] This insight impressed itself powerfully upon me when I heard Newbigin say, "I wish someone had told me in seminary that the Christological and Trinitarian controversies of the second and third century were first and foremost issues of contextualization." If the church is missional by its nature, then church history will be concerned with how the gospel as it is articulated and embodied by the church encounters the various cultures of the world. As Newbigin laments, church history is taught not "in terms of the missionary advance in successive encounters of the gospel with different forms of human culture and society, but rather as a story of the doctrinal and other conflicts within the life of the church."[60]

Both the controversies of the second and third centuries and of the Reformation offer vivid and paradigmatic examples of how a proper attention to mission can reframe church history. When the Hebrew gospel was translated into Greek culture it encountered a very different way of understanding the world. Among other things it engaged a world that explained meaning in terms of "being" arranged in a hierarchical ontology. How does one understand Christ and his relation to the Father in this cultural context? In terms of his being, is he God or man or both? If both, how? In terms of the hierarchical ontology, where do Christ and God sit on that ladder? The struggle was how to translate the gospel into this new cultural milieu.

Prior to the Reformation, the gospel was contextualized in a tribal

57. Bosch, "Theological Education in Missionary Perspective," 28.

58. Church historians interested in a missional telling of the church's history also highlight another concern: the story is told only in terms of the Western church. It neglects the way church history may be told from the standpoint of the church in Latin America or Africa or Asia, for example. This is an important issue that I will not pursue here.

59. Bosch, "Theological Education in Missionary Perspective," 28.

60. Newbigin, *Honest Religion*, 102.

setting throughout the medieval period. A tribal culture emphasizes the solidarity of community and plays down individuality. But a new humanistic spirit began to take hold in Western culture from the late medieval period into the early Renaissance. This new spirit gave fresh attention to the individual, something that was suppressed in medieval theology. Thus, in the Reformation, biblical themes were rediscovered that emphasize how individuals are included in God's cosmic and communal salvation, along with the benefits they receive and how they receive them.

These examples do not move us into the gray twilight of relativism. But both illustrate how church history unfolds in terms of a missionary encounter with cultural forces, which manifest both creational insight and idolatrous twisting. We may use the language of "orthodoxy" when we see the gospel faithfully contextualized in a particular setting, and of "heresy" when the gospel is overpowered by idolatrous forces. But this is never a matter of who, on which side of the historical debate under examination, correctly represented the timeless ideas of Scripture in their theological formulation.

If we follow Newbigin in seeing church history as a series of missional encounters, we can see how such a way of teaching church history could equip missional leaders. As they traced the church's trek through history and various cultures, they would, on the one hand, deepen their understanding of the gospel and Scripture's teaching by observing the theological gains and insights made by these successive encounters. But, on the other hand, they would learn that they too are involved in such encounters. They would be warned by the record of unfaithful contextualizations and challenged by faithful ones. Such leaders would be taught to be aware of their cultural settings, of their necessary embodiment of the gospel in those settings, of the danger of idolatry, and of the way forward to faithfulness.

Mission interrupts the theological conversation of church history with the words "among the nations." It probes the way the story is being told. If the church is set among the nations to embody the life-giving creational insights and to reject the death-dealing idolatry of each culture, then church history must tell this story.

Congregational Theology

This branch of theology, or rather this aggregation of various branches of theology, is variously called "pastoral" or "practical" theology. These adjectives point to problems. The first is the assumption that biblical or systematic or historical theology is neither pastoral nor practical. The second is the deeply problematic distinction between theory and praxis. Practical theology applies the theory learned in biblical studies, systematic theology, and church history. What binds the disparate subjects together is the need to apply theological theory to clerical ministry. The third problem is the way pastoral theology is connected to a certain understanding of the church that has become thoroughly introverted. The church is reduced to an institution concerned only for its pastoral role to channel salvation to individual believers: in this case, pastoral theology is about institutional maintenance.

I suggest the alternative term "congregational" theology. However, as long as an inward and nonmissional view of the church is assumed, this word will hardly clear up matters. It is tempting to abandon this category altogether. However, another vision of church is possible that perhaps can shape this area of theological study.

Congregational theology may be an area in which theological education reflects on the calling of the pastor within the local congregation and asks how the pastor might lead that congregation to be a faithful missional church. Our ecclesiology needs to be framed in terms of the inseparable connection between its communal gathering and its outward facing, the church gathered and the church scattered. The church is an institution in which various ministries are undertaken, all with the purpose of ministering Christ and the gospel to the members. It is a community where various spiritual gifts build up the body for their calling in the world. But the church cannot be understood only in terms of its communal and institutional character. The goal of its existence is to be oriented to the world, and it is only as the gathered life of the church is directed to this end that it is faithful.

What is the pastor's role in the life of a missional congregation? Congregational studies may revolve around nurturing our new life in Christ for the sake of the world (preaching, prayer, worship, sacraments, pastoral visitation, counseling, fellowship, formation, and so on), our new life in the midst of the world (evangelism, mercy and justice, cross-cultural missions, training laity for their callings, living as a contrast community, equipping to understand culture and other religions, and so on), and structures that enable and equip the nurturing and outward ministries to thrive (leadership, congregational, ecumenical, and financial structures).[61] The question is al-

61. This is how I structured a course I taught at Calvin Theological Seminary from 2012 to 2015 entitled "Introduction to Missional Ministry." It is also the way we structure the

ways: How does a missional orientation of the church to the world shape the various dimensions of pastoral ministry in contrast to a maintenance or institutional-church vision?

These subjects must not be limited to applying the theories of the other disciplines. There must be a theological reflection on the praxis of congregational leadership that is at least as rigorous as the other theological disciplines.

Mission interrupts the conversation of congregational theology with the words "among the nations," asking whether it has cast pastoral ministry in terms of institutional maintenance and reduced the life of the congregation to nurturing new life in believers.

Challenging the Theory-Practice Dichotomy

At the heart of traditional theological education is a dichotomy between theory and praxis. In the curriculum this translates into a distinction between theoretical and practical subjects. We have "sciences of sheer understanding" and "sciences of technique and function."[62] This deeply problematic dualism is doing great damage to the preparation of church leaders.

It is not difficult to see how this dichotomy distorted theological education. When theoretical reflection is lifted out of its living context and given a life of its own, knowledge becomes abstract, divorced from its contextual source. Truth becomes a defined, prepackaged set of propositions that must be cognitively mastered before being acted upon. Only subsequently is theory applied to ministry. Paulo Freire calls this the "banking concept of education" because the teacher deposits knowledge in the minds of the students only to expect interest later in the future.[63]

There are enormous problems[64] with this whole distorted mindset.[65]

---

whole "congregational theology" component of our curriculum at Missional Training Center in Phoenix.

62. Edward Farley, "The Reform of Theological Education as a Theological Task," *Theological Education* (Spring 1981): 102.

63. Paulo Freire, *Pedagogy of the Oppressed* (New York: Continuum, 1993), 71–86.

64. Cf. Ott, *Beyond Fragmentation*, 224–34, for a good discussion of the impact of the theory-praxis dichotomy on theological education. He lists a number of problems when this is in place in the curriculum (227).

65. Albert M. Wolters argues that the source of this dichotomy is Aristotle's pagan idolatry. He singles out the reasoning function (*theoria*) and idolatrously gives it the absolute status of God. Having fallen into the idolatry of rational, theoretical aspect, all the rest of hu-

Pedagogically this is not how learning works; students who have no involvement or experience find it difficult to master decontextualized knowledge. They may give up and simply succumb to a pragmatic mindset or (if they are bright) remain fascinated with the world of theory—both dangerous possibilities for pastors. Epistemologically this is not how knowledge works; knowledge does not stand above context but arises out of a context and is directed toward a context. Moreover, it is an almost impossible task to bridge the chasm between abstract theory—passed off as timeless, but really arising from *another* context—and concrete ministry.

In the curriculum, problems manifest themselves in the way these theoretical and practical subjects are taught. The theoretical disciplines become pure sciences that are seemingly not directed toward any particular goal or context. They are left without a mandate in theological education to direct the teaching toward the church-in-mission. The practical disciplines, on the other hand, are shorn of the deep theological reflection that is needed and reduced to clerical skills and techniques. Practical theology becomes "more and more functional and pragmatic. Practical is that which can be *used* immediately and that which *works* within a short period of time. With this emphasis practical theology tends to lead to a 'preoccupation with technique.'"[66] For example, preaching is one of the most complex hermeneutical activities one can undertake, and yet homiletics classes are often reduced to teaching communication techniques on the assumption that in hermeneutics and biblical studies classes students have already received the exegetical grist for the homiletical mill.

Theological reflection is a necessary and important rational exercise that stands back at a theoretical distance from the context and reflects on and evaluates that particular setting in the light of certain criteria, supremely the word of God. But deep involvement and experience in the local congregation is absolutely necessary if that reflection is to be authentic.[67] Thus theoretical reflection must be of a piece with concrete ministry life; it must flow from it and be directed back to it. Theological education, then, is a process in which one reflects in the light of Scripture on the missional context to which one is committed and in which one is deeply involved.

---

man functioning and activities are lumped together and downgraded and mindlessly labeled "praxis" or "practical"; *Ideas Have Legs* (Toronto: Institute for Christian Studies, 1987), 8–9.

66. Ott, *Beyond Fragmentation*, 225.

67. Robert Banks says, "theological education can only enhance ministry in progress, not prepare people for ministry"; *Reenvisioning Theological Education: Exploring a Missional Alternative to Current Models* (Grand Rapids: Eerdmans, 1999), 136.

Can attention to mission help us resist this dichotomy?[68] The following examples may show how theological reflection can be set in the context of ministerial practice. Setting biblical hermeneutics in the context of listening for God's address for the sake of preaching and teaching the Bible to form and equip God's people for mission does not in any way diminish the depth of reflection on the grammatical, historical, cultural, literary, and theological dimensions of the text. On the contrary! Yet this setting keeps hermeneutics from becoming an exercise in methodological reason. The context and direction of this reflection is to deepen one's ability to listen to what the Spirit is saying to the churches in context, and it thus equips leaders for their ministry of God's word. If we are careful to set discussions about God, Christ, or salvation, for example, within the context of real questions that congregants are asking, or of real distortions at work in the theology of the church, or of real gaps in understanding, then systematic theology will arise out of the mission of the church and may be directed toward equipping leaders for their ministry. Setting church history in the context of how the church in its particular time struggled to be faithful to the gospel in its culture offers living examples of contextualization that will equip students in their own settings.

Two Additions: Cultural Studies and Spiritual Formation

The fourfold theological curriculum has neglected areas of study that are absolutely essential to equipping faithful leaders. At least two areas should be nonnegotiable: cultural studies and spiritual formation.

In the latter half of the 1960s, missionaries and Third World theologians began to question Western standards for theological education: that conversation would ultimately lead to the terminology of "contextualization" in 1972. Their rethinking of theological education revolved around the insight that understanding cultural context could no longer be a side issue in the curriculum.[69] Taiwanese theologian Shoki Coe says that the goal of theological education should be a "deeper understanding of the Gospel in the context of the particular cultural and religious setting of the Church,

68. I do not believe curriculum design alone can break the powerful hold of this dichotomy. The theory-praxis dichotomy is so woven into the fabric of theological education in its pedagogical, epistemological, and structural assumptions that much more is needed.

69. Cf. Conn, "Theological Education and the Search for Excellence."

so that the Church may come to a deeper understanding of itself as a missionary community sent into the world, and to a more effectual encounter within the life of the society."[70] Colombian theologian Hugo Zorrilla critiques traditional theological education as abstract because its curriculum lacks "dialogue with the world to which it ministers," thus hampering students from developing "creativity and understanding of the historical moment" in which they live.[71] Japanese theologian Kosuke Koyama argues that a missionary pastor needs "two kinds of exegesis: exegesis of the Word of God and exegesis of the life and culture of the people among whom he lives and works."[72]

The gospel is always embodied and expressed in some cultural context. Thus, it is essential to understand both the creational and the idolatrous currents at work in any culture, if we are to be faithful to the gospel. A study of culture, therefore, cannot be an optional extra in theological education. In the twentieth century, no mission organization worth its salt would ever think of sending a missionary into a cross-cultural setting without a rigorous training in the particular culture to which he or she was going. They understood well that to be faithful to the gospel, both by holding fast its biblical message and by making it relevant, one *must* own a deep understanding of the culture.

And yet, somehow, here in the twenty-first century, it is deemed acceptable to send out Christian leaders into the Western cultural context without a thorough knowledge of that culture. This shortsightedness is all the worse because Western culture has now become a global culture—the most powerful in the world and perhaps the one most dangerous to the Christian faith. The problem, according to Newbigin, is that we have been blinded by two myths: the myth of a Christian culture and the myth of a neutral secular culture. But Western culture is neither Christian nor neutral: it is a culture shaped by the powerful religious vision of humanism.

Cultural studies needs to equip the student by deepening insight into the cultural story that shaped the worldview at work today, by carefully noting the way a religious vision unifies and shapes the various elements of

70. Shoki Coe, "In Search of Renewal in Theological Education," *Theological Education* 9.4 (1973): 236.

71. Hugo Zorrilla, "Crucial Issues in Theological Education in Latin America," in *Mission Focus: Current Issues*, ed. Wilbert Shenk (Scottsdale: Herald, 1980), 374–75.

72. Kosuke Koyama, *Water Buffalo Theology*, 25th anniversary ed. (Maryknoll, NY: Orbis, 1999 [orig. 1974]), 65. In fact, says Koyama, we maintain our "missionary identity" *only if* we are "entangled in" or "sandwiched between" these two realities.

a culture, by examining the current spiritual currents of a culture, by noting how these currents shape the institutions and structures of the culture, by asking how the cultural worldview is shaping church life, and by probing pastoral ways of dealing with church members whose lives are woven into these idolatrous patterns.

Spiritual and moral formation is also important. If leaders are set aside for prayer and the word (Acts 6:4), and if leaders must be examples in their godly conduct (1 Tim. 3:1–8), then the intellectual formation that has been the traditional emphasis of the seminary is simply not enough. It is here that the disconnect between church and academy demands to be addressed.

Yet there is also a curricular side. Dealing with prayer and family life, for example, within the curriculum will be important. But the importance of spiritual formation arises at other points in the curriculum. For example, we often reduce hermeneutics to a methodological analysis of the text. However, if interpreting Scripture is a matter of listening to God's address in Scripture, and if the various hermeneutical techniques are part of hearing God, then our hermeneutics courses must do more than simply teach a method that accounts for the grammatical, cultural, historical, literary, and theological dimensions of the text. Many good seminary graduates master hermeneutical methods, yet never acquire the spiritual disposition to hear God speak.

Conclusion

The rediscovery of mission as central to the biblical story in the middle part of the last century followed a historical logic that raised fundamental questions about the relationships among congregation, theology, and theological education. Yet we are a long way off, both theologically and structurally, from realizing even some of the dreams of mission advocates and Third World leaders a half century ago. I believe they pointed the way forward. The health of the church, the faithfulness of theology, and the renewal of theological education are, in part, tied to a recovery of the centrality of mission in our reading of Scripture.

Missional Hermeneutics Bibliography

Tim J. Davy and Michael W. Goheen

The aim of this bibliography is to give a comprehensive orientation to writings on the missional interpretation of the Bible. It is more focused than simply a list of books and articles connecting the Bible and mission. Rather, it notes titles that consciously adopt the method of "missional hermeneutics," or those whose work is very closely aligned with this approach, as developed since the mid–1990s. It includes books, articles, and chapters in edited volumes. The bibliography also includes a selection of key works that are considered to have been foundational to the emergence of missional hermeneutics.

For updates to this bibliography, including web links for unpublished works and other digital resources, please visit bibleandmission.redcliffe .org/missional-hermeneutics-bibliography.

Key Forerunners

Barth, Karl. "An Exegetical Study of Matthew 28:16–20." In *The Theology of the Christian Mission*, edited by Gerald H. Anderson, 55–71. London: SCM, 1961.

Bavinck, Johannes Herman. *An Introduction to the Science of Missions*. Philadelphia: Presbyterian & Reformed, 1960 (especially 11–76).

Blauw, Johannes. *The Missionary Nature of the Church: A Survey of the Biblical Theology of Mission*. London: Lutterworth, 1962.

Boer, Harry R. *Pentecost and Missions*. Grand Rapids: Eerdmans, 1961.

Bosch, David J. "Hermeneutical Principles in the Biblical Foundation for Mission." *Evangelical Review of Theology* 17.4 (1993): 437–51.

———. "Mission in Biblical Perspective." *International Review of Mission* 74 (1985): 531–38.

———. "Reflections on Biblical Models of Mission." In *Toward the Twenty-First Century in Christian Mission*, edited by J. M. Phillips and R. T. Coote, 175–92. Grand Rapids: Eerdmans, 1993.

———. "The Scope of Mission." *International Review of Mission* 73 (1984): 17–32.

———. "The Scope of the BISAM Project." *Mission Studies* 6.1 (1989): 61–68.

———. "Towards a Hermeneutic of 'Biblical Studies and Mission.'" *Mission Studies* 3.2 (1986): 65–79.

———. *Transforming Mission: Paradigm Shifts in Theology of Mission*. Maryknoll, NY: Orbis, 1991 (especially 15–178).

———. "The Vulnerability of Mission." *Baptist Quarterly* 34.8 (1992): 351–63.

———. "The Why and the How of a True Biblical Foundation for Mission." In *Zending Op Weg Naar De Toekomst*, edited by J. Verkuyl, 33–45. Kampen: Kok, 1978.

Burnett, David. *The Healing of the Nations: The Biblical Basis of the Mission of God*. 2nd edition. Carlisle: Paternoster, 1996.

Cullmann, Oscar. "Eschatology and Missions in the New Testament." In *The Theology of the Christian Mission*, edited by Gerald H. Anderson, 42–54. London: SCM, 1961.

De Ridder, Richard R. *Discipling the Nations*. Grand Rapids: Baker, 1971.

DuBose, Francis M. *God Who Sends: A Fresh Quest for Biblical Mission*. Nashville: Broadman, 1983.

Guder, Darrell L. *Be My Witnesses: The Church's Mission, Message, and Messengers*. Grand Rapids: Eerdmans, 1985.

Jeremias, Joachim. *Jesus' Promise to the Nations*. Translated by S. H. Hooke. Studies in Biblical Theology 24. London: SCM, 1958.

Legrand, Lucien. *Unity and Plurality: Mission in the Bible*. Translated by R. R. Barr. Maryknoll, NY: Orbis, 1990.

Lohfink, Gerhard. *Jesus and Community: The Social Dimension of the Christian Faith*. Translated by John P. Galvin. Philadelphia: Fortress, 1982.

Martin-Achard, Robert. "Israel's Mission to the Nations." *International Review of Missions* 51 (1952): 482–84.

———. *A Light to the Nations: A Study of the Old Testament Conception of Israel's Mission to the World*. Translated by John Penney Smith. London: Oliver & Boyd, 1962.

Rowley, H. H. *Israel's Mission to the World*. London: SCM, 1939.

———. *The Missionary Message of the Old Testament*. London: Carey, 1945.

Senior, Donald, and Carroll Stuhlmueller. *The Biblical Foundations for Mission*. Maryknoll, NY: Orbis, 1983.

Taber, Charles. "Missiology and the Bible." *Missiology* 11.2 (April 1983): 229–45.

Van Swigchem, Douwe. *Het Missionaire Karakter van de Christelijke Gemeente Volgens de Brieven van Paulus en Petrus*. Kampen: Kok, 1955 (detailed English summary on 256–66).

Verkuyl, Johannes. *Contemporary Missiology: An Introduction*. Translated by D. Cooper. Grand Rapids: Eerdmans, 1978 (especially 89–117).

Wright, G. Ernest. "The Old Testament Basis for the Christian Mission." In *The Theology of the Christian Mission*, edited by Gerald H. Anderson, 17–30. London: SCM, 1961.

Books

Ashford, Bruce Riley, ed. *Theology and Practice of Mission: God, the Church, and the Nations*. Nashville: B&H, 2011.

Barram, Michael. *Mission and Moral Reflection in Paul*. New York: Peter Lang, 2006.

Bartholomew, Craig G., and Michael W. Goheen. *Drama of Scripture: Finding Our Place in the Biblical Story*. 2nd edition. Grand Rapids: Baker, 2014.

———. *The True Story of the Whole World: Finding Your Place in the Biblical Drama*. Grand Rapids: Faith Alive, 2009 (revised shorter version of *Drama of Scripture*).

Bauckham, Richard. *Bible and Mission: Christian Witness in a Postmodern World*. Carlisle: Paternoster, 2003.

Beeby, Harry Daniel. *Canon and Mission*. Harrisburg, PA: Trinity, 1999.

Blackburn, W. Ross. *The God Who Makes Himself Known: The Missionary Heart of the Book of Exodus*. Downers Grove, IL: InterVarsity, 2012.

Brownson, James V. *Speaking the Truth in Love: New Testament Resources for a Missional Hermeneutic*. Harrisburg, PA: Trinity, 1998.

Davy, Tim J. *The Book of Job and the Mission of God: An Application of a Missional Hermeneutic to the Book of Job*. Eugene, OR: forthcoming.

Flemming, Dean. *Contextualization in the New Testament: Patterns for Theology and Mission*. Downers Grove, IL: InterVarsity, 2005.

———. *Recovering the Full Mission of God: A Biblical Perspective on Being, Doing, and Telling*. Downers Grove, IL: InterVarsity, 2013.

———. *Why Mission?* Nashville: Abingdon, 2015.

Glasser, Arthur F., with Charles E. Van Engen, Dean S. Gilliland, and Shawn B. Redford. *Announcing the Kingdom: The Story of God's Mission in the Bible*. Grand Rapids: Baker, 2003.

Goheen, Michael W. *Introducing Christian Mission Today: Scripture, History, Issues*. Downers Grove, IL: InterVarsity, 2014 (especially 35–72).

———. *A Light to the Nations: The Missional Church and the Biblical Story*. Grand Rapids: Baker Academic, 2011.

Gorman, Michael J. *Becoming the Gospel: Paul, Participation, and Mission*. Grand Rapids: Eerdmans, 2015.

Grams, Rollin G., et al., eds. *Bible and Mission: A Conversation between Biblical Studies and Missiology*. Schwarzenfeld: Neufeld, 2008.

Guder, Darrell L., ed. *Missional Church: A Vision for the Sending of the Church in North America*. Grand Rapids: Eerdmans, 1998.

Haydock, Nicholas. *The Theology of the Levitical Priesthood: Assisting God's People in Their Mission to the Nations*. Eugene, OR: Wipf & Stock, 2015.

Laansma, Jon, Grant R. Osborne, and Ray Van Neste, eds. *New Testament Theology in Light of the Church's Mission: Essays in Honor of I. Howard Marshall*. Eugene, OR: Cascade, 2011.

LaGrand, James. *The Earliest Christian Mission to "All Nations" in the Light of Matthew's Gospel*. Grand Rapids: Eerdmans, 1994.

Nissen, Johannes. *New Testament and Mission: Historical and Hermeneutical Perspectives*. 2nd edition. Frankfurt: Peter Lang, 2002.

Okoye, James Chukwuma. *Israel and the Nations: A Mission Theology of the Old Testament*. Maryknoll, NY: Orbis, 2006.

Penner, Peter F. *Missionale Hermeneutik: Biblische Texte Kontextuell und Relevant Lesen*. Schwarzenfeld: Neufeld, 2012.

Porter, Stanley E., and Cynthia L. Westfall, eds. *Christian Mission: Old Testament Foundations and New Testament Developments*. Eugene, OR: Pickwick, 2010.

Redford, Shawn B. *Missiological Hermeneutics: Biblical Interpretation for the Global Church*. Eugene, OR: Pickwick, 2012.

Russell, Brian D. *(Re)Aligning with God: Reading Scripture for Church and World*. Eugene, OR: Cascade, 2016.

Schnabel, Eckhard J. *Early Christian Mission*. 2 volumes. Downers Grove, IL: InterVarsity, 2004.

Schwanz, Keith, and Joseph Coleson. *Missio Dei: A Wesleyan Understanding*. Kansas City, MO: Beacon Hill, 2011.

Wagner, Ross. *Heralds of Good News: Paul and Isaiah "in Concert" in the Letter to the Romans*. Leiden: Brill, 2002.

Wright, Christopher J. H. *The Mission of God: Unlocking the Bible's Grand Narrative*. Nottingham: Inter-Varsity, 2006.

———. *The Mission of God's People: A Biblical Theology of the Church's Mission*. Grand Rapids: Zondervan, 2010.

———. *Truth with a Mission: Reading the Bible Missiologically*. Cambridge: Grove, 2005.

Articles and Book Chapters

Amstutz, Neil. "Response and Waterford Story." *Mission Focus: Annual Review* 15 (2007): 142–46.

Barram, Michael. "The Bible, Mission, and Social Location: Toward a Missional Hermeneutic." *Interpretation* 61 (2007): 42–58.

———. "'Fools for the Sake of Christ': Missional Hermeneutics and Praxis in the Corinthian Correspondence." *Missiology* 43.2 (2015): 195–207.

———. "'Located' Questions for a Missional Hermeneutic." 2006 paper available at gocn.org/resources/articles/located-questions-missional-hermeneutic.

———. "'Occupying' Genesis 1–3: Missionally Located Reflections on Biblical Values and Economic Justice." *Missiology* 42.4 (2014): 386–98.

———. "A Response at AAR to Hunsberger's 'Proposals . . .' Essay." *The Gospel and Our Culture Newsletter* eSeries 2 (2009). Available at gocn.org/resources/articles/response-aar-hunsberger-s-proposals-essay.

Barton, Mukti. "A Missional Reading of Susanna and the Woman Accused of Adultery." *Rethinking Mission* (July 2012). Available at rethinkingmission.org.uk/pdfs/barton_july_12.pdf.

Bauckham, Richard. "Mission as Hermeneutic for Scriptural Interpretation." *Currents in World Christianity Position Paper* 106 (1999).

Beeby, Harry Daniel. "A Missional Approach to Renewed Interpretation." In *Renewing Biblical Interpretation*, edited by C. Bartholomew, C. Greene, and K. Möller, 268–83. Grand Rapids: Zondervan; Carlisle: Paternoster, 2000.

Bekele, Girma. "The Biblical Narrative of the *Missio Dei*: Analysis of the Interpretive Framework of David Bosch's Missional Hermeneutic." *International Bulletin of Missionary Research* 35.3 (2011): 153–58.

Brownson, James V. "A Response at SBL to Hunsberger's 'Proposals . . .' Essay." *The Gospel and Our Culture Newsletter* eSeries 2 (2009). Available at gocn.org/resources/articles/response-sbl-hunsbergers-proposals-essay.

———. "Speaking the Truth in Love." *International Review of Mission* 83 (1994): 479–504.

Carriker, Timothy. "The Bible as Text for Mission." In *Bible in Mission*, edited by Pauline Hoggarth, Fergus Macdonald, Bill Mitchell, and Klaus K. Jørgensen, 29–39. Oxford: Regnum, 2013.

Cerny, Pavel. "The Relationship between Theology and Missiology: The Missional Hermeneutics." *European Journal of Theology* 19.2 (2010): 104–9.

Choi, Hunn. "Multicultural Hermeneutics and Mission." *Asbury Journal* 70.1 (2015): 111–39.

Flemming, Dean. "Exploring a Missional Reading of Scripture: Philippians as a Case Study." *Evangelical Quarterly* 83.1 (2011): 3–18.

———. "Revelation and the *Missio Dei*: Toward a Missional Reading of the Apocalypse." *Journal of Theological Interpretation* 6.2 (2012): 161–78.

———. "A Sent and Sanctified Community: Missional Holiness in the Gospel of John." *Wesleyan Theological Journal* 51.1 (2016): 133–44.

———. "'Won Over without a Word': Holiness and the Church's Missional Identity in 1 Peter." *Wesleyan Theological Journal* 49 (Spring 2014): 50–66.

Goheen, Michael W. "Bible and Mission: Missiology and Biblical Scholarship in Dialogue." In *Christian Mission: Old Testament Foundations and New Testament Developments*, edited by Stanley E. Porter and Cynthia L. Westfall, 208–32. Eugene, OR: Pickwick, 2010.

———. "Continuing Steps toward a Missional Hermeneutic." *Fideles* 3 (2008): 49–99.

———. "A Critical Examination of David Bosch's Missional Reading of Luke." In *Reading Luke: Interpretation, Reflection, Formation*, edited by C. G. Bartholomew, J. B. Green, and A. C. Thiselton, 229–64. Grand Rapids: Zondervan, 2005.

———. "The Importance of Narrative Theology for Mission." In *Engaging the Nations: Contours of Mission Theology in Global Perspectives*, edited by Robert L. Gallagher and Paul Hertig. Maryknoll, NY: Orbis, forthcoming.

———. "The Mission of God's People and Biblical Interpretation: Exploring N. T. Wright's Missional Hermeneutic." Paper for "A Dialogue with N. T. Wright. Jesus: A Public Figure Making a Public Announcement. Mission, Worldview, and the People of God," Scripture and Hermeneutics Seminar, San Francisco, 18 November 2011. Available at 64.64.27.114/~mission/wp-content/uploads/2013/01/Missional-Hermeneutic-A-Dialogue-with-NT-Wright.pdf.

———. "A Missional Approach to Scripture for the Theological Task." In *The End of Theology: Shaping Theology for the Sake of Mission*, edited by Jason S. Sexton and Paul Weston. Minneapolis: Augsburg Fortress, forthcoming.

———. "The Urgency of Reading the Bible as One Story." *Theology Today* 64 (2008): 469–83.

Goheen, Michael W., and Christopher J. H. Wright. "Theological Interpretation and a Missional Hermeneutic." In *A Manifesto for Theological Interpretation*, edited by Craig G. Bartholomew and Heath Thomas, 171–96. Grand Rapids: Baker, 2016.

Gorman, Michael J. "Missional Musings on Paul." *Catalyst On-line* 37.2 (2011). Available at catalystresources.org/missional-musings-on-paul/.

Green, Joel B. "Neglecting Widows and Serving the Word? Acts 6:1–7 as a Test Case for a Missional Hermeneutic." In *Jesus Christ, Lord and Savior: Essays in Honor of I. Howard Marshall*, edited by J. Laansma, G. Osborne, and R. Van Neste, 151–60. Carlisle: Paternoster; Eugene, OR: Wipf & Stock, 2011.

Guder, Darrell L. "Biblical Formation and Discipleship." In *Treasure in Clay Jars: Pat-

terns in Missional Faithfulness, edited by L. Y. Barrett, 59–73. Grand Rapids: Eerdmans, 2004.

———. "Missional Hermeneutics: The Missional Authority of Scripture—Interpreting Scripture as Missional Formation." *Mission Focus: Annual Review* 15 (2007): 106–21.

———. "Missional Hermeneutics: The Missional Vocation of the Congregation—and How Scripture Shapes That Calling." *Mission Focus: Annual Review* 15 (2007): 125–42.

———. "Missional Pastors in Maintenance Churches." *Catalyst On-line* 31.3 (2005). Available at catalystresources.org/missional-pastors-in-maintenance-churches/.

Hendriks, H. Jurgens. "Contextualising Theological Education in Africa by Doing Theology in a Missional Hermeneutic." *Koers: Bulletin for Christian Scholarship* 77.2 (2012).

Hesselgrave, David J. "A Missionary Hermeneutic: Understanding Scripture in the Light of God's Mission." *International Journal of Frontier Missions* 10.1 (1993): 17–20.

Hunsberger, George R. "Proposals for a Missional Hermeneutic: Mapping a Conversation." *Missiology* 39.3 (2011): 309–21.

———. "Proposals for a Missional Hermeneutic: Mapping the Conversation." *The Gospel and Our Culture Newsletter* eSeries 2 (2009). Available at gocn.org/resources/newsletters/2009/01/gospel-and-our-culture.

Hwang, Jerry. "'My Name Will Be Great among the Nations': The Missio Dei in the Book of the Twelve." *Tyndale Bulletin* 65.2 (2014): 161–80.

Jabini, Frank S. "Witness to the End of the World: A Missional Reading of Acts 8:26–40." *Conspectus* 13.1 (2012).

Keene, Timothy. "A Missional Reading of 2 Corinthians 5:11–6:2; especially 5:21." *Transformation* 30.3 (2013): 169–81.

Kelly, Michael B. "Biblical Theology and Missional Hermeneutics: A Match Made *for* Heaven . . . on Earth?" In *Eyes to See, Ears to Hear: Essays in Memory of J. Alan Groves*, edited by P. Enns, D. J. Green, and M. B. Kelly, 61–76. Phillipsburg: P&R, 2010.

Lee, Byungohk. "A Missional Hermeneutic of the Other: A Dialogue between Levinas and Confucianism." *Missiology* 41.4 (2013): 416–26.

Lee, Kyuboem. "An Urban Missional Reading of Genesis 1." *New Urban World Journal* 3.1 (2014): 59–66.

LeMarquand, Grant. "From Creation to New Creation: The Mission of God in the Biblical Story." In *Waging Reconciliation: God's Mission in a Time of Globalization and Crisis*, edited by I. T. Douglas, 9–34. New York: Church Publishing, 2002.

Lines, Kevin P. "Exegetical and Extispicic Readings of the Bible in Turkana, Kenya, and North America." *Asbury Journal* 66.1 (2011): 65–94.

Magda, Ksenija. "A Missional Reading of Rom 15:1–12." *Evangelical Journal of Theology* 2.1 (2008): 39–52.

Nugent, John. "Response to Kyuboem Lee: An Urban Missional Reading of Genesis 1." *New Urban World Journal* 3.1 (2014): 67–68.

Okure, Teresa. "'In Him All Things Hold Together': A Missiological Reading of Colossians 1:15–20." *International Review of Mission* 91 (2002): 62–72.

Penner, Peter F. "Practising Community in the Early Church: A Missional Reading of the Summary Texts in Acts." In *Mission in Context: Explorations Inspired by J. Andrew Kirk*, edited by J. Corrie and C. Ross, 77–91. Farnham: Ashgate, 2012.

Russell, Brian D. "What Is a Missional Hermeneutic?" *Catalyst On-line* 36.4 (2011). Available at catalystresources.org/what-is-a-missional-hermeneutic/.

Schertz, Mary. "Response." *Mission Focus: Annual Review* 15 (2007): 122–24.

Sexton, Jason. "Reading the Parables Theologically to Read Them Missionally: Test Cases from the Early Galilean Parables in Luke's Gospel." *Currents in Theology and Mission* 40.3 (2013): 165–78.

Stone, Lawson G. "Inhabiting the Garden: Bible, Theology and Mission." *Asbury Journal* 66.1 (2011): 6–30.

Wagner, Ross. "*Missio Dei*: Envisioning an Apostolic Reading of Scripture." *Missiology* 37.1 (2009): 19–32.

Wieland, George. "Reading Acts Missionally in a City of Migrants." In *God's People on the Move: Biblical and Global Perspectives on Migration and Mission*, edited by VanThanh Nguyen and John N. Prior, 144–58. Eugene, OR: Pickwick, 2014.

Wielenga, Bob. "Renewal and Reconstruction: Holy Writ in Ezra-Nehemiah—A Missional Reading." *In die Skriflig/In Luce Verbi* 47.1 (2013).

Wolters, Albert M. "Mission and the Interpretation of Zechariah 8:20–23." In *That the World May Believe: Essays on Mission and Unity in Honour of George Vandervelde*, edited by Michael W. Goheen and Margaret O'Gara, 1–13. Lanham, MD: University Press of America, 2006.

Wright, Christopher J. H. "'According to the Scriptures': The Whole Gospel in Biblical Revelation." *Evangelical Review of Theology* 33.1 (2009): 4–18.

———. "Lamentations: A Book for Today." *International Bulletin of Missionary Research* 39.2 (2015): 59–64.

———. "Mission and Old Testament Interpretation." In *Hearing the Old Testament: Listening for God's Address*, edited by Craig G. Bartholomew and David J. H. Beldman, 180–203. Grand Rapids: Eerdmans, 2012.

———. "Mission as a Matrix for Hermeneutics and Biblical Theology." In *Out of*

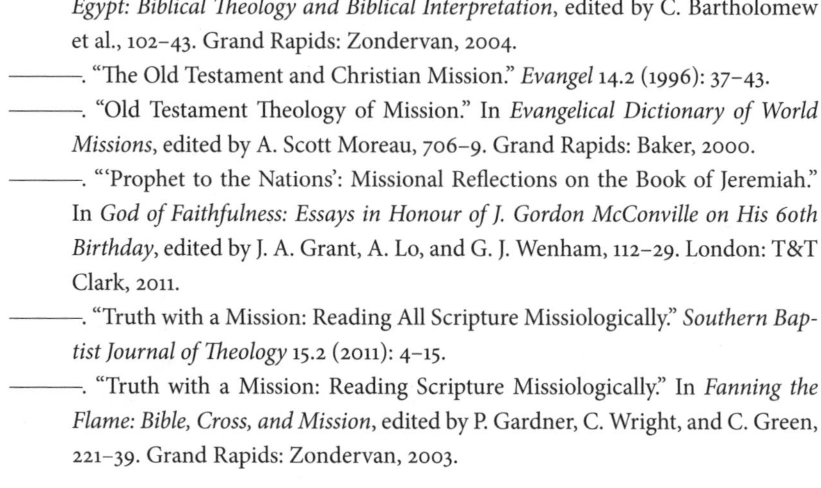

Egypt: Biblical Theology and Biblical Interpretation, edited by C. Bartholomew et al., 102–43. Grand Rapids: Zondervan, 2004.

———. "The Old Testament and Christian Mission." *Evangel* 14.2 (1996): 37–43.

———. "Old Testament Theology of Mission." In *Evangelical Dictionary of World Missions*, edited by A. Scott Moreau, 706–9. Grand Rapids: Baker, 2000.

———. "'Prophet to the Nations': Missional Reflections on the Book of Jeremiah." In *God of Faithfulness: Essays in Honour of J. Gordon McConville on His 60th Birthday*, edited by J. A. Grant, A. Lo, and G. J. Wenham, 112–29. London: T&T Clark, 2011.

———. "Truth with a Mission: Reading All Scripture Missiologically." *Southern Baptist Journal of Theology* 15.2 (2011): 4–15.

———. "Truth with a Mission: Reading Scripture Missiologically." In *Fanning the Flame: Bible, Cross, and Mission*, edited by P. Gardner, C. Wright, and C. Green, 221–39. Grand Rapids: Zondervan, 2003.

Journal Issues Devoted to the Topic of Missional Hermeneutics

Encounters Mission Journal 29 (June 2009): "The Bible and Mission."

Encounters Mission Journal 33 (May 2010): "The Psalms and Mission."

Missio Dei: A Journal of Missional Theology and Praxis 5.1 (February 2014): "Missional Hermeneutics."

Index